This is a collection of original studies on the new international health and welfare organisations between the First and Second World Wars. The diversity of such organisations and their many-sided activities make this a rich and complex area of historical investigation which has direct relevance to current issues in international health.

Multilateral organisations such as the League of Nations and a variety of types of non-governmental organisations are discussed. The role of scientific and professional factors, as well as the priorities of women's employment, eugenics and pronatalism are also considered. Together, the various chapters present a cohesive and integrated view of a hitherto neglected area of study. The book also complements comparative studies of welfare states by emphasising the importance of international interactions between expert groups in a broader political and social context.

Cambridge History of Medicine

EDITORS: CHARLES WEBSTER and CHARLES ROSENBERG

International health organisations and movements, 1918–1939

Cambridge History of Medicine

EDITED BY

CHARLES WEBSTER
Senior Research Fellow of All Souls College, University of Oxford,

CHARLES ROSENBERG
Professor of History and Sociology of Science,
University of Pennsylvania

For a list of titles in the series, see end of book

International health
organisations and movements,
1918–1939

EDITED BY
PAUL WEINDLING
Wellcome Unit for the History of Medicine, University of Oxford

CAMBRIDGE
UNIVERSITY PRESS

Published by the Press Syndicate of the University of Cambridge
The Pitt Building, Trumpington Street, Cambridge CB2 1RP
40 West 20th Street, New York, NY 10011–4211, USA
10 Stamford Road, Oakleigh, Melbourne 3166, Australia

First published 1995

Printed in Great Britain at the University Press, Cambridge

A catalogue record for this book is available from the British Library

Library of Congress cataloguing in publication data
International health organisations and movements, 1918–1939 /
edited by Paul Weindling
p.   cm. – (Cambridge history of medicine)
ISBN 0 521 45012 8 (hardback)
1. World health – Societies, etc. – History – 20th century.
2. Public health – International cooperation – History – 20th century.
I. Weindling, Paul. II. Series.
[DNLM: 1. Health policy – history. 2. International Agencies – history.
3. World Health. 4. International Cooperation.
WA 11.1 I605 1995]
RA441.I586 1995
362.1'06'01 – dc20
DNLM/DLC for Library of Congress   94–26570   CIP

ISBN 0 521 45012 8 hardback

Contents

Contents

Notes on the contributors

MARTA ALEKSANDRA BALIŃSKA, Wellcome Unit for the History of Medicine, 45–47 Banbury Road, Oxford OX2 6PE, Great Britain. She studied Polish literature at the Institut National des Langues Orientales. She subsequently completed a doctoral course in Soviet and East European Studies at the Institut d'Etudes Politiques, Paris. She studied questions of Polish and international public health, completing a doctoral thesis on Ludwik Rajchman. She is currently writing a biography of Rajchman and, with a Wellcome Trust Fellowship awarded for 1994–5, she is engaging on a study of the Warsaw Institute of Hygiene.

MARTIN BULMER, Department of Sociology, University of Surrey, Guildford, Surrey GU2 5XH, Great Britain. He previously taught at the London School of Economics and Political Science, and the University of Southampton. He has interests in the history of American philanthropic support for the social sciences in the early twentieth century, and is the author of *The Chicago School of Sociology* (Chicago: University of Chicago Press, 1984) and of articles in *Minerva* on this subject.

MARCOS CUETO, Instituto de Estudios Peruanos, Horacio Urteaga 694, Lima 11, Peru. He received his PhD in history from Columbia University. He is a researcher at the Instituto de Estudios Peruanos and is the editor of *Missionaries of Science: The Rockefeller Foundation and Latin America* (Bloomington, Ind.: Indiana University Press). He is also the author of articles on the history of science and medicine in Latin America.

MARTIN DAVID DUBIN, Department of Political Science, Northern Illinois University, DeKalb, Illinois 60115–2887, USA. He is an Associate Professor of Political Science and is currently completing a book on the League of Nations Health Organisation.

JOHN FARLEY, Biology Department, Dalhousie University, Halifax, Nova Scotia, Canada, B3H 4J1. His research interests are the history of tropical medicine and parasitology. Among his numerous publications are: *The Spontaneous Generation Controversy* (Baltimore: Johns Hopkins University Press, 1977); *Gametes and Spores, Ideas about Sexual Reproduction 1750–1914* (Baltimore: Johns Hopkins University Press, 1982); *Bilharzia: A History of Tropical Medicine* (Cambridge University Press, 1991).

JOHN F. HUTCHINSON, Department of History, Simon Fraser University, Burnaby, British Columbia, Canada, B3H 3J5. He is a Professor of History and is interested in the history of philanthropy and public health. He is presently completing a full-length history of the Red Cross. His *Politics and Public Health in Revolutionary Russia, 1890–1918* appeared in 1990, as did *Health and Society in Revolutionary Russia*, a collection of essays co-edited with Susan Gross Solomon.

LENORE MANDERSON, Tropical Health Program, University of Queensland Medical School, Herston Road, Herston, Brisbane QLD 4006, Australia. Her teaching and research interests are in medical anthropology and public health, and she has published extensively on topics related to gender and sexuality, the anthropology of infectious disease, and the social history of medicine. Much of her research has been conducted in Peninsular Malaysia.

CAROL MILLER, 95 Route des Fayards, 1239 Collex, Switzerland. She is a research assistant on a gender and development project at the United Nations Research Institute for Social Development, Geneva, and a social science tutor for the European branch of the Open University. She completed her DPhil at Oxford in 1992 on 'Lobbying the League: Women's International Organisations and the League of Nations' which is currently under revision for publication. She has published articles on the international activities of interwar women's organisations.

ANNE MARIE MOULIN, U-158 INSERM, Hôpital Necker-Enfants Malades, 149 Rue de Sèvres, 75743 Paris Cedex 15, France. She is a researcher and the author of *Le dernier langage de la médecine, histoire de l'immunologie de Pasteur au Sida* (Paris: Presses Universitaires de France, 1992) and co-edited *Science and Empires* (Dordrecht, Boston and London: Kluwer Academic Publishers, 1992).

ANNE MARIE RAFFERTY is Lecturer within the Department of Nursing and Midwifery Studies, Medical School, University of Nottingham. She is co-author of *Introduction to the Social History of Nursing* (London: Routledge, 1988) with Robert Dingwall and Charles Webster and is preparing her doctoral dissertation, 'The Politics of Nursing Education, 1860–1948', for publication as a book by Routledge. She is consultant historian to the International Council of Nurses

Centennial Project, University of Pennsylvania, where she will be a Harkness Fellow from 1994–5.

PATRICIA T. ROOKE, Department of Educational Foundations, University of Alberta, Edmonton, Alberta, Canada, T6G 2E5. RUDY SCHNELL, Faculty of Education, Department of Educational Policy and Administrative Studies, University of Calgary, 2500 University Drive N.W., Calgary, Alberta, Canada, T2N 1N4. Their major research interests are history of child welfare and of international women's organisations. They are the co-authors of *Discarding the Asylum* (Lanham: University Press of America, 1983) and *No Bleeding Heart: Charlotte Whitton, Feminist on the Right* (Vancouver: University of British Columbia Press, 1987).

MATHEW THOMSON, Department of History, University of Sheffield, Sheffield S10 2TN, Great Britain. He is a Wellcome Research Fellow and a Lecturer at the University of Sheffield. He completed his DPhil at Oxford in 1992 on 'The Problem of Mental Deficiency in England and Wales, *c*. 1913–1946'. He is currently revising his thesis for publication and is also engaged on an international and comparative study of mental hygiene. He has published articles on sterilisation, segregation and community care of mental defectives. His interests lie in the history of the interrelation between psychiatry and social policy.

BRIDGET TOWERS, Department of Social Sciences, Kingston University, Penrhyn Road, Kingston-upon-Thames, Surrey GT1 2EE, Great Britain. She is Senior Lecturer at Kingston University where she teaches social policy and is a member of the Gender Studies Group. Her research and publications are in the field of the history of medicine, with a particular focus on the politics of international health organisations.

PAUL WEINDLING, Wellcome Unit for the History of Medicine, 45–47 Banbury Road, Oxford OX2 6PE, Great Britain. He is Senior Research Officer at the Wellcome Unit and the author of *Health, Race and German Politics between National Unification and Nazism, 1870–1945* (Cambridge: Cambridge University Press, 1989; paperback 1993), and of *Darwinism and Social Darwinism in Imperial Germany* (Stuttgart: Gustav Fischer Verlag, 1991). He co-edits *Social History of Medicine*, and currently researches on infectious disease in twentieth-century Europe.

Preface

The essays in this volume arise from a recent convergence of interest in the history of international health and welfare organisations. The sheer diversity of organisations and their many-sided activities make this a rich and complex area of historical investigation, which has direct relevance to current issues in international health

Although contributors to this volume are dispersed throughout the world, an informal network arose in what is very much a new field of study. I therefore wish to express my appreciation of how contributors have co-operated to bring this volume to fruition within a relatively short period of time. The exchange of papers meant that there was much interchange on topics of mutual interest, while perspectives have remained refreshingly diverse. I am particularly indebted to contributors for comments on my introduction and my essay on social medicine. It meant that arguments were refined, and, in order to avoid duplication of analysis on central issues, several contributors generously agreed to omit material dealt with elsewhere in the volume. Their efforts have meant that an exceptionally cohesive, integrated and intellectually coherent volume has taken shape. It is hoped that this collection will provide solid foundations for other projects on twentieth-century international health that are already under way.

I would like to express my appreciation to the archivists at the International Labour Office, League of Nations Archives and Historical Collections Section and at the Rockefeller Foundation Archive Center who provided copious material and judicious advice. A number of contributors had the pleasure of stimulating encounters with the former League of Nations archivist, Sven Wielander. I know that authors will join with me in stating my appreciation of the help given by these institutions and individuals, while also wishing to thank other bodies and persons, whose contribution will be clear in various chapters. I would also like to thank Humaira Ahmad, Florence Bazin and Daniella Freeden at the Wellcome Unit, Oxford, for administrative, secretarial and indeed technological help in bringing this volume together. Valuable advice was also provided by Leo van Bergen (Nijmegen), Virginia Berridge (London School of

Hygiene and Tropical Medicine) and Susan Solomon (Toronto). Finally, I would like to express my appreciation to Charles Webster, co-editor of this series and mentor over many years, for his enthusiasm for this area of study leading to the incorporation of this volume in the Cambridge History of Medicine, a series that is both pioneering and prestigious.

Paul Weindling

Abbreviations

AJJDC	American Jewish Joint Distribution Committee
ARA	American Relief Administration
ARC	American Red Cross
ASSI	Archives of the State Serum Institute, Copenhagen
CICR	Comité international de la Croix Rouge
FAO	United Nations Food and Agriculture Organisation
FNIF	Florence Nightingale International Foundation
GNC	General Nursing Council
IAPCW	International Association for the Promotion of Child Welfare
ICN	International Council of Nurses
ICRC	International Committee of the Red Cross
ICSU	International Council of Scientific Unions
IHB	International Health Board of the Rockefeller Foundation
ILO	International Labour Office
LN	League of Nations
LNA	League of Nations Archives, Geneva
LNEC	League of Nations Epidemic Commission
LNHO	League of Nations Health Organisation
LRCS	League of Red Cross Societies
LSHTM	London School of Hygiene and Tropical Medicine
MRC	Medical Research Council
NCMH	National Committee for Mental Hygiene
NEPB	National Epidemic Prevention Board, Peking
OIHP	Office international d'hygiène publique
PRO	Public Record Office, London
RAC	Rockefeller Archive Center
RF	Rockefeller Foundation
RFA	Rockefeller Foundation Archives
SCF	Save the Children Fund
SCIU	Save the Children International Union

List of abbreviations

UCH	University College Hospital, London
UN	United Nations
UNESCO	United Nations Educational, Scientific and Cultural Organisation
UNICEF	United Nations International Children's Emergency Fund
UNRRA	United Nations Relief and Rehabilitation Administration
USCB	United States Children's Bureau
WHO	World Health Organisation

1

Introduction: constructing international health between the wars

PAUL WEINDLING

Whereas the development of welfare states has been the subject of sustained academic scrutiny, international aspects of welfare have been much neglected.[1] It is possible for national systems to retain a diversity of locally administered elements (for example, involving municipalities, social insurance corporations or occupational health schemes) while providing centralised funding and administrative and legal frameworks. But international organisations have vital roles and demand far greater attention from historians and social scientists than they have hitherto received.[2]

As any localised system could suffer from inequalities and lack resources, and states could manipulate health and welfare issues for the purposes of political expediency, international organisations became an attractive option for promoting reforms. International bodies may remedy local deficiencies, set optimal standards and improve the quality of the systems of care and the training of personnel. While some of these functions can be fulfilled by the state, it should be recognised that the state as a provider of welfare can be problematic, because its multifunctional character may render health and welfare low political priorities, or distort welfare as caught up in the politics of interest groups and financial expediency. The interwar rise of fascist and kindred authoritarian regimes that perverted welfare systems for purposes of political discrimination and genocide was in marked contrast to the humane ideals of internationalists. Many international health reformers were frustrated by the deteriorating political conditions in state-administered systems, or were even driven into exile. Yet international organisations often became fraught with tensions between national interests and idealists, as humanitarians and pacifism clashed with *Realpolitik*.

The voluntary sector has maintained a vital role at the local, national and international levels. Its flexibility and ethos of care and of altruistic dedication have to be set against disadvantages of uneven resource distribution and paternalist (or for some theorists, maternalist) ideologies, as well as a

1

stigmatising tendency in the direction of 'cringe or starve'.[3] While the League of Nations (LN) remained primarily state-oriented, a variety of voluntary organisations provided alternative forms of organisation. Universalist concepts of human rights extended into the sphere of entitlement to welfare, and supranationalist ideals have given international organisations important roles in pioneering innovations, monitoring conditions and organising assistance.

The first heroic generation of studies on international health organisations was by physicians and administrators who were themselves involved in international work.[4] Their publications were inward looking – written by and for insiders in order to advance expertise. Despite the popularity of internationalist and pacifist ideals in the LN and kindred associations between the wars, there were few attempts to enlighten the general public about the League's international health work or to provide (as did the German Hygiene Museum, Dresden) international health education exhibitions.[5] Interwar health propaganda, using the new media of the cinema and radio as well as taking advantage of new forms of leisure and physical culture, remained cast in a nationalist rather than an internationalist mould.

There has recently been a convergence of interest in interwar health and welfare, breaking out of the single-country paradigm of the welfare state. This volume brings together the first-fruits of a number of sustained research projects on the interwar period. These complement the burgeoning numbers of single-country studies, as well as international comparisons of national welfare systems and of public health.[6] Issues relating to gender, population studies and eugenics, particularly studies of international aspects of eugenics and of population agencies, are as crucial to discussions of international agencies as they were for welfare states.[7]

The justification for focusing on the interwar period is that it marks the transition from treaties and conventions between nation states to the establishment of a brave new world of international organisations, designed to promote health and welfare. A number of themes come to the fore:

(i)   The interaction of voluntary and state organisations on the international plane.
(ii)   The innovative, modernising role of corporate philanthropies (e.g. the Rockefeller Foundation – hereafter RF), and of supranational organisations (notably the LN).
(iii)   The place of these organisations as part of broader patterns of international relations.
(iv)   The role of what might be construed as autonomous scientific and professional factors.
(v)   The priorities of women's employment, eugenics and pronatalist measures to encourage the birth rate.

The volume focuses on multilateral projects and organisations, rather than on any bilateral health and welfare schemes, despite their importance during this period. It is, however, important to note that multilateral agencies had a varying membership, and that they attempted to publicise their activities among member states, in ways that could be politically controversial.[8] International political tensions affected policies relating to Germany, the United States, the Soviet Union and Japan, which were all noteworthy for being either wholly or partially absent from the LN. Yet, as in the case of Germany before 1926 and the United States, states could participate in the Health Organisation without necessarily being LN members. Within the LN certain powers emerged as influential (notably Britain and France) although their policies often did not agree. To compensate, bilateral relations developed between political outcasts, such as Germany and the Soviet Union which launched programmes of medical and scientific exchanges.[9] Participation in health and welfare schemes was not always in step with membership of the LN as a political organisation. Moreover, the power of US foundations mitigated the effects of isolationism.

While the studies in this volume focus on international interactions, comparative conclusions can be drawn (and indeed Bulmer's concluding chapter does just this). Several contributors demonstrate that the LN was a complex organism with a number of technical branches that differed in ethos, organisation and scope. Similarly the RF had diverse programmes, such as the International Health Board, the Laura Spelman Foundation (which sponsored social studies) and a core foundation programme which from 1927 was research oriented. Two studies compare the Comité international de la Croix Rouge (CICR) and the League of Red Cross Societies (LRCS), and the constituent Red Cross organisations also varied in scope.

Comparative studies of interwar health and welfare systems agree in identifying the period as crucially innovative in establishing welfare states. Weimar Germany, Sweden, the Soviet Union and the USA under President Roosevelt's New Deal all launched pioneering schemes. However, in seeking the sources of innovation within single-country contexts the broad interaction of international expertise in health and welfare is lost from view. This book's interactive perspective enables analysis of specific links between organisations and demonstrates how their activities promoted the interchange of ideas and expertise. International organisations undertook comparative evaluations, both quantitative – with a range of statistical data presented so as to facilitate international comparisons – and qualitative, particularly dealing with organisational structures, service provision and social conditions. Such inter-actions and surveys were politically problematic because member states often feared the violation of their national sovereignty, and it was at times difficult to overcome political divisions and arrange programmes including, for example, German and Soviet experts. But that such programmes were possible provides important testimony to the effectiveness of the international ideal – at least at a professional and scientific level.

Two crucial themes that emerge are the founding of international organisations with semi-permanent staffs, and the consequent professionalisation and scientisation of policies. There was a shift away from relief in the form of food aid, emergency hygiene measures and the distribution of clothing, etc. Here the famine-relief measures in the Soviet Union between 1921 and 1924 are instructive. These represented one of the first instances of modern disaster relief with efforts to co-ordinate the work of relief teams. Fridtjof Nansen, the Arctic explorer and naturalist, took a leading role in mobilising international support and in co-ordinating relief programmes. The most ambitious aid agency, the American Relief Administration, was directed by the former mining engineer, Herbert Hoover.[10] The fear of migrants 'carrying' cholera and typhus, amounting to a 'new Black Death' which would overwhelm Western European civilisation exposed the self-interest of the West in sponsoring epidemic relief. There continued to be active relief programmes elsewhere, especially to cope with the refugees resulting from the redrawing of frontiers and during the 1930s from the heightened international tensions during the Spanish Civil War.[11] Scrutiny of relief work during the Depression shows novel scientific concerns, as with the testing of new diets and therapies. Moreover, the whole concept of relief *in situ* contrasted sharply with the freedom of movement allowed to refugees during the nineteenth century. Migration was a safety valve in the event of poverty and persecution. The spirit of national self-determination had its reverse side as restrictive policies on migration were imposed, necessitating relief work in disaster areas. The futility of arranging relief *in situ* was exposed by the rise of Nazi racism and military expansionism which made evacuation and migration the only realistic courses of action.[12]

As science assumed an increasing role in professionally administered systems, there was a move away from charitable relief with the effort to establish on a scientific basis the causes of poverty and disease. The universalism of science found natural affinity with internationalist ideals. Modern analysts, notably E. B. and P. M. Haas, have developed the concept of a transnational epistemic community in discussing the role of scientific experts in international questions like conservation and pollution.[13] The concept of an epistemic community (used in this volume by Dubin) has much to recommend it, particularly in drawing on the historical sociology of sciences as developed by Ludwik Fleck in the 1930s (explicitly referring to irrational factors in the League of Nations Health Organisation (LNHO)'s standardisation work) and Thomas Kuhn in the 1960s.[14] However, in going back to these roots, questions of nationalist biases and interest groups arise, which might be obscured by an unreflective application of this concept. Dubin emphasises how the LN built up an international network of experts, a theme further pursued by Moulin's study of centre–periphery relations of the Pasteur Institutes, concentrating on what was essentially an organisation finding its prime rationale in medical research. Farley shows how the RF was influential in promoting the switch to modern causal and laboratory-based approaches. Rooke and Schnell examine the shift from 'sentiment to science' in the case of child welfare, while Miller reviews the development of social work, and Thomson demonstrates the coexistence of moralistic and scientistic strategies in the mental hygiene movement. Rafferty shows that scientised and professional approaches were to the fore in international nursing organisations. Bulmer concludes the volume by examining the sociological implications of the modernisation of health and welfare agencies.

Despite the modernist ethos of international health work between the wars, as well as the replacement of the nineteenth-century concept of a balance of power by notions of collective security, the diverse and often conflicting strategies drew on nineteenth-century precedents. These can be classified as:

(i)   quarantine and containment of infectious diseases,
(ii)   international sanitary conferences and conventions which ultimately spawned authorities,
(iii)   the Red Cross societies oriented to war-relief,
(iv)   conferences on medical issues that were of direct social relevance, and finally
(v)   international standard-setting agencies.

More commercially and popularly oriented international expositions seem to have contributed less to international health work than to publicising the work of the LNHO.[15]

(i) Quarantine authorities drew on Enlightenment schemes of medical police and inspection. A Superior Council of Health was founded in 1838 in Constantinople (Istanbul) with both Ottoman and European representation.[16] The Health, Medicine and Quarantine Board functioned in Alexandria, Egypt, from the 1830s until 1938, with foreign delegates from at least 1881 and representation on the LN Health Committee from 1924. An International Board of Health was established in 1840 in Tangier, and functioned as an autonomous authority until 1923. In order to prevent the spread of infectious diseases through pilgrimages to Mecca, there was an Ottoman quarantine station on Kamaran Island in the Red Sea from 1882 (until 1956).[17] The European Commission of the Danube, established in 1856, also took on certain powers over health issues. While quarantine became unfashionable with the rise of free trade ideologies, the shift back to protectionism gave quarantine approaches a new lease of life. The initial function of the Ottoman stations was more the defence of European health rather than concern for individual migrants. This was also true for the German port stations where migrants travelling from Eastern Europe to the United States were confined. The quarantine model shaped the development of port health authorities during the twentieth century, which served to impose health checks on migrants and to provide treatment and prevention of sexually transmitted diseases. It was modified by the LNHO's support for a sanitary iron curtain between Russia and the rest of Europe (see chapter 5).[18]

(ii) Howard-Jones has documented the series of international sanitary conferences which first took place in 1851 as a response to cholera. By the early twentieth century, organisations with permanent staffs were beginning to be established, albeit on a modest scale. The International Bureau for the Suppression of Traffic in Women and Children (1899) provides an early example. In 1902 the Pan-American Sanitary Bureau was established in Washington, DC, largely under US influence. In 1907 it was agreed to establish the Office international d'hygiène publique (OIHP) which was based in Paris. Although imperial rivalries posed obstacles to the participation of major powers (notably Germany), the OIHP was to constitute an important element of the LNHO.

(iii) The bodies which eventually became the CICR and national Red Cross societies grew out of international meetings held in Geneva in 1863–4. The extent to which such organisations could engage in peacetime welfare work remained problematic.[19] The late nineteenth-century patriotic ethos of women's nursing organisations, notably in Germany, accelerated the development of social work during the First World War.[20]

While the Red Cross represented a secular approach to international relief (its symbol is a reversal of the Swiss flag), missionary societies and confessional organisations remained active. The Roman Catholic Church was well placed to undertake international medical and welfare work through organisations like Caritas, while Protestant churches assumed dynamic international roles.

(iv) Coincident with the rise of international scientific congresses, there appeared another more socially oriented species of congress: in 1856 an International Congress of Charities, Correction and Philanthropy was held, and in 1889 a Congrès internationale d'assistance.[21] Further initiatives in establishing non-governmental organisations were prompted by social problems. Controversial social problems were often forced onto the international level, because of intractable difficulties in securing action at a national level. International federations were generated by concerned groups in a particular country; the existence of a federation that required national associations to be constituted elsewhere, thereby providing a stimulus to domestic social policies. Infant welfare exemplifies this. In 1894 an infant welfare clinic was opened at Fécamp in France to provide working mothers with pasteurised milk. The clinic provided the nucleus of an international movement which became entangled with imperialist ideologies and was dogged by controversy surrounding the issues of the morality of working mothers and the medical issues of bottle as opposed to breast milk.[22] The politics of international associations against alcoholism was even more complex with diverse competing organisations, differing in extremism on the issue, their moral or medical approach, and the social target groups. Although the tuberculosis problem rapidly came to secure both national and international support at the turn of the century, international tensions (as between Pasteurians and German supporters of Robert Koch's bacteriology) and sociopolitical differences remained. After a series of international congresses on tuberculosis in Paris in 1867, 1888, 1894 and 1898, in Berlin in 1899 and in Naples in 1900, an International Central Bureau for the Campaign against Tuberculosis was founded in 1902 in Berlin.[23] Most controversial of all were sexually transmitted diseases, with medicalised approaches attempting to secure consensus between feminists and moral purity organisations.[24] The politics of attempts to secure an international eugenics organisation was also fraught with imperialist tensions, international boycotts and finally the rise of National Socialist racism.[25]

(v) National scientific federations such as the Gesellschaft deutscher Naturforscher und Ärzte or the British Association for the Advancement of Science were part of the liberal agenda of freeing science from state interference. From 1852 there was a series of international congresses on hygiene and demography. One type of congress was a mainly scientific congress that migrated round the cities of Europe: in 1857 there occurred the International Ophthalmological Congress, and coinciding with the Universal Exposition held in Paris in 1867 the first International Medical Congress was held. At the same time there occurred a related movement for national and international standard setting in science and technology. Notable areas of activity concerned weights and measures: in 1875 a Bureau Internationale des Poids et Mesures was established at Sèvres, outside Paris. These conferences promoted universal standards in scientific and medical terminology, and established standard weights, measures and other types of standard units, leading to specialised, permanent committees from the 1890s.[26]

Before the First World War standard setting for drugs and vaccines was primarily a national affair (although international surveys were periodically undertaken). The LNHO was unable to establish its own laboratories, but it designated international laboratories at the National Institute of Medical Research in London, and at the State Serum Institute in Copenhagen: these represented the attempt to overcome national rivalries, although this was at the cost of the German Institute for Serum and Medical Research in Frankfurt.[27]

The above-mentioned conferences and organisations suffered from imperial rivalries and national interests. It required further developments to establish an organisation which could overcome problems of sectional interests with permanent staffs, whose dynamism ensured that these organisations represented far more than just the aggregated opinions of national representatives. Sections of the Treaty of Versailles directed the LN 'to take steps in matters of international concern for the prevention and control of disease'. Positive policies were formulated to promote health and welfare on a wide range of issues. However, the diversity of prior trends in international health work meant that the LNHO itself became a battleground for conflicting strategies of international health work.

The LN rapidly rose to prominence on the international stage after the First World War. The war itself had been a testing ground for relief agencies, and post-war epidemics, notably the influenza epidemic, braced the world for a global onslaught of typhus. Although this never materialised, the chapter by Balińska demonstrates the lasting effects in facilitating the emergence of an international health organisation. Several chapters in this volume deal with the LN's technical agencies, particularly its Health Organisation (LNHO) (Balińska, Dubin, Manderson), the Social Section (Miller, and Rooke and Schnell), and the International Labour Office (ILO) (Weindling). These case-studies complement already published work on other LN technical agencies such as that for Intellectual Co-operation.[28]

Geneva combined with the advantages of a location in a politically neutral state distinctive socio-cultural features as a canton, with its Calvinist sobriety, its interwar radical politics and at times riots. It provided a rarefied atmosphere – a sort of interwar Magic Mountain – where diplomats and welfare experts interacted. Its situation at the heart of Europe raises the question as to how Eurocentric international organisations were. Although such infectious diseases as typhus, malaria and syphilis were international problems, LNHO responses were Eurocentric. However, women members of the Mandates Commission regularly raised questions concerning infant mortality, the training of midwives, maternity protection and sanitation. The LN's authority over mandated territories gave it the chance to improve health and welfare conditions in a wide variety of locations.[29] Yet there were glimmers of a genuinely more internationalist approach. Rajchman and Štampar became preoccupied with Chinese public health during the 1930s, and there were attempts to internationalise nutrition research. Rooke and Schnell demonstrate how initial concerns with demographic reconstruction after the First World War gave way to more internationalist perspectives by the mid-1920s. Manderson's study confirms global priorities endorsed by the RF and LNHO, although it should also be kept in mind that epidemic intelligence in the Far East constituted an early-warning system for public health experts concerned with the defence of Europe's and North America's health. Cueto's study of South America confirms the increasing prominence of this region in international health promotion. Although British and French influence at the LN served to discourage intervention in colonial health, there were occasional initiatives in the fields of African child welfare and Asian diets.

The LN was a complex and evolving organisation, and the chapter by Dubin provides a pivotal overview of the structure of the LNHO and its place in the LN. The LNHO underwent several phases. Initially targeted towards epidemic control (Balińska) and monitoring infectious diseases (Manderson), it shifted to international standard setting; from this emerged a social agenda (Weindling) that represented one of the most ambitious theoretical schemes of interwar public health and was in pronounced contrast to the racialisation of health in fascist and kindred authoritarian states during the 1930s. Rivalries persisted between agencies, as for example in the problematic relations with the OIHP located in Paris.[30] Perhaps in contrast to the League's Secretariat, its technical agencies became increasingly dynamic and able to take initiatives that transcended the interests of member countries.[31] The personalities, despite idiosyncracies, of such as Ludwik Rajchman of the LNHO or Albert Thomas of the ILO emerge as visionary figures, and there is much scope for further investigation of the medical internationalism of experts such as René Sand (for a time a technical expert with the LRCS) and Andrija Štampar (a former director of Yugoslav public health who in exile worked for the LNHO).[32] Indeed, international organisations have attracted writers (notably the novelist Céline), and have furnished modern novelists with powerful characterisations and plots.[33] Against the cult of personality should be set the new emphasis on professional expertise and on the development of equitable and efficient systems of health provision. Here health centres were pivotal and demanded new expertise in public health and, as Rafferty demonstrates, in various aspects of nursing. Moreover, professionalism reinforced the supranationalist agenda.

Relations between the LN and the voluntary sector emerge as complex, as there were initially voluntaristic models for a world health authority. The tensions between state-sponsored and voluntary initiatives are central to the study of child welfare by Rooke and Schnell. Other chapters (by Hutchinson and Towers) focus on voluntary organisations (notably the CICR and the League of Red Cross Societies – hereafter LRCS), or on philanthropic foundations (Farley), for which Bulmer provides an analysis of their role as intermediary organisations. While having considerable interaction with the LN – indeed for a time the voluntary sector was poised through the LRCS to take the leading role in international health (see Towers and Hutchinson) – there ensued a division of labour between the voluntary organisations and between the more state-oriented LN and the Red Cross and other voluntary organisations.

The voluntary sector was itself undergoing a process of modernisation linked to professionalisation of social and public health work. Professionalisation and the associated process of the scientisation of social policy have been historically controversial, as is well borne out by studies of the RF.[34] The LNHO as oriented to scientific medicine was a largely male preserve, and issues like birth control and abortion were taboo. As Miller demonstrates, it had a female counterpart in the LN's Traffic in Women Commission. Another solution was to leave issues like birth control and sexually transmitted diseases to autonomous organisations: examples are the Union international contre le péril vénérienne, and the International Union for the Scientific Investigation of Population Problems.[35] By way of contrast to the LNHO as a scientistic male preserve, the family and social work were very much the preserves of women. Gender and professional issues are discussed by Miller in her chapter on the LN Social Section and by Rafferty in her chapter on nursing organisations in relation to the Red Cross.

The promotion of positive health, particularly of the physical and psychological health of the normal child and of adolescents, left unresolved issues about the fate of civilian populations in an age of total war. Whereas the LN's welfare programme was designed in part to shore up societies, to prevent them from slipping into war by ameliorating underlying social tensions, the problems of civilian populations in wartime remained (as Rooke and Schnell observe) unresolved. After the First World War the CICR provided relief to civilian refugees, notably from Russia (aided by the Czarist Red Cross organisation in exile). But the CICR and national Red Cross organisations continued to give priority to military relief. Indeed, the fact that a convention on civilian populations under military occupation was drawn up but never ratified was to have tragic consequences in shaping the priority of the Red Cross organisations during the Second World War when the CICR failed to act on behalf of civilian victims of the Nazi occupying forces and to inform the world of conditions in concentration camps and of the Holocaust.[36] Indeed Nazi racism and anti-Bolshevism may be construed as fascist perversions of the international health ideal.

The introduction of the Nobel Prizes in 1900 had augured a new era of scientific internationalism.[37] Scientific aspects of medicine emerge as crucial in the chapters by Moulin on the network of Pasteur Institutes, and in the studies focusing on the Rockefeller Foundation (RF) (Cueto and Farley). The RF had crucial interactions with the LN and its agencies (Balińska, Bulmer, Dubin, Rooke and Schnell, and Weindling), as well as with voluntary organisations (Thomson) and was itself a powerful modernising force. The RF's increasing scientific priorities establish a further important theme, which has been investigated elsewhere. Again, there was considerable rivalry for scientific prestige and influence, exemplified by the rivalry between the RF and the Pasteur Institutes in South America, which Cueto and Moulin consider in chapters 11 and 12. Particularly important are Schroeder-Gudehus' studies of the international politics of scientific organisations, arising from the politics of the Allied boycott of the Central Powers in the wake of the First World War. Scientists were active in the LN Committee on Intellectual Co-operation and in the International Council of Scientific Unions (ICSU), a non-governmental organisation founded in 1931.[38] The scientisation of social policy resonates with parallel developments in industrial organisation, notably Taylorism and the more welfarist corporatism of Fordism. The status of individual scientists, notably Fridtjof Nansen, assisted in their dynamic international roles, while others, such as Albert Schweitzer, adopted more quietist profiles.

The achievements of the LN's technical organisations can be contrasted to its diplomatic and political failures. The short time span, the lack of resources and the numerous political obstacles must be taken into account as they make the achievements of international health organisations all the more remarkable. Yet the health and humanitarian work should not be viewed uncritically. If compared to certain phases of the post-Second World War work of the United Nations and of other international agencies (like the Food and Agriculture Organisation (FAO), the United Nations Educational, Scientific and Cultural Organisation (UNESCO) and the United Nations International Children's Emergency Fund (UNICEF)), the LN emerges as excessively Eurocentric, professionalised, scientised and gender-biased in its strategies.[39] Here comparisons might be drawn with more populist approaches (notably the Health for All primary health care programme of the World Health Organisation (WHO)), intermediate technologies, and birth control and health education programmes.[40] Another line of comparison might be with the flowering of non-governmental, transnational idealism among internationalists like Julian Huxley and Joseph Needham in the late 1940s; yet their ideals succumbed to the power politics of the Cold War.[41] In looking back on the restricted sphere of activity of interwar organisations, it could be argued that the low priority given to relief meant that the world was ill equipped to respond to the need to save the lives of those falling prey to the military oppression and racial ideologies of the Axis powers during the Second World War. The spirit of the brave new internationalist world was not without its more sinister aspects.

Notes

1 For introductory texts see C. Webster (ed.), *Caring for Health: History and Diversity*, revised edn (Buckingham: Open University Press, 1993); A. de Swaan, *In the Care of the State: Health Care Education and Welfare in Europe and the USA* (Cambridge: Cambridge University Press, 1988). For exemplars of the comparative genre: H. M. Leichter, *A Comparative Approach to Policy Analysis. Health Care Policy in Four Nations* (Cambridge: Cambridge University Press, 1979); P. Evans, D. Rueschemeyer and T. Skocpol (eds.), *Bringing the State Back In* (Cambridge: Cambridge University Press, 1985); P. Flora and H. Heidenheimer (eds.), *The Development of Welfare States in Europe and America* (New Brunswick: Transaction Books, 1981); P. Baldwin, *The Politics of Social Solidarity. Class Bases of the European Welfare State 1875–1975* (Cambridge: Cambridge University Press, 1990); D. M. Fox, *Health Policies, Health Politics: The British and American Experience 1911–1965* (Princeton, N.J.: Princeton University Press, 1986); J. R. Hollingsworth, *A Political Economy of Medicine: Great Britain and the United*

States (Baltimore: Johns Hopkins University Press, 1986); M. Weir, A. S. Orloff and T. Skocpol (eds.), *The Politics of Social Policy in the United States* (Princeton, N.J.: Princeton University Press, 1988); D. Porter (ed.), *The History of Public Health and the Modern State* (Amsterdam: Editions Rodopi B.V., 1994); for the way in which international studies can neglect international agencies see 'The Health of Nations', *International Social Science Journal*, 29, 3 (1977), focusing on medical sociology and health indicators.

2 'Approaches to the Study of International Organizations', *International Social Science Journal*, 29, 1 (1977); 'International Organizations. Theoretical Perspectives and Current Trends', *International Social Science Journal*, 45, 4 (1993).

3 'Cringe or starve' satirised the activities of the Charity Organisation Society (or COS).

4 René Lacaisse, *L'Hygiène internationale et la Société des Nations* (Paris: Editions du 'Mouvement Sanitaire', 1926). C. W. Hutt, *International Hygiene* (London: Methuen, 1927). H. B. Eisenstadt, 'Aufgaben und Ziele der Hygienesektion des Völkerbundes', medizinische Dissertation, Berlin, 1930. H. van Blankenstein, *L'Organisation d'Hygiène de la Société des Nations* (Purmerend: J. Musses, 1934). N. M. Goodman, *International Health Organisations and Their Work* (London: Churchill, 1952). F. Brockington, *World Health* (Harmondsworth: Penguin, 1958). W. Hobson, *World Health and History* (Bristol: John Wright, 1963). N. Howard-Jones, *International Public Health between the Two World Wars: The Organisational Problems* (Geneva: WHO, 1978). N. Howard-Jones, *The Scientific Background of the International Sanitary Conferences 1851–1938* (Geneva: WHO, 1975). Howard-Jones, *The Pan-American Health Organization: Origins and Evolution* (Geneva: WHO, 1981). A recent contribution to this genre is M. I. Roemer, 'Internationalism and Public Health', *Companion Encyclopaedia of the History of Medicine* (London: Routledge, 1993), pp. 1417–35. See also M. I. Roemer, *National Health Systems of the World* (Oxford: Oxford University Press, 1991–3), 2 vols. An important aid for LNHO historians is: 'Bibliography of the Technical Work of the Health Organisation of the League of Nations, 1920–1945', *Bulletin of the Health Organisation*, 11 (1945), 1–235.

5 On the German Hygiene Museum see P. J. Weindling, *Health, Race and German Politics between National Unification and Nazism, 1870–1945* (Cambridge: Cambridge University Press, 1989). R. Beier and M. Roth (eds.), *Der gläserne Mensch – eine Sensation* (Stuttgart: Gerd Hatje, 1990).

6 Roemer, *National Health Systems*.

7 M. S. Teitelbaum and J. M. Winter (eds.), *Population and Resources in Western Intellectual Traditions* (Cambridge: Cambridge University Press, 1989); also in *Population and Development Review*, 14 supplement (1988). G. Bock and P. Thane (eds.), *Maternity and Gender Policies. Women and the Rise of the European Welfare States 1880s–1950s* (London: Routledge, 1991). T. Skocpol, *Protecting Soldiers and Mothers: The Political Origins of Social Policy in the United States* (Cambridge, Mass.: Harvard University Press, 1992). S. Koven and S. Michel (eds.), *Mothers of a New World. Maternalist Politics and the Origins of Welfare States* (New York: Routledge, 1993). V. Fildes, L. Marks and H. Marland (eds.), *Women and Children First: International Maternal Welfare, 1870–1945* (London: Routledge, 1993).

8 The impact and perceptions of the LNHO are beyond the scope of this book. See for example, G. E. Brooke, 'A System of Intelligence as a Handmaiden of Hygiene', *The Malayan Medical Journal*, 2 (1927), 6–11, and issues of the *Straits Times* (my thanks to Lenore Manderson for these references). For Britain see *Second Annual Report of the Ministry of Health* (1920–1), 44–6, and following years. For a German nationalist critique see W. Rimpau, 'Der geistige Krieg gegen Deutschland und wir', *Münchener Medizinische Wochenschrift*, 72 (1925), 1889–90. This journal carried frequent hostile notices of LNHO activities; see P. J. Weindling, 'The Divisions in Weimar Medicine: German Public Health and the League of Nations Health Organisation' (unpublished paper).

9 On the boycott of German science see B. Schroeder-Gudehus, *Deutsche Wissenschaft und Internationale Zusammenarbeit 1914–1928* (Geneva: Dumaret & Golay, 1966). On Soviet social hygiene see S. G. Solomon and J. F. Hutchinson (eds.), *Health and Society in Revolutionary Russia* (Bloomington and Indianapolis: Indiana University Press, 1990). On the German–Soviet special relationship see P. J. Weindling, 'German–Soviet Medical Co-operation and the Institute for Racial Research, 1927–c. 1935', *German History*, 10 (1992), 177–206.

10 Most studies of Soviet famine relief focus on the American Relief Administration under Herbert Hoover: see H. H. Fisher, *The Famine in Soviet Russia 1919–1923* (New York: Macmillan Co., 1927); B. M. Weissmann, *Herbert Hoover and Famine Relief to Soviet Russia 1921–23* (Stanford: Stanford University Press, 1974).

11 M. Marrus, *The Unwanted. European Refugees in the Twentieth Century* (New York and Oxford: Oxford University Press, 1985).

12 See references to the Red Cross below. The topic is large and complex. For a significant organisation in the sciences see N. Baldwin, *The Society for the Protection of Science and Learning Archive* (Oxford: Bodleian Library, 1988).

13 P. M. Haas, 'Introduction [to Special Issue: Knowledge, Power and International Policy Coordination]: Epistemic Communities and International Policy Coordination", *International Organizations*, 46, 1 (1992), 1–35. E. B. Haas, *When Knowledge is Power: Three Models of Change in International Organizations* (Berkeley: California University Press, 1990).

14 See foreword by Thomas Kuhn to L. Fleck, *Genesis and Development of a Scientific Fact* (Chicago: Chicago University Press, 1979), 1st edn 1935. R. S. Cohen and T. Schnelle (eds.), *Cognition and Fact – Materials on Ludwik Fleck* (Dordrecht: Reidel, 1986).

15 *Die Hygiene-Organisation des Völkerbundes. Kurzer allgemeiner Überblick über ihre Aufgaben und Ziele. (Verteilt auf der Hygiene-Ausstellung in Düsseldorf 1926)* (nd. np).

16 B. Freiherr von Toll, *Der oberste Gesundheitsrat von Konstantinopel in seiner völkerrechtlichen Bedeutung (1838–1914)* (Munich: Piloty and Loehle, 1922).

17 J. Baldry, 'The Ottoman Quarantine Station on Kamaran Island 1882–1914', *Studies in the History of Medicine*, 2, 1–2 (1978), 3–138.

18 H. Wehberg, *Theory and Practice of International Policing* (London: Constable, 1935), pp. 37–71. H. M. Kallen, *The League of Nations Today and Tomorrow* (Boston: Marshall Jones, 1919), pp. 133–5. F. B. Sayre, *Experiments in International Administration* (New York and London: Harper and Brothers, 1919), pp. 48–56. H. E. Gear and Z. Deutschmann, 'Disease Control and International

Travel. A Review of International Sanitary Regulations', *Chronicle of the World Health Organisation*, 10 (1956), 273–344. N. M. Goodman, 'Disease Knows No Frontiers. The Story of Quarantine and the World Health Organisation', *Progress*, 44 (1955), 237–40.

19 J. F. Hutchinson, 'Rethinking the Origins of the Red Cross', *Bulletin of the History of Medicine*, 63 (1989), 557–78. J. Bleker and H.-P. Schmiedebach (eds.), *Medizin und Krieg. Vom Dilemma der Heilberufe 1865 bis 1985* (Frankfurt am Main, 1987). The history of national constituent organisations remains fragmented. For case-studies see: F. R. Dulles, *The American Red Cross, a History* (New York: Harper, 1950); H. Seithe, *Das Deutsche Rote Kreuz und Nationalsozialismus* (Frankfurt am Main: Mabuse-Verlag, 1994); H. Lichtenstein, *Angepasst und treu geblieben. Das Deutsche Rote Kreuz im Dritten Reich* (Cologne: Bund-Verlag, 1988); W. Gruber, *Das Rote Kreuz in Deutschland* (Wiesbaden: Wirtschaftsverlag, 1985); L. van Bergen, *Voor Onze Jongens Een Sigaar. 'Een geschiedenis van het Nederland Indisch Roode Kruis' 1870–1945* (Nijmegen, n.d.); S. M. Best, *The Story of the British Red Cross* (London: Cassell, 1938); M. Poulter, 'The Archives of the British Red Cross', *Social History of Medicine*, 6 (1993), 143–8.

20 E. V. Heyen, *Bürokratisierung und Professionalisierung der Sozialpolitik in Europa (1870–1918)* (Baden-Baden, 1993). 'La Première conférence internationale de service social, juillet 1928', *Vie Sociale*, 5–6 (1988).

21 *Congrès internationale d'assistance* (Paris, 1889).

22 D. Dwork, *War is Good for Babies and Other Young Children: A History of the Infant and Child Welfare Movement in England, 1898–1918* (London and New York: Tavistock, 1987), pp. 94–102. For the critical German response see Weindling, *Health, Race and German Politics*, p. 199. See also L. Manderson, 'Bottle Feeding and Ideology in Colonial Malaya: The Production of Change', *International Journal of Health Services*, 12 (1982), 597–616.

23 L. Bryder, *Below the Magic Mountain* (Oxford: Oxford University Press, 1988), p. 16.

24 *Conférence internationale pour la prophylaxie de la syphilis et des maladies vénériennes, Bruxelles, Septembre 1899* (Brussels: H. Lamertin, 1899). P. J. Weindling, 'The Politics of International Co-ordination to Combat Sexually Transmitted Diseases, 1900–1980s', in V. Berridge and P. Strong (eds.), *AIDS and Contemporary History* (Cambridge: Cambridge University Press, 1993), pp. 93–107.

25 S. Kühl, *The Nazi Connection: Eugenics, American Racism, and German National Socialism* (Oxford: Oxford University Press, 1993). P. J. Weindling, 'The "Sonderweg" of German Eugenics: Nationalism and Scientific Internationalism', *British Journal for the History of Science*, 22 (1989), 321–33. Weindling, *Health, Race and German Politics*. D. Kevles, *In the Name of Eugenics* (New York: Knopf, 1985). M. P. Adams (ed.), *The Wellborn Science: Eugenics in Germany, France, Brazil and Russia* (Oxford: Oxford University Press, 1990).

26 E. Crawford, *Nationalism and Internationalism in Science, 1880–1939* (Cambridge: Cambridge University Press, 1992), pp. 38–43.

27 W. C. Cockburn, 'The International Contribution to the Standardization of Biological Substances. I: Biological Standards and the League of Nations, 1921–1946', *Biologicals*, 19 (1991), 161–9.

28 F. Northedge, *International Intellectual Co-operation within the League of Nations: Its Conceptual Basis and Lessons for the Present* (London, 1953).

29 C. Miller, 'Lobbying the League: Women's International Organisations and the League of Nations', DPhil. dissertation, University of Oxford, 1992.

30 N. Howard-Jones, *Les bases sciéntifiques des conférences sanitaires internationales 1851–1938* (Geneva: WHO, 1975). R. Carvais, 'La maladie, la loi, et les moeurs', in C. Salomon-Bayet (ed.), *Pasteur et la Révolution pastorienne* (Paris: Payot, 1986), pp. 279–330, 413–22.

31 A. Loveday, *Reflections on International Administration* (Oxford: Oxford University Press, 1956).

32 M. D. Grmek (ed.), *Serving the Cause of Public Health. Selected Papers of Andrija Štampar* (Zagreb: Andrija Štampar School of Public Health, 1966). M. A. Balińska, 'Ludwik Rajchman, International Health Leader', *World Health Forum*, 12 (1991), 456–65. M. A. Balińska, *Ludwik Rajchman. Médecin sans frontière* (forthcoming).

33 For Louis-Ferdinand Destouches as a budding novelist at the LNHO between 1924 and 1927 see: F. Vitoux, *La vie de Céline* (Paris: Grasset, 1988) (transl. New York: Paragon House, 1992); P. Alméras, *Les idées de Céline* (Paris: Université Paris 7, 1987). P. Alméras, *Céline: entre Haines et Passion* (Paris: Laffont, 1994). M. Cournot, 'Céline avant', *Le Monde* (4–5 October 1992). M. A. Balińska, 'Céline face à Rajchman', *Le Monde* (17 October 1991). For a modern historical novel see: Frank Moorhouse, *Grand Days* (London: Picador, 1993).

34 See chapter 7 by Weindling on social medicine, and chapter 15. The Rockefeller Archive Center (15 Dayton Avenue, Pocantico Hills, North Tarrytown, NY 10591–1598, USA) is a major resource for the history not only of the RF but also of foundations. See: Rockefeller Archive Center, 'A Bibliography of Published Works Citing Resources at the Rockefeller Archive Center 1975–1991' which demonstrates the richness of this literature. K. W. Rose (ed.), *The Availability of Foundation Records: A Guide for Researchers* (Pocantico Hills: Rockefeller Archive Center, 1990). *Rockefeller Archive Center Newsletter*. Also: E. R. Brown, 'Public Health in Imperialism', *American Journal of Public Health*, 66 (1976), 897–903.

35 *Population. Journal of the International Union for the Scientific Investigation of Population Problems*, 1 (1933–). For subsequent developments see R. Symonds and M. Carder, *The United Nations and the Population Question 1945–1970* (London: Chatto & Windus, 1973); S. P. Johnson, *World Population and the United Nations. Challenge and Response* (Cambridge: Cambridge University Press, 1987).

36 J.-C. Favez, *Une Mission Impossible? Le CICR, les déportations et les camps de concentration nazis* (Lausanne: Payot, 1988), transl. *Das internationale Rote Kreuz und das Dritte Reich* (Zurich: Verlag Neue Zürcher Zeitung, 1989). M. Dworzecki, 'The International Red Cross and its Policy vis-à-vis the Jews in Ghettos and Concentration Camps in Nazi-occupied Europe', *Rescue Attempts During the Holocaust* (Jerusalem: Yad Vashem, 1977), pp. 71–110. A. Ben-Tov, *Facing the Holocaust in Budapest. The International Committee of the Red Cross and the Jews in Hungary 1943–1945* (Dordrecht: Nijhoff, 1988).

37 E. Crawford, *Nationalism and Internationalism in Science 1880–1939* (Cambridge: Cambridge University Press, 1992).

38 A history of ICSU is in progress under the direction of Frank Greenaway.

39 For UNESCO see J. Sewell, *Unesco and World Politics* (Princeton: Princeton University Press, 1975). P. Lengyel, *International Social Science: The UNESCO Experience* (New Brunswick: Transaction Books, 1986) and the UNESCO-sponsored *International Social Science Journal*, 1, 1– (1959–). For UNICEF see M. Black, *The Children and the Nations: the Story of UNICEF* (New York: UNICEF, 1986). Also: M. Wyman, *DP. Europe's Displaced Persons 1945–1951* (Philadelphia: Balch Institute Press, 1989). George Woodbridge, *UNRRA. The History of the United Nations Relief and Rehabilitation Administration* (New York: Columbia University Press, 1950), vol. I, p. 306.

40 A definitive history of the WHO remains a desiderata. See *The First Ten Years of the World Health Organisation* (Geneva: WHO, 1958); *The Second Ten Years of the World Health Organisation 1958–1967* (Geneva: WHO, 1968); *Four Decades of Achievement. Highlights of the Work of the WHO* (Geneva: WHO, 1988). P. Morpurgo, 'The Role of Outside Expertise', *International Social Science Journal*, 20 (1977), 46–57.

41 M. Finnemore, 'International Organizations as Teachers of Norms: The United Nations Educational, Scientific and Cultural Organisation and Science Policy', *International Organizations*, 47 (1993), 565–98.

2

'Custodians of the sacred fire': the ICRC and the postwar reorganisation of the International Red Cross

JOHN F. HUTCHINSON

The Italian War of 1859 helped to create the Red Cross; the First World War precipitated efforts to reorganise it. These may be divided into two quite different categories: those which sought to consolidate and extend the traditional role of the International Committee of the Red Cross (ICRC) and the national societies, and those which asserted the need to create a new kind of Red Cross for the anticipated new era of peace and international co-operation. Support for the idea of a limited reorganisation came primarily from the ICRC (entirely Swiss in membership since its inception in 1863), and from the national Red Cross societies of the smaller European states; proposals for a much more ambitious reform came principally from America and Japan. What rapidly took shape was a power struggle between the Red Cross societies of the victorious Allies, led by the Americans, and the ICRC, which understandably feared for its own survival if the reformers were to triumph. In one form or another, this struggle lasted until 1928, when a settlement of the main issues was finally reached.

More was at stake in this conflict than was apparent on the surface: at its heart lay a fundamental disagreement over what role the Red Cross ought to play in modern society. The advocates of sweeping change sought to shift its focus from war and wounds to illness and misfortune, from assisting the military medical services in wartime to assisting the public health services in peacetime; consequently they believed that a new international Red Cross organisation was called for. On both counts, they soon found that they would receive only limited co-operation from the ICRC, which had its own, considerably less ambitious, plans for the future. In an era which spawned numerous international health and welfare organisations right and left, most members of the ICRC sought to retain as much as possible of the traditional role of the Red Cross, the rationale for which seemed to them as strong in the 1920s as it had in the 1860s. Their determination was not always appreciated: as one exasperated critic put it, they appeared to think of themselves as 'the custodians of the sacred fire'.[1]

Within days of the signing of the Armistice, the ICRC sent a circular letter to all of the national societies and to the governments of the erstwhile belligerents concerning the post-war activity of the Red Cross.[2] It reveals much about how the members of the ICRC initially saw the post-war role of the Red Cross. After expressing 'joy and gratitude' at the ending of 'this butchery', the circular went on to note that the major focus of ICRC activity during the war, the care and treatment of prisoners of war, would soon end; now was the moment to consider in what other ways the sufferings of war could be diminished. The circular noted that efforts to assist these needy groups were already under way in some countries, and were sponsored either by the state or by private societies. However, the ICRC suggested that a greater degree of co-operation might ensue if governments and national Red Cross societies were to exchange information about their intentions at a conference to be held for this purpose.[3] The circular concluded by asking recipients to respond to these suggestions.

There are no surprises in this document for anyone familiar with the prewar history of the ICRC. From the 1860s the ICRC had always taken the view that the most important peacetime tasks of the national societies included caring for the victims of the last war while preparing improved ambulance services for the next. To be sure, the colossal scale of the war just ended meant that immediate needs far exceeded all previous governmental or philanthropic endeavours on behalf of the wounded and other victims of war. In these circumstances, an exchange of information and intentions among governments and national societies was therefore especially appropriate. Nor was there anything remarkable in its expressed concern for the ravages of tuberculosis; as the ICRC was well aware, the French and especially the German national societies had for decades been heavily involved in campaigns to reduce the incidence of tuberculosis among their civilian populations, particularly among men of military age and among young women who might bear the next generation of soldiers.[4] Nor was there anything novel in the proposal for an international conference: in the past the ICRC had frequently nudged the national societies towards what it regarded as a desirable course of action by proposing that it be the subject of an international conference. The November circular made it plain that, while recipients of this letter were at liberty to suggest whatever they pleased, the ICRC for its part had no intention of proposing a substantial reordering of the priorities of the Red Cross movement.

During these very weeks an entirely different vision of the future of the Red Cross was taking shape in the mind of Henry P. Davison, the New York banker who in 1917 had been appointed Chairman of the War Council of the American Red Cross (ARC) by Woodrow Wilson. Davison was a relative newcomer to the Red Cross movement; his own involvement dated from 1910, when he had run a successful fund-raising drive for the ARC in New York City. About the European Red Cross societies and the International Committee in Geneva he understood only what he had been able to pick up during the war, and that had not impressed him very much. Understandably proud of what the ARC had achieved in a very few years, Davison soon convinced himself that the Red Cross everywhere needed to be rejuvenated by an infusion of American enthusiasm and American money.

Once Davison realised that the ARC would finish the war with a surplus of close to $75 million in its treasury, he put forward an idea which, he claimed, would be both 'a great service to mankind and a creditable finish to our Red Cross movement'; to a close associate he wrote that if he could secure the approval of President Wilson and the adherence of the British, French and Italian Red Cross Societies, he planned to

> go to Geneva and suggest to the International Red Cross that they immediately invite . . . delegates from the various Red Cross organizations throughout the world for a conference . . . [and] I would there organize a real International Red Cross . . . there is common ground in the Red Cross which would bring together all the nations, leading to a better understanding . . . [and] there could be cooperation at least along humanitarian lines. For instance, I can see a medical force organized which would formally adopt a regime for fighting tuberculosis and that there would be a world-wide fight against the plague. There would also be adopted a recognized formula for treating with other plagues incident to certain localities, such as yellow fever, typhus, etc. It is not beyond reason to believe that there might develop a plan of cooperation for treating with the destitute where they are in masses resulting from the war . . . many moves . . . might be made . . . which would evolve from a getting together and exchange of views . . . [including] The adoption of a system of reports relative to health conditions, disasters, etc., which would be cleared through the International Red Cross.[5]

This passage reveals the full extent of Davison's bold vision for the future: the need to create a 'real' international Red Cross that would take the lead in such humanitarian enterprises as the struggle against epidemic diseases and the organisation of relief for those made destitute by war. Coupled with this vision was a timetable for its speedy realisation:

> if anything is going to be done along this line, it must be done immediately, because minds are now more or less groping and pliable, whereas in a few months they will become cold and it will be difficult. Of course, at the outset, the Red Cross organizations of the Central Powers would not be invited, but as soon as peace is declared they should be invited.[6]

Whilst conceding that at the moment his plan was little more than a daydream, he nevertheless alerted his associate in Paris that he might require at short notice a villa on the Riviera, several top-ranking legal and medical advisers, and a secretarial staff, not to mention 'a first-class car and the best chauffeur in France'. A senior partner at J. P. Morgan & Co., Davison was used to thinking big and acting decisively.

Only a week after his return to America, Davison had an interview with

President Wilson at the White House, at which he outlined his plan for creating '[a] virile effective international Red Cross'.[7] Wilson's reaction was positive: he liked the idea of the Red Cross societies of the world being reorganised 'under the not too obtrusive leadership of the American Red Cross', and urged Davison 'to proceed to Geneva as quickly as possible' and confer with the 'rather amiable gentlemen' who made up 'the present international committee'.[8] Wilson appears to have been under the impression – as perhaps Davison was – that the projected world conference of Red Cross Societies would be competent to produce a new or revised Geneva Convention; in fact, it could have produced no more than a draft, because such an agreement would have required the full diplomatic congress that included representatives of the states party to the 1906 Convention. This went well beyond the sort of post-war Red Cross conference that the ICRC had in mind.

Encouraged by the President's support, Davison spent considerable time explaining his plan to William E. Rappard of the Swiss Legation in Washington; Rappard, a recently appointed member of the ICRC, had arrived in Washington in June of 1917 carrying a letter of introduction from its President, Gustave Ador, to President Wilson.[9] Rappard apparently greeted the proposal with enthusiasm and, somewhat rashly perhaps, assured Davison of the co-operation of the ICRC in Geneva.[10] This was all that he needed to hear. After securing the approval of the War Council of the ARC and the agreement of his associates at J. P. Morgan & Co., he made his second Atlantic crossing in a month; scarcely had he disembarked before he was explaining his idea to Sir Arthur Stanley of the British Red Cross.[11]

Over the next few weeks, more pieces of the plan fell into place: with Wilson's approval, Colonel House approached Lloyd George and the other allied leaders while Davison spoke to the leaders of the allied Red Cross Societies.[12] Keeping to his original intention, Davison went to Cannes to develop his plans; the necessary money for the enterprise was readily available thanks to a special appropriation of $2.5 million granted him by the ARC War Council.[13] On 25 January, Colonel House wrote from Paris that the allied governments were lining up behind the plan, and that he (House) would be discussing this 'splendid' idea with the ICRC President, Gustave Ador, who was to see him the following day.[14] On 1 February, Davison formed a 'Committee of Red Cross Societies', representing the United States, Britain, France, Italy and Japan; its stated purpose was to prepare and present 'to the Red Cross Societies of the whole world an enlarged program of action in the general interest of humanity.'[15] The time had come for direct talks with the ICRC, and Davison telegraphed to arrange a meeting of the 'Cannes Committee' with the ICRC in Geneva on 12 and 13 February.[16]

Members of the ICRC were understandably concerned about both the scope of Davison's proposal and the seemingly breakneck speed with which he expected it to be implemented. This was by no means the first time in the long history of the Red Cross that someone had proposed transforming it into an international welfare society. At the Berlin Conference in 1869, for example, no less a figure than Rudolf Virchow had suggested that the misfortunes of soldiers in wartime ought to take second place to those experienced by most people in peacetime.[17] However, the ICRC had always rejected such arguments on the grounds that the original and special purpose of the Red Cross – assistance to sick and wounded soldiers – would easily become lost amidst the countless rival claims for assistance. Davison's plan was far more sweeping in its scope than more modest plans that had been discussed and rejected in the past; moreover his manner of proceeding smacked too much of steamroller tactics. What gave the Americans the right to assume that it was their duty to reorganise the work of Red Cross societies throughout the world? The ICRC knew better than to regard the Committee of Red Cross Societies as anything other than an American operation in disguise: Davison was its heart and soul, as well as its banker. He seemed to expect that the ICRC would endorse in advance whatever proposals the Cannes Committee chose to elaborate.

On the other hand, President Wilson's enthusiastic support for Davison's scheme put the ICRC in a quandary: despite their reservations, they could scarcely appear to be uncooperative without appearing to set themselves against the rising tide of optimism. In any case, Rappard had already led the Americans to believe that there would be no difficulties in Geneva, and the ICRC itself had already hailed President Wilson 'as the indefatigable defender, on the world stage, of the principles of humanity and justice which it [the ICRC] labours itself to make prevail'.[18] Moreover, it was impossible to ignore Davison's arguments about the need to move quickly in this new atmosphere of co-operation. Prudence therefore dictated the greatest tact and restraint in dealing with the Davison plan.

Ador and the other members of the ICRC met Davison and his associates in Geneva on 12 February, at the splendid Athenée, chosen, no doubt, because it had been the scene of the 1863 Conference which founded the Red Cross. Members of the ICRC wished to make it clear that they were no temporary wartime creation, invented only so that belligerents could communicate with one another through a neutral intermediary; rather they were the trustees of the Red Cross movement, the direct heirs of its founders, who had collectively accumulated nearly sixty years of activity and experience on its behalf. They were not about to be thrown into the 'dustbin of history' merely because some influential Americans had recently discovered the usefulness of Red Cross organisations.

Virtually the only thing that all could agree on was that a reconsideration of the role of Red Cross societies was both timely and necessary. Davison wished the ICRC to endorse the proposals of his Committee of Red Cross Societies but this they refused to do, on the grounds that such an endorsement would pre-empt the invitation that had already been sent to all national societies, asking them to make suggestions for the future work of the Red Cross. Davison's proposals enjoyed the apparent support of five national societies, but from the Genevans' point of view, they should be taken no more – or less – seriously than proposals advanced by any five national societies. Davison wished the ICRC to call an international conference immediately, without including the national societies of the Central Powers; again the ICRC refused, on the grounds that the universalism of the Red Cross precluded the very idea of exclusion, temporary or otherwise. Davison stated the intention of his Committee to submit their proposals to a conference of experts which they planned to hold at Cannes as soon as practicable; the ICRC replied that, while the five associated societies could seek whatever expert advice they chose, it would be up to them to persuade other national societies to support the Cannes proposals at the international conference.[19] As a gesture of goodwill after all its refusals, the ICRC did agree that it would take steps to convene a full international Red Cross conference within thirty days of the signing of the peace treaty. Davison's group retired, not without some disappointment, to Paris, to make plans for convening the conference of public health experts in Cannes.

On 13 February, while the allied Red Cross representatives were still in Geneva, the ICRC issued an Appeal concerning the forthcoming conference.[20] One of the most carefully worded documents ever issued by the ICRC, the Appeal contrived to suggest that Davison and his associates were simply responding with enthusiasm to the idea of an enlarged, peacetime Red Cross, for the instigation of which the ICRC now credited its own Circular of 27 November 1918. The visit to Geneva by representatives of the five Red Cross societies was described as an opportunity 'to explore, with the International Committee, the best means of attaining the immediate goal. In this visit, where a complete agreement was noted between the International Committee and the Red Crosses, the questions which will be taken up at the Conference were examined'.[21] The ICRC noted that the five Red Cross societies had their own agenda for peacetime health work; pointed out that other national societies might be especially interested in the plight of victims of war, or in the formation of nursing corps; and emphasised that 'there is no question of providing ready-made solutions which will be imposed by a vote'.[22] Finally, it announced unambiguously that the task of leading the way to this Red Cross of Peace would become part of its own work, which it was beginning by calling the Conference. Thus the Appeal underlined the primacy of the ICRC, while studiously avoiding the real differences which had surfaced at the Geneva meeting, thereby giving the rest of the Red Cross world a quite misleading impression of harmony.

Members of the ICRC were not against all change; but they instinctively mistrusted sweeping and headlong changes. They disliked any changes over which they might lose control. Davison himself was so full of his own desire to create a 'real' Red Cross that he was unable to appreciate the basis of their apprehension. In a private letter to Woodrow Wilson, he confessed that he was 'much disappointed' in the ICRC; 'I find the organization very weak and without imagination or courage.'[23] Yet from the Genevan perspective, Davison's plan not only threatened to alter drastically the traditional Red Cross concern with soldiers and victims of war; it also threatened to relegate the ICRC to the limited and occasional role of wartime neutral intermediary, and to replace its moral leadership of the international movement with some as yet undefined but probably representative executive body; most ominous of all, perhaps, it implied that what had been, for more than half a century, a successful voluntary organisation of amateurs now needed the guidance of scientific experts in public health and philanthropy. That Davison was disappointed by his reception in Geneva is a measure of how little he understood the role of the ICRC within the Red Cross movement.

The lukewarm response in Geneva led Davison to solicit Woodrow Wilson's help in tying the new Red Cross organisation to the League of Nations. He had originally thought of rewriting the Geneva Convention to make provision for the new organisation, but the impossibility of holding a fully international Red Cross conference in the strained atmosphere of post-war Europe prevented this. Members of the Allied Red Cross societies refused to sit down with those whom they believed guilty of gross violations of the existing Geneva Convention. As a result, Davison explained in a letter to Wilson, there were only two alternatives: either to postpone the Geneva conference indefinitely, which would be tantamount to abandoning his plan for a reorganised international Red Cross; or, as he delicately put it, 'to proceed in some relation to the League of Nations'.[24] Hinting strongly that he had really given up on the ICRC, Davison made it clear that he now saw Wilson's League of Nations as his only hope. Luckily for him, Wilson and his advisers were looking for some immediate and practical demonstration that the 'international spirit' they were invoking in Paris was not simply a figment of their own imaginations. Needless to say, Davison made no public statement about the possibility of an alliance with the League, nor did he, so far as one can tell, discuss the idea formally with the Committee of Red Cross Societies. The ICRC was purposely left completely in the dark. With the Cannes conference scheduled to meet from 1 to 10 April, Davison was obviously hoping for a positive response from Wilson before the conference had finished its business. His personal timetable still called for returning to New York in late May, as he reaffirmed in a letter to J. P. Morgan.[25]

Wilson, anxious to capitalise on such a concrete demonstration of the benefits of internationalism, quickly sent Davison a positive response, in which he proposed that they 'tie the Red Cross up in some proper way with the League of Nations and arrange for the admission of other nations to the Red Cross

International Organization when they are admitted to the League of Nations'.[26] Meanwhile, Colonel House supplied Wilson with alternative drafts of an article concerning the Red Cross that could be included in the Covenant of the League.[27] Both cited the improvement of public health as the chief, though not the only, goal of the Red Cross; one referred to 'the principle of international cooperation through the action of national Red Cross organizations, while the other specifically mentioned an "International Red Cross League"'.[28] Presumably these draft articles were discussed by House and Davison when they met on 27 March, just before Davison left Paris for the Conference in Cannes.[29]

It was at this point that the alarm bells started to ring in Geneva. After the February meeting, Ador had sent two members of the ICRC, Rappard and Alfred Gautier, to Paris to keep an eye on the unpredictable Davison. On 28 March, Rappard learned from Colonel House what was being discussed, and reported on these developments to the ICRC. Although its members were well aware of President Wilson's favourable attitude towards Davison's general plan, it had never occurred to them that these three Americans would cook up a plan to reorganise the Red Cross without the approval and participation of the ICRC. The immediate issue was, of course, the timing of the Geneva Conference, which Davison's Committee had asked the ICRC to call on 5 May, provided that the peace treaty had been signed by then. Colonel House had apparently told Rappard that 'in view of the mood that he had noted on the part of some of the Allies, though deploring it himself, he thought it better in any case to convene two successive and separate conferences for the Societies of the Allies and neutral countries on the one hand and for the Societies of the Central Powers on the other'.[30] Greatly irritated by this news, the ICRC wired Davison in Cannes and asked him to clarify the situation. Davison, unwilling to show his hand until he had received further assurances from Wilson about the League Covenant, coyly replied, 'Owing to a recent and important development, I am unable for the moment to reply more fully to your telegram, much as I regret this.'[31] Instead, he invited the ICRC to send delegates to Cannes in order to keep it abreast of developments. The tail was indeed wagging the dog.

The Cannes Conference met from 1 to 10 April in the lavish surroundings of the Cercle Nautique. When the ICRC representatives arrived on 3 April, they found themselves surrounded by experts in public health, epidemiology, sanitary science, hygiene and nursing. Davison had invited more than fifty of the most illustrious medical and scientific names of the day, among them Aldo Castellani from Italy; Emile Roux and Albert Calmette from France; and Sir Arthur Newsholme, Sir Ronald Ross and Henry Kenwood from Great Britain. The American delegation was a veritable 'who's who' of medicine, public health and philanthropy, including Hermann Biggs, Hugh Cumming, Emmett Holt, Wycliffe Rose, Frederick Russell, Richard Pearson Strong and William H. Welch. In a separate Nursing Section of the Conference, social reformer Lilian

Wald from America joined seven recognised leaders of military nursing from Britain, France and Italy.

The Cannes Conference did what Davison wanted: it put the scientific stamp of approval on his vision of the future. Participants shared his belief that the recent war had proved the Red Cross could be 'an agency for good of unparalleled force and power', and held that 'for the prevention of disease and the betterment of the health and the general welfare of the people in all countries . . . the potential usefulness of the Red Cross . . . is unlimited . . . No other organization is so well prepared to undertake these great responsibilities at the present time.'[32] Accordingly, the Conference endorsed the idea that an association or league of national Red Cross societies should be organised, and that an international bureau of hygiene and public health should be attached to it. Strong and Castellani, well known for their work in containing the typhus epidemic in Serbia in 1915, were the foremost advocates of the formation of this bureau, but of course they were largely preaching to the converted. An emergency campaign against typhus and the rapid development of child welfare work were singled out as the two highest priorities for the new bureau to undertake; in addition, the Conference drew up a series of resolutions and memoranda relating to preventive medicine, tuberculosis, malaria, venereal diseases and nursing, to indicate 'some of the lines of activity which the new organization may wisely follow'.[33] Once the bureau was established, it would be expected to formulate programmes in other fields, such as mental hygiene, industrial hygiene, foods and nutrition. Further resolutions called upon Red Cross societies everywhere to encourage 'wise Public Health Legislation and efficient Public Health Administration', to prepare suitable plans and designs for 'proper housing for workingmen', and to erect as war memorials buildings that could be used as health and community centres.[34] Seemingly, no aspect of health and hygiene, whether personal or public, was to be left unattended.

Now that the programme had been formulated by the experts, Davison could organise his 'real' international Red Cross. In the middle of the Conference, word came from Paris that – at Wilson's urging – the Covenant of the League of Nations (LN) would contain the following Article 25: 'The members of the League agree to encourage and promote the establishment and co-operation of duly authorized voluntary national Red Cross associations having as purposes the improvement of health, the prevention of disease and the mitigation of suffering throughout the world.'[35] On the initiative of Biggs and Welch, delegates replied with a telegram to the Allied leaders, setting out graphically the threat posed by the typhus epidemic already raging in Central Europe, and offering the services of Davison's Committee of Red Cross Societies to fight the epidemic and provide relief to those stricken by famine.[36] As soon as he learned the news from Paris, Davison told Edouard Naville of the ICRC that he had decided to proceed immediately to transform his Committee into a League of

Red Cross Societies (LRCS), without waiting for the proposed Red Cross conference in Geneva.[37] In short, he was presenting the ICRC with a *fait accompli*. Although some of its members tried to dissuade him and his associates, the momentum that Davison had built up was now unstoppable. Two weeks later, in Paris, Davison announced that Articles of Association had now been signed, creating a League of Red Cross Societies, composed initially of the five Allied Red Cross societies, but which other societies could join with the approval of the League's Board of Governors, which Davison himself would chair.[38] The League would immediately establish its headquarters in Geneva, and the campaign against typhus would be organised by Richard Pearson Strong, who would become the first Director of its Medical Department. Davison himself, having kept to his original timetable for seizing the golden moment, now returned to New York, leaving the day-to-day running of the League in the hands of Strong and the new (British) Director-General, Sir David Henderson, whose appointment, it was claimed, exemplified the new spirit of international co-operation.[39]

Taken aback by the speed at which this had all happened, the ICRC was forced to put the best possible face upon events which it may have deplored, but had been unable to prevent. Since Davison had publicly announced the formation of the League, it was vital that the ICRC speedily communicate with the other national societies, in order to remove any possible confusion about its own future in the wake of the creation of the League. On 20 May, therefore, the ICRC issued another circular letter in which it briefly summarised what had happened since its February meeting with the Committee of Red Cross Societies. While it applauded the eagerness of Davison and his associates to begin their expanded programme of peacetime activity, the ICRC was careful neither to welcome the formation of the League, nor to approve the manner of its creation. Instead, the circular reaffirmed that the ICRC 'remains the medium of all the Red Cross Societies, which it has always been by virtue of the successive decisions of the [international] Conferences. The organization now created should in no way supplant it, but rather spread and extend its activities.'[40] Shrewdly, the ICRC quoted liberally from the conciliatory letter which Davison had sent to Geneva just before announcing the formation of the League; in it he had described the League as 'a plan of action whose way must be considered as purely transitory', and had affirmed his intention that the League should become a universal body as soon as circumstances permitted.[41] The ICRC did not explicitly promise to co-operate with the League; rather, they claimed to be studying what kind of support and collaboration they might be able to give without compromising their principles of impartiality, balance and neutrality. The circular concluded by restating the urgency of convening the proposed international conference as soon as the peace treaty had been signed and ratified. One perceptive senior member of the ARC commented after reading the circular that 'The Committee is trying to be very careful to see that the Red Cross societies do not take the League too seriously.'[42]

In truth, the ICRC could do little else. Since it had taken the position that the future direction of the movement could be determined only by an international conference, any delay in signing the peace worked to its own disadvantage, while providing the League with an opportunity to establish its separate identity. During this interval, the prudent course was to appear to be co-operating with the League – a posture which was affirmed when Rappard became Secretary-General of the League while continuing to serve as a member of the ICRC – while doing nothing whatever to persuade other national societies either to join the League, or to endorse the programme drafted at the Cannes Conference. Thus a façade of legitimacy was created, one which concealed – at least for the moment – the ICRC's profound conviction that the League was an unwelcome and illegitimate child, foisted upon the Red Cross world by the urgency and determination of Harry Davison.

This uneasy relationship between the ICRC and the League lasted much longer than had been expected. For reasons that need not be explored here, the Tenth International Conference could not be convened in Geneva until the spring of 1921. Only then did the ICRC obtain the opportunity at long last to assert its revised vision of the future of the Red Cross. This vision was necessarily different from the one articulated in its November 1918 circular, and reflected the altered circumstances in which the ICRC now found itself, not only because of the formation of the League, but also because the world of the Red Cross was not entirely exempt from the political dynamics of the post-war decade. It is to these altered circumstances that attention must now turn.

Three salient facts emerge from this two-year period. First, Davison had obviously been right to believe that there was considerable sympathy among national Red Cross societies for an expanded peacetime programme of activities, and for the effort to establish new national societies all over the world. Between May 1919 and July 1921, LRCS membership grew from the original five to thirty-five national societies.[43] To be sure, enthusiasm for its programme was not the sole consideration: newly independent states such as Finland, Czechoslovakia and the Kingdom of the Croats, Serbs and Slovenes naturally took every opportunity to assert their elevated status by joining international organisations; so did the incipiently autonomous British dominions of Canada, Australia, New Zealand, India and South Africa. Moreover, membership in the LRCS was regarded in some quarters as desirable simply because it enabled poorer countries to receive additional aid from richer ones, particularly from the United States.

Secondly, whatever their reasons for joining, the adherence of so many national societies to the LRCS demonstrated that they did not share the ICRC's belief that nothing new or fundamental could be done in the world of the international Red Cross unless it had first been discussed and approved at a duly constituted conference. If they had endorsed this view, they need only have declined the invitation to join the LRCS and put forward alternative proposals for discussion at the Geneva conference. It is no surprise that the ICRC's 'constitutional' objections to the LRCS carried so little weight: the ICRC itself took important initiatives whenever it felt them appropriate, whether or not there had been prior consultation or discussion with the national societies. An outstanding example of this phenomenon in the post-war years was its response to the Russian Revolution: not only did the ICRC decide to treat the Bolshevik reorganisation of the Russian Red Cross quite differently from the way it had treated previous, arguably more drastic, reorganisations of other national societies, but it also decided to continue recognising the tsarist Red Cross in emigration while withholding recognition of the Soviet Red Cross.[44] Both these decisions were taken without prior discussion at an international conference. To be sure, matters to do with the recognition of national societies had long been within the purview of the ICRC; however, since the Geneva Convention specified that there could only be one recognised Red Cross society in a country, there was, at the very least, room for discussion. In the circumstances, it was perhaps a little hypocritical for members of the ICRC to complain that Harry Davison had acted unilaterally in creating the LRCS.

Thirdly, individuals and agencies outside the Red Cross neither understood nor cared about the issues and rivalries that divided the ICRC and the LRCS; for them, the existence of two uncoordinated Red Cross bodies, both with international pretensions, was perplexing and sometimes aggravating. What were their separate spheres of influence? Which organisation was the proper one to deal with? Both the secretariat of the League of Nations (LN) and the organisers of other international welfare organisations found it awkward, not to say incomprehensible, that the Red Cross seemed unable to put its house in order. From many quarters, therefore, the ICRC felt pressure to clarify its relationship to the LRCS.

For most of those connected with the LRCS, and for many of those outside the movement, the simplest and most obvious course was for the LRCS to take charge of the peacetime work of the international Red Cross, and for the ICRC to lie dormant unless another war should require it to function as an intermediary in a world of belligerents and neutrals. Such a sharp division of roles was precisely what the ICRC feared most, and tried to prevent by every means at its disposal. To be sure, the LRCS had no power either to abolish or to impose a more limited peacetime role upon the ICRC; by the same token, the ICRC had no power to abolish the LRCS, but it could and did rethink its own role, and it used its influence at Red Cross conferences to strengthen its position *vis-à-vis* the LRCS. Durand himself notes that the ICRC took its first tentative step into the broader world of international welfare when it agreed to become 'patron' of the Save the Children Fund International Union (SCIU) (yet another important decision taken without prior reference to an international Red Cross conference).[45] There were three peacetime functions which the ICRC had traditionally exercised, functions to which it clung tenaciously whenever others threatened to limit this role: it was the principal medium of communication among the national societies, it was the organiser of their international conferences, and it was the publisher of the *Bulletin International de la Croix-Rouge*. These recognised functions gave the ICRC considerable advantage in any possible showdown with the LRCS.

A showdown of sorts took place in the spring of 1921, at a moment when the LRCS appeared to be extremely vulnerable. Both of its most important leaders were by then seriously ill: Davison with 'neuritis in the head' (which proved to be a brain tumour) and Sir David Henderson with the cancer to which he succumbed in August 1921.[46] Davison made his last trip to Geneva in March of that year to chair the LRCS Board of Governors meeting; he returned home shocked by Henderson's obviously failing health. In addition, the LRCS suffered from tensions that were almost inevitable in an organisation that tried to combine professional administrators, technical experts and volunteers. Eminent medical scientists found it difficult to leave their universities and institutes for more than a few months, and in Geneva the League could offer little or nothing in the way of laboratory and research facilities. Thus, despite the best efforts of Richard Pearson Strong and Hermann Biggs, both of whom had served brief stints as its Medical Director, the League was still a long way from achieving the place that had been envisioned for it by the delegates in Cannes. True, it had played a minor role in fighting typhus and famine in post-war Europe, but its work in promoting public health was limited to the creation of training programmes for public health nurses and to the publication of the *International Journal of Public Health*. A great deal of time and effort went into promoting the creation of new Red Cross societies, planning regional conferences, and popularising the Junior Red Cross. However, the LRCS never managed to become *the* international health organisation of the post-war world, a situation that was underlined when the League of Nations created its own health organisation in 1921.

The LRCS was largely an American creation, and it remained heavily dependent on the financial support of the American Red Cross. Davison had used ARC money, as well as his prestige as ex-Chairman of its War Council, to create the LRCS, but his mandate to do so had come from the War Council, itself an interim body; once the ARC had returned to a peace footing, the LRCS became vulnerable to the same tide of post-war isolationism that kept America from joining the LN. Many Americans were understandably irked that the other national societies which joined the League contributed so little money for its operations. In 1921 the LRCS turned to the Rockefeller Foundation in the hope that it might provide a subsidy for the *International Journal of Public Health*, but the application was unsuccessful.[47] Moreover, both the American Relief Administration (ARA), headed by Herbert Hoover, and the ARC Commission in Europe, headed by Robert Olds, did their best to keep the LRCS from becoming a serious player in the business of post-war relief.[48] The Americans seemed to be turning their backs on their own creation.

All in all, the achievements of the LRCS in its first two years of operation were considerably less than breathtaking. Doubtless it was a similar evaluation of the situation that led the ICRC to attempt a complex outflanking strategy. This involved, on the one hand, quietly undermining the credibility of the LRCS while publicly appearing to co-operate with it, and on the other hand using the 1921 Geneva Conference to marginalise the LRCS while strengthening substantially the position of the ICRC. The LRCS was even more vulnerable than might be appreciated from what has been said above because of its ambiguous legal status: Article 25 of the League Covenant referred to co-operation among national Red Cross societies, but did not specifically mention the LRCS, so that arguably its existence was justified neither by the Covenant nor by a resolution adopted at an international Red Cross conference. Since it had not achieved the status of an official League agency, the LRCS had to find some basis for survival in the Red Cross world, or it would be in danger of becoming an institutional orphan. Thus its need for legitimation put an additional advantage in the hands of the ICRC.

Once the Tenth Conference was fixed for March 1921, the ICRC set about persuading some national societies that the LRCS could be ignored or replaced by a more suitable body. In January 1921, ICRC delegates visited Rome, Athens and Sofia to canvass the idea of forming an International Red Cross Union, 'under the direction of the Comité International, with the assistance and advice, and perhaps cooperation, of a committee of delegates from the various national Red Cross societies'.[49] The LRCS discovered what was afoot when one of its staff members, T. B. Kittredge, was told about the plan by the President of the Bulgarian Red Cross, Ivan Gueschoff. Evidently what was envisioned was the establishment in Geneva of 'an office that would coordinate and reinforce the efforts of the national societies in their struggle against physical and moral destitution, and would administer an international fund meant to support activities undertaken for the benefit of the victims of such misery. This fund should be sustained by subventions from the national Red Cross societies.'[50] Kittredge also reported that he had been told that the LRCS was regarded as 'pronouncedly Anglo-Saxon in membership, ideas, and its direction. It is suspected of being a form of propaganda machinery for Anglo-Saxon and particularly for American ideas and influence.'[51] The Bulgarian Red Cross, he was told, believed that 'a genuine union must be accomplished under a leadership and direction, whose real neutrality, and whose genuine international character cannot be doubted, that is, under the Comité International'.[52] Sensibly, Kittredge concluded 'that the Red Cross Societies of the world will never contribute from their funds to support two international organizations. If the Union International de la Croix Rouge is established, and maintained by contributions of member societies, the fate of the League [LRCS] is clear.'[53]

Yet at the same moment when its delegates in the Balkans were doing their best to undermine the LRCS, the ICRC itself proposed, and eventually signed, a one-year working agreement with the LRCS, under which a Joint Relief Commission was established, composed of members of both bodies.[54] This policy was arguably less contradictory than it might seem at first glance. By signing such an agreement on the eve of the Tenth Conference, the ICRC secured four important advantages: first, it was now able to reassure outsiders that the two Red Cross bodies were co-operating; secondly, if accused by member societies of the LRCS of working to undermine that body, it could point to the working agreement as evidence of its good intentions; thirdly, this agreement to co-operate in organising peacetime relief was tantamount to an admission by the LRCS that the role of the ICRC was far broader than that of wartime neutral intermediary; fourthly, the one-year term of the agreement effectively removed the question of ICRC/LRCS relations from the agenda of the Tenth Conference, leaving the ICRC with a perfect opportunity to secure from the Conference further recognition of its special role and broad sphere of action within the Red Cross movement. There is no doubt that the ICRC obtained far more from this agreement than did the LRCS; as one knowledgeable American commented on learning of its terms, 'it struck me as exactly the sort of agreement I should want if I were in the place of the Comité International and intended eventually to put the League [LRCS] out of business'.[55] To make assurance doubly sure, an unpublicised 'side agreement' stipulated that the Chairman of the Joint Relief Commission would be named by the ICRC; not surprisingly, Gustave Ador himself assumed this position.

With this advantageous agreement in hand, the ICRC was able to obtain from the Tenth Conference resolutions that not only confirmed but extended its role. With the LRCS representatives confined to the role of 'guests' – a status they shared with delegates of the League of Nations – they were in no position to challenge the ICRC's masterful orchestration of the occasion. The passage of Resolution XVI was a triumph for the ICRC; not only did the Conference confirm the existing organisation and all of the previous mandates of the ICRC, but it added a crucial clause which implicitly but effectively diminished the international aspirations of the LRCS:

> The Conference approves the activity of the International Committee in peacetime.
> It recognizes the Committee as the guardian and propagator of the fundamental, moral and legal principles of the organization and appoints it to watch over their dissemination and application throughout the world.[56]

Only two years had elapsed since Harry Davison had arrived in Geneva determined to create a completely new international Red Cross. At that time, the ICRC feared for its own survival amidst the tide of international benevolence which produced the LRCS; but now, with the flow running in the other direction, it was clear that the LRCS would either be eliminated or, if it survived at all, it would do so only on the terms set by the ICRC.

Had the choice been left to Gustave Ador, there is little doubt that the LRCS would have been superseded by something like the Union International de la Croix-Rouge. However, the ICRC's very insistence on the supreme role of the Red Cross conference to some extent limited its options: if ill-informed but well-intentioned conference delegates insisted – as they did repeatedly – that both the ICRC and the LRCS should survive and find ways to live with one another, then efforts had to be made to find a basis for co-operation. This is not the place to review the tortuous 'fusion' negotiations which occupied both bodies for the next eight years; no less than four separate attempts were made to bring the ICRC and the LRCS closer together. The details of these negotiations have been examined elsewhere.[57] It was hardly a coincidence that a workable agreement was eventually reached shortly after Gustave Ador's death in 1928. Under its terms, a truncated version of the LRCS survived, primarily as an international co-ordinating agency for disaster relief. What is clear from the events of 1919–21 is that the ICRC had little or no sympathy for the idea of a new peace-time Red Cross organisation that would devote itself to broad programmes for the improvement of health and welfare.[58] Thanks to a fortuitous combination of circumstances, the ICRC was able to weather the challenge posed by Harry Davison's audacious vision, and to emerge from the post-war contest with its traditional organisation and methods confirmed, and its historic mission modestly but enthusiastically extended. The keepers of the sacred flame had not only preserved and defended it; they had even managed to augment it.

Notes

1 American Red Cross Library. Henry P. Davison Papers. Robert E. Olds to Otis Cutler, 31 August 1921.
2 National Archives and Record Administration (NARA), Record Group 200: Records of the American National Red Cross (ANRC), Box 52, File 041: International Red Cross Committee. ICRC Circular No. 174, 27 November 1918.
3 *Ibid.* p. 3.
4 See, for example, Dr P. Bouloumier, *L'effort antituberculeux de l'Union des Femmes de France. Son programme, ses réalisations* (Paris: Vigot, 1919) and Bodo von dem Knesebeck, *Das Deutsche Rote Kreuz und die Tuberkulosebekämpfung* (Berlin and Charlottenburg: Das Rote Kreuz, 1921).
5 Davison Papers. Davison to Harvey D. Gibson, 22 November 1918, pp. 2–3.

6 *Ibid.* p. 3.

7 Davison used these words in his cable no. 10580, to Harvey D. Gibson, 10 December 1918, quoted in Clyde E. Buckingham, *For Humanity's Sake. The Story of the Early Development of the League of Red Cross Societies* (Washington, DC: Public Affairs Press, 1964), p. 32.

8 Davison Papers. Woodrow Wilson to Davison, 3 December 1918.

9 Library of Congress, Division of Manuscripts. Woodrow Wilson Papers. Gustave Ador to Wilson, 23 June 1917.

10 ARC cable no. 10580, Davison to Gibson, 10 December 1918, quoted in Buckingham, *For Humanity's Sake*, p. 32.

11 Sir Arthur Stanley, 'Recollections of the Early Days of the League', *Red Cross Courier*, 8, 9 (1 May 1929), 5.

12 House to Lloyd George, 14 January 1919, in Charles Seymour, *The Intimate Papers of Colonel House* (Boston: Houghton, Mifflin, 1928), vol. IV, pp. 257–9; see also Buckingham, *For Humanity's Sake*, pp. 36–7.

13 War Council minutes, 15 January 1919, quoted in Buckingham, *For Humanity's Sake*, p. 40. However, this sum was only half of the $5 million that Davison had requested; members of the War Council evidently thought it prudent to withhold some of the funds until more was known about how Davison's plans were working out. Davison Papers. Davison to Eliot Wadsworth, ? January 1919, cable no. 17267.

14 Woodrow Wilson Papers. Edward House to Davison, 25 January 1919.

15 Georges Milsom, 'The History of the Red Cross', *World's Health*, 3, 1 (January 1922), p. 20.

16 According to André Durand (*From Sarajevo to Hiroshima. History of the International Committee of the Red Cross*. Geneva: Henry Dunant Institute, 1984, p. 149), the ICRC received telegrams from Davison on 4 and 6 February. Regrettably, copies of these telegrams have not been preserved in the Davison Papers.

17 *Compte rendu des travaux de la Conférence Internationale tenue à Berlin du 22 au 27 avril 1869* (Berlin: J. F. Starcke, 1869), pp. 185–7.

18 Woodrow Wilson Papers. Edouard Naville, interim President of the ICRC, to Wilson, 9 December 1918. Naville was serving as interim President during the absence in Berne of Gustave Ador, who had been serving on the Swiss Federal Council, and who was elected President of the Confederation for 1919.

19 The ICRC's version of what took place at these meetings may be followed in *Bulletin International de la Croix-Rouge*, 15 March 1919, pp. 334–51. The text of Davison's Memorandum was published in *Revue Internationale des Sociétés de la Croix-Rouge*, 1, 4 (15 April 1919), 393–402. This account draws on several additional sources: Durand, *From Sarajevo*, pp. 148–53; Buckingham, *For Humanity's Sake*, pp. 45–6; Davison Papers, Robert E. Olds to Otis Cutler, 31 August 1921.

20 Davison Papers. 'Appel du Comité international de la Croix-Rouge à Genève' (13 February 1919).

21 *Ibid.* p. 1.

22 *Ibid.* p. 2.

23 Davison Papers. Davison to Wilson, 9 March 1919, p. 2.

24 *Ibid.* p. 2.

25 Davison Papers. Davison to J. P. Morgan, 15 March 1919.

26 Davison Papers. Wilson to Davison, 26 March 1919.

27 Buckingham, *For Humanity's Sake*, pp. 63–4. In all probability these drafts were prepared by Chandler Anderson, the former State Department legal adviser whom Davison had hired as counsel to the Committee of Red Cross Societies.

28 For the text of these draft articles, see David Hunter Miller, *The Drafting of the Covenant* (New York: Putnam, 1928), vol. I, p. 400.

29 Woodrow Wilson Papers. Davison to Wilson, 27 March 1919: 'This afternoon I have had an opportunity to go over the whole subject with Colonel House, who says he will speak to you about it, so I will not take up your time by writing.'

30 Rappard's report is quoted, presumably from the ICRC Archives, in Durand, *From Sarajevo*, p. 156.

31 Quoted by Durand, *From Sarajevo*, p. 156.

32 *Proceedings of the Medical Conference Held at the Invitation of the Committee of Red Cross Societies, Cannes, France, April 1 to 11, 1919* (Geneva: The League of Red Cross Societies, 1919), p. 12.

33 *Ibid.* p. 13.

34 *Ibid.* pp. 13–14.

35 Davison read the text of the Article to the Seventh Session of the Conference on 7 April 1919: *ibid.* p. 82.

36 The text of this telegram is reproduced in *ibid.* pp. 162–4.

37 Durand, *From Sarajevo*, p. 157.

38 A copy of the Articles of Association is preserved in NARA/RG 200 ANRC Box 55, Folder 041, LRCS Origins 1919.

39 On the choice of Henderson, see Buckingham, *For Humanity's Sake*, pp. 78–9.

40 A copy of ICRC Circular No. 182 is preserved in NARA/RG 200 ANRC Box 55, Folder 041. LRCS Origins 1919, p. 2.

41 *Ibid.* p. 2; Davison to ICRC, 3 May 1919, in NARA/RG 200 ANRC Box 55, Folder 041. LRCS Origins 1919.

42 George Murnane to Livingston Farrand, 11 July 1919, in NARA/RG 200 ANRC Box 55, Folder 041, LRCS Origins 1919.

43 *The League of Red Cross Societies – Its Work and Aims* (Geneva: League of Red Cross Societies, 1921), p. 3.

44 Durand does his best to provide an explanation for this behaviour; see *From Sarajevo*, pp. 97–108.

45 *Ibid.* pp. 164–5.

46 For the impact of these illnesses on the work of the LRCS, see Buckingham, *For Humanity's Sake*, pp. 161–91.

47 There is an extensive correspondence on this subject in the papers of C.-E. A. Winslow at Yale; Sterling Memorial Library, Winslow Papers, Group 749, Series III, Box 80, Folders 1244–1253: LRCS.

48 This story is well told by Buckingham, *For Humanity's Sake*, pp. 88–107.

49 See the Memorandum from T. B. Kittredge in Sofia to LRCS headquarters in Geneva dated 21 March 1921; Hoover Institution Archives, League of Red Cross Societies, Box 1, Folder 7, Bulgarian Red Cross, p. 1.

50 *Ibid.* p. 2.

51 *Ibid.* p. 1.

52 *Ibid.*
53 *Ibid.*
54 Durand, *From Sarajevo*, p. 168; see also Buckingham, *For Humanity's Sake*, pp. 179–80.
55 Davison Papers. Robert E. Olds to Otis Cutler, 31 August 1921; quoted in Buckingham, *For Humanity's Sake*, p. 180.
56 Quoted in Durand, *From Sarajevo*, p. 171.
57 See *ibid.* pp. 174–94.
58 Even Miss Cramer, who like Rappard was not unsympathetic to an extended peacetime programme, warned that the Red Cross could never hope to become a panacea for the woes of humanity. See Renée-Marguerite Cramer, 'La tâche de la prochaine Conférence internationale des Croix-Rouges', *Revue Internationale des Sociétés de la Croix-Rouge*, 1, 4 (15 April 1919), 403–11.

3

Red Cross organisational politics, 1918–1922: relations of dominance and the influence of the United States

BRIDGET TOWERS

Introduction

The theme of this chapter is the influence of the United States of America on the development of international health organisations in Western Europe. The period focused upon is the short four-year span between 1918 and 1922 during which new international organisational bases were being created for the health work of the League of Nations (LN) and major conflicts were occasioned among existing organisations. It was a time of the building of new power bases and political structures in the context of the Paris Peace Conference; it was also the period in which domestic health policies were being negotiated in separate national discourses.

I will argue that American influence in international health organisations was exercised through the powerful corporate philanthropic organisations of the American Red Cross (ARC) and the Rockefeller Foundation (RF). The influence of the RF, through the International Health Board, on public health in Europe has been documented and researched.[1] The role of the American Red Cross, under the chairmanship of Henry Davison, and its War Council has been less studied, although Howard-Jones suggests it may have been pivotal in the formation of the Health Section of the LN.[2]

Background

The United States played a major role in the post-war construction, financing and design of what were two of the largest international health organisations in the world, the League of Red Cross Societies (LRCS) and the League of Nations Health Organisation (LNHO), the forerunner of the World Health Organisation (WHO). Additionally, through the International Health Board (IHB) of the RF, American influence on public health was exercised in a series of large-scale aid and development projects in Europe.[3]

American influence was expressed directly and indirectly, openly and

36

secretly, through formal organisational representation and informally through personal and group associations and networks. It was realised not only in organisational practices, work processes and institutional forms but also at the level of constituting the nature of an 'international health' discourse.

While there was not one determinant level or sphere of influence, considerable emphasis should be placed upon the primacy of the political realm within which American influence was internationally expressed. It is self evident that international agreements between states in the field of co-operation on health matters are likely to be subject to political considerations, particularly with respect to foreign policy. This is likely in so far as the implications of such agreements incur expense and loss of freedom of mobility which in turn might affect trade and communications and in the past might have involved whole networks of colonial government and administration.

Attempts to make international agreements between states on a limited number of quarantine regulations began in 1851 with the setting up of the International Sanitary Conference in Paris. These met irregularly every seven or eight years but failed to secure any significant binding agreements even with the apparent emergency concerns of cholera epidemics. Their deliberations and meetings were characterised by a conservatism and deep suspicion about any regulatory controls which might interfere with trade; agreements were frequently called off if it was apparent that any one country might fail to co-operate or exclude itself. Incrementally by the turn of the century some agreements had been reached on quarantine regulations concerning yellow fever and cholera, more as a result of mutual self interest than of any shift in philosophy.

The 1912 Sanitary Conference agreed to establish a more permanent forum for the administration of co-operation between states on health controls and the Office international d'hygiène publique (OIHP) was established in Paris. It was not established to have any role in promoting or expanding the sphere of international public health. It was firmly rooted in the mid nineteenth-century philosophy of minimum quarantine controls and has been described as: 'a club of senior public health administrators, mostly European, whose main preoccupation was to protect their countries from the importation of exotic diseases without imposing too drastic restraints on international commerce'.[4]

Provided that public health agreements were confined to these narrow conservative limits, while there might be difficulties in enforcement and agreements on particular details there were no fundamental conflicts over health policy or philosophy between states. It was when demands came for a more positive concern for the promotion of health and the 'prevention' of disease rather than the reactive 'control of epidemics' that conflicts emerged. These occurred not only between different states and countries but also between different groups within countries and different international organisations.

Although these conflicts were about different public health philosophies and policies, they were not always focused upon identified 'health issues'. They were often expounded and discussed at the level of political theories of the role of the state in the provision of welfare goods and services. More frequently they were expressed at the basic level of the responsibility for finance and funding.

These debates in international public health were echoes of the broader challenges being made in many western industrial societies to *laissez-faire* philosophies in their governance not only of the relationship between citizens and the state, but the relationships between states themselves. At this time in the United States there had been a shift within the economic and political philosophy of industrial capitalism away from individualistic free enterprise towards corporate capitalism involving the linking of interests and offices of the state and capital through new regulatory and co-ordinating agencies, and inter-locking directorates.[5] This managerial principle of maintaining hegemony through negotiated agreements within a planned and regulated framework was coming to be defended and expanded to cover not only industrial production, trade and economic policy in the industrial capitalist societies but also health and welfare planning at an international level. In each of the agencies examined in this chapter one can see the American promotion and defence of this new ideology against what they impatiently perceived as the forces of reactionary traditionalism.

Brown has argued that members of the American corporate class during the Progressive era 'acting mainly through philanthropic foundations articulated a strategy for developing a medical system to meet the needs of a capitalist society'. Whilst his analysis attributes low significance to international public health, a number of his observations are helpful in understanding the connec-tions between the emergence of new philosophies of public health, the formation of new professional classes and the corporatist philosophy of Rockefeller philanthropy.[6] The Rockefeller Commission always affirmed the importance of the partnership between the state and the private sector in the provision of health and welfare services. The Americans through the interwar period remained persistently critical of any attempts to make public health provision a state monopoly. However their interpretation of what constituted 'private' or 'voluntary' provision was somewhat elastic and many bodies and institutions receiving 100 per cent state financing which characterised themselves as 'private' retained only notional autonomy. By the same token they seemed willing to interpret such large transnational organisations as the LRCS, with its heavy political representation, as 'voluntary' bodies.

Braverman identifies this as the period in the United States which saw the emergence of a new form of scientific management, 'Taylorism', based on an attempt to locate and exercise control within the structure of work processes and organisations, rather than externally through personally imposed orders and disciplinary codes.[7] The new leadership of the ARC and the Rockefeller IHB came from the ranks of top business and financial management and brought with them the style and some of the practices of Taylorism, particularly their concern for strategic planning, strict budgeting controls, efficiency and cost effectiveness. It also featured in their early organisational planning and rhetoric on the importance of a strong executive management and specialist sub-units linked in a line of accountability upwards. This was particularly apparent in the Rockefeller Mission to France under Dr Livingston Farrand and the ARC Commission in Europe under Robert Olds. However, the principles of scientific management often were of little avail or credibility in matters that touched on foreign policy. There was a constant tension between the rational planning approach of the American leadership and the self-interested political pragmatism of the Europeans. Although the organisational reality of this new management style often fell far short of the ideal, it was rehearsed as part of the rhetoric of legitimation of change during this formative period.

The League of Red Cross Societies (LRCS)

The LRCS was a new international health organisation composed of a federation of national Red Cross Societies. Created after the Armistice, largely by the leaders of the ARC, to co-ordinate and promote health work during peacetime, it was distinct from the older Comité international de la Croix Rouge (CICR) which was a neutral (i.e. private, independent and autonomous) organisation composed of Swiss citizens and formed in the 1864 Geneva Convention.

The ARC played an active part in the 1914–18 European war zone, particularly in France; and the Rockefeller Mission to France relied heavily upon their personnel and organisation in Paris. The co-operation between the Rockefeller Mission and the ARC was forged back in America at the highest levels of management. Before launching the Rockefeller Commission to France discussions were held with the Executive Committee of the ARC in Washington. The new standards of the Rockefeller international philanthropy represented on its IHB had tended to disparage the past work of the ARC, but the appointment in 1917 of Henry Pomeroy Davison, a leading business financier, as Chairman of the War Council of the ARC was greeted with enthusiasm and believed to herald a new era of strong management.[8] The War Council became the steering group of the whole executive and brought a new emphasis upon the efficient co-ordination of all war work and the deployment of the most available expert advice and personnel. On his arrival Davison announced that a new spirit of professionalism would be found in the ARC; the business men who had assumed control were prepared to think in large financial budgets and were expecting to attract trained experts to the organisation.[9]

Davison's plan for the development of the ARC did not stop at the simple

co-ordination of war relief work; more ambitiously he envisaged the transformation of the International Red Cross with the ARC at its core into a new
international health organisation. In America the National Red Cross Societies
had developed a range of social and health programmes during peacetime and it
was this work that Davison hoped to co-ordinate and expand as an international
function. In contrast to America, Red Cross societies in many other countries,
although active and often operating on a large scale, engaged in activities which
were essentially linked to conditions generated by war.

There have been a number of interpretations of Davison's decision to extend
the ARC. House histories of the ARC have tended to stress the evolutionary
inevitability of the development of the agency during peacetime.[10] Howard-
Jones links Davison's view of an international health agency to a broader
development of international thinking in America, but does not examine the
source of such ideas.[11] He also places much emphasis on Davison's charismatic
personality, a factor however which needs putting in the context of the new type
of executive management adopted by the ARC. It seems likely that factors which
were involved in the setting up of the Rockefeller IHB were relevant to the
policy development of the War Council of the ARC; namely, a new corporate
strategy of working closely with the political agencies of the state, and a new
management style based on a strong and independent executive looking to the
profitable and efficient expansion of its markets or sectors of influence. The
wartime programme of the ARC had given the leadership a familiarity with
Europe as a theatre of operations which they were eager to retain and expand in
peacetime.

As early as November 1918 Davison was outlining his plans for expansion to
Harvey Gibson, ARC Commissioner for Europe:

> if the President requests me I would accept the responsibility of representing the
> ARC to go at once to Paris to meet there by arrangement the representatives of
> the British Red Cross, French Red Cross and Italian Red Cross. If in accord with
> me, or possibly if they were not, I could then go to Geneva and suggest to the
> International Red Cross that they immediately invite by telegram and cable
> delegates from various Red Cross organisations to a conference – I would then
> organise a *REAL* international Red Cross.[12]

Davison had a strong sense of political opportunism but was constantly frustrated by the international dimension of the political environment in which he
had to operate. He apparently saw the furtherance of American interests as
synonymous with progress and was at a loss to understand the reluctance of the
Europeans to co-operate eagerly and willingly with his initiatives. He sensed that
there was a unique opportunity for action immediately after the Armistice: 'if
anything is going to be done . . . it must be done immediately because new minds
are more or less groping and pliable, whereas in a few months they will become

cold and it will be difficult'.[13] Even at that stage he was considering the possibility of making a new international Red Cross an arm of the putative League of
Nations (LN):

> I have a feeling that if there is anything whatever in the question of the League of
> Nations there is a common ground in the Red Cross which would bring together all
> the nations leading them to a better understanding: for instance I can see a medical
> force organised which would formally adopt a regime for fighting tuberculosis and
> that there would be a worldwide fight against the plague.[14]

It was true that there was nothing new in the idea of expanding the work of the
CICR in peacetime.[15] What was new was a specific plan of how to realise such
an idea and a climate in which an international agency could be fitted into the
planning of new agencies for international co-operation.

The plan was quickly put into operation with letters sent to the Italian, French,
British and Japanese Prime Ministers (who were present in Paris for the
Versailles Peace Talks) outlining Davison's plan to enlarge the scope of
the CICR.[16] The letters had the imprimatur of President Wilson and reflected the
lobbying Stockton Axson, secretary to the ARC, had engineered in Washington.
There were some difficulties in securing the President's co-operation since
most of the senior ARC personnel were Republicans. Regretting that more
Democrats had not been brought into the organisation at the time of the change,
but by some tortuous reasoning, Axson assured Wilson that: 'the absence of
Democrats is a sign of the nonpolitical motive of Mr Davison and his organising
Association'.[17]

The ARC had a broader charter than the Geneva Convention: under its federal
charter 1905–6 it was empowered to carry out a system of national and international relief in time of peace and it was precisely this sort of extension that
Davison wanted to see in a revision of the Geneva Convention. But for the CICR
to consider such a change a conference was necessary and that was only likely
to be convened if the national Red Cross societies, particularly those of the 'Big
Five' powers, petitioned for one. Davison therefore went to Paris in January
1919 and set up a series of informal meetings. He arrived with full accreditation
from President Wilson who stressed from the outset the political dimension of
the plan:

> Although the Red Cross is not strictly a governmental agency but rather a
> voluntary organisation, it is clear that a moral endorsement on the part of the most
> important governments is essential to insure the fullest possibilities of the plan . . .
> The success of the Conference would seem assured if it can be made clear that the
> movement has at the outset the unqualified approval and support of the govern-
> ments named.[18]

In Paris Davison relied heavily on the political and diplomatic figure of
Colonel Edward Mansell House who was a special representative of the US

Government at the Paris Peace Conference. Appointed by Wilson in 1918 as a personal adviser, he had no formal part in the government but was recognised everywhere as confidante and adviser to Wilson.

Following these informal negotiations in which an agreement to work together on the plan had been reached, a formal meeting of representatives of the 'Big Five' Red Cross Societies was organised in Cannes later in the same month. The convening of this meeting was very rapid and indicated the urgency with which Davison was pursuing the plan. Davison anticipated being elected Chairman and being given complete executive freedom, and with the granting of that authority he told the powerful J. P. Morgan, a supporter of the project, that he was 'ready to begin to operate'.[19] From the beginning the dominance of the Americans in the enterprise was an important factor in guaranteeing political backing in America and was taken for granted by Davison: 'For obvious reasons the ARC must be the leader and it has been made clear that they will follow us about anywhere, whereas any other Red Cross organisation cannot command the following'.[20]

Notwithstanding the support of the 'Big Five', Davison was concerned that the existing CICR should be seen as party to the development, but Gustave Ador, Chairman of the CICR, was not enthusiastic about the plan, recognising that the mantle of organisation and control of the Red Cross would pass from the Swiss to the Americans.[21] During the year the CICR's opposition to the plan grew steadily into a firm refusal to integrate with the LRCS. This provided Davison with a continued focus for resentment and embarrassment. Being unable to secure the patronage or co-operation of the CICR, Davison decided to fight them and to gain political and press promotion to back the project. Seeking House's help he requested maximum attention and publicity: 'in order to insure the highest degree of success this project must be presented to the world in a very effective and high-toned manner'.[22] To give an idea of the level of promotion he envisaged he asked House to have the subject presented at a banquet in Paris attended by Clemenceau, Lloyd George, Orlando (the Prime Minister of Italy) and the Japanese representative. This promotional work was also active in eliciting the support of leading medical and scientific experts, which was mainly achieved through academic networks.

There was, however, one significant stumbling block which Davison failed to anticipate and that was the strength of the anti-German feeling amongst the French and British Red Cross leadership. Even though the Armistice had been signed and the International Peace Conference had been called, the French and British Red Cross delegates refused to meet with representatives of the German Red Cross until all accusations of German violations of the Geneva Convention had been examined and answered. Davison was exasperated and unable to understand this attitude as anything more than stubbornness which could jeopardise the whole plan. But recognising that he was unlikely to move their position he suggested to House that a possible solution would be: 'to tie up the plan alongside the League of Nations, in fact, practically identical in its form; its headquarters to be the same as that of the League of Nations'.[23] Although Davison had from the beginning linked his vision of a new international peace-time Red Cross to that of the emerging LN, this was the first time the nature of the link was specified.[24]

House and Davison's promotion was successful and the Cannes medical conference was convened on 1 April 1919. The conference was mainly concerned with formulating the scope and purpose of the medical section, which later became the General Medical Department of the LRCS. Policy, administration and co-ordination were left to an Executive Committee based in Paris. A Board of Governors was appointed, composed of representatives of the 'Big Five' founders. Davison's position as Executive Chairman was confirmed and Sir David Henderson was appointed as Director General. On 5 May 1919 the Committee formally agreed on the establishment of 'The League of Red Cross Societies', its declared purpose being: 'To associate the Red Cross Societies of the world in a systematic effort to anticipate, diminish and relieve the misery produced by disease and calamity'.[25]

The high point of the Conference was Davison's dramatic announcement that he had received an official but confidential telegram from Sir Eric Drummond, Secretary-General of the LN, confirming the official recognition of the LRCS in Article 25 of the Covenant of the League of Nations.[26] This recognition was to have strategic importance for the status of the organisation and proved later to be something of an embarrassment to the Health Organisation of the League of Nations when it was created. Davison had lobbied hard and long for that recognition, against opposition from those who argued that official recognition of a voluntary organisation at the very beginning of the League of Nations work was inadvisable. Drummond throughout his dealings with Davison and Henderson remained confident in the personnel and administration of the LRCS and wanted them integrally involved in any international public health agency that might be set up; he judged that any loss of goodwill would jeopardise the potential efficacy of the health work of the League of Nations.[27]

With this acknowledgement, the LRCS under Davison's direction decided to set up its headquarters in Geneva rather than Paris. In January 1919 he cabled the War Council of the ARC for an appropriation of $5,000,000 to be used at his discretion for the new work; he was given $2,500,000.[28] This was clearly a very large sum and it was particularly remarkable that this initial funding was subject to the exclusive personal control of the Chairman. This largesse contrasted markedly with the paucity and rigidity of funding with which the other international health organisations based in Europe had to manage. It was also indicative of the style and form of the ARC initiative, with its emphasis upon speed, opportunity and results, and with a chairman's large private budget it had the opportunity and facility to bypass the traditional political and organisational channels.

The Epidemic Commission

The politics and interests involved in the establishment of the Epidemic Commission provide a good example of the importance of the organisational dimension in defining and legitimating what constitutes 'health' issues. One of the earliest activities the LRCS undertook as a formal organisation was to be responsible for the campaign against the typhus epidemic in Eastern Europe. Davison had sent a telegram to the leading participants at the Paris Peace Conference from the Cannes medical conference urging action to be taken, and specifically suggesting that the new LRCS should be the organisation responsible for this work: 'the Committee of Red Cross Societies of the Allied Nations is in our opinion the natural and at present only, agency available to undertake this work if the required resources are placed at its disposal and if it is invested with proper power'.[29] From the view point of a new organisation such work was significant in that it would put the LRCS on the map in terms of its ability and operational reality. As early as May 1919 Davison was outlining his plans for the involvement of the LRCS in the typhus epidemic. He noted that the Allied Relief Board would be wound up in July and recommended that the LRCS take over the relief function completely. He was jubilant at the opportunity and confided to Colonel House: 'both you and I would realise much sooner than we had expected the benefits of LRCS if it were in a position to occupy the field immediately after July 1st . . . and the psychological effect would in my opinion be very great and very important'.[30]

At the first preliminary meetings of the Council of the LN it was agreed that the epidemic was an emergency and that some relief organisation would have to be funded to take action. But it was a sensitive matter deciding *which* organisation should be sponsored and how it should be funded. Davison had volunteered the LRCS on the understanding that funds and supplies would come from the League, transport from the Allied armies and that the responsibility for organisation would rest on the ARC network still operating in Europe. However the British Imperial War Famine Fund was already operating in the same area and they were very put out that they were being lobbied by an organisation they saw as a 'newcomer' to help 'dole up' the £2 million for famine relief.[31] The British Red Cross was strongly in favour of using the LRCS, on which it had executive Board membership, and it mounted a publicity campaign in Britain on the ravages of the epidemic and calling for government and LN funding. However the British Treasury and the government in power were not minded to contribute funds through the LN to any campaign of relief. Treasury officials were in no mood to contribute generously even to their own national health care scheme and Christopher Addison was a familiar target for abuse in *The Times* for his spending record at the newly established Ministry of Health.

Lord Balfour, as president of the Council of the LN had written on 15 May, on his own initiative, to the LRCS asking for their help with the epidemic.[32] However, the British Treasury was firmly opposed to such a move and in a letter to the Secretary of State at the Foreign Office made it clear that on no account should British representatives at the LN commit Britain to spending British money on the typhus relief campaign:

> the doctrine that the British government should tax the British taxpayer for the purpose of combating typhus in Poland on the grounds that it would be open to HMG to look for assistance from the Polish taxpayers (among others) for assistance in meeting the cost of an outbreak of typhus in UK should such occur appears to their Lordships a manifest absurdity.[33]

The Treasury suggested that a straightforward loan should be paid to the Polish government, and even this loan arrangement would be conditional on the involvement of other countries, particularly the United States.

In the British Cabinet's League of Nations Committee there was almost unanimous opposition to funding any campaign coming from the LN. It was felt that Britain had no commercial or hygienic interest in the epidemic and therefore the only possible reason for involvement in a relief programme was 'benevolence'. Lord Curzon captured the distrust for such motives and the fear that they might constitute a precedent in his claim that if the first action the League took was a humanitarian appeal, then South America might start, and then Persia and Siam would ask for the League's largesse.[34] Chamberlain was even stronger in his opposition and view that it was a case of 'pouring money into Poland whilst she was pouring money into aggression in Lithuania'.[35] The Cabinet Committee was willing to contribute funds if it could be shown that it was genuinely a case of averting another 'Black Death' but only at a maximum of £50,000 and only if the USA, France, Holland and Spain contributed the same amount.[36]

The problem was that limited funds could be collected by special appeals but no government was prepared to acknowledge the precedent of an international peacetime relief agency funded by the LN. The LRCS was willing to undertake the function but wanted some security of tenure in the field. Against this background of the devastating typhus epidemic the possibility of a joint organisation, a commission, was discussed at an informal conference on international public health held in London in July 1919.

The conference was called by the British, and chaired by the British Minister of Health, Addison, to act as a steering group to plan a formal conference on the health and relief work of the League of Nations and its relationship with other international health organisations. The typhus epidemic was a priority issue since the OIHP refused to allow the LRCS to impose a *cordon sanitaire* at the Eastern front. The responsibility for these sorts of classic international public health controls lay with the OIHP; it was jealously guarded and based upon a complex set of agreements and treaties carefully worked out over the years to avoid infringements on trade and commerce, and the OIHP was adamant that the LRCS should not trespass into this area. The conference agreed therefore to send an interallied Commission of Inquiry to Poland in August.

The Polish government had already made a bilateral appeal to the LRCS to undertake an epidemic relief project; this was not surprising since the ARC had been involved in relief work since March, operating canteen trains, mobile hospitals, etc., and the ARC had, as has been seen, been the dominant influence in the LRCS. The Poles were unwilling to accept the dictatorial powers of any epidemic 'commission' and wanted to make their own arrangements through the LRCS.[37] In order to deal with this impasse the Polish Minister of Health appointed his own team under Ludwik Rajchman of the National Institute of Health in Warsaw. Rajchman handled the situation with great diplomacy and was quickly co-opted into the international public health elite, and within a year was appointed the first medical director of the Provisional Health Committee of the LN.[38]

The importance of the Polish campaign for getting organisations off the ground can also be seen in Rajchman's appointment. The Portuguese delegate to the OIHP (Professor Jorge) voiced concern and suspicion about the speed and '*fait accompli*' circumstances of the appointment of the Health Committee of the League of Nations; he complained that the Council of the League had arbitrarily selected certain public health experts to form a committee, and that the excuse that the epidemic of typhus made it necessary was not justified.[39] The Secretary-General, Drummond, acknowledged the speed and partiality of appointments but affirmed the need to get the work of the technical committees started.[40] The LRCS was prepared to continue its work; it had the personnel and organisation, but it demanded funding. The bargaining continued, but governments showed great reluctance to become financially involved; eventually Drummond hammered out a compromise: the Epidemic Commission would be organised and staffed by the LRCS but appointed and financed by the League out of a special emergency budget.[41]

The field staff of the Epidemic Commission were almost exclusively those who had been working in the area since the war began under a variety of ARC or other army or relief agencies. Whilst all the discussion on organisational structure and funding was taking place, Davison had realised that it was important for the LRCS to be in on 'the ground floor'; and the typhus epidemic was the sort of opportunity the LRCS had to respond to if it wanted to establish itself as an efficient international organisation. The LRCS secured a permanent place in the Epidemic Commission and thereby representation on the LNHO.

The Epidemic Commission was not by itself sufficient to secure for the LRCS the dominant position within the LN that Davison wanted: there were other organisations which campaigned more effectively or had the advantage of being directly politically allied.

The Comité international de la Croix Rouge (CICR)

By December 1920, Davison had become extremely frustrated with the delays and political intrigues at the LN. The Director-General, Henderson, was prompted therefore to write to Drummond spelling out his belief that at the bottom of the delay and intriguing was an attempt to give a new lease of life to the CICR and hinting that the ARC funding of the Epidemic Commission might be withdrawn; he warned: 'if the Assembly through ignorance or original sin or from any other course give to the Comité International any mandate to deal with such problems as epidemic disease, such action would be deeply resented by many of the Red Cross Societies who organised the LRCS expressly to deal with such matters'.[42]

The relationship with the CICR was a difficult and sensitive matter for the LRCS. The fact that both organisations styled themselves as Red Cross organisations and referred to a common history and adopted the same logo, and had their headquarters in the same city, meant that in popular perception they were one organisation: '*The* Red Cross'.

The question of why the two organisations remained separate was periodically reviewed throughout the interwar years. From the beginning of the LRCS in May 1919, Davison claimed that the founders had been in constant communication with the CICR and had sought an organic union between the two organisations.[43] However the evidence suggests that Davison's early planning was to create a totally new organisation. The new organisation clearly presented itself as a federated group of national societies, quite different from the CICR which was a centralised, neutral, international and autocratic organisation. Acknowledging that the centralised autocratic structure of the CICR might be necessary for its neutrality during times of warfare Henderson argued that it was a wholly unsuitable structure for peacetime activities: 'in the first place it is no way representative; its continuity is preserved by nomination of the Committee itself, and its members are not removable. No Red Cross society has any voice in its composition or any weight in its deliberations.'[44] It was this exclusion which particularly irked the 'Big Five' societies, which were unused to being in a subordinate position: 'no national society would entrust their joint business in peacetime to a body which was outside and above their control'.[45]

The LRCS gave an interesting twist to the CICR's argument by suggesting that whilst its neutrality and undemocratic structure were absolutely necessary for its supranational role in wartime, it was precisely that very characteristic which made it unsuitable for peacetime and therefore necessitated the LRCS stepping in to take control of the peacetime activities. What the CICR had traditionally defended now became the grounds the LRCS used for justifying its exclusion from the new venture. The LRCS' position was that they were two complementary organisations between which there was no need for rivalry or even overlap provided there was a clear identification of and agreement on areas of operation. However, such demarcation proved difficult to agree and there were constant misinterpretations of the parameters. Whilst the LRCS believed that its responsibilities included matters of public health, especially epidemics, and co-ordinating the efforts of the national societies in cases of grave calamity, the CICR felt it was also responsible for peacetime civil calamities as well as for victims of war and sickness.

In the small city of Geneva the conflict was public and hostility was often expressed in print but it entered a particularly acute phase over the typhus epidemic when the CICR issued a communiqué at the Assembly of the LN announcing its intention to take part in the epidemic relief work. This was perceived by Henderson as 'muscling-in' and he angrily condemned it: 'The claim of the Comité International to organise and co-ordinate the peace work of the Red Cross societies dates from the hour when those societies organised another body to fulfil these very duties.'[46] The CICR's claim was that it had been undertaking campaigns against public disasters since 1869 and up until the recent Armistice had been the co-ordinator of all international relief work.

It was an unedifying wrangle between two organisations which were claiming the mantle of international care and relief functions. The particular issue of the responsibility for the Polish epidemic was made more inglorious by the fact that the need for funding for actual relief work and the scale of suffering was being largely ignored by the rest of the world. It was in order to create an appearance of proficiency and to push for funding for the epidemic that Drummond instructed the CICR and the LRCS to create a joint committee 'to co-ordinate all relief work in all countries in Europe'.[47] In March 1921 Ador and Henderson hammered out a temporary agreement for separate spheres of action. The CICR was to be the 'moral and legal adviser of the National Societies', it was to be responsible for the observance of international conventions, it was to be the 'competent authority for dealing with national societies and governments on general questions with the *exception of those relating to public health*, which came within the province of the League of Red Cross Societies' (my italics).[48] The CICR was responsible for all negotiations and correspondence with the League of Nations and national governments in the field of calamities and disaster relief. The publicity surrounding the agreement claimed somewhat fulsomely that the two organisations would 'work together in absolute trust and agreement'.[49]

The following year, at the expiration of the agreement, a conference was convened by the Italian Red Cross to consider the case for expanding the terms of the Geneva Convention. This conference was interesting for the way it reflected clearly the political links between national governments and their national Red Cross societies, a good example being the British case, in respect of the Foreign Office and the British Red Cross. The Secretary of the British Red Cross, Sir Anthony Balfour, was privately briefed before the conference by the Foreign Office, unofficially and verbally.[50] The Cabinet had sought Foreign Office advice on the attitude that their delegates should take at the LN on the extension of the Geneva Convention to cover peacetime activities.[51] The British Red Cross was enthusiastic about the scheme but the Foreign Office was resolutely opposed. The War Office deprecated any change to the Convention; they wanted it to remain simply as a means of ameliorating the conditions of war between belligerents. They were even in favour of restricting further the use of the words 'Red Cross' and its emblem to specific wartime activities.[52]

As was seen in the case of the typhus epidemic the British Foreign Office and the Cabinet opposed any extension of League of Nations activity beyond the narrowly political and diplomatic and any extension of Red Cross activity was similarly considered unacceptable:

> we should certainly have nothing to do with such a scheme, especially when it is proposed by the Italians. Our experience is that they have never subscribed to any refugee work. If other nations would only pay their subscriptions towards the carrying out of the Warsaw Conference instead of putting forward fantastic schemes we should get something done.[53]

Although nothing came of the Italian initiative, the LRCS had begun to feel increasingly that, through the joint committee, they were being exploited by the CICR. Their funds, their innovations and their achievements were being absorbed whilst the CICR was contributing very little, and credit was not accruing to them.[54] Internal discussions in the LRCS centred on the importance of disengaging from the CICR; if co-operation could not be achieved then it was agreed that it should be better for clear and separate institutions to be maintained. One of the ways in which this was held to be achievable was by moving away from Geneva back to Paris, thereby physically separating the two organisations. It was not just the negative effects of the CICR and Geneva which prompted the move; there were real political advantages. Paris was the 'capital' of inter- national public health work at this time and the LRCS wanted to be closely tied in with any new developments:

> as we wish to associate ourselves through our health programme with the health programme of the League of Nations, we must be in Paris to do so. The League of Nations has approved the Office International d'Hygiène Publique as its official health organ and this association has its headquarters in Paris. I feel that a certain co-operation can be established, but if we are in Geneva we will only be privileged

to attend (through our representative) a yearly meeting. It is natural to suppose that the OIHP will establish its own connections and select its associates among those nearest at hand, *we may establish the connection we have some right to expect and have worked to prepare ourselves for.* If we were established in Paris we would be constantly receiving visits from the many travellers in the city, and these would carry our message back to their countries.[55]

There was one further reason for moving that the LRCS took into account, and that was the negative effect it would have upon the CICR: 'to move away from Geneva will weaken the peace programme of the CICR more than anything which we can do by remaining. The organisation welcomes the competition with us and hopes to bring about an open discussion leading to a re-adjustment which might not be entirely in our favour.'[56]

This strategic thinking, in addition to more mundane cost-effective considerations, resulted in the LRCS moving its headquarters from Geneva to Paris in August 1922. However the hoped-for expansion did not occur because by then the initial high funding of the LRCS by the American Red Cross had begun to tail off and the budget had to be severely cut back. The financial strength of the LRCS began to wane and its lobbying position within the LN public health section declined in comparison to other organisations and so the ambitious designs and optimism that Davison had shown in 1919 also shrank. With the death of Henderson in 1921 and Davison in 1922 the new executive leadership under the Secretary-General René Sand was renowned for its public health work but it was no longer directed towards issues of organisational dominance or territoriality.[57]

Conclusion

In summing up the relationship between the two Red Cross organisations, it can be said that the founders of the LRCS showed little interest in the CICR, having failed to take it over at the beginning. Davison simply bypassed it, using the finance and the organisational basis of the American Red Cross as the nucleus of his new vision. The CICR, with its headquarters in Geneva, was primarily concerned with the enforcement and arbitration of the Geneva Convention. However, many of the national Red Cross societies had expanded their peace-time work in the general field of public health and preventive health care including tuberculosis and infant welfare programmes; it was this expansion of function which found a focus in the LRCS. The CICR retained the dominant position in prestige and access to national governments although the LRCS commanded by far the larger budget. It was through the LN that Davison hoped to anchor the LRCS as the major agency, but there was strong political opposition to the creation of a peacetime international health and welfare organisation that would need to be funded by member countries. If it remained as a voluntary body then it would be impossible for the LN member states to be compelled to subscribe to it; if it were a 'League of Nations' organisation then the member states would not fund it for anything more than very residual 'epidemic' work. The compromise with the CICR was forced upon the LRCS by the Council of the LN, which was only prepared to recognise and fund Red Cross activity if it was a limited organisation. The division of functions was worked out at a time when the LRCS was still well funded by the ARC and concerned to expand and put itself on the international health map. The sphere in which the LRCS then began to move extensively and gain primacy as a result of the American influence was public health education and publicity.

This narrowing of policy and programmes was the result of a number of factors: the loss of the heavy ARC subsidy that Davison had engineered at the beginning; the change in leadership following the deaths of Davison and Henderson; but most significantly the development and expansion of other governmental health agencies through the LN Provisional Health Committee and the OIHP. Although in the early 1920s the budget of the LNHO was severely limited, and it called upon the LRCS to help out, as its budgets and staffing increased and its political support and prestige grew so its dependence on the LRCS lessened and its voluntary status became more of an anomaly than an asset. The agreements made with the CICR from 1920 progressively restricted the scope of operations of the LRCS to health education, which although regarded at the time as a triumph of securing a monopoly of an area of work progressively became seen as a hollow victory in so far as health education received neither large budgets nor high-status work rewards. It was deemed an area of 'popular' non-medical work by the LNHO and hence could be easily discarded.

The underlying factor in the waning of a dominant role of the LRCS in international health policy was, most probably, the changed position of America towards the League of Nations. Davison had acknowledged in 1918 that the American attitude towards the putative League was vitally important to the success of his call upon the ARC to be the dynamo for the LRCS; but the Head of the Medical Department, Charles Winslow, on his return to America in 1921 noted a changed attitude of isolationism and nationalism in the ARC and was not surprised at the progressive reduction of American funding of the League.[58] As the American attitude towards the LN hardened to the extent of discouraging co-operation even in the technical committees, so the lobbying strength of Davison was reduced. At one point it had seemed as if the LRCS representative could provide a convenient cover for American participation in the technical committees, but as the strength of national representatives – either directly or through delegates or indirectly from the OIHP – increased, this LRCS vehicle became redundant and its constituency was covered by other representatives.[59]

Acknowledgements

I have been much influenced by N. Howard-Jones who gave me encouragement and help to pin down source material to substantiate what had been house-gossip and folklore in the League of Nations Health Section during his working life.

I owe a great debt to Suzanne Macgregor for her close and critical interest in this research from its beginnings, and particularly to David and Alice-Claire Painting who have been a sustaining presence since 1991.

Notes

1 P. Weindling, 'Public Health and Political Stabilisation: The Rockefeller Foundation in Central and Eastern Europe Between the Two World Wars', *Minerva*, 31, 3 (1993), 253–67; B. A. Towers, 'The Politics of Tuberculosis in Western Europe 1914–40', unpublished PhD dissertation, University of London (1987); D. Fisher, 'Rockefeller Philanthropy and the British Empire: The Creation of the London School of Hygiene and Tropical Medicine', *History of Education*, 7, 2 (1978), 129–43.

2 N. Howard-Jones, *International Public Health Between the World Wars* (Geneva: WHO, 1978), p. 73. John F. Hutchinson has also documented its significance in the formation of the League of Red Cross Societies (see chapter 2 and, for a critical re-appraisal of the history of the Red Cross, 'Rethinking the Origins of the Red Cross', *Bulletin of the History of Medicine*, 63 (1989), 557–78).

3 Weindling, 'Public Health'.

4 Howard-Jones, *International Public Health*.

5 G. Kolko, *The Triumph of Conservatism* (Chicago: Quadrangle Press, 1963).

6 E. R. Brown, *Rockefeller Medicine Men* (Berkeley: University of California Press, 1979).

7 H. Braverman, *Labour and Monopoly Capitalism* (New York: Monthly Review Press, 1974).

8 RAC 500T. Memo from Vincent and Rose to IHB on Interview with Eliot Wadsworth Vice Chairman ARC, 28 May 1917.

9 RAC 500T. Report on a conference with Davison, Rose, Vincent and others, 27 May 1917.

10 C. E. Buckingham, *For Humanity's Sake* (Washington: Public Affairs Press, 1964).

11 Howard-Jones, *International Public Health*.

12 LRCS Papers. The American Contribution in the Founding of the LRCS. Selected Source Documents (hereafter US Source Docs.). Document 4. Letter from Davison to Harvey Gibson, 22 November 1918.

13 *Ibid.*

14 *Ibid.*

15 LRCS Papers. US Source Docs. A Japanese Red Cross Mission proposed this formally in 1915 to President Ador (Swiss Minister of the Interior and the President of the CICR), Arata Ninagawa, *The Facts about the Formation of the LRCS* (nd).

16 LRCS Papers. US Source Docs. Draft letter. France, Italy, Japan, Britain and the United States were known as 'the Big Five' (nd).

17 LRCS Papers. US Source Docs. Document 8. Letter from Stockton Axson to Woodrow Wilson, 3 December 1918.

18 LRCS Papers. US Source Docs. Davison to Signor Orlando (nd).

19 LRCS Papers. US Source Docs. Letter from Davison to J. P. Morgan, 22 February 1919.

20 *Ibid.*

21 RAC 500T. Letter from Davison to Harvey Gibson, 22 November 1918.

22 LRCS Papers. US Source Docs. Letter from Davison to House, 9 February 1919.

23 LRCS Papers. US Source Docs. Letter from Davison to House, 2 March 1919. Apparently this problem had been anticipated by Wilson at the outset of American involvement in the war: according to Bendiner, Wilson told House that although England and France had different views from the United States with respect to the peace, when the war was over they could be forced to the American way of thinking since by that time they would be financially in American hands (E. Bendiner, *A Time for Angels* (London: Weidenfeld and Nicolson, 1975)).

24 LRCS Papers. US Source Docs. Letter from Davison to House, 6 May 1919.

25 *Proceedings of the Medical Conference Held at the Invitation of the Committee of Red Cross Societies, Cannes, France, April 1 to 11, 1919* (Geneva: The League of Red Cross Societies, 1919). Cited in Howard-Jones, *International Public Health*, p. 12.

26 Article 25 of the Covenant of the League of Nations reads: 'The members of the League agree to encourage and promote the establishment and co-operation of duly authorised voluntary national Red Cross Associations having as purposes the improvement of health, the prevention of disease and the mitigation of suffering throughout the world.' Proceedings of Meetings of General Council (1920) March, LRCS, Geneva.

27 Addison Papers Box 61. Conference. Minister, Drummond, Astor, Newman at the Ministry of Health, 18 August 1919. During private discussions with the British Ministry of Health at the time of the Informal London Conference, Drummond expressed his concern to get LRCS representatives on the governing body of a LN Health Committee.

28 LRCS Papers. US Source Docs., Document 13. Cable No. 17627, 15 January 1919.

29 *Proceedings of the Medical Conference Cannes*, p. 13.

30 LRCS Papers. US Source Docs. Letter from Davison to House, 10 May 1919.

31 LNA Health. 12B. Docs. 3895/1719. Letter from Drummond to Sir Arthur Stanley, LN correspondence with LRCS, 21 June 1920. LRCS Papers. US Source Docs. Letter from Davison to House. As early as 1919, Davison had suggested to Colonel House that the LRCS 'occupy the field' of the Allied Relief Board (10 May 1919).

32 PRO CAB 27/98. Report of Balfour to Cabinet Committee, 15 May 1920.

33 PRO FO 371 3930. Note to Secretary of State, Foreign Office.

34 PRO CAB 27/98. Cabinet Committee Proceedings, LN Committee 1920–1, 1 June 1920.

35 *Ibid.*

36 *Ibid.*

37 PRO FO 371 3930. Report from British Legation, H. Rumbold, 19 February 1920.

38 LN Health. C471. Minutes of Provisional Health Committee, Paris 1921 and PRO
    FO 371/8303. Report by Sir George Buchanan to MOH, Paris, October 1921.
39 PRO FO 37-8303. Report of Delegate to OIHP, October 1921.
40 *Ibid.*
41 LN Health. 12B. 220723. Correspondence of LRCS 20723. Letter from Henderson
    to Drummond, 8 June 1920. The budget was organised in co-operation with the
    LRCS and the LN. In a letter to Drummond, Henderson (Director-General of the
    LRCS) suggested that if the LN needed money for the typhus campaign 'the best
    way is to go via the LRCS, which will approach the ARC . . . owing to the very close
    relationship between that society and the US government, the ARC could furnish a
    suitable channel of communication with the latter'.
42 LRCS Papers. Letter from Henderson to Drummond, 3 December 1920.
43 Article 1 of the Articles of Association of the LRCS claimed that the 'co-operation
    will in due time lead to an organised union with the International Committee'.
44 D. Henderson, 'The International Red Cross Committee and the LRCS', *Bulletin
    of the LRCS*, 2, 3 (December 1920). Robert Olds, an ARC Commissioner, was
    sceptical of the CICR's claim to neutrality: 'I have noted in the declarations of the
    Comité itself, as well as of others, an implied assumption that neutrality is a rare
    flower that flourishes continually only in Switzerland.' LN Health. R637. LN
    Memo, Olds Report on Internal Organisation of the Red Cross, 3 May 1924.
45 Henderson, 'The International Red Cross Committee', p. 108.
46 *Ibid.*, p. 110.
47 *League of Nations Official Journal*, 2 (1921), 157–8.
48 Meeting of the Board of Governors of the LRCS, 28 March 1921. Report in *Bulletin
    of LRCS*, 2, 8 (May 1921), 281.
49 *Ibid.*, p. 284.
50 PRO FO 371/8330, 27 December 1922.
51 PRO FO 371/8330. Note from Cabinet Office to Under Secretary of State Foreign
    Office, 22 August 1922.
52 PRO FO 371/8330. War Office position paper, B. Cubitt, 22 July 1922.
53 PRO FO 371/8330, 22 August 1922, minute. 'The Warsaw Conference' alluded to
    is a reference to the fact-finding mission to Poland of the Advisory Board to the
    Epidemic Commission in April 1921, which formulated a relief plan in conjunction
    with the Polish Epidemic Commissariat in Warsaw. It seems that the issue of
    refugees and displaced persons caused by British foreign policy would have placed
    the British government in a 'difficult position' if the Convention had been changed
    to cover peacetime relief. In a note to Curzon, the Foreign Office cautioned that such
    a convention 'might impose definite and far reaching obligations on this country, the
    fulfilment of which might be very costly and might also in any given emergency run
    counter to the general policy of HMG'. Such calculations have continued to inform
    immigration policy (PRO FO 371/8330, 23 August 1922).
54 LRCS Papers. File 24. Memo M. Rappard, 'Why it is advisable to get away from
    Geneva' (nd).
55 LRCS Papers. File 24. Centanini, Supplementary remarks to memorandum (nd).
56 PRO FO 371/8330 Rappard.
57 René Sand (1877–1953) contrasted greatly with his fellow Belgian, Oscar Velghe,
    the traditional and conservative president of the Permanent Committee of the OIHP

from 1919 to 1932. Sand was a major figure nationally and internationally as a writer, academic and manager in the field of social medicine. Appointed Secretary-General to the LRCS in 1921, he later became Secretary-General of the Belgian Ministry of Health and from 1934 was a member of the LN Health Committee. He held the Chair in Social Medicine at the University of Brussels until 1952 (*Who's Who in Medicine*, 1939).

58 LRCS Papers. Winslow collection. Letter. Winslow to Sand, 8 November 1921.
59 Howard-Jones, *International Public Health*, p. 29.

4

The League of Nations Health Organisation

MARTIN DAVID DUBIN

An elite of biomedical and health specialists functioning through the League of Nations Health Organisation (LNHO) in the interwar decades contributed to the development of the public health profession.[1] They served as a co-ordinating body – a sort of executive committee – for a worldwide biomedical/public health episteme that recently had acquired confidence in its ability to alleviate human suffering by reducing, if not eliminating, disease.[2] This new confidence reflected new consensual knowledge about the aetiology and epidemiology of many diseases and the physiological conditions and socio-economic factors contributing to human illness. It stimulated their humanitarian instincts, leading them to devise the LNHO, a novel institution at the centre of the interwar health regime. This regime had the unusual quality of being largely self-transforming in response to new scientific knowledge developed within the episteme. It also led to the creation in various countries of new national health institutions.

Health co-operation before 1919

During much of the nineteenth century, little consensual knowledge existed about the causes of illness or how diseases are transmitted. The social devastation and fear generated by plague and cholera, nevertheless, induced some governments to seek protection against epidemics emanating from the Middle and Far East and Asia Minor.[3] Diverse, arbitrary, and often contradictory opinions about these diseases prevented effective action. Only in December 1903 was there shared knowledge sufficient for a useful convention to be negotiated.[4] It attempted to erect a cordon sanitaire around parts of Europe and America against plague and cholera by establishing regulations for ships, rules governing quarantine and a system of diplomatic notices from infected ports. Pursuant to the December 1907 Treaty of Rome, the Office international d'hygiène publique (OIHP) was formed in Paris to oversee the convention.[5] The Permanent Committee of the OIHP was dominated by French diplomat Camille Barrère and included foreign diplomats resident in Paris. The OIHP's small, almost entirely French, secretariat was directed by Jacques de Cazotte, a retired French diplomat.[6] A new convention, which did not come into force until 1920, was drafted in January 1912. It recognised that healthy humans may carry the cholera vibrio and made yellow fever a reportable disease. These pre-1914 diplomatic arrangements were designed to protect certain states against external threats; they were not intended to ameliorate conditions universally. The biomedical community was not yet emboldened to propose co-operative measures reducing, if not eliminating, diseases.

Scientific knowledge, however, was advancing rapidly. In recent decades, new knowledge in microbiology, biochemistry, immunology, and pharmacology had laid the intellectual foundations for preventive medicine.[7] This goal increasingly animated health professionals on both sides of the Atlantic. It was reflected in OIHP discussions;[8] the activities of the Rockefeller Foundation (RF), established in 1913 to promote 'public sanitation and the spread of the knowledge of scientific medicine';[9] the work of the Inter-Allied Sanitary Commission established in Paris in 1917; and Red Cross societies providing wartime medical relief.[10]

At the end of the First World War, members of the biomedical/public health episteme were eager to organise preventive medicine on an international basis. This sentiment was manifested in two separate initiatives: one by the American Red Cross Society (ARC), and the other by public health officials of the Allies and the United States. The former proposed creating a new Red Cross agency and the latter an intergovernmental organisation to improve human health and alleviate suffering. Their goals corresponded to the pledge of the RF at the war's end 'to put its policies, personnel, and resources at the service of the world'.[11] These words were understood by George E. Vincent, the Foundation's president, to signify an intention to take part in 'world-wide team work for preventing disease and bringing about improved conditions of health'.[12] The RF would assume a major role in this effort. The initiatives of both the Red Cross and the public health officials were provided for in the League of Nations Covenant.[13]

The Red Cross programme was the first to take shape and rather quickly ran out of steam. The ARC in November 1918 proposed to President Woodrow Wilson that a new international Red Cross agency be formed to improve human health.[14] This ideal, embraced by Wilson and through him by the leaders of the Allies, resulted in the creation of the League of Red Cross Societies (LRCS) following an April 1919 international conference at Cannes, France.[15] The conference was attended by prominent biomedical experts, leading health officials, and key Rockefeller Foundation figures, many of whom would be important in developing the LNHO.

The Red Cross scheme called for a permanent headquarters at Geneva, near the League of Nations (LN), staffed by health professionals, who would stimulate research, collect vital statistics and promote improved health administration, amelioration of socio-economic causes of illness and upgrading of nursing and popular health education. Special attention would be paid to suppressing venereal diseases and tuberculosis.

The LRCS embarked upon an ambitious programme and tried to counter epidemics of typhus, relapsing fever and cholera in Eastern Europe. Its efforts soon began to sputter. Feuding with the rival International Committee of the Red Cross (ICRC), the LRCS had uncertain relations with national Red Cross societies, and it lacked funds and the means of implementing necessary measures.[16] In late 1921, the LRCS contracted its programme to concentrate on popular health and nursing education, relocated to Paris, and assumed a position at the periphery of the intergovernmental health regime.[17]

The second initiative was taken by public health officials. The bureau of the US Public Health Service complained about the limited scope of the OIHP, the defective nature of the unratified 1912 sanitary convention and the absence of international arrangements for preventive medicine.[18] The subsequent appointment of Dr Alberto Lutrario, Italian director-general of public health, to the inter-allied commission in Paris signalled that health questions would probably arise at the peace conference. In fact, the Eastern European epidemics produced extensive consultation, Red Cross activity and emergency relief by the US and the Allies.

The public health officials, however, had a broader agenda. A number of them, including Otto Velghe, Belgian director-general of health and new OIHP president; Alberto Lutrario; Thorvald Madsen, director since 1902 of the State Serum Institute in Copenhagen; Sir George Buchanan, senior medical officer in the British Ministry of Health; and Assistant US Surgeon-General Hugh S. Cumming, also discussed reorganising the OIHP as part of the LN.

Following extensive consultations, a resolution authorising a health organisation as part of the LN was approved by the League's Assembly in December 1920.[19] Meanwhile, the League's Council in May 1920, following evidence of the LRCS's inability to cope with European epidemics, had created a temporary Epidemic Commission, employing voluntary contributions.

The League of Nations Health Organisation

After the Assembly acted in December 1920, approval for the reorganisation and transfer to the LN of the OIHP was required by signatories to the 1907 Treaty of Rome. Pending what was regarded as likely to be quick action, the Council in March 1921 established a Temporary Health Committee.

The United States, however, unexpectedly complicated matters. It had participated in the early planning for the new Health Organisation, but now it vetoed the project. Having refused to join the LN, the US refused to approve making the OIHP part of the LN. The Temporary Health Committee, nonetheless, led by Léon Bernard, Professor of Clinical Tuberculosis and secretary-general of the International Union Against Tuberculosis, backed by French elder statesman Léon Bourgeois, recommended creating the health organisation while further steps were taken to obtain OIHP representation, 'if only in an advisory capacity'.[20]

On the basis of this advice, the Council in June 1921 formed a Provisional Health Committee which held six sessions before being replaced in 1924.[21] The new Health Committee, reformed during the years 1935–7, held thirty-one sessions. Apart from occasional participants, between 1921 and 1939 fifty-nine health professionals, drawn from around the world, served on the Committee.[22]

The organisation's nerve centre, however, was its secretariat, headed by a medical director, a mid-level LN official, who also served as secretary to the Health Committee. From October 1921 to February 1939, this position was held by Dr Ludwik Witold Rajchman, a brilliant, although controversial, Polish bacteriologist highly respected for his imagination, energy and skills. His conception of a social medicine serving humanity reflected the highest aspirations of the biomedical/public health episteme and corresponded to the goals of the health administrators and experts composing the Health Committee.[23]

The LNHO's major contributions to the development of public health may be summarised as follows:

(a) Provided a worldwide clearing-house which elevated public health values, institutions and practices, quickened scientific discoveries and expanded the boundaries of preventive medicine. It directed international expert committees, technical commissions, and specialised conferences, studying specific diseases and numerous aspects of biomedical and health administration, research and education.

(b) Created a Service of Epidemiological Intelligence and Public Health Statistics in Geneva, collected data on diseases not covered by the International Sanitary Convention, established the Eastern Bureau at Singapore to improve the collection and dissemination of regional data, and developed a system to communicate reports of epidemic diseases by telegraph and radio.

(c) Established an international epidemiological database essential for systematic public health work. This required devising, and convincing national officials to employ, a standard nomenclature; instituting uniform reporting methods; and standardising reports submitted to Geneva. In time, this database covered virtually the whole world and resulted in the publication of data serving administrative and research needs. This database was inherited after the Second World War by the World Health Organisation (WHO) which continues to refine it.

(d) Conducted public health personnel interchanges to socialise officials into a shared value system and to diffuse modern practices from advanced to less-advanced health administrations.[24] These interchanges identified common problems experienced in different countries and issues requiring continuing attention. Underwritten by the RF, they created new and intensified existing networks among health professionals and contributed to an international perspective that had not existed outside elite circles before the 1920s. The LNHO in a similar way helped to create and encouraged communication among schools of public health.

(e) Through a laboratory-based programme created international standards for numerous biological agents, including antitoxins; sera; vaccines; hormones and vitamins.[25] Directed by Thorvald Madsen and the eminent British pharmacologist, Sir Henry Dale, this activity engaged institutes around the world in trials and evaluations of biological products. Many of the standards were embodied in an international convention signed in 1935. By the late 1930s, sample standards were being provided at League expense to national centres in many lands.[26]

(f) Expanded the boundaries of social medicine by studies of the social and natural environments affecting human health. Among these were studies of nutrition,[27] physical education, the purity of milk and water supplies, housing, rural hygiene and medical insurance. The interest in rural hygiene was extended to 'rural life', and resulted in the 1930s in several pan-European conferences, a Far Eastern conference, and plans for similar conferences in Latin America and Africa.

(g) Furnished technical assistance to governments needing external help to suppress epidemics, conduct health surveys, evaluate health services, advise on port sanitation and sewage systems, train personnel and reorganise health administrations. Among the places given technical assistance were countries in the Balkans, Central Europe and Latin America, and China, Iraq, Liberia and Persia.

The LNHO's activities evolved, partly in response to external political, social and technological factors, but largely to changes in consensual scientific knowledge within the biomedical/public health episteme. This new knowledge also transformed state health agencies which were directed by members of the episteme.

The Provisional Committee

The League Council, in forming the Provisional Health Committee, appointed fourteen biomedical experts, a majority of whom sat on the OIHP's Permanent Committee and a number of whom had LRCS connections. Among those named was the chief of the Industrial Health Section of the International Labour Office. A German expert was added to facilitate German co-operation, and efforts were made to appoint representatives of the US Public Health Service and of the

Soviet government.[28] However, Cumming, who in February 1920 had become US Surgeon-General, entered the Committee only after it was reconstructed in 1923.[29] The USSR joined only in 1936, after entering the LN.

The 1923 and 1935–7 reforms

The 1923 reform permitted the US to pretend that it did not belong to any LN organ, while participating in its Health Committee. The reform made the OIHP's Permanent Committee the (General) Advisory Health Council of the Health Organisation.[30] Its president and nine other members elected by it, including nationals of states with permanent League Council seats, were to serve on the (Standing) Health Committee. The Health Committee itself was to suggest six additional members for appointment by the Council. It was understood that the OIHP would select Cumming, its US member, for one of its seats. Technically, the United States would not belong to the LNHO, although its chief public health official would be one of its most influential members.

Health Committee members served three-year terms and were eligible for reappointment. The Committee, moreover, was entitled to add assessors with the same status as members, and experts without votes. The medical director also could invite persons to attend specific sessions. The Health Committee, as a consequence, grew in size. The British and French manoeuvred to obtain places for their colonial health services, and the great powers acquired multiple representation.

Effective leadership, however, resided in the Committee's bureau, and particularly with the medical director. At the bureau's centre were the president, the OIHP president, who was vice-president ex officio and the medical director. In addition, the bureau contained vice-presidents (growing in number over time) with one-year terms.

Thorvald Madsen, elected president in 1921, and again in 1924, 1927, 1930 and 1934, and Otto Velghe, vice-president ex officio until his death in 1932, were at the centre. So were Sir George Buchanan, who succeeded Velghe, Léon Bernard and, to a lesser degree, Alberto Lutrario. They commanded attention by virtue of their reputations, personalities and national identities. Madsen's right to exercise discretion between sessions was used to back Rajchman.

Committee members appreciated Rajchman's leadership, but Buchanan and Cumming, both social and political conservatives, were repelled by his radicalism and accused him of manipulative ways. The former grudgingly co-operated with him, while railing against Genevan 'politics', the growth of Rajchman's 'bureaucracy' and League intrusion in domestic affairs.[31] Cumming was ever mindful of Washington's desire to distance itself from the League. He also was eager to protect his prerogatives as director of the Pan American Sanitary Bureau. He placed US Public Health Service resources at Rajchman's disposal, but sought to derail League health activities in Latin America and disparaged those in China.[32] This small group of critics was enlarged at the end of 1934 with the appointment, following Bernard's death, of Jacques Parisot, Professor of Hygiene and Social Medicine, and director of the Institute of Hygiene, at the University of Nancy. Like Cumming, Buchanan and the latter's successor, Montague T. Morgan, Parisot decried Rajchman's radicalism and methods. Moreover, Rajchman's extraneous political activities in the 1930s increased his vulnerability by engendering the hostility of Joseph Avenol, the League's Secretary-General after June 1933.[33]

To constrain Rajchman, Morgan and Parisot, with Avenol's connivance, engineered the Health Committee's reorganisation. In 1935, the Committee's bureau was expanded, composed largely of representatives of the LN's great powers, and required to meet quarterly as a means of supervising Rajchman. Also, the Health Committee, at the end of its term in 1936, was reduced from twenty-six to twelve members, consisting of the OIHP president and eleven other persons in whom their governments had confidence. The latter, including representatives of the leading public health administrations, were to be selected by the Council's rapporteur on health questions in consultation with the League's Secretary-General.[34] The review function of the OIHP also was revised. It was to hold an annual meeting in Paris, attended by its members and League members not belonging to the OIHP, to examine the LNHO's activities.

This reform was intended to reduce Rajchman's freedom. Rajchman, however, rose to the occasion. Before the Committee was reconstructed, he manoeuvred the creation of a special committee for 'technical studies' under Madsen to implement new activities, and, thereby, evade control. In revenge, when the Health Committee was reappointed for the years 1937–1940, Morgan, Parisot and Cumming arranged Parisot's replacement of Madsen as president.[35] The Polish government, as part of this scheme, replaced Chodźko, a Rajchman ally.[36] The powerful coalition that achieved these reforms, however, did not dare to move directly against Rajchman, whose support remained strong.

The Health Committee within the League of Nations

The Health Committee was formally subordinate to the LN's political organs, but, in fact, enjoyed an extraordinary autonomy.[37] It was formed by, and reported to, the Council, which approved its membership, agenda, recommendations, communications to the Assembly and governments and changes in its budget. This budget was drafted by the medical director, reviewed by the Health Committee, and with its amendments forwarded to the League's Secretary-General. The latter's recommendations were vetted by the Supervisory Commission, a panel of fiscal conservatives, and then debated and approved by the Assembly. The Assembly also reviewed the LNHO's performance and made recommendations to it through the Council.

League rules would seem to have placed the LNHO at the bottom of a hierarchical structure. The appearance, however, is misleading. Members of the Council, diplomats and foreign ministers, knowing little about public health, and having been assured by their own health ministries of what had been proposed, usually rubber-stamped Health Committee recommendations.

The Assembly was another matter. Governments represented on the Health Committee and others, for humanitarian reasons or because they benefited from technical assistance, supported health activity. More generally, however, Assembly delegations lacked homogeneity. They were composed of politicians, officials from diverse ministries, and individuals with personal standing. As a result, the Assembly contained an active lobby supporting health programmes. Moreover, its procedures facilitated that lobbying.

The LNHO's work was examined in the Assembly's Second Committee, a core of whose members returned year after year.[38] Among them were health officials, persons identifying with health associations, and even Health Committee members who often proposed new health programmes and enlarged budgets.[39] The Assembly, thus, was an arena in which transboundary coalitions supported health co-operation.

The LNHO, moreover, formulated special programmes in Latin America and Asia for countries with few stakes in the League's Euro-centred agendas. These programmes were pay-backs for League dues that otherwise were hard to justify. Fearful of a massive desertion by Latin American countries, the Assembly in 1927 authorised funding – beyond the ordinary health budget – for projects on that continent.[40] Discretionary funds also were spent in India for the same reason. In 1928, after the Nationalists seemed to consolidate their hold in China, extra funds also were appropriated for Chinese projects.[41]

The LNHO grew rapidly. While its initial budget in 1922 was 392,000 Swiss francs, in 1925 its budget (excluding funds from the RF) was capped at one million Swiss francs to avoid overwhelming other programmes.[42] In 1929, however, with Latin American and Asian projects under way, the Assembly relaxed its cap.[43] The health budget continued to grow, but the world economic depression took its toll on League finances. Cushioned by Rockefeller largess, the health budget then declined, but less steeply than others.

The Health Committee in action

The Health Committee was a dynamic body. Its agenda and the bodies reporting to it changed over time, partly in response to its external environment, as exemplified by its growing attention to social medicine in the 1930s, when governments turned toward social welfare policies. More generally, however, these changes reflected the advance of knowledge within the biomedical/public health episteme.

An outstanding feature of the Committee was the remarkable continuity and dedication of a core of its members. Madsen, for example, president until 1937, and then honorary president, worked closely with Rajchman. He lent the Health Committee his immense prestige, negotiating agreements, attending meetings, travelling extensively, and directing its Permanent Commission on Biological Standards. Velghe, vice-president ex officio until 1932, and Madsen helped soothe differences between Paris and Geneva and strongly endorsed the Geneva secretariat's work in the League's Assembly. Other long-term members included George Buchanan, Velghe's successor as OIHP president and Health Committee vice-president ex officio; Léon Bernard; Jean Cantacuzene, Professor of Bacteriology and director of the Institute of Experimental Medicine at the University of Bucharest; H. Carrière, director of the Swiss Federal Public Health Service; Witold Chodźko, Polish Minister of Health; H. S. Cumming; Josephus Jitta, president of the Public Health Council of The Netherlands, and after Buchanan OIHP president; Ricardo Jorge, director-general of Public Health in Lisbon; Alberto Lutrario; and Gustavo Pittaluga, Professor of Parasitology in the Faculty of Medicine at the University of Madrid.

Among the more interesting members who served for shorter periods were Jules Bordet, 1919 Nobel prize-winner for work in immunology and director of the Pasteur Institute in Brussels; Albert Calmette, a protégé of Louis Pasteur and co-discoverer of the controversial BCG anti-tuberculosis vaccine; Carlos Chagas, director of the Oswald Cruz Institute in Rio de Janeiro; J. Heng Liu, a Harvard Medical School graduate, professor at the Peking Union Medical College and the leading Chinese Nationalist public health official; Mikinosuke Miyajima, director of the Kitasato Institute for Infectious Diseases in Tokyo; Lucien Raynaud, inspector-general of the health service of Algeria; René Sand, secretary-general for health in the Belgian Ministry of Home Affairs and former secretary-general of the LRCS; A. Sordelli, director of the Bacteriological Institute in the Argentine Department of Health; and Andrija Štampar, inspector-general of public health in Yugoslavia. Štampar developed an exemplary system of rural health centres regarded as models for similar centres throughout Central Europe. He spent most of the 1930s, however, associated with Rajchman, for a short time in his secretariat and for years in China. In 1948, Štampar represented Yugoslavia at the First World Health Assembly which elected him president.

Many Health Committee members also chaired or served on expert bodies, maintained relations with each other through their ministries or institutes, participated in the OIHP Permanent Committee, were active in regional health bodies, collaborated in associations and enjoyed in their personal and/or official capacities RF support. There were, in fact, dense communications among

Committee members that extended through much of the biomedical/public health episteme.

The Health Committee was only the apex of a complex structure that brought into active association thousands of health workers worldwide. Among them were administrators, researchers and educators affiliated with state services, laboratories, schools, professional societies, associations and philanthropies. The specialised bodies in which they participated assessed knowledge in their respective fields, established research agendas, allocated tasks and promoted public education. They sponsored laboratory and field studies; provided training; disseminated information; and prompted the creation of new national institutions.

The Committee thus functioned as a superordinate co-ordinating body, a reviewing agency, and a sounding board. It appointed the specialised bodies and their chairs, established their jurisdictions, and allocated financial support, subject to League Council approval. The subordinate bodies were, in turn, at the centre of their own specialised networks. They dealt with a wide range of matters, including addictive drugs, child welfare, Chinese drugs, classification of diseases, health insurance, hospital administration, housing, infant mortality, the list of the causes of death, maternal welfare, medical education, milk supplies, nutrition, opium, penal administration, physical education, port sanitation, public health education, quarantine regulations, radiation, rural hygiene, schools of public health, ship fumigation, statistics, the unification of pharmacopoeias, vaccination, water quality and numerous individual diseases and health defects.

Many bodies were formed jointly with other League organs, especially the International Labour Organisation, and with independent associations. Studies also were conducted by the health secretariat, outside experts and agencies, such as the Pasteur Institutes, national government laboratories and university centres. Among the Health Committee's own organs, apart from the Permanent Commission on Biological Standards, the most prominent was the Malaria Commission.[44] It investigated the virulence of various strains of the disease, the different environmental conditions under which they occurred and the possibility of eliminating mosquitoes; conducted study tours and surveys; presented courses in the latest methods of control and treatment of malaria; and sponsored a synthetic substitute for quinine, which was in short supply and expensive.

The medical director

The structure of the LNHO and its interaction with the biomedical/public health episteme were necessary, but not sufficient, conditions for successful health co-operation. The elaborate system did not function automatically. It depended upon intelligent stimulation and effective co-ordination. That leadership could be provided only by the medical director, who was a full-time official at the centre of intersecting networks that had to be managed.

To this task, Ludwik Rajchman brought great talents.[45] It was said that, if his methods were not always orthodox, 'his objectives were nearly always admirable, and that he had the good of humanity at heart'.[46] Rajchman possessed professional credentials in biomedical research and public health administration. He exhibited a passion for social justice, a large vision of what might be accomplished and extraordinary organising skills. A gifted speaker, in one-to-one and small group discussions, he often was charming and persuasive.

Born in Warsaw on 1 November 1881, Rajchman received a medical degree from the University of Cracow in July 1906, worked in a Warsaw hospital, and engaged in Polish Socialist Party activity. After being detained by the Warsaw police, he left for France. There he attended a course at the Pasteur Institute in Paris.[47] He returned to Cracow as an assistant in the University's Department of Veterinary Medicine. From October 1910 to 1913, Rajchman was at the Royal Institute of Public Health in London teaching bacteriology and assisting in laboratories. From October 1910 to November 1911, Rajchman wrote a column in the Institute's journal, and in 1912 served as one of its assistant editors. Among those on the journal's advisory board were Albert Calmette and Thorvald Madsen with whom he would be associated in his LN career. Rajchman also lectured at King's College, did investigations for the London Hospital, and was employed in editorial and research projects by the newly founded Medical Research Committee. During the First World War, Rajchman was active in Polish emigré circles in collaboration with August Zaleski, a follower of Piłsudski. Zaleski, who would become the Polish Foreign Minister from May 1926 to November 1932, remained friendly with Rajchman, whom he sometimes used to communicate with foreign leaders. Rajchman's political activities brought him into contact with the British Foreign Office and British Labour politicians, including the future Prime Minister, J. Ramsay MacDonald.

In October 1918, Rajchman travelled through revolution-torn Germany, arriving in Warsaw as the armistice of 11 November was being declared. He played a leading role in devising Poland's attack upon a widespread typhus epidemic and in enlisting Western medical and relief assistance. He established the State Central Epidemiological Institute in Warsaw and bacteriological laboratories throughout Poland which were extremely important in the anti-epidemic fight.[48]

Rajchman's knowledge, skills and contacts in the West made him invaluable to the Polish Government. In Paris, in the summer of 1919, he appeared 'bright and frank'[49] in enlisting support for Poland; and in Poland, he impressed visitors with the way in which the fight against typhus was being conducted.[50] In April

1920, he accompanied Chodźko, then Poland's Deputy Minister of Health, to a conference in London to discuss epidemic conditions. There, he presented what Léon Bernard, who was to become one of his staunchest allies in the League's Health Committee, called an extraordinary report on the Polish anti-typhus campaign.[51]

Rajchman's reputation grew as a member of the League's Epidemic Commission. In October 1920, Red Cross observers reported that 'Rajchman has impressed us as being the most competent public health worker we have met in this part of Europe.' Rockefeller officials concurred.[52]

Soon after joining the League as medical director in October 1921, Rajchman articulated a view of international health co-operation that embodied the aspirations of the biomedical/public health episteme. His vision, corresponding to those entertained by the RF and the LRCS, sharply contrasted with the limited view reflected in the prewar sanitary conventions. He spoke of building the intellectual foundation for systematic advances in scientific knowledge, creating a worldwide standard among rank-and-file public health workers, and employing the LNHO as an engine for improving human well-being.[53] The health secretariat should 'regard as its duty' initiating actions which 'no single administration . . . can undertake', and 'of investigation of international concern and importance'. It should be a clearing-house for national health administrations, review national reports and collect and standardise epidemiological data. It should conduct surveys, help create international biological standards, analyse data on diseases in the colonial world, and institute conferences and conventions with the object of 'exterminating or limiting' tropical diseases. Agreements also should be promoted on child welfare, tuberculosis, venereal diseases and perhaps opium.

Health workers, however, currently lacked 'a common "esprit de corps"' and 'an equal realisation of the ideals of common service' necessary for it to be possible to 'count seriously on the realisation of projects based on international cooperation'. To inculcate these ideals, he proposed international interchanges of medical officers and the temporary assignment of some of them to his staff. Recognising the paucity of LN funds, Rajchman requested financial help from the RF.[54] It regarded the proposed interchanges and epidemiological service as fundamental contributions to improving public health and provided funds for them. The resulting collaboration would become multidimensional. It rested upon the Foundation's respect for Rajchman's leadership and the need for an intergovernmental body to do things a private foundation could not do by itself.

The Foundation's support came amidst other successes by Rajchman. He obtained Soviet co-operation in fighting epidemics; initiated statistical publications on Russia and Eastern Europe;[55] masterminded, in March 1922, a European Health Conference in Warsaw[56] and bilateral sanitary conventions by

Soviet authorities and Poland with each other and with their neighbours; extended the Epidemic Commission into Soviet territory; and, in 1923, helped negotiate the back-door entry of the United States into the LNHO.[57]

Subsequently, Rajchman had a major role in expanding Rockefeller support, creating the Eastern Bureau, introducing programmes in Latin America, initiating assistance to China, reconstructing Greece's public health administration, emphasising rural hygiene and other aspects of social medicine and relentlessly pursuing the establishment of a worldwide epidemiological database.

Rajchman was committed to improving health conditions in less-developed countries, and much of his effort was directed toward that goal. The reasons can be found in the universal threat posed by tropical diseases, and in Rajchman's humanitarian and anti-colonial sentiments, which especially fuelled his interest in China.[58]

Rajchman's success, however, cannot be explained solely by reference to the global nature of the biomedical/public health episteme, the structure of the Health Committee or the merits of its programme, or his personal vision and skills. It requires, as well, understanding of the medical director's structural position in the League of Nations secretariat, the LNHO, and the biomedical/public health episteme.

As a secretariat official, Rajchman relied on LN rules and practices to protect or expand his authority and to fend off restrictions suggested by Health Committee critics; supervised documentation transmitted to the Council and Assembly; mobilised or lobbied delegates to League meetings; developed health programmes for political purposes defined or endorsed by the Assembly and Secretary-General; and served the secretariat as an information source and as a go-between with national governments. The esteem with which he was held in the secretariat served him within the LNHO, and his success as medical director enlarged his standing with his Secretariat colleagues and contributed to the autonomy granted him by the Secretary-General.

Rajchman's dual functions within the LNHO as secretary to the Health Committee and director of the health secretariat made him a traffic controller and patronage dispenser. He monitored the flow of information, shaped the Committee's agenda, prepared documents, presented at each session a report that formed the basis for deliberations and implemented decisions. He suggested persons for appointment to the Committee and to attend specific sessions. He played a major role in selecting expert body members; arranging inquiries, personnel interchanges and study tours; allocating the budget; and negotiating with Committee members, officials, experts, association representatives and foundation executives. He dispensed patronage through budgetary and staffing decisions, and by proposing programmes and recommending projects or awards to countries or persons.

Enhancing Rajchman's power was his use of external resources to supplement those provided by the League. His ability to enlist Rockefeller funds and the widespread knowledge that he enjoyed the Foundation's confidence were among these power resources. They dovetailed into and reinforced the broader support he enjoyed within the biomedical/public health episteme.[59]

Rajchman also drew upon his socialist humanism and political activism to expand his resources, although they would eventually undermine his position. No shrinking violet, he identified openly with the democratic Left. In Great Britain, he was on excellent terms with leaders of the Labour Party who helped neutralise Buchanan.[60] In France, centrist politicians and socialist friends performed a similar function.[61] In combination, his support within the Secretariat, Health Committee, biomedical/public health episteme, and important political circles enabled him to maintain the support of governments whose co-operation was essential, despite the presence in them of influential critics. As the 1930s progressed, however, Rajchman became distracted by the rise of totalitarianism. He became embroiled in political controversies extrinsic to his responsibilities, and he compromised his position as an international official.

The health secretariat

Rajchman was not a one-man band. He required backing from the LN's secretariat and the Health Committee and broad co-operation from within the biomedical/public health episteme. He also had to rely upon his staff. This multinational unit was small, but highly proficient and widely respected.[62] Its members prepared studies, drafted documents, liaised with health administrations, conducted surveys, attended conferences, serviced expert bodies and supervised or carried out technical assistance. They were two-way transmission belts extending Rajchman's outreach and bringing to him information about developments in the field.

A mainstay of his secretariat in the 1920s was F. Norman White, formerly of the Indian Medical Service, and, since 1920, the LN's chief epidemic commissioner. White was a field epidemiologist who supervised the Epidemic Commission; studied Asian ports in 1922/23; drafted a Far Eastern sanitary convention, which influenced provisions of a 1924 Pan American Sanitary Code and of the 1926 International Sanitary Convention; surveyed the south Pacific; represented the League at a conference in Melbourne; and in 1929 took charge of developing a school of public health in Athens.

The success of the Epidemiological Intelligence Service in implementing Rajchman's dream of a worldwide database rested with a number of talented statisticians. Among these were Knud Stouman, a Dane, who in 1921 transferred from the LRCS to the health secretariat; and Americans were recruited with

Rockefeller help. The first, Edgar Sydenstricker, was borrowed from the US Public Health Service. He instituted standardising statistical methods and training national officials in these methods. Following him were Otto Eichel, of the New York State health department, and then Frank G. Boudreau, of the Ohio health department. Boudreau served from March 1925 to June 1937, acting as Rajchman's assistant, or, in Rajchman's absence from Geneva, in his stead. Boudreau resigned to become executive director of the Milbank Memorial Fund, a New York health philanthropic organisation. In 1939, when contraction of the League's secretariat was forced on Geneva by declining revenues, he drafted a plan combining the Health, Opium and Social Sections.[63]

Another invaluable official was Raymond Gautier, a Swiss doctor. Gautier, among other assignments, directed the Eastern Bureau and was secretary to the Permanent Commission on Biological Standards. After Rajchman's departure at the end of January 1939, Gautier became acting medical director. His strenuous efforts maintained a core of the health secretariat during the Second World War.[64]

Other members included C. L. Park, an Australian, who headed the Eastern Bureau and filled in as acting medical director; Yves Biraud, a Frenchman, who served as secretary to expert bodies on tuberculosis, leprosy and social medicine, in the 1930s worked in epidemiology, and later directed the World Health Organisation's (WHO) division of epidemiology; Melville D. Mackenzie, a Briton recruited into the secretariat after serving in Russia with the Friends' Emergency and War Victims' Relief Committee and with the Epidemic Commission, who studied rural health centres, directed technical assistance in Chile and the League's humanitarian work in Liberia, examined hospital administration and, in the late 1930s, purchased medical supplies used to fight epidemics in China; W. R. Aykroyd, another Briton, who joined the secretariat in 1931, brought to Geneva expert knowledge of nutrition and with Etienne Burnet wrote the basic study on the subject;[65] Etienne Burnet, a French physician who, in addition to working on nutrition, surveyed epidemic conditions in the Soviet Union, travelled to Latin America as secretary to the Leprosy Commission, planned for the proposed International School of Advanced Health Studies in Paris, which he was slated to head, and in the late 1930s became director of the Pasteur Institute in Tunis; Otto Olsen, a German hired in 1925 in anticipation of German entry into the League, who in the 1930s was secretary to the Commission on Housing and liaised with Madsen; Mihai Ciuca, a Romanian protégé of Cantacuzene who also served in China; and Emilio Pampana, an Italian malaria specialist, who became chief malariologist at the WHO.

Rajchman also brought to Geneva for short periods Europeans, Chinese, Japanese and Latin Americans to serve particular needs or to gain experience they would use at home. He employed extremely able health professionals in China, among them refugees from Nazi Germany and Yugoslavia. Pre-eminent among the latter were Štampar and B. Borcic, his colleague from Zagreb.

Rajchman's dismissal

In the 1930s, Rajchman's political engagements increasingly compromised his status as an international official. In 1931, he advised the Chinese on responding to Japanese aggression in Manchuria, and in 1933, with the reluctant acquiescence of London and Paris, he went to China to prepare an economic plan to strengthen the Chinese government.[66] His indiscretions antagonised the Japanese, annoyed the British and French, and infuriated Secretary-General Joseph Avenol.[67] His political leanings and intimate contacts in Moscow contributed to his loss of support by the right-wing Polish government,[68] and his anti-fascism, ties to the Popular Front and vigorous objection to appeasing Hitler increased his vulnerability.[69] The 1935–7 reorganisation of the LNHO would probably not have been achieved without Avenol's support. However, only after the October 1938 Munich agreement did Avenol dare to dismiss him in a 'purge' of 'leftists' from the secretariat.[70] His dismissal came as the LN was collapsing and Europe was plunging into the Second World War.

The OIHP and the LNHO

In the interwar years, the OIHP retained legal and administrative jurisdiction over sanitary conventions, and became a vehicle for other diplomatic agreements.[71] The Permanent Committee held semi-annual meetings, but its role as the LNHO's Advisory Health Council was nominal. Most health professionals regarded the OIHP as ineffective, for its Paris staff had a minuscule budget, inadequate facilities and a narrow sense of mission.[72] The OIHP was so heavily dependent upon Geneva that the Health Committee became the *de facto* lead agency in preparing for a new sanitary convention.

While the 1920 sanitary convention failed to reflect existing knowledge, political turmoil in Turkey delayed the preparation of a new convention. The Health Committee, nevertheless, invested in epidemiological studies. It collected data, conducted surveys and created the Eastern Bureau before a conference finally met in Paris in May 1926.

The resulting convention made typhus and smallpox, as well as plague, cholera and yellow fever, reportable diseases.[73] The conference recognised the excellence of the LN's epidemiological work, and sentiment existed for transferring to Geneva responsibility for the convention's notification provisions. Buchanan, Cumming and Barrère predictably insisted upon maintaining the OIHP's authority, and carried the day. The convention, however, empowered the OIHP to 'make necessary arrangements' for assistance.[74] The Pan American Sanitary Bureau, the Eastern Bureau and the Egyptian Sanitary Maritime and Quarantine Council were designated regional agencies for this purpose. The Permanent Committee also reached agreement with the Health Committee for consultation, the use of League publications to disseminate information, and the delegation of research activity to Geneva.[75] Even so, rivalry between the secretariats continued unabated.[76]

The Rockefeller Foundation

The LNHO and the RF enjoyed a symbiotic relationship in which the former acted in important respects as a surrogate for the latter. The LNHO could pursue strategic goals beyond the reach of a private foundation, while the Foundation made available essential resources. Their partnership served the global biomedical/public health episteme.

To create an epidemiological intelligence service and implement a health personnel interchange programme, as suggested by Rajchman, the RF in 1922 made a five-year grant to the LN of $492,000. Subsequent grants were made to train officials in vital and epidemiological statistics, establish the Eastern Bureau and create a public health documentation centre. Grants for the interchanges were extended through 1929, and for the intelligence service through 1937. During the years 1922–1930, the RF invested about $1.3 million in the LNHO, and for the years 1930–4 another $723,000 were awarded. Residual funds lasted through 1937.

These grants were a pittance in the Foundation's total public health budget, but they were a life-line for Rajchman.[77] They permitted him to carry out important projects the League probably would not have financed, and, by conferring prestige on him and the LNHO, probably stimulated the LN to appropriate more funds than it might otherwise have provided.

Relations between the RF and LNHO were complex. The RF helped Rajchman recruit staff; awarded travel grants to individuals visiting Geneva; recommended persons for expert bodies; made its own staff available for special purposes; helped assess requests for technical assistance; provided additional help to governments receiving LN assistance; and funded its own schools, laboratories and institutes of persons engaged in the LNHO.

Of mutual interest was the upgrading of Chinese medical and health institutions and practices. The Foundation had formed the Peking Union Medical College, and by the early 1920s was eager to develop Chinese public health institutions. Political chaos in China prevented orderly progress, although White's Asian mission led to the creation of the Eastern Bureau. The LNHO's Chinese programme rested upon Rajchman's enthusiasm and European interest in stabilising the Chinese government. The Foundation provided the League with expert advice on China, and the Chinese programmes of each benefited from the activities of the other.[78]

Conclusions

The international sanitary regime before the First World War was a narrow, defensive arrangement intended to protect European and American enclaves from epidemics of plague and cholera endemic in other regions. It was embodied in diplomatic agreements conceived in the national security interests of the signatories.

Scientific advances and practical achievements in disease prevention prior to and during the war transformed the goals and mechanisms for health co-operation. They instilled into the biomedical/public health episteme a belief that scientific research and preventive measures organised on an international basis would reduce or eradicate many diseases and socio-economic causes of human illness.

Postwar co-operation aimed at improving the health of all humans and was centred within the biomedical/public health episteme. The interstate character of the LN did not detract from the technocratic character of its Health Organisation. Both the Health Committee and its professional proactive Secretariat, directed by the energetic visionary Ludwik Rajchman, were innovative institutions. They penetrated deeply into national societies drawing domestic administrative, research and educational agencies into a transboundary biomedical/public health infrastructure. They also developed new intellectual resources essential for systematic public health work, most notably standardised nomenclature and statistical methods, a worldwide epidemiological database and international standards for important biological agents.

Especially important was Rajchman's leadership. He embodied the most advanced ideals of the biomedical/public health episteme and possessed exceptional skills. He was strategically located within communication networks and brought to the LNHO external resources which made much of what it achieved possible. A central feature of the regime was the public–private partnership in which the RF, by endorsing and funding the intergovernmental LNHO, enhanced not only its effectiveness but also its legitimacy.

The interwar health regime was largely self-transforming. New consensual knowledge led to frequent modifications in the Health Committee's agenda and to new domestic, as well as international, institutions. That is not to say that the regime was unresponsive to external influences. New scientific knowledge and significant changes in the political, social and technological setting after 1945 would bring further changes in the health regime almost as dramatic as those after the First World War.

Notes

1 The LNHO is examined in Fraser Brockington, *World Health* (London: Churchill Livingstone, 1975), and Neville M. Goodman, *International Health Organisations and Their Work*, 2nd edn (Philadelphia: The Blakiston Co., 1971).

2 Literature on organisation theory, network analysis, international regimes, epistemic communities and international organisation leadership helps to explain LNHO dynamics. A portion of this literature is examined in Martin David Dubin, 'International Regime Theory and International Health Cooperation in the Interwar Era', a paper presented at the 34th Annual Conference of the International Studies Association, 25 March 1993, Acapulco, Mexico.

3 Richard N. Cooper, 'International Cooperation in Public Health as a Prologue to Macroeconomic Cooperation', in Richard N. Cooper, et al., *Can Nations Agree? Issues in International Economic Cooperation* (Washington, DC: The Brookings Institution, 1987), pp. 178ff; and Norman Howard-Jones, *The Scientific Background of the International Sanitary Conferences, 1851–1938* (Geneva: WHO, 1975), pp. 12–92.

4 Howard-Jones, *The Scientific Background*, pp. 1–88; and Goodman, *International Health Organisations*, pp. 49ff.

5 In 1902 an Inter-American Sanitary Bureau (renamed in 1923 the Pan American Sanitary Bureau) had been formed, but was little more than a paper organisation until after the First World War. Norman Howard-Jones, *The Pan American Health Organization, Origins and Evolution* (Geneva: World Health Organisation, 1981), pp. 5–10.

6 *Vingt-cinq ans d'Activité de l'Office International d'Hygiène Publique (1909–1933)* (Paris: OIHP, 1933). Barrère dominated sanitary conferences from 1892 to 1938 and the OIHP until his death in 1940. Howard-Jones, *The Scientific Background*. Barrère's role is documented in H. S. Cumming, 'Memoir', H. S. Cumming Papers, University of Virginia.

7 Sir George Newman, 'Fifty Years' Progress in Public Health', in *Interpreters of Nature, Essays by Sir George Newman* (reprint, Freeport, NY: Books for Libraries, Inc., 1968), pp. 251–71.

8 Howard-Jones, *The Scientific Background*, pp. 87ff.

9 Raymond B. Fosdick, *The Story of the Rockefeller Foundation* (New York: Harper & Brothers, Publishers, 1952), and RF annual reports, the first of which is dated 1913–14. The RF by December 1919 had an endowment of $174.5 million. Between 1913 and 1932, it devoted over $48 million to public health, and large additional sums to medical research and medical and nursing education. The Rockefeller Foundation, *Annual Report, 1932* (New York: The Rockefeller Foundation, nd), pp. 156–7.

10 For First World War Red Cross activities, see American Red Cross, *The Work of the American Red Cross During the War* (np; nd); Henry P. Davison, *The American Red Cross in the Great War* (New York: The Macmillan Co., 1919); Foster Rhea Dulles, *The American Red Cross, A History* (New York: Harper & Brothers, Publishers, 1950); and Dame Beryl Oliver, *The British Red Cross in Action* (London: Faber & Faber, 1966).

11 The Rockefeller Foundation, *Annual Report, 1918* (New York: The Rockefeller Foundation, nd), p. 59.

12 Late in 1920, the Foundation refused to help the League's Epidemic Commission due to the political controversy in the US over League membership. George E. Vincent to Starr Murphy, 15 September 1920, RG 1.1., Series 789, Box 2, Folder 11, Rockefeller Foundation Archives (hereafter RFA), Rockefeller Archives Center (RAC). Vincent's comment appears in RF, *Annual Report, 1921*, (New York: The Rockefeller Foundation, n. d.), p. 73.

13 The Covenant in Article 23 stipulated: 'Subject to and in accordance with the provisions of international conventions existing or hereafter to be agreed upon, the Members of the League: . . . (f) will endeavour to take steps in matters of international concern for the prevention and control of disease.' Article 25 approved the Red Cross activity: 'The members of the League agree to encourage and promote the establishment and co-operation of duly authorized voluntary national Red Cross organizations having as purposes the improvement of health, the prevention of disease and the mitigation of suffering throughout the world.'

14 Davison, *The American Red Cross*, pp. 282–90, and Clyde E. Buckingham, *For Humanity's Sake. The Story of the Early Development of the League of Red Cross Societies* (Washington, DC: Public Affairs Press, 1964).

15 *Proceedings of the Medical Conference held at the Invitation of the Committee of the Red Cross Societies, Cannes, France, April 1 to 11, 1919* (Geneva: The League of Red Cross Societies, 1919).

16 Simon Flexner and James Thomas Flexner, *William Henry Welch and the Heroic Age in American Medicine* (New York: Dover Publications, 1966), p. 380, and Simon Flexner to C.-E. A. Winslow, 28 April 1921, William H. Welch Papers, The Johns Hopkins School of Hygiene and Public Health.

17 The LRCS's Medical Advisory Board advised against activities covered by existing organisations, including the Health Section of the League of Nations. 'Second Meeting of the General Council of the League of Red Cross Societies. Geneva, March 28th–March 31st, 1922', *The World's Health*, 3, 4 (April 1922), 153–83, esp. p. 174.

18 'Memorandum for the Secretary', 22 November 1918, attached to Rupert Blue to H. S. Cumming, 7 February 1919, Papers of the USPHS, RG 90, General Files, Group XII, OIHP, Box 1, US National Archives, Washington, DC.

19 LN, *The Records of the First Assembly, Plenary Meetings (Meetings held from the 15th of November to the 18th of December 1920)* (Geneva: LN, 1920), pp. 323–51, 371–92 and 411.

20 LN, Temporary Health Committee of the League of Nations, 'Minutes of the first and second meetings of the Committee, held in Paris on May 5th and 6th, 1921.' C.27.1921.III; and C.-E. A. Winslow to R. Rajchman, 28 January 1935, C.-E. A. Winslow Papers, Yale University.

21 The organisation and work of the Health Committee in the 1920s are examined in H. R. G. Greaves, *The League Committees and World Order* (London: Oxford University Press, 1931), pp. 85–110. An 'emergency sub-committee' of the Health Committee met in March 1940.

22 A membership list appears in LN, *Bulletin of the Health Organisation*, 11 (1945), 206.

23 See below, p. 65.

24 Charles W. Popkin, 'The Interchange of Public Health Personnel Under the Health Organization of the League of Nations, A Study of the Creation of an International Standard of Public Health Administration' (Geneva: League of Nations Non-Partisan Association, 1928).

25 W. C. Cockburn, 'The International Contribution to the Standardization of Biological Substances. 1. Biological Standards and the League of Nations, 1921– 1946', *Biologicals*, 19 (1991), 161–9.

26 In November 1939, free samples were being distributed to seventy-five laboratories. LN, Health Committee, 'Record, Thirty-First Session of the Health Committee, Geneva, November 20th–24th, 1939.' C.H. 31st Session, p. 31.

27 W. R. Aykroyd, 'International Health – A Retrospective Memoir', *Perspectives in Biology and Medicine*, 2, 2 (Spring 1968), 273–85; E. Burnet and W. R. Aykroyd, 'Nutrition and Public Health', *Quarterly Bulletin of the Health Organization*, 4, 2 (June 1935) and LNHO, 'Report on the Physiological Bases of Nutrition, drawn up by the Technical Commission of the Health Committee at the meeting held in London (November 25th–29th, 1935), Reviewed and amplified at the Meeting held at Geneva (June 4th–8th, 1936)', 15 June 1936. C.H.1197(1).

28 'Memorandum', 22 June 1921, Cumming Papers, and Edward T. Steegman to H. S. Cumming, 28 October 1921, Papers of the USPHS, RG 90, General Files, Group XII, League of Nations, Box 6. In response to feminist pressure, S. Josephine Baker, an American child welfare expert, was appointed to the Health Committee, but she never attended a Committee meeting. In April 1922, Rajchman arranged for a special commission that would have given the Soviets *de facto* Health Committee membership. The Commission met only once. L. Rajchman, 'Report on Trip to Moscow', 19 June 1924, LNA 12B/36769/15255.

29 W. R. Castle, Jr., to The Secretary, 14 and 23 May 1923, Papers of the US Dept. of State, RG 59, Decimal File 1910–1929, 500.C1191/9 and 23, US National Archives, Washington, DC.

30 LN, 'Scheme for the Permanent Health Organisation of the League of Nations', 9 June 1923. C.391.1923.III.

31 Buchanan even tried to discredit Rajchman's negotiations with the Rockefeller Foundation. See the Buchanan–Rose correspondence starting with G. S. Buchanan to W. Rose, 23 June 1922, in RAC RF R.G. 5, Series 1.2, 1922, 400 Great Britain, Folder 1845, and G. S. Buchanan to Dear President [Madsen], 27 July 1922, RG 1.1, Series 100. Box 20, Folder 165, RFA; G. S. Buchanan to Sir Eric Drummond, 15 July 1922, 1520 League of Nations, Health Section I, Papers of the British Medical Research Council, London; and L. Rajchman to W. Rose, 7 August 1922, LNA 12B/26222/21836.

32 H. S. Cumming, 'Memo', 19 September 1929, Papers of the USPHS, RG 90, General Files, Group XII, League of Nations, Box 8.

33 See below, p. 71.

34 LN, 'Composition of the Health Committee, Report by the Representative of New Zealand', 29 January 1937. C.92.III.1937.

35 M. T. Morgan to Dr Carnwath, 30 May 1935, and H. Carnwath to A. Salusbury McNalty, 21 October 1935, Papers of the British Ministry of Health, MH 58/60, Public Record Office, Kew. Cumming explained that 'it was felt . . . that Dr.

Madsen's influence has possibly been lessened by advancing age and more or less complete compliance with the desires of the Director of the Health Section'. H. S. Cumming to The Honorable Secretary of State, 29 December 1937, Papers of the US Dept. of State, RG 59, Decimal File 1930–1939, 500.C1191/186.

36 To reduce Rajchman's influence, Parisot formed a sub-committee composed of himself and Morgan to draft Committee resolutions and reports. LN, Health Organisation, Twenty-fourth Session of the Health Committee (5–9 February 1937), 'Note on the Composition of the Committee', 6 February 1937. C.H. 1231. Rajchman, nonetheless, attempted to control appointments to the Committee. G. S. Buchanan to H. S. Cumming, 27 January 1937, and H. S. Cumming to J. C. Dunn, 16 February 1937, Cumming Papers.

37 LN, 'The Records of the First Assembly, Plenary Meetings (Meetings held from the 15th of November to the 18th of December 1920)' (Geneva: LN, 1920), 337ff.

38 This changed in 1938 when the Health Organisation was reviewed by a new Seventh Committee. On certain questions, the two committees met jointly.

39 At the Third Assembly in 1922, Chodzko presided over the Second Committee. At the Sixth Assembly in 1925, Velghe, as rapporteur on health questions, aided by Lutrario, was instrumental in increasing the health budget despite British efforts inspired by Buchanan to trim it. LN, 'Records of the Sixth Assembly, Meetings of the Committees, Minutes of the Second Committee (Technical Organisations)', *Official Journal Special Supplement No. 35* (Geneva: LN, 1925), 11ff, and 'Minutes of the Fourth Committee (Budget and Financial Questions)', *Official Journal Special Supplement No. 37* (Geneva: LN, 1925), 26ff.

40 Buchanan in September 1927 sarcastically observed 'that it is desirable to encourage the League of Nations to prove its utility in technical matters in the Pacific region, as it is now endeavouring to do by other health missions in India and Latin America'. Note to the Colonial Office by Sir G. Buchanan, 'Recommendations of the International Pacific Health Conference, Melbourne, 15th–22nd December 1926', 30 September 1927, Copy in 1520/HS 3, Papers of the British Medical Research Council.

41 On LN aid to China see Cheryl Ann Payer, 'Western Economic Assistance to Nationalist China, 1927–1937, A Comparison with Postwar Foreign Aid Programs', PhD dissertation, Dept. of Government, Harvard University, September 1971.

42 LN, 'Records of the Sixth Assembly, Text of the Debates', *Official Journal Special Supplement No. 33* (Geneva: LN, 1925), 94 and 377.

43 LN, 'Records of the Tenth Ordinary Session of the Assembly, Meetings of the Committees, Minutes of the Fourth Committee', *Official Journal Special Supplement No. 79* (Geneva: LN, 1929), 75–6, 131, and 139.

44 Hughes Evans, 'European Malaria Policy in the 1920s and 1930s: The Epidemiology of Minutiae', *Isis*, 80, 301 (March 1989), 40–59.

45 For a sketch of Rajchman, see Henryk Korczyk's article in Polska Akademia Nauk, *Polski Slownik Biograficzny*, 30, 3 (1987), 464–68.

46 Aykroyd, 'International Health', and Aykroyd's obituary of Rajchman in *The Lancet*, 7407 (14 August 1965), 349.

47 Rajchman claimed to have spent 1907–9 at the Pasteur Institute, but Institute records show only that he attended the study course. A. Perrot, Conservateur du Musée Pasteur, to Martin David Dubin, 8 April 1987.

48 Rajchman directed the Institute until 1931. He may have been the only official to retain a national post while serving in the LN's secretariat.

49 H. S. Cumming, 'Memoir', June 1919, Cumming Papers.

50 J. T. Elliott, A. Ruth Fry and V. C. Stephens, 'Poland', 15 May 1919, Friends' War Victims' Relief Committee, circulated with Sir Wm. Goode's Compliments, Papers of the American Relief Administration, Paris Office, Poland. May 1919, Box 9, The Hoover Institution on War, Peace and Revolution.

51 'Minutes of the Fifth Meeting of the International Health Conference held in London at the Ministry of Health, Whitehall, on Thursday, 15th April 1920, at 11:00 a.m.', LNA 20/51/5.

52 F. E. Longley and H. A. Shaw to H. Biggs, 8 October 1920, RFA and S. M. Gunn to W. Rose, 8 July 1921, RG 1.1, 789 Poland, Box 1, Folder 1, RFA. See also E. R. Embree, 'Poland, Warstruck and Woebegone', 20 September 1920, Edwin R. Embree Papers, Yale University.

53 L. Rajchman to the Secretary-General, 20 January 1922, LNA 12B/18772/18772.

54 L. Rajchman to W. Rose, 18 November 1921, RG 5, IHB 1920, Switzerland 803, and L. Rajchman to W. Rose, 18 February 1922, RG 1.1, Series 100, Folder 165, RFA.

55 LN, Health Section, 'Epidemiological Intelligence, No. 1, Eastern Europe in 1921' (Geneva: LN, 14 January 1922).

56 LN, 'European Health Conference held at Warsaw from March 20th to 28th, 1922' (Geneva: LN, 3 April 1922), Papers of the British Foreign Office, FO 371/8136.

57 See above, n. 29.

58 Rajchman's strong anti-colonial sentiments are revealed in William Martin, typescript of an interview: 'M. Rajchman, *Chine*, 17 février 1926', copy in LNA.

59 American Public Health Association leaders reminded Cumming that 'the sentiment of the American public health workers is very strong in favor of the admirable work that is being done at Geneva'. C.-E. A. Winslow to H. S. Cumming, 18 June 1926, Winslow Papers. In Great Britain, Rajchman was supported by Buchanan's chief, George Newman. G. Newman to H. S. Cumming, 4 July 1927, Cumming Papers, and G. Newman to Dr Morgan, 25 February 1935, Papers of the British Ministry of Health, MH 58/60. In France, Léon Bernard, by the late 1920s president of the Conseil supérieur d'Hygiène and Robert Debré, were among his very active supporters.

60 G. S. Buchanan to H. S. Cumming, 6 August 1931, Cumming Papers. Buchanan observed: 'If I hadn't a Labour Ministry, . . . I would try to stir the thing up at the Assembly!'

61 Rajchman in 1930 obtained Aristide Briand's support for an International School of Advanced Health Studies in Paris. The school never materialised, but French cabinets throughout the 1930s endorsed the idea. As late as October 1937, the French were organising a conference to assess plans for the school. LN, 'Conference of the Ministers of Public Health of Europe', 2 October 1937. C.463.1937.III.

62 A list appears in LN, *Bulletin of the Health Organisation*, 11 (1945), 207. In 1931, the Health Section topped out at 51 members. The professionals never exceeded 21.

63 Joseph Avenol to Frank G. Boudreau, 9 November 1938, Frank G. Boudreau Papers, New York Academy of Sciences. Frank G. Boudreau, 'Memorandum on the

Reorganization of the Health, Opium and Social Sections of the League of Nations', August 1939, Copy in the Clark Eichelberger Papers, New York Public Library.

64 The LNHO's wartime activities are reviewed in LN, *Chronicle of the Health Organisation*, Special Number (December 1945).

65 Aykroyd, 'International Health', and Burnet and Dr Aykroyd, 'Nutrition and Public Health'.

66 LN, Council Committee on Technical Co-operation Between the League and China, 'Report of the Technical Agent of the Council on His Mission in China, from the date of his appointment until April 1st, 1934', Geneva, 30 April 1934. C.157.M.66.1934.

67 Avenol told Rajchman to choose between serving China and remaining in the Secretariat. J. Avenol to L. Rajchman, 13 June 1934, Ludwik Rajchman Papers, possessed by Mrs Balińska-Taylor, Chenu, France. The British backed Avenol, suggesting that, if necessary, he might enlist support from the Polish government. William Strang to Monsieur Avenol, 19 July 1934, Joseph Avenol Papers, Quai d'Orsay, Paris.

68 Polish officials in April 1935 labelled Rajchman's news of a war scare as coming from 'Jewish-masonic circles, and from the 2nd and 3rd International', *Diariusz i Teki Jana Szembeka (1935–1945)* (4 cols.; London: Polish Research Centre, 1964–72), vol. I, p. 262. In January 1937, the Polish government, through its controlled press, accused Rajchman of interfering with the selection of a League of Nations High Commissioner for Danzig. *Ilustrowany Kuryer Codzienny*, 30 January 1937, p. 13. Subsequently, the Polish government purged Chodzko from the Health Committee.

69 Rajchman in 1936 was accused of expressing 'avowed Communistic feelings'. H. S. Cumming to The Honorable, The Secretary of State, 22 August 1936, Papers of the US Dept. of State, RG 59, Decimal File 1930–1939, 500.C119/164. When he blocked the International Relief Union, an Italian Red Cross offshoot, from receiving League approval for work in civil-war-ridden Spain, former League Secretary-General Sir Eric Drummond, then British ambassador at Rome, accused Rajchman of 'distinct communist leanings'. Sir Eric Drummond to Sir Gregory Mounsey, 23 December 1937, Papers of the British Foreign Office, FO 371/20557, Public Record Office, Kew. Rajchman in 1938 appealed to the French foreign ministry for arms to aid China. In July 1938, he was an organiser of a scheme to raise a private airforce for China. This scheme is documented in the Rajchman Papers and in the Lord Noel-Baker Papers, Churchill College, University of Cambridge.

70 James Barros, *Betrayal from Within, Joseph Avenol, Secretary-General of the League of Nations, 1933–1940* (New Haven: Yale University Press, 1969), pp. 185–8.

71 The OIHP was responsible for the International Agreement of Brussels of 1 December 1924 on the treatment of venereal diseases among sailors; the June 1926 International Sanitary Convention and the October 1938 revision recognising Egyptian sovereignty; and the Air Navigation Sanitary Convention of 12 April 1933. It was jointly responsible with the Health Committee for (1) assisting Turkey in carrying out sanitary provisions in the Lausanne Treaty of 24 July 1923 and (2) for implementing the International Opium Convention of 11 February 1925.

72 Cumming in 1919 called the director of the OIHP secretariat 'quite moss-back'. In 1926, he declared it an 'indisputable fact' that the OIHP 'under dominance of the French Government had failed to perform the duties assigned it by the Conventions of Rome and Paris'. H. S. Cumming, 'Memoir', 11 July 1919, Cumming Papers, and H. S. Cumming to The Honorable, The Secretary of State, 26 July 1926, Papers of the US Dept. of State, RG 59, Decimal File 1910–1929, 512.4B2/30.

73 'International Sanitary Convention and Protocol of Signature. Signed in Paris, June 21, 1926', LN, *Treaty Series*, 78 (1928), 229–347.

74 *Ibid.* pp. 248–51. This was insisted upon by many delegates. Unsigned memo, 'The Paris International Sanitary Conference of May and June 1926', RG 1.1, Series 100, Box 22, Folder 183, RFA. Rajchman and Madsen wanted to merge the secretariats, and Buchanan recognised that strong support existed for eliminating the Paris secretariat. L. Rajchman to Th. Madsen, 9 February 1926, LNA 12/33149/31035, and 'Memorandum of conversation between Dr. Cumming, Sir George Buchanan and Mr. Castle, on February 8, 1926 on the subject of the Office international and the League Health Committee', 9 February 1926, Papers of the US Dept. of State, RG 59, Decimal File 1910–1929, 512.4A1a/286; H. S. Cumming to the Hon. Robert Work, and H. S. Cumming to the Hon. McKenzie Moss, 2 June 1926, Cumming Papers; W. R. Castle, Jr to Mr Grew, 13 July 1926, Papers of the US Dept. of State, RG 59, Decimal File 1910–1929, 512.4B2/29. Cumming notes the difficulty in blocking Geneva, for 'the Health Section of the League of Nations, well organized chiefly by able Americans, and generously subsidized by the . . . Rockefeller Foundation, under an able and aggressive Polish subject, had done excellent work both in research and in establishing an international epidemiological intelligence service'. H. S. Cumming to the Honorable, The Secretary of State, 26 July 1926, Papers of the US Dept. of State, RG 59 Decimal File 1910–1929, 512.4B2/30. Buchanan admitted that the Office had to get its 'house in order'. G. S. Buchanan to H. S. Cumming, 2 June 1926, Papers of the USPHS, RG 90, General Files, Group XII, League of Nations, Box 6.

75 LN, Health Committee, 'Minutes of the Tenth (Extraordinary) Session Held at Paris on Tuesday, April 26th, and Wednesday, April 27th, 1927', 30 July 1927. C.350.M.124.1927.III.

76 This rivalry is documented in the Cumming Papers, and in the Taliaferro Clark Papers in the National Library of Medicine, Bethesda, Md.

77 The RF provided over 30 per cent of the LNHO's budget, but this amounted to less than 2 per cent of its public health expenditures. RF expenditures to fight tuberculosis in France between 1917 and 1926 – $2,359,178.52 – alone exceeded the $1,733,560.42 appropriated for the LNHO between 1922 and 1934. These data are derived from RF accounts. For the French expenditures, see E. R. Embree to C.-E. A. Winslow, 17 September 1927, Winslow Papers.

78 The RF–LNHO links in China are documented in their archives and in John B. Grant's oral memoir in *Columbia University Oral History Collection* (Glen Rock, NY: Microfilming Corp. of America, 1973–).

5

Assistance and not mere relief: the Epidemic Commission of the League of Nations, 1920–1923

MARTA ALEKSANDRA BALIŃSKA

It is a curious and heartening fact that international cooperation in the prevention of epidemics placidly continues, however hostile or competitive other relationships may become. (Hans Zinsser, *Rats, Lice and History* (1935), p. 293)

The Epidemic Commission of the League of Nations (LNEC) was considered at the time of its creation to be the 'first essay in international cooperation',[1] in that, contrary to other health and relief organisations, its funds proceeded not from a charitable public, but from national governments. The Commission acted exclusively through local health administrations, basing its work on 'the necessity of strengthening the public health and sanitary organisation of the country as the most effective and the most lasting means of checking the spread of epidemics'.[2] Although the Epidemic Commission lasted little over three years (April 1920–December 1923) and worked in only five countries (Poland, Soviet Russia and Ukraine, Latvia and Greece), it marks one of the early 'success stories' of the League of Nations Health Organisation (LNHO) which it preceded and, indirectly, had a large part in creating.

Typhus and the First World War

The Epidemic Commission (initially called the Typhus Commission) was born to fight the louse, as the vector of typhus, a rickettsial infectious fever which leads 'the quiet bourgeois existence of a reasonably domesticated disease'[3] in times of peace and flares up into epidemics when basic sanitary conditions break down.

Typhus was a major fear from the onset of the First World War, but contagion was somewhat surprisingly avoided in the West, owing perhaps to the systematic delousing of Allied troops. In Serbia, where it was endemic, the fever broke out a mere three months after hostilities began and is thought to have caused the deaths of over 150,000 people.[4] Generally speaking, it is difficult to estimate the incidence and spread of typhus in Central and Eastern Europe

81

during and after the war. There seems little doubt that Eastern Poland and Russia were worst hit, but countries such as Germany, Austria, Romania, Hungary, Czechoslovakia and Lithuania were also affected in varying degrees. According to the man who was to lead the anti-epidemic campaign in Poland, Dr Ludwik Rajchman, in countries where local administration and government continued to function, such as Germany and Austria-Hungary, typhus did not take on epidemic proportions, whereas in Poland, for example, which was being continuously occupied by different armies, numbers of cases of typhus rose throughout the war, despite the efforts of the Prussian and Austro-Hungarian authorities to contain the disease.

When, soon after the November 1918 armistice, news came of the increasing incidence of typhus in Poland and particularly in Russia (where the disease was endemic), the threat was taken seriously by European statesmen. Lord Balfour warned of 'a calamity which, following hard on war, seems almost worse than war itself', while Lenin prophesied: 'either the louse will defeat socialism or socialism will defeat the louse'.[6]

The reason for the renewed flourishing of the vermin was simple. The Germans had managed to keep the epidemic under relative control in the parts of Poland they occupied, but when they withdrew, they took with them all their sanitary and medical supplies, leaving the Poles with next to nothing. Simultaneously, the Bolshevik take-over had sunk Russia into civil war and turmoil, causing entire populations to flee westwards. The Red Army invaded Poland in February 1919, a mere three months after the armistice. By 1919–20, typhus was affecting an estimated 6 million Russians;[7] hundreds of thousands of Polish repatriates and prisoners of war and White Russians were spreading the disease in their attempt to cross the Polish border. Poland became a veritable clearing-house for European migration with – in addition to Eastern immigration – a West–East flow of Russian prisoners of war returning home from Germany. From November 1918 to January 1921, the Poles registered over 2.5 million persons at their border control stations.[8]

The origins of the Epidemic Commission

The first foreign organisation to bring succour to Poland was Herbert Hoover's American Relief Administration (ARA) which was to remain in Poland, playing an active role in national reconstruction, until the end of 1922. As former Food Administrator, Hoover and his organisation had done much to assuage the famine in Belgium during the war.[9] One month after Poland regained independence, in December 1918, the US government despatched a Food Mission to Warsaw, composed of Dr Kellogg, Colonel William R. Grove and Count Jan Harodyski; preliminary investigations indicated that more than a third of the population 'were unable to provide themselves with enough food to maintain health'.[10] Within six weeks, the first food deliveries arrived and the ARA undertook a children's feeding programme which was soon providing 400,000 Polish children with a daily meal of American food.[11] In June 1919, Poland appealed to the West for help in fighting the worsening typhus epidemic. Hoover introduced a resolution to the Supreme Economic Council that Poland be aided in her struggle against the disease with Allied army supplies on credit and, with Woodrow Wilson's support, arranged to send 6.5 million dollars' worth of steam laundries, linens, beds, soap, motorised bath plants, underclothes, ambulances, etc., requiring 'thirty-two trains and over fifty cars to transport to Poland'.[12] At the same time, the American surgeon who had been in charge of delousing the Allied armies, Colonel Gilchrist, arrived in Eastern Poland (the worst affected area of the country, due to its proximity to Russia) with a contingent of 500 men, all of whose expenses were borne by Washington. Soon thereafter, the British government opened a credit of £100,000 for the purchase of medical and sanitary supplies and promised to deliver 'two freights of hospital *matériel*'.[13] The League of Red Cross Societies (LRCS, founded in May 1919 by the League of Nations (LN) to encourage the creation of and co-operation among national Red Cross Societies) delegated, also in June 1919, a medical commission composed of Dr Hugh S. Cumming (USA), Sir George Buchanan (GB), Dr Aldo Castellani (Italy) and Dr Visbecq (France) to investigate sanitary conditions in Poland. Consequent to their findings, the LRCS issued a report in September, stressing the seriousness of the epidemic situation in Eastern Europe.[14]

In Poland, the local health authorities were doing their utmost to tackle overwhelming circumstances. In November 1918, a State Institute of Hygiene (Państwowy Zakład Higieny) was set up by Rajchman in rudimentary conditions in Warsaw, with subsidiaries around the country.[15] He and his colleague Dr Czesław Wroczyński (both future members of the Epidemics Commission) followed the retreating German troops to buy back the sanitary and laboratory equipment they were taking out of Poland. Doctors were mobilised and sent to the most contaminated regions: medical students were put in charge of sanitary inspection at railways; humanitarian organisations such as National Red Cross Societies, the British and American Quakers, the Save the Children Fund (SCF), the American Jewish Joint Distribution Committee (AJJDC) and various Polish–American associations sent teams of volunteers and supplies. The American Red Cross was particularly active, but missions of the Austrian, Belgian, British, French, Japanese, Portuguese, Romanian, Serbian and Swedish Red Cross Societies also provided aid. Yet all these measures proved unequal to the task in a country which was also struggling with the aftermath of over 120 years of partitions: different local administrations, currencies, legal codes and even width of railroad tracks.

On 29–30 July 1919, the first post-war British Minister of Health, Dr Christopher Addison, called an informal conference in London to examine a 'certain number' of health matters, and most especially the question of typhus in Eastern Europe.[16] Its main purpose was to discuss the part that the League of Nations (which was to come into being when the Treaty of Versailles was ratified in January 1920) should take in the field of health, but no definite conclusions were reached.[17] Although the League had been invested with important functions regarding health, national governments were having a hard time determining just what these should be, in view of the existing health organisations, especially the Office international d'hygiène publique (OIHP, founded in 1907) in Paris and the LRCS. Poland, which had appealed to the LRCS for help, was now spending the exceptionally high proportion of 1.5 per cent of its total national budget on the fight against typhus[18] and it seemed imperative that some intergovernmental agency take charge of co-ordinating a major anti-epidemic campaign.

In January 1920, the Polish Prime Minister and world-famous pianist, Ignacy Paderewski, went to Geneva to attend the first session of the League of Nations Assembly, taking Rajchman – who was already recognised as an expert in epidemiology – with him.[19] Rajchman had trained in Cracow and specialised in bacteriology at the Pasteur Institute under Elie Metchnikoff before spending the war years in Britain as demonstrator and researcher at the Royal Institute of Public Health, King's College and the Medical Research Committee. He came from a prominent Warsaw family and had been closely involved in Józef Piłsudski's victorious struggle for Polish independence. His Franco-British connections made him an attractive interlocutor for Poles and Westerners alike. In Geneva, he called attention to the threat of typhus to public health. In January 1920 alone, 100,000 cases had been reported in Poland, causing some 12,000 deaths.[20] A few weeks later Lord Balfour issued an urgent appeal to the LRCS as the only organisation capable of providing sufficient relief to the Polish crisis.[21] According to Rajchman (who later analysed the situation with a view to post-Second World War relief), the LRCS drew up a plan proposing to send 'thousands' of medical personnel to Eastern Europe, complete with the necessary means of transportation, on the condition that it be granted control of 'railroad and automobile traffic throughout all affected areas' as well as 'overall authority in relation to local administration and technical services'. This was, purportedly, 'flatly rejected by national governments'.[22]

It was once again Addison who, citing the League of Nations resolution for the constitution of a permanent health organ, proposed that a conference be convened in London in April 1920 to deal specifically with the typhus epidemic in Poland and 'with a view to protecting all of Europe against the spread of this terrible sickness towards the West'.[23] The particular fear was that typhus might spread to Germany and Austria, as it had to Holland the previous year, introduced by prisoners of war and causing some 500 deaths.[24] His suggestion was formally adopted by the League Assembly[25] and it was agreed that the setting up of a 'permanent organ' at the LN for matters of health should be studied, with representatives from the Polish Ministry of Health and the LRCS being invited to attend. The French were keen that the OIHP also be present and that the British should not be the only ones to choose the participants.[26] Presided over by Viscount Astor, the Conference assembled health experts from seven countries: France (Drs Brisac, Léon Bernard, Thiebault, Boujard); Great Britain (Sir George Buchanan, Sir George Newman); Canada (Dr Edward Steegman); Italy (Drs Alberto Lutrario and B. Forniciaria); Japan (Drs Yoneyi Miyagawa and Kachichi Kwaita), Poland (Drs Witold Chodźko and Ludwik Rajchman) and the United States (Surgeon-General Rupert Blue); as well as representations of three organisations: the LRCS (Sir David Henderson, Colonel R. P. Strong), the OIHP (Dr H. Pottevin) and the secretariat of the LN (Dame Rachel Crowdy, Mr Broch). The outside specialists Dr Frederick Norman White, Mr Teesdale and Colonel Smallman were also asked to take part in the discussions.

The Conference decided that the LN was the only body endowed with sufficient power and authority to take the required measures. These were to consist, basically, in reinforcing those already taken by the Polish authorities. The Conference recommended that the existing 12 quarantine and delousing stations, 13,077 hospital beds for contagious diseases and 294 disinfecting columns be brought to the respective numbers of 24, 30,000 and 1,000. In order to do so, a League of Nations Typhus Commission was to be named to raise money and oversee operations in collaboration with the Extraordinary Epidemic Commissariat which the Poles had recently (March 1920) instituted themselves.[27]

The question may be asked why the Polish government, aided by the LRCS and the OIHP, could not have taken the action themselves and what need there was for yet another relief organisation. The Conference's answer to this was that the Polish government and military authorities were already doing their utmost 'to obtain enough [sic] essential materials which, even if they could be purchased in the ordinary way, would be far beyond [their] resources'; the supplies lent by the American army had by now been exhausted; the LRCS had declared that any contributions on its part would be subsidiary and the OIHP did 'not possess the staff, organisation or funds to admit of its taking the required action'.[28]

The new Typhus Commission was to consist of a Chief Commissioner, who would take 'the necessary measures in order to buy, assemble and despatch the required *matériel* to Poland', a Medical Commissioner, who would organise and send 'to Poland the necessary health staff and medical personnel' and one or two other Medical Commissioners, to be based in Poland. The Conference resolved that the Commission would 'be able, when they see fit, to extend their action to all countries other than Poland' and take any steps 'in order to prevent the spread of typhus and other serious epidemics'.[29] An international board (composed of Drs Blue, Buchanan, Castellani and Visbecq) was appointed to name the Commissioners and their choice fell upon Dr Frederick Norman White (who had been Assistant Director-General of the Indian Medical Service during the war) as Chief Commissioner, and Dr Kenyon Vaughan Morgan (GB) and Dr Rajchman as Medical Commissioners. Their immediate task was to 'consult the competent authorities of various governments in order to register the available war *matériel* and transport it to Poland'.[30] A list of necessities was drawn up detailing sanitary and medical equipment, hospital supplies, food, clothing and vehicles, estimated at a cost of £3.25 million, which goods, it was hoped, could reach Poland by the end of August 1920, to be followed by 65 medical doctors, 150 nurses and 10 sanitary inspectors.[31] The complete list was as follows: 272 apparatus for vapour disinfection; 72 apparatus for hot air disinfection; 500 mobile disinfecting units; 100 showers with a 12-person capacity; 2,000 tons of soap; 96 iron tubes; 15,000 razors; 30,000 hospital beds; 60,000 mattresses; 60,000 pillows; 180,000 pairs of sheets; 10,000 blankets; 90,000 pillow cases, hand towels and rags; 2,000,000 shirts; 1,000,000 pairs of long underwear; 500,000 sets of underwear; 10,000 nurses' smocks; 3,750 tons of flour; 300 tons of sugar; 500 tons of preserves; 1,000 tons of cereals; 500 tons of condensed milk; 100 tons of coffee; 500 tons of fats; 100 ambulances; 40 'tourism cars'; 10 large motor cars; and 3 automobile repair units.

After the Conference, Rajchman returned to Warsaw with Norman White whom he led on an extensive tour of Eastern regions in May–June 1920. Norman White came back to Geneva more than ever convinced that the crisis required co-ordinated international action: 'How serious [the menace of typhus] may prove to be depends primarily on the efficiency of the barrier which the health authorities of Poland and neighbouring states are endeavouring to erect against the westward spread of the communicable disease'. He stated soon after his return in August 1920:

> In these days of economic stress the health authorities of no country can fail to be apprehensive of the results that are likely to follow the importation of typhus infection into other countries. That there is likely to be an ever increasing risk of such importation . . . unless the Polish health administration be reinforced, I fully believe. It would be preferable, and cheaper, to defeat the disease in Eastern Europe, than to fight it in our midst.[32]

Contributions to the Epidemic Commission

Soon after the November 1918 armistice, the Poles had started setting up a cordon sanitaire along their Eastern border, three-quarters of which were destroyed by the Red Army's invasion in February 1919. Once an armistice had been signed between the two warring countries a year and a half later (October

1920), the cordon sanitaire had to be rebuilt and reinforced if Poland and possibly the West were to be protected from further contagion.

The London Conference had come up with the figure of £3.25 million as the amount necessary to bring relief to Poland. The LN accordingly divided up the sum among the countries, including non-League members, basing their calculations on the Universal Postal System, international trade and risks of contagion, those countries considered most concerned by the threat of typhus being expected to pay proportionally more. Thus, Germany was asked to contribute £579,000; Great Britain – £260,000; Italy – £155,850; France – £152,000; Poland – £121,900; United States – £114,550; Austria – £73,500; Hungary – £73,150, and so on, with a country like Venezuela being called on to subscribe the amount of £5,850.[33]

The response to the League's appeal was – none, possibly because many states felt they had already donated generously (even if indirectly) through their volunteer aid agencies to the humanitarian crisis in Eastern Europe and particularly in Poland. Food was being supplied to Austria, Romania and Poland by the ARA, the ARC, the Save the Children Fund (SCF), the AJJDC and at least two other European organisations (the Comité de Secours des Amis des Victimes de la Guerre and the Comité de Secours de Vienne); the United States had sent to Poland vehicles and sanitary equipment worth $2 million; Great Britain had despatched 3.2 million yards of ticking, more than 200,000 pairs of shoes and £500,000 for transportation (in Poland *and* Romania); Holland had contributed 17 million florins to the Polish cause and the American Liquidation Commission and the ARC had sent medicines worth $9 million;[34] the French military health service had delivered medical supplies worth 1,284,750 francs,[35] while the Conference on Relief Credits (held in Paris on 21/22 April 1920) had voted that credits for wool and other materials be attributed to Poland.[36]

When Great Britain, however, declared herself ready to make a new contribution of £50,000 to the League of Nations Typhus Commission, rechristened the Epidemic Commission (henceforth LNEC), in June 1920, Lord Balfour called on Léon Bourgeois, President of the French Senate and League representative for France, to make a 'similar' donation.[37] The French Service at the LN was quick to point out to its superiors in Paris that France could hardly remain aloof in the face of international efforts to favour Poland (it should be remembered that the French had a military mission in Poland and that the medical supplies she had sent through it – cited above – were thus not considered by the League as direct donations to Poland), especially given the large contributions forthcoming from the American and British governments. While France might be less threatened than other countries, she had an obligation to 'international solidarity', the French Service in Geneva argued, pointing out the dire consequences which might arise if, from sheer lack of funds, typhus spread unchecked to the right bank of the Rhine. Was not Poland rendering France a great service by her defeat of the Soviets – what better cordon sanitaire against bolshevism was there than the Polish army?[38]

The French Minister of War, André Lefèvre, was offended by the fact that the medical supplies sent by his health service to Poland had not been cited by the League and Sir Eric Drummond, Secretary-General of the LN, was asked to rectify the mistake.[39] The Minister for Foreign Affairs, Alexandre Millérand, put forward a motion to Parliament in June 1920 asking for credits for Poland,[40] but the issue went no further, for France and Great Britain had declared themselves willing to contribute £50,000 each to the LNEC only on the condition that at least three other states do the same.[41]

In Poland, Rajchman was feeling the weight of being the sole commissioner on the 'spot', his desperate pleas for aid being repeatedly disappointed by a helpless Norman White.[42] By the autumn of 1920, the LNEC was reduced to two members, Vaughan Morgan having resigned in July since no money was forthcoming and because he had other pressing responsibilities.[43] The French were anxious that one of their nationals should be nominated for the LNEC (despite their reluctance to make a financial contribution) and suggested Colonel Aimé Gauthier,[44] the chief and longest-serving physician of the French army in Poland (not to be confused with the Swiss Dr Raymond Gautier, who later joined the League of Nations Health Organisation (LNHO) and replaced Rajchman as its Director in 1939).

There were, however, quite a few problems surrounding French relations with the LNEC. Besides their apparent unwillingness to contribute materially (as demonstrated by the fact that the promised £50,000 would not be voted by the French Parliament for a full eighteen months), there seems to have been some resentment of what was seen as the League's 'usurpation' of the OIHP in health matters, even though certain members of the Ministry of Health fully recognised that the Office had neither the mandate nor the power to take the measures the LNEC had set itself.[45]

By mid-October 1920, only six members of the League of Nations Council had responded to the LNEC's appeal: Great Britain and France had pledged £50,000, contingent, as has been said, on three other countries doing likewise; Italy had declared herself unable to help; Spain had expressed willingness but nothing else. Only Belgium and Greece had contributed – £1,000 and £10,000 respectively – whilst no replies had been forthcoming from Japan or Brazil. 'It thus appears . . . ', Drummond reported, 'that the campaign against typhus may be threatened with complete failure unless new measures are quickly taken or unexpected relief comes soon'.[46]

A few weeks later, Norman White again visited Eastern parts of Poland, accompanied by Dr Pottevin (Vice-Director of the OIHP) and the Danish bacteriologist Thorvald Madsen. They reported that there were still 'numerous cases' of typhus, although the disease was not as prevalent as in the spring. There was, on the other hand, a total dearth of sanitary organisation. 'As an example of the lack of information', they stated upon their return, 'we may cite our experience at Zuraki. This small village in the Bohorodczany district had reported no cases of typhus to the sanitary authorities: all the same, half an hour's house to house inquiry in a portion of the village resulted in the discovery of 2 typhus patients in one house, 3 in another, 5 in a third and in a fourth we found all occupants convalescent from a recent attack of the disease.'[47]

Drummond now called on the international community to subscribe a sum of at least £2 million for the LNEC.[48] In Warsaw, Rajchman informed the head of the French Military Mission, (General?) Niessel, that the LN had made an 'urgent appeal to all countries of the world'. Niessel appears to have supported French involvement in the LNEC since, when recommending that Colonel Gauthier be nominated to the Commission, he pointed out that if France continued to help Poland in isolation – that is, through her military mission and not through the League – Geneva might well refuse Gauthier's nomination.[49]

The same month, December 1920, Czechoslovakia informed the League that she too was faced with an outbreak of typhus which was entailing 'enormous expenditure', supported by the state, local authorities and private associations. As such, the government did not have the means to contribute to the Polish campaign.[50] Hungary also reported that typhus, spread by prisoners of war returning from Soviet Russia, had taken on 'epidemic' proportions: given her meagre resources, she could not respond positively to Drummond's appeal for Poland either; indeed she was in need of help herself.[51]

The French Deputy-Secretary General of the League, Jean Monnet (the future 'father of Europe') now intervened, pressing his Prime Minister, Aristide Briand, to contribute 'immediately' the promised £50,000 and urging the Minister of War, André Maginot, to name Gauthier Epidemic Commissioner.[52] Norman White was being paid by the British government, Rajchman by the Polish, but the French insisted that the League cover the larger part of Gauthier's salary.[53] They still could not, however, come to an agreement regarding their promised contribution. There was some tension on the subject between the War and Foreign Ministries, the former arguing that its health service had already despatched to Poland, in late 1919, medical material amounting to nearly 1.3 million francs and insisting that that sum be subtracted from the £50,000. But Jean Gout (Council President at the Quai d'Orsay) pointed out in a somewhat stiff letter that if money was not given through the League, it could hardly be considered part of the subscribed sum. 'It is absolutely necessary, both from the point of view of our influence in Poland and of our public finances that the efforts of the Government of the Republic be coordinated.'[54]

At this point, the British withdrew their initial condition and agreed to hand over the £50,000 without other states doing likewise, thus finally allowing the LNEC to send its first supplies to Poland in April 1921. The League of Nations Assembly promised to supplement that amount by raising a further £220,000, but by September little over half (£126,000) had reached the LNEC's coffers. The Commission had had to scrap their plan of sending foreign medical staff to Poland, but had been able, according to the League's Swiss representative, Gustave Ador, 'with the available funds, to obtain much better results than had been initially foreseen . . . Given the lack of resources, [the LNEC] was obliged to concentrate their efforts on the worst affected areas . . . It is certain that by working with the national administration and concentrating on the areas of contagion only, the Commission acted with great wisdom and had made great savings.' Had the funds been greater, he pointed out, they would have been able to extend their help to Lithuania (which had appealed to the League for help in May 1921),[55] Czechoslovakia and Romania. Ador also hoped that the LNEC would be able to collaborate with the Soviet government in order to help Russia, Georgia and Armenia.[56]

In recognition of 'the successful results achieved by the LNEC' the Assembly recommended, on 21 September 1921, that its work be continued and made a pressing appeal to those countries which had hitherto not contributed to do so now and for all members to show 'liberal support'.[57] Czechoslovakia promised to make available 'up to one million crowns' as of 1922.[58] Drummond and Monnet both pressed the French government to take action[59] and finally, on 28 December 1921, the Chamber of Deputies voted its contribution of 2.5 million francs.[60]

The 'zone sanitaire'

It was thus not until nearly a year after its appointment that the LNEC was at last able to ship the first supplies to Eastern Poland (via Danzig, to Warsaw by the Vistula and, by rail, on to Grodno, now part of Byelorus). Given the limited funds, material assistance took the form of those supplies which were both most needed and hardest to obtain in Poland – especially soap, medicines and medical equipment, but also ambulances, food for hospitals, equipment for a fifty-bed hospital, clothing for quarantine stations, subsidies for constructing and repairing bathing and disinfection installations and hospitals.[61] The area of the LNEC's activities was also reduced from what had originally been planned to the region of Grodno–Lida–Walkowysk–Brześć-Litowsk–Białystok (see figure 5.1). Help was concentrated at the control stations of Rowno and Baranowicze which were supposed to 'process' all migrating Polish and Bolshevik prisoners of war.

The LNEC set up their main headquarters in Warsaw, where the State Institute of Hygiene graciously offered its offices and personnel. Gauthier came

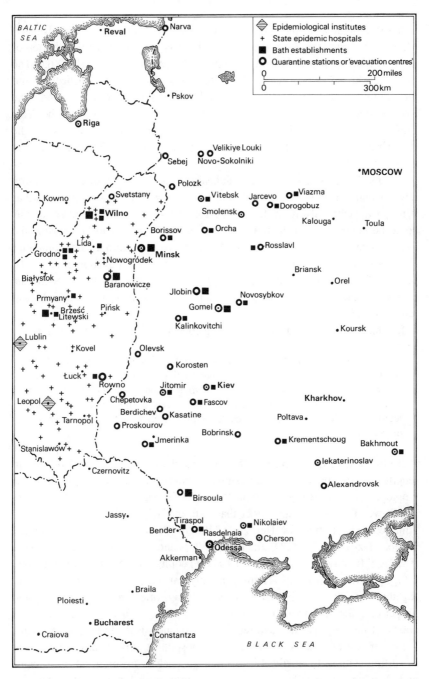

Fig. 5.1 Epidemic hospitals, quarantine stations and epidemiological institutes on the Polish–Russian frontier. *Source:* AFMFA SDN SG 1560, League of Nations Report on Health Situation in Eastern Europe in 1922.

to assist Rajchman in the spring of 1921 and was followed by the (British?) Major Fitzhugh, delegate of the LRCS, who was to oversee the distribution of the LRCS's supplies to Poland through the LNEC (valued at £10,000).[62] The Polish health service provided the LNEC with facilities for inspection and the commissioners were allowed to call on its staff in case of need. The Commission could also seek counsel from their advisory board: the Yale professor C. E. A. Winslow (LRCS); Dr Frick (International Committee of the Red Cross, ICRC), Dr Frédéric Ferrière (ICRC) and Dr Thorvald Madsen (OIHP).[63]

The most urgent task for the Polish health authorities was, of course, to stop new contagion from entering the country, yet this was not as straightforward as it might appear: railway traffic and persons passing through frontier stations could be controlled, but thousands of others were thought to be crossing the border undetected. Thus the 'cordon' had to be widened into a 'zone sanitaire'. Besides supplies and subsidies for the construction and renovation of hospitals, the LNEC set up observation posts along the Russian frontier, oversaw the sanitary control of repatriates and lent their expertise to bacteriological laboratories.[64]

Rajchman (who is credited with having conceived the 'zone')[65] explained:

> The system consisted in (a) as wholesale as possible sanitary control at the 'frontiers' of the area, and (b) a systematic delousing and cleansing of larger villages, townships and cities and (c) *above all*, the establishment of two, three, or more chains of emergency hospitals and sanitary centres throughout the affected region, one behind the other, so as to allow rapid detection, isolation and treatment of cases and contacts.[66]

By the time of its completion, the 'zone sanitaire' covered over 1,000 km in length and was made up of 20 sanitary centres and 132 epidemic hospitals employing 189 medical officers and 450 nurses. The largest was at Baranowicze, which was finished in April 1921 thanks to the help of the ARA, the Polish-American Committee for Help to Children (Polsko–Amerykański Komitet Pomocy Dzieciom, PAKPD), the Polish White and Red Cross Societies and the YMCA.[67] It could quarantine up to 10,000 people at a time with around 3,000 refugees arriving per day. Trains generally carried the healthy and the sick, together with dozens who had died on the way, often from lack of food and proper clothing. The mode of reception of incoming refugees at sanitary posts was the following: (1) sick and repatriated prisoners isolated in sanitary trains; (2) on arrival at base, sick evacuated to hospital, trains cleaned, others sent to sorting station; (3) medical inspection; (4) sick to hospital, others to baths and disinfection installations; (5) disinfection of belongings and clothing; (6) distribution of underclothing; (7) second medical inspection; (8) vaccination against smallpox; (9) period of quarantine.[68]

The European Sanitary Conference

While the money raised by the LNEC helped to achieve some improvement, it was not enough to sway the epidemic tide. However effective the 'zone sanitaire' might prove in itself, it was a palliative measure and as such could lessen but not eradicate contagion coming from elsewhere. Unless Russia herself instituted effective sanitary control, her endemic diseases – and typhus to begin with – would present a permanent danger to border states. The only way to proceed was to seek the co-operation of the Soviet health officials, which is what Norman White and Rajchman had in mind when they went to Moscow in November 1921, hoping to persuade the Bolsheviks to let themselves be helped and come to an agreement with Poland on common sanitary measures.[69] The Soviet Health Ministry greeted the two men with 'suspicion and hostility', but after six days of negotiations, they succeeded in their endeavour.[70]

The next step was to get European health experts around the same table, decide on concerted action and sign bilateral sanitary conventions. In August 1921, Drummond had named Rajchman Director of the League of Nations Health Section, specifying that he should stay in Poland until November to continue his direction of the anti-epidemic campaign.[71] Why Rajchman? Many reasons and hypotheses could be suggested, including that of the extraordinary international 'network' which existed at the time, rendering it not unlikely that Drummond and/or Frank Walters (another prominent British member of the secretariat) had known Rajchman in London during the war.[72] In the meantime, Rajchman had acquired quite a brilliant reputation in Rockefeller Foundation (RF) and ICRC circles, the former soon attributing him with having set up one of the best public health services in Europe, after Denmark.[73] Rajchman had also considerable influence with the Polish government (where a number of his pre-independence socialist friends now held prominent positions) and was undoubtedly behind Poland's proposal to convene a League-sponsored sanitary conference in Warsaw. In view of the serious deterioration of the epidemic situation in the winter of 1921–2 (the famine in Russia was thought to be affecting 30 million people, with typhus and cholera on the rise),[74] the meeting was quickly organised to take place in March. It was to be attended by health and government officials only. Rajchman was particularly anxious that (despite the Polish government's request) volunteer organisations, that is the LRCS and Hoover's and Nansen's (see below) organisations, should *not* be represented. He wished the conference to be purely technical[75] and believed that LRCS presence would 'provide the governments with an easy way of escape from possible financial obligation', since they were 'all too ready to hand over to the Red Cross Societies any questions which require material assistance'. He believed that 'the chief strength of the Epidemics Commission lay in the fact that it dealt through governments and not through Red Cross Societies . . . it was the duty of the governments to bring assistance and not mere relief'. (Rajchman's attitude in this instance to voluntary aid organisations is arguable and it would be interesting to know the LRCS's and the ICRC's reaction to their exclusion from the Conference. Later in his career, Rajchman advocated collaboration between UNICEF and the Red Cross Societies, notably in the International Tuberculosis Campaign.)[76] He had hoped, however, that Lord Robert Cecil, Drummond and Monnet could be persuaded to come but Drummond declined, fearing that their presence would transform the meeting into a 'political demonstration'.[77]

The Polish Minister of Foreign Affairs, Konstanty Skirmunt, opened the Conference by stating that the economic reconstruction of Europe (which was to be studied at the forthcoming Genoa Conference) was 'impossible without an overall effort of all states to stop the progress of epidemics' and Rajchman went on to give a detailed overview of the incidence of typhus in Europe, stressing the risks of a prolonged sanitary crisis for the reconstruction of the continent.[78]

The resolutions drawn up by the conference were simple and straightforward: immediate aid for the Russian and Ukrainian health authorities, bilateral sanitary conventions, mutual recognition of medical degrees in order to facilitate exchange, new regulations in the notification of contagious diseases, public health campaigns and specialised training for medical personnel in Warsaw, Kharkov and Moscow. But what were obvious and necessary measures for the assembled health experts were not always interpreted as such by their governments at home. Politicians regarded the Warsaw Conference first and foremost as a testing ground for international relations since, for the first time since the war, all European states (except Albania and Portugal) were represented. Somewhat curiously, Japan also participated, while the United States, despite the Polish government's invitation,[79] did not. Why this was so is not clear. Japan was known for being a very enthusiastic League member during its first decade, but it is surprising that no American officials were present, given the leading American role in aid to Eastern Europe. From the start, the meeting was highly politicised, the more so because it came just one month before the Genoa summit conference which was intended to restore more normal relations between the international community on the one hand, and Germany and Soviet Russia on the other. Normalisation notwithstanding, the French were outraged that the LNEC had allowed German to be one of the official languages in Warsaw (English at the League had already been enough of a shock!). The Germans (represented by Dr Frey and Professors Otto and Mühlens) showed general reluctance towards anything to do with the LN, but ended up by agreeing to the Conference resolutions when they were promised a seat on the League's Health Committee (Germany would not enter the League itself until

1926). Jean Monnet urged his government not to oppose the nomination of a German to the Health Committee, pointing out that Germany could thus not object to League involvement in the execution of the Genoa resolutions since she could not claim lack of representation in League technical organisations, but his suggestion was not well received by the Quai d'Orsay. On second thoughts, however, the French realised that too open a hostility to the proposition might turn against them and make other states vote in favour of the Germans, so they decided to propose that a German be named instead to the LNEC which was, of course, conceived as a temporary body. They appear to have been particularly worried that a German member of the Health Committee might exploit Franco-British divergences on questions of quarantine in the colonies (some of which had been formerly German) and thus indirectly affect political and commercial interests.[80]

The Soviets paradoxically, albeit not surprisingly, caused the greatest trouble even though they stood to benefit the most. At first, they had refused to come to Warsaw altogether, but relented on the condition that they do so unofficially, in a 'personal' capacity, and ended up sending one of the largest delegations. (The Russian delegation was composed of I. L. Lorenc (First Secretary of the Legation of the Soviet Republic of Russia in Warsaw); I. Siak (First Secretary of the Legation of the Soviet Union in Warsaw); Dr J. P. Kalina (Head of the Bureau of Foreign Information of the People's Commissariat); Dr A. N. Syssin (Head of the Epidemiological Section of the People's Commissariat); and the Ukrainian delegation consisted of Drs J. Siak and J. Kholodny.) Upon arrival, however, they promptly changed their minds and, threatening to leave the conference, demanded to see Rajchman (who was acting as Secretary-General) forthwith. They wanted reassurances that the Soviet government would not be held 'responsible' for the epidemic crisis, that they would be able to negotiate directly with other governments and not pass through League channels, that epidemics in the West would also be discussed and that – amazingly – no funds would be raised for assisting Russia. Rajchman agreed to the two first points, tactfully stated that there happened to be no epidemics in the West at the moment, but could not hide his surprise at their last demand: had not the Soviet authorities handed him 'a long list of necessary items' when he was in Moscow? This was the case, they finally admitted, but preferred their needs to be presented in kind and not in terms of monetary value.[81]

Nor was that an end of their objections. On the last day of the conference, they refused to accept the clause which entrusted the Warsaw resolutions to the League of Nations Health Section and warned that they might disrupt the meeting with a 'militant' anti-League declaration. Rajchman (whom they had gone to inform during the night) admitted that such a scene would 'pain' him, but held his ground, unwilling to change a single word.[82] He probably guessed that the Soviets would eventually agree to League sponsorship provided that they were given certain compensations in return. He also realised how important it was to insist on international arbitration, as nationalistic feelings were still running high after the recent war.

The Warsaw resolutions were a grave source of preoccupation for the French also. The Quai d'Orsay thought it was premature to be collaborating with the Germans and the Soviets and hardly saw why they should contribute to sanitary measures against epidemics which did not even touch their country. France had by now donated the promised equivalent of £50,000 to the LNEC and was not ready to give any more financial aid, possibly partly because the OIHP had been completely left out of the resolutions.[83] But thanks to relentless lobbying on the part of the League delegation (headed by Rajchman, who urged his friend Monnet once again to intervene in favour of the League's health activities),[84] British, Italian and Japanese support was won and the Genoa Conference adopted the controversial Warsaw resolutions.

This must have come as a great relief to the Polish government, for in 1922 the typhus epidemic is believed to have reached its peak, with an estimated 4 million cases in Poland and between 25 and 30 million in Russia.[85] In view of these figures, it seems indeed miraculous that within a year the situation in Poland had so much improved that the LNEC was able to close down its offices in Warsaw.

The Epidemic Commission in Soviet Russia and Ukraine

When Norman White and Rajchman went to Moscow in 1921, their main objective had been to establish a dialogue with the Soviet authorities. They were aware of the numerous obstacles any action on their part would encounter, given the administrative chaos following the Revolution and the vastness of the country (rendering transportation problems overwhelming), not to mention the regime's hostility to the West and vice versa. Furthermore, epidemics were only part of the problem: from October 1921 to June 1922, approximately 5 million people are thought to have died from the famine which affected two-thirds of the country.[86]

The Volga region was worst hit, but southern areas were also very badly off; even in Moscow Rajchman noted that nurses were fed only once every other day.[87] Hoover was again the first to respond to the humanitarian crisis, sending over 200 Americans to distribute food. Smaller relief organisations also wanted to help, but needed some overall co-ordination as well as greater means. So the LN named Fridtjof Nansen (the famous Norwegian zoologist and explorer) High Commissioner for Aid to Russia and he was soon confronted with the same difficulties in raising money for the Russian famine as the LNEC had been for the cordon sanitaire. Member-states were just not willing to give and Nansen was rewarded for his untiring efforts with accusations of being pro-Soviet. Not until he appealed to the public for private donations did he manage to send any substantial aid through and even so it was very limited.[88]

Nansen recognised in Rajchman a man who 'thoroughly share[d] his views with regard to the danger to Europe of allowing the famine and epidemics to go on'[89] and naturally enough the two Commissioners decided to work together. It was Nansen who wrote to Drummond, requesting the appointment of a Medical Officer for the LNEC, who would remain under his orders whilst in Russia. Nansen agreed to hand over to the LNEC 'considerable consignments of drugs presented by the International Trade Union Federation' as well as 'all sanitary supplies' and to entrust the Medical Officer with 'the supervision of the Red Cross work in Russia'.[90] (The British Red Cross had been given by the government war stocks worth £100,000, which were waiting in Constantinople to be shipped to Russia.) Rajchman already had his eye on a suitable candidate for the LNEC post in Moscow: Dr Reginald Farrar, formerly of the British Ministry of Health, who was an 'epidemiologist of considerable reputation' and had been British representative on the International Manchurian Plague Commission in 1911. He had also been 'very keen . . . to engage in hygiene work in Russia'. In addition to these attributes, Rajchman was also influenced in his decision by the fact that the British Red Cross named Farrar to be in charge of their supplies for Russia.[91]

Farrar set out for Moscow in December 1921 with the instructions that he was to be 'in charge of the Sanitary Section of Dr. Nansen's Relief Organisation'. It was stressed that he was to oversee 'the distribution of all medical and sanitary stores supplied by the Nansen Organisation and the Epidemics Commission', as had been agreed by Nansen and the Soviet government. He was to have 'the right of inspection of all Hospitals, Quarantine Stations, Refugee Centres, etc., where such stores are utilised and distributed'. Further, he was expected to submit 'weekly reports of the incidence of the chief epidemic diseases in Russia' (without releasing any information to the press) and to seek to 'facilitate the conclusion of Sanitary Conventions between the Soviet Government and the Governments of adjacent countries . . . It must be remembered', Rajchman concluded in his instructions for the British doctor, 'that the *raison d'être* of the Epidemics Commission is to bring assistance in the task of preventing the spread of epidemic disease from Russian foci.'[92]

The League envoys faced a harrowing spectacle. In a joint telegram to the LNEC in Geneva, they spoke of a mortality rate of thirty to forty daily in certain refugee homes. 'In villages visited only eleven hundred left while two thousand died and fled westwards. Survivors also threatened with extinction. Waiting immediate help on large scale in near future or [prospects] whole region very dark.'[93]

The relief supplies requested by Nansen and Farrar (who, soon after Christmas – the very same day that the French Parliament voted its contribution to the LNEC – succumbed fatally to typhus) were subject to controversy. The French had clearly stated that their donation was to be used for Poland only; they (including Gauthier) believed that it was useless to assist such a chaotic regime as the Soviet government and argued that all funds should be devoted to Poland if the West was to be effectively protected from typhus.[94] Prime Minister Raymond Poincaré was particularly vehement on the subject: 'It is out of the question for the French Government, and the Chambres would certainly not accept it, to employ part of the resources furnished to the Treasury by tax-payers for works which are certainly praiseworthy, but would take place in conditions which, do what we might, would give no guarantee of efficiency or good use.'[95] The Soviet authorities had apparently not respected their agreement with the Poles, and were sending over the border four times as many refugees as initially agreed, thus totally overwhelming the reception structures at Baranowicze. According to Gauthier, the Soviets never sent sick refugees to hospital, nor did they remove the dead from the unheated trains in which the dying and the healthy travelled for anything from fourteen days to one month.[96]

Although the Soviet government did not always facilitate the LNEC's work (diplomatic privileges were hard to obtain and, once secured, were occasionally violated, while re-entrance visas could be refused on the grounds of 'anti-bolshevist' activities),[97] medical experts and local health workers were very eager to collaborate with the League commissioners. Even the People's Commissar for Health, Nicolai Semashko (an intimate of Lenin and participant in the October Revolution), welcomed the LNEC's assistance (after some initial nervousness), although he admitted privately to Rajchman that in order to overcome his government's objections to the League's presence, it was essential that the aid proffered be not only technical, but material as well.[98]

Health Committee reports on aid to Russia are not as complete as those concerning Poland. Besides the activities cited above, the LNEC provided technical assistance in vaccination campaigns against cholera, typhoid fever and dysentery throughout Soviet Russia and the Ukraine (the LNEC set up offices for a short time in Kharkov) and, following the Warsaw sanitary conference, organised courses for health personnel in Kharkov and Moscow.[99] Expenditure on Russia was very much reduced compared to that on Poland. LNEC accounts record that £8,528 was spent on supplies for Russia, as against £142,797 for Poland.[100] It should be remembered, however, that these figures concern the expenditure of the LNEC proper and not the other supplies furnished by the international community which the Commission oversaw. In view of Western attitudes towards aid for Poland and Soviet Russia, the question may legitimately be asked – though no answer can be given – as to whether Poland was not seen as a buffer more against bolshevism than against typhus and whether the epidemic itself did not become somewhat of a metaphor for communist contagion.

When the LNEC withdrew from Russia in 1924, Soviet collaboration with the League's Health Section continued. In 1922, although the Soviets had not yet recognised the League, they set up an International Sanitary Commission consisting of an official from the Soviet Ministry of Health and a representative of the League of Nations Health Organisation. Since that time, relations between the LNHO and the Soviet health administration had developed 'from day to day',[101] Semashko himself visiting Geneva as early as January 1923. This was no mean achievement, since the Soviet Union would not join the League until 1934 and thus public health was one of the few channels of communication left open between Russia and the West for a decade. However, as the President of the Health Committee, Thorvald Madsen, was to point out, it took over ten years 'to establish closer relations with the Soviet health authorities . . . the impression remained that their delegates to our meetings, if they turned up at all, at best behaved as if they were observers. It was in fact Dr. Rajchman who cleared the way during a visit to Moscow in 1935.'[102]

The Epidemic Commission in Greece

In November 1922, when the Polish health crisis was nearing its end, the Greek government called on the LNEC to assist them in the sanitary control of their refugee population, their own department of sanitation consisting only of three or four officials. Subsequent to the Treaty of Lausanne which forced Greece to return to Turkey the territories she had won during the war, over a million Greeks and nearly half as many Turks were migrating to their respective countries. This presented a major danger to public health, particularly as the 1,250,000 Greeks had been brutally expelled from Asia Minor, taking with them no more than the clothes they were wearing. Of these refugees, 70 per cent had settled in urban areas, causing the population of certain towns to double practically overnight.[103]

The numerous breeding grounds of typhus and smallpox throughout the Greek islands gave reason to fear the spread of epidemics. Two members of the LNEC, Gauthier and Dr W. E. Haigh, were asked by the Greek Ministry of Health to set up quarantine stations for containing typhus and, above all, to co-ordinate a mass vaccination campaign against smallpox, cholera and typhoid fever. The country was divided into two zones, one centred around Athens, the 'Old Greece', and the other around Salonica, the 'New Greece'. Vaccinations began in January 1923, thanks to £5,000 made available by Nansen who donated half of his Nobel Prize money to relief work in favour of Greek refugees and half for a development project in the Ukraine. Rajchman reckoned that this funding would not last more than six months and instructed that the vaccinations be completed by May. (As it turned out, Gauthier remained in Greece a further three months, on the request of the Greek government, who asked him to co-ordinate an anti-dysentery campaign.) After Haigh's departure (see table 5.1), he was joined by his Polish colleague Czesław Wroczyński and, in agreement with the Hellenic Ministry of Health, they hired teams of Greek doctors and medical students to carry out the operations. Even so, four months left little time for immunising the most vulnerable segments of the population – not enough time, in any case, for propaganda to have much effect, although the ARC helped out by printing posters and the clergy, both Christian and Moslem, did their best to convince the faithful. Thus, obligatory vaccination seemed the only recourse. This gave rise to different reactions on the part of the Greek authorities. In the New Greece, they not only consented, but provided police reinforcement, which led to very positive results, particularly when the needle was linked to bread ration cards! In the Old Greece, however, permission was refused. Without resorting to coercive measures, Gauthier nonetheless managed to vaccinate 67,000 persons in his area of operations. By 1 April the LNEC was responsible for having immunised 1,674,585 individuals against smallpox, cholera and typhoid fever and could note with satisfaction that only 8,000 cases of smallpox and 6,500 of typhus had been recorded during its stay in Greece.[104]

The Epidemic Commission in Latvia

The LNEC extended its help also to Latvia, albeit in a limited capacity, simply because it had run out of funds. Initially, the plan was to assist the Latvian government in establishing quarantine stations at Dvinsk (Daugavpils) and supplying the existing station at Rezekne. To do so, however, would have required £35,000, or at least £18,000 in order to allow the partial functioning of the station at Dvinsk. Since this money was not available, and since the LNEC had only £10,000 to devote to the project, a presumably smaller maritime quarantine station was set up at Libau. The LNEC further arranged for two Latvian specialists to visit Hamburg and Bremen to study the functioning of their quarantine systems.[105]

Attempts to make the Epidemic Commission a permanent body

Human nature being what it is, as soon as the immediate fear of epidemics had receded, governments (which had already been reluctant to support the LNEC) saw no point in contributing to an anti-epidemic fund, even in view of possible future emergencies. At the end of 1923, when Gauthier left Greece, the LNEC came to a halt: quite simply, it had run out of money. The only donation forthcoming that year had been 173,000 Swiss francs from Czechoslovakia, while Great Britain had pledged half as much.[106] Various members of the Health Organisation, Rajchman to begin with, advocated making the LNEC a permanent body. In 1921, Rajchman rightly pointed out that epidemic control

Table 5.1. *Commissioners of the LNEC*

Name	Country of origin	Country of mission	Length of mission
(Dr Henri J. Cazeneuve	France	Russia	July–August 1924)
Dr Reginald Farrar	GB	Russia	December 1921
Major Fitzhugh	GB? (LRCS)	Poland	1920[a]–December 1921
Col. Aimé Gauthier	France	Poland	Spring 1921–December 1922
		Greece	December 1922–September 1923
Dr W. E. Haigh	GB?	Russia	3 months in 1922
		Greece	December 1922–September[a] 1923
Dr Frederick Norman White	GB	(Chief Epidemics Commissioner)	April 1920–1923[a]
Dr M. Pantaleoni	Italy	Russia	July 1922–August 1923
		Ukraine	
Dr Ludwik Rajchman	Poland	Poland	April 1920–November 1921
Dr Czesław Wroczyński	Poland	Greece	December 1922–May 1923

[a]Indicates doubt as to month

was the problem that (a) best lent itself to international legislation and (b) was of most concern to the public. He suggested that a permanent LNEC be composed of a limited executive board and a Chief Commissioner who could call on experts and engage temporary commissioners in the region of operations and would carry out special missions only on the request of national governments.[107] Even though Léon Bernard supported it,[108] his plan was rejected outright by the French, who protested that 'nothing could justify such an institution', since 'the Office International d'Hygiène Publique is particularly qualified for studying epidemics and proposing the most appropriate means for combating them'.[109] French opposition to a permanent LNEC was to be expected. A relationship of rivalry with the OIHP persisted throughout the interwar period and prevented the League from having a permanent Health Section until 1923. What certain French public servants failed (or refused) to see, was that Rajchman was proposing to create a Commission endowed with *funds* for preventive and relief work in case of epidemic crises, whereas the Office did not sponsor public health projects and had, up to that time, dealt only with cholera, yellow fever and plague, thus proving of little use during the typhus epidemic.

The British delegate to the League's Health Committee, Sir George Buchanan, shared Rajchman's views. He believed that the LNEC was the best propaganda the League could possibly have and that its permanent institution would warrant even a change in the League's Covenant. The Italian Red Cross had also suggested creating an epidemic fund for management by national Red

Cross Societies, but Britain, in the person of Lord Balfour, preferred League sponsorship. Rajchman, with typical optimism, hoped that member-states could be persuaded to contribute from 5 per cent to 10 per cent over and above their LN dues to an anti-epidemic fund[110] and, as early as 1920, Drummond had said that while the LNEC was being created especially for the Polish emergency, it might later extend its activities to China and South America.[111] On the suggestion of the Japanese member of the Health Committee, Dr Miyajima, Norman White set out in November 1922 on an eight-month tour of the Far East to study the incidence of plague and cholera. His report led to the decision to create a Far Eastern Branch of the Health Organisation. The Singapore Bureau did not take over the LNEC's mission in the Far East, but acted as an epidemiological intelligence processing centre: in 1924 the LNEC came to an end and was never revived. (The official date for the closing down of the LNEC is not clear. It would appear that the bulk of its activities ceased with Gauthier's departure from Greece. By that time, in any case, it had run out of funds, but it seems that it continued to provide technical assistance in Russia to an anti-malaria campaign, in July–August 1924.)

Conclusion

In the light of Drummond's proposition, one wonders why no one argued that while the LNEC might have lost its immediate utility in Europe, it could still play an important role on the African, Asian and South American continents, where the incidence of contagious diseases was far higher. Members of the Health Committee who might have advocated such a plan probably realised that if member-states had been reluctant to help Poland, they would have been even less inclined to spend money on non-European countries. Moreover, the issue would have been immeasurably complicated by disagreements from and among colonial powers. This was already a preoccupation for the French in 1922 and when Rajchman wrote, three years later, to the Inspector-General of the Algerian Public Health Service, asking to be notified of the first case of cholera or plague, his letter went unanswered, at the express demand of the French government: Algeria was to have no direct relations with the League.[112] One cannot help seeing a certain parallel with UNICEF which was initially created for Second World War stricken countries and only later, after much debate, extended its assistance to what became known as the 'Third World'.

But the parallel between the LNEC and UNICEF does not stop there. Both were set up as *temporary* bodies to deal with post-war crises; both – unlike other LN and UN agencies – were endowed with funds for humanitarian action and, last but not least, both had as a central figure Ludwik Rajchman. It is hardly surprising, therefore, that the basic 'philosophy' of UNICEF bears so much resemblance to that of the LNEC. Had he been given half a chance (after the

Second World War Rajchman was excluded from all preliminary talks leading to the creation of the WHO), Rajchman would have made – rather than a World Health *Organisation* – a United Nations Health *Service*, much more on the model of an epidemics commission, that is, a service catering to the specific needs of each country and endowed with funds through taxation of member-states. The 'health tax' was to amount to 1 per cent of what each country contributed to its own public health service.[113]

In matters of international public health, Rajchman stressed three fundamental rules which characterised both the LNEC and UNICEF:

(a) Public health is first and foremost the responsibility of national govern-ments. Charitable organisations should exist only to deal with emergencies, but to encourage their development would be to lessen the primary obligation of governments with regard to the state of health of their citizens.

(b) It follows that an international health agency should work uniquely in agreement with and through national health authorities and, as much as possible, call on local health personnel to carry out operations. This favours limited staff on the part of the international agency and easier acceptance of operations by the local population. In order to ensure full government involvement, countries should never receive totally free international assistance, but must be made to contribute, even if symbolically.

(c) Finally, an international health agency must provide 'assistance and not mere relief':[114] 'Relief organisations are as a rule interested in the immediate alleviation of sufferings, or in satisfying immediate needs of a situation, with the result that when assistance has been withdrawn, former conditions prevail again and no permanent system of benefit accrues.' Whereas for the LNEC, 'epidemiological intelligence work, intimate and constant cooperation with health services and material relief [were] bound up together'.[115]

In our days of growing bureaucratisation and expenditure, one is struck by the high degree of efficiency attained by the LNEC, despite its very limited means and small staff. The Commission was conceived to 'provide such "missing links" in the chain of the complex system of sanitary defense as were required to make the system work'.[116] If 'an international agency stands and falls by its ability to serve common needs',[117] then the Epidemics Commission of the League of Nations can claim a fair amount of success.

Notes

1 Archives of the French Ministry of Foreign Affairs, Paris (henceforth AFMFA) Société des Nations (SDN) Secrétariat Général (SG) 1560; F. Norman White, 'Minutes of the First Meeting of the Advisory Board of the Epidemics Commission of the League of Nations held in Warsaw April 15, 1921'.

2 Archives of the League of Nations, Geneva (henceforth LNA) 12B 18772/18772: L. Rajchman, 'The Main Functions of the Health Organisation . . . ', memorandum addressed to Sir Eric Drummond, 20 January 1922.

3 Hans Zinsser, *Rats, Lice and History* (Boston: Little, Brown and Co., 1935), p. 294.

4 Neville M. Goodman, *International Health Organisations and Their Work* (Edinburgh and London: Churchill Livingstone, 1971), p. 11; LNA 12B 19529/ 19529: 'Report by Dr. Rajchman. The incidence of typhus in Europe', February 1922.

5 *Ibid.*

6 AFMFA SDN SG 1578: 'The Epidemic of Typhus in Poland' (Geneva: LN, April 1920); G. Schultz, *Sanitarnaya i protivoepidemicheskaya rabota v SSSR* ('Sanitary and anti-epidemic work in the USSR') (Munich: Institut für Erforschung der Geschichte und Kultur der UdSSR, 1951), p. 8.

7 'Report by Dr. Rajchman'. See also K. David Patterson, 'Typhus and Its Control in Russia, 1870–1940', *Medical History*, 37 (1993), 361–81.

8 Archives of the United Nations, New York, PAG4, Records of UNRRA, PAG4/1.0.0.0.B.2: L. Rajchman, 'General Observations and Recommendations', February 1944.

9 See: Herbert Hoover, *Memoirs I: The Years of Adventure* (New York: Macmillan Co., 1951) and Joseph Wechsberg, 'At the Heart of UNICEF', *The New Yorker*, 2 December 1961.

10 H. H. Fisher, *America and the New Poland* (New York: Macmillan Co., 1928), p. 126.

11 *Ibid.* p. 225.

12 *Ibid.* p. 240.

13 AFMFA SDN SG 1557: 'Conférence internationale d'hygiène' (London, April 1920).

14 Bibliothèque de Documentation Internationale Contemporaine (BDIC), Collection SDN: 'La Campagne contre les maladies épidémiques dans l'Europe centrale et orientale, Document d'Assemblée SDN 212', 14 December 1920.

15 On the history of the Polish State Institute of Hygiene, see Ludwik Hirszfeld, *Historia jednego życia* ('The Story of One Life') (Warsaw: Czytelnik, 1946); Ludwik Hirszfeld, 'Państwowy Zakład Higieny. Wspomnienia i rozważania z okazji 10-lecia Niepodległości Państwa Polskiego ('The State Institute of Hygiene. Reminiscences and Considerations on the 10th Anniversary of Polish Independence'), *Warszawskie Czaspismo Lekarskie*, 38–9 (11 November 1928); Janina Opieńska-Blauth, *Drogi i spotkania – wspomnienia profesora* ('Paths and Encounters – Reminiscences of a Professor') (Lublin: Wydawnictwo Lubelskie, 1979); Feliks Przesmycki, 'Wspomnienia' ('Reminiscences') (unpublished manuscript, Warsaw, 1976, archives of the State Institute of Hygiene); Edmund Wojciechowski, 'Państwowy Zakład Higieny – Rys historyczny' ('The State Institute of Hygiene – Historical Sketch'), *Polski Tygodnik Lekarski*, 41 (7 October 1968).

16 AFMFA SDN SG 1557: Le Sous-Préfet de Saint-Jean d'Angély to Ministre de l'Hygiène, 24 February 1920.

17 See Norman Howard-Jones, *International Public Health Organisations between the Two World Wars: the Organisational Problems* (Geneva: WHO, 1978), p. 15.

18 'Conférence internationale d'hygiène'.
19 Hirszfeld, *Historia jednego życia*, p. 71.
20 BDIC, Collection SDN: *Report of the Epidemic Commission of the League of Nations* (Geneva: LN, 1921).
21 AFMFA SDN SG 1578: Lord Balfour to H. P. Davidson, 24 February 1920.
22 Rajchman, 'General Observations and Recommendations'.
23 AFMFA SDN SG 1578: 'Résolution adoptée à la troisième séance de la Société des Nations', Paris, 13 March 1920.
24 *Ibid.*
25 AFMFA SDN SG 1557: Addison to Ministre de la Santé, 12 March 1920.
26 Le Sous-Préfet de Saint-Jean d'Angély to Ministre de la Santé, 24 February 1920.
27 AFMFA SDN SG 1557: 'Rapport', 13 April 1920; 'Conférence internationale d'Hygiène'.
28 AFMFA SDN SG 1578: 'The Epidemic of Typhus in Poland', Council Document 40/12/3419/1719 (Geneva: LN, April 1920).
29 'Conférence internationale d'hygiène'.
30 AFMFA SDN SG 1578: 'Note sur le typhus en Pologne', Service Français de la SDN, 21 April 1920.
31 'Conférence internationale d'hygiène'.
32 LNA 12B 6442/4479: 'Statement by Dr. Norman White, Medical Commissioner of the Typhus Commission on Trip to Poland', August 1920.
33 AFMFA SDN SG 1578: 'Le typhus en Pologne', Document du Conseil 44 12/4171, 27 April 1920.
34 AFMFA SDN SG 1579: 'Prévention des Epidémies en Europe Centrale', Document du Conseil 46 12/4188/1719 (nd).
35 AFMFA SDN SG 122578: Ministre de la Guerre to Ministre des Affaires Etrangères, 28 June 1920.
36 'Prévention des épidémies'.
37 AFMFA SDN SG 1578: Lord Balfour to Léon Bourgeois, 12 June 1920.
38 AFMFA SDN SG 1578: 'Note sur le typhus en Pologne', Service Français de la SDN, 21 June 1920.
39 Ministre de la Guerre to Ministre des Affaires Etrangères, 28 June 1920.
40 AFMFA SDN SG 1578: Ministre des Affaires Etrangères to M. Paléologue, 23 June 1920.
41 AFMFA SDN SG 1578: 'Le typhus en Pologne: Mémorandum présenté par le Secrétaire Général', 18 October 1920.
42 AFMFA SDN SG 1578: 'Télégramme du Dr. Rajchman au Dr. Norman White', 5 October 1920.
43 AFMFA SDN SG 1578: 'Le typhus en Pologne. Note du Secrétaire Général', 20 July 1920.
44 AFMFA SDN SG 1578: Ministre de la Guerre to Président du Conseil, 20 July 1920.
45 Le Sous-Préfet de Saint-Jean d'Angély, 24 February 1920.
46 'Le typhus en Pologne: Mémorandum présenté par le Secrétaire Général', 18 October 1920.
47 AFMFA SDN SG 1578: 'Report on the Special Commission on Typhus in Poland' (nd).

48 Frank Walters, *A History of the League of Nations* (Oxford: Oxford University Press, 1952), p. 101.

49 AFMFA SDN SG 1578: Niessel to Ministre de la Guerre, 20 December 1920.

50 AFMFA SDN SG 1579: Cyrill Durek to Eric Drummond and Jean Monnet, 7 February 1921.

51 AFMFA SDN SG 1579: Kanya to Thomas Beaumont Hohler, 5 January 1921.

52 AFMFA SDN SG 1579: Jean Monnet to Président du Conseil du Gouvernement Français, 24 January 1921.

53 AFMFA SDN SG 1579: Eric Drummond to Jean Gout, February 1921.

54 AFMFA SDN SG 1579: Jean Gout to Ministre de la Guerre, 18 March 1921.

55 AFMFA SDN SG 1579: Sidzikauskas. 'Typhus in Lithuania', 10 May 1921.

56 AFMFA SDN SG 1579: 'Rapport présenté le 20 septembre 1921 par M. Gustave Ador, représentant de la Suisse au nom de la 5ème commission de l'Assemblée, sur la question de la lutte contre le typhus en Europe orientale.'

57 AFMFA SDN SG: 'Second Assembly. Resolution adopted on 21 September, 1921'.

58 AFMFA SDN SG 1579: 'Communiqué de Prague à la Société des Nations', 18 October 1921.

59 AFMFA SDN SG 1579: Eric Drummond to Quiñones, 21 October 1921 and 'Note du Ministère des Affaires Etrangères' (signature illegible), 18 October 1921.

60 AFMFA SDN SG 1579: 'Note du Ministère des Affaires Etrangères', 21 January 1921.

61 AFMFA SDN SG 1560: F. Norman White, 'Travaux de la Commission des Epidémies de la Société des Nations', 1 August 1921.

62 AFMFA SDN SG 1560: 'Commission des Epidémies de la Société des Nations, Second Rapport', 24 August 1928.

63 AFMFA SDN SG 1579: 'SDN. Communiqué du Conseil. Note du Secrétaire Général sur le typhus', 11 May 1921.

64 Marcin Kacprzak, 'La lutte contre les maladies épidémiques', in *L'hygiène publique en Pologne*, ed. Marcin Kacprzak (Warsaw, 1933).

65 According to Dr Józef Parnas, interviewed by author, Copenhagen, August 1991.

66 Rajchman, 'General Observations'.

67 *Report of the Epidemics Commission of the League of Nations* (1921).

68 AFMFA SDN SG 1579: 'Rapport du Col. Gauthier', A. de Panafieu to Président du Conseil, Ministère des Affaires Etrangères, 27 December 1921; AFMFA SDN SG 1557: 'Première Séance du Comité Provisoire d'Hygiène tenue à Genève. Procès verbaux, 25–29 août 1921'.

69 See 'Première Séance du Comité Provisoire d'Hygiène'.

70 Walters, *History of the League of Nations*, p. 101.

71 'Première Séance du Comité Provisoire d'Hygiène'.

72 According to Jean-Claude Comert, interviewed by author, Paris, July 1993. See also M. A. Balińska, 'Ludwik Rajchman (1881–1965); Précurseur de la santé publique moderne' (PhD thesis, Institut d'Etudes Politiques, Paris, December 1992).

73 RAC RG5 IHB/D 1921: 789 Poland; Box 125; Folder 1676: 'Minutes of the International Health Board', 23 May 1922.

74 AFMFA SDN SG 1560: 'League of Nations Report on the Health Situation in Eastern Europe', January 1922.

75 AFMFA SDN SG 1560: 'League of Nations Report on the Health Situation in Eastern Europe', January 1922.

76 LNA 18702/18792: Ludwik Rajchman to Bernardo Attolico, 28 February 1922.

77 LNA 12B 18792/18792: Eric Drummond to Bernardo Attolico, 3 March 1922. J. Holm, *The History of the ITC (International Tuberculosis Campaign)* (Copenhagen, 1984).

78 AFMFA SDN SG 1580: 'Conférence sanitaire européenne réunie à Varsovie du 20 au 28 mars 1922'.

79 AFMFA SDN SG 1580: J. Wielorzycki (?) (Polish Legation in France) to Ministère des Affaires Etrangères, 29 March 1922.

80 AFMFA SDN SG 1580: Jean Monnet to Léon Bourgeois, 7 April 1922; Maurice Herblette, 'Note pour le Service Français de la SDN', 21 April 1922; SDN SG 1558: 'Note du Service Français de la SDN', 3 May 1922.

81 AFMFA Relations commerciales 1920–1939, 91: Pierre Comert, 'Note sur l'attitude de la Délégation soviétique et ukrainienne à la Conférence Sanitaire de Varsovie', 31 March 1922.

82 *Ibid.*

83 AFMFA Délibérations internationales, Carton 82, Conférence de Gênes, 92: 'Note pour la direction des affaires administratives et techniques. Service Français de la SDN', 7 April 1922.

84 LNA 40 A 20136/20136: Ludwik Rajchman to Bernardo Attolico (?), 7 May 1922.

85 Dr Marcin Kacprzak, unpublished speech given in 1961 at the State Institute of Hygiene, Warsaw. Similar figures are cited by Rajchman and Tarassevitch, see AFMFA SDN SG 1578: 'Rapport du Dr. Rajchman sur sa mission en Russie. Procès verbaux de la quatrième session du Comité d'Hygiène tenue à Genève du 14 au 21 août 1922'.

86 S. G. Wheatcroft, 'Famine and Epidemic Crises in Russia, 1918–1922. The case of Saratov', *Annales de démographie historique* (1983), 329.

87 'Rapport du Dr. Rajchman sur sa mission en Russie'.

88 See Tim Greve, *Fridtjof Nansen* (Lausanne: Fondation Jean Monnet pour l'Europe, 1989), pp. 53–9.

89 LNA Archives de l'Office Nansen C 1117: ? (Assistant to Nansen) to L. Rajchman, 19 February 1922.

90 Archives of the State Serum Institute, Copenhagen (ASSI): L. Rajchman to T. Madsen, 28 October 1921.

91 *Ibid.*

92 ASSI: L. Rajchman, 'Instructions for Dr. Farrar' (in letter to T. Madsen, 24 November 1921).

93 LNA 12B 17902/15255: F. Nansen and R. Farrar to Epidemics Commission, 6 December 1921.

94 A. de Panafieu to Ministère des Affaires Etrangères, 27 December 1921.

95 AFMFA SDN SG 1560: Raymond Poincaré to Count Sforza, 24 July 1922.

96 AFMFA SDN SG 1579: 'Rapport du Médecin Principal Gauthier, membre de la Commission des Epidémies, au sujet d'une visite de la station de quarantaine de Baranowicze effectuée du 7 au 10 décembre 1921'.

97 AFMFA SDN SG 1579: 'Note rédigée par le Dr. Cazeneuve de la Section d'Hygiène et remise à M. Guerlet, Service Français de la SDN', 4 November 1924.

98　LNA 12B 26104/15255: L. Rajchman to Dr M. Pantaleoni, 29 January 1923.

99　Unfortunately, very little information is available on the nature of these courses. Lectures were given in Warsaw to 67 health workers by Polish and foreign experts (Ion Cantacuzino – Romania; Col. Liston – GB (?) and Prof. Abel – Germany). Prof. Abel also gave courses in Kharkov (attended by 65 health workers) and in Moscow, where the courses lasted the longest.

100　AFMFA SDN SG 1579: 'Rapport du Directeur Médical', 3 January 1923.

101　AFMFA SDN SG 1558: 'Procès verbaux de la 4ème session du Comité d'Hygiene', 14–21 August 1922.

102　E. Schelde-Moller, *Thorvald Madsen. I Videnskabens og Menneskehendes Tjeneste* (Copenhagen: Thorvald Madsens Legat, 1970), p. 158.

103　AFMFA SDN SG 1579: 'Situation sanitaire en Grèce. Audition du Dr. Wroczyński', 27 May 1923, Sixth Session of the Health Committee.

104　*Ibid.*

105　AFMFA SDN SG 1559: 'Rapport du Directeur Médical', 3 January 1923.

106　*Ibid.*

107　AFMFA SDN SG 1560: 'Note du Dr. Reckmann' (Rajchman), 28 December 1921.

108　AFMFA SDN SG 1560: Léon Bernard, 'Note sur la Commission des Epidémies de la SDN', 24 December 1922.

109　AFMFA SDN SG 1560: 'Note par Maurice Herblette', 21 December 1921.

110　Minutes of the Sixth Session of the Health Committee, 27 May 1923.

111　AFMFA SDN SG 1578: 'Mémorandum du Secrétaire Général. Document du Conseil 44'.

112　AFMFA SDN SG 1581: 'Note pour le Service Français de la SDN', 17 May 1925.

113　L. Rajchman, 'A United Nations Health Service. Why Not?', *Free World* (September 1943).

114　AFMFA SDN SG 1558: Minutes of the third session of the Provisional Health Committee, 11–16 May 1922.

115　*Ibid.*

116　Rajchman, 'General Observations'.

117　*Ibid.*

6

Wireless wars in the eastern arena: epidemiological surveillance, disease prevention and the work of the Eastern Bureau of the League of Nations Health Organisation, 1925–1942

LENORE MANDERSON

Introduction

The Eastern Bureau of the League of Nations Health Section was established in 1925 to collect and disseminate epidemiological information. Until February 1942, when Singapore was invaded by Japanese troops, the Bureau served a variety of functions; the receipt, compilation and dissemination of health statistics, quarantine procedures and other information related to the control of disease were only part of its wider role. Its functions included the co-ordination and review of scientific research; the provision of in-service training of sanitation, public health and medical officers through staff interchanges, study tours and from 1934 annual short-course training programmes for malariologists; and sponsorship of and participation in scientific conferences and symposia. Through these various activities, the Bureau helped to identify the primary public health concerns of the region, facilitate co-operation between individual researchers and research institutions, and develop public health expertise. Less easily documented, the Bureau also played a role in fostering a sense of common purpose among countries in the region. Its primary function and central activity, however, as noted, was the collection and dissemination of epidemiological information; this is the focus of this chapter.

The Commission of Enquiry in the Far East

Epidemic disease in East Asia was first brought before the Health Committee of the League of Nations (LN) at its second session in October 1921, when the Japanese delegate, Dr Miyajima, drew attention to the incidence of pneumonic plague in Manchuria and Siberia.[1] Miyajima, Professor in the Faculty of Medicine at Keio University and a member of the Kitasato Institute for Infectious Diseases, Tokyo, reopened the discussion at the third session of the

Committee in May 1922, when he presented a paper concerning the continued high rates of infection of plague and cholera in the region; the public health threat this posed; the lack of 'sanitary organisation'; the spread of typhus and relapsing fever due to population movement in Siberia and neighbouring territories; and the especial public health threat posed by cholera.[2] Miyajima called for a committee to be appointed, similar to that for the Near East, to investigate the physical conditions and sanitary regulations applying in ports in the region.

The reaction to Miyajima's request was negative. Although the chair, Sir George Buchanan, canvassed the possibility of a representative of the Committee 'study[ing] the position on the spot',[3] others cautioned against the high cost of an enquiry and the lack of people with epidemiological and regional knowledge who could conduct it. Calmette's alternative proposal was to establish correspondence between the Pasteur Institutes and other medical laboratories in the Far East, including in this context French Indochina, China, Japan and the Dutch East Indies. Dr Ludwik Rajchman, Medical Director of the Health Section of the League, supported this, although he argued that data collection be centralised, for example in the Pasteur Institute in Paris. At its fourth session in August 1922, Miyajima again drew attention to the continued 'march of epidemics in the Far East',[4] and again he argued for a small Commission to investigate the incidence of infectious diseases in the major ports in the region; the systems used for the notification of cases and deaths and preventive measures taken to control epidemic diseases; and to explore the possibility of introducing a uniform system of collecting, publishing and disseminating such vital statistics. He argued too that the work of the Commission would result in a 'vast educational campaign' within the Far East on questions of hygiene, would facilitate the development of a sanitary convention for the region, and 'would give a concrete proof that [the League's] work was not limited to European affairs, as unfortunately, the peoples of the Far East seemed more and more inclined to suspect'.[5]

The Committee took Miyajima's final point to heart. Its primary concern had been with the spread of infectious diseases in Eastern Europe, and the threat that this posed to central and western Europe. Mindful of the strategic value of the mission, the need to demonstrate that the League was an international organisation and the need to control infectious disease, the Committee resolved 'to despatch a small commission to get information on epidemic diseases . . . in important ports',[6] which would include Dr Josephus Jitta, President of the Public Health Council of the Netherlands, and Dr Norman White of the Health Section of the League. Jitta could not get leave to make the journey, and hence it was decided that White should go alone, participating in the Red Cross Conference in Bangkok in early December and including in his tour Bombay, Calcutta, Singapore, Batavia, Bangkok, Saigon, Hanoi and Haiphong, Hong

Kong, Formosa, Shanghai, Kobe, Yokohama and ports of the Philippines. The US Public Health Service appointed Dr Howard Smith, based in Manila, to accompany White from late January to April, visiting with him Hong Kong, Shanghai, Japan and the Philippines.[7] Miyajima joined White when he visited Japanese ports and travelled to Formosa; Wu Lien Teh accompanied him to Beijing and Dairen.

Most governments supported the Commission and provided White with considerable assistance: hence the voluminous report. However, the Government of India opposed the Commission, and stated that it was 'not in a position to afford facilities to this Mission in so far as the ports of India were concerned'.[8] Geneva interpreted this as related to 'some misunderstanding and confusion regarding the objects' of the mission, its terms of reference and its relationship to the Office internationale d'hygiène publique (OIHP). White had hoped for someone from India to join him on the mission because of its direct interest in the issues and outcomes. India rejected the invitation, and the India Office advised the Secretary-General that 'it would be undesirable to press for the grant of facilities for the proposed medical commission'; it did not regard the mission as necessary since it already distributed epidemiological information each week by telegram, post and press, and because a revision of the International Sanitary Convention was already under way.[9] White was stung by statements that India wished to have nothing to do with the tour at all except through prescribed official channels,[10] and he described India's formal position as 'too miserably pitiable for words'.[11] However, he visited and included in his report both the Bombay and Bengal Presidencies.

White sailed from Marseille on 3 November 1922, and returned to the port on 29 July the following year. His itinerary covered thirty-four ports from Aden to Korea. The resultant document includes epidemiological overviews of plague, cholera and smallpox in the Far East; country reports covering general public health issues, environment and sanitation, medical and port health administration, staff and quarantine provisions; and information about port health procedure and equipment to determine the suitability or otherwise of the Convention. As an outcome of the enquiry, White recommended a special Sanitary Convention for the Far East to replace the International Sanitary Convention of 1912, and the establishment of an International Epidemiological Intelligence Bureau for the Far East.[12]

White's commentary port by port provides us with a valuable description of conditions in ports and adjacent residential and industrial areas, and the inefficacy of port administrations that hindered the monitoring, control and prevention of epidemics. Of Hong Kong, he reports that 'I am sadly disappointed with the inefficiency of public health administration . . . perhaps I should say the absence of public health administration. I have spoken very bluntly and plainly to the various high officials of the Colony'; the Philippines health administration he described as 'a great disappointment'.[13]

White's discussion of the International Sanitary Convention and its applicability to Far Eastern ports was lengthy.[14] A primary objection to it related to its ethnocentrism and primary purpose 'to protect the countries of the West from invasion by infection from the East'.[15] White argued the need for a convention that fitted with 'Oriental conditions' and that would not place 'too great a burden on free commercial intercourse [that] they will be honoured rather in the breach than the observance'.[16] He argued that the classification of ships as 'infected', 'healthy' and 'suspected', under the terms of the International Sanitary Convention, failed to take account of conditions at the port of departure. He recommended the classification of ports rather than ships, with a subdivision of ports into classes that reflected the presence or absence of health staff, laboratories, an infectious disease hospital, and a quarantine station, potable water, fumigation equipment, staff and equipment to catch and scrutinise rats, and the capacity to collect vital statistics. This system would be based on local conditions. Systematic and objective information would be collected and transmitted to other ports and ships in the region: hence the recommendation for regional bureaux to receive weekly information regarding cases of infectious diseases and measures taken to control transmission.[17] White's recommendations to substitute ports for ships, to determine protective and preventive sanitary measures to be applied in order to prevent the transmission of infectious disease and to entrust a central bureau with the power to classify ports, was opposed by the Government of India. It argued that the surveillance of ships was adequate to control infection; that proposed changes to the dissemination of information had no advantages over procedures set out in the International Sanitary Convention of 1912; and that creation of an external body to determine preventive sanitary measures constituted 'an infringement of international sovereignty'. It argued too that individual governments should be responsible for declaring ports as sanitary risks, that the obligations on sanitary staff of ports, implicated in White's recommendation, were impossible to discharge without interfering with the civilian population, and that the recommendations would 'react disastrously on the commerce of a country'.[18] Australia shared the view that the proposed classification of ports was not 'based on sound scientific foundations' and that the use of 'human case incidence' was unreliable; it shared with India a preference for continued use of the International Sanitary Convention.[19] Other governments were more positive and suggested only minor amendments.[20]

The recommendation for an epidemiological bureau flowed from the need to modify the Convention to improve the flow of epidemiological information collected by governments – bills of health, consular reports, reports from the health authorities, from medical officials attached to consulates and from newspaper articles – and to allow its communication to neighbouring countries. A bureau would need to be centrally located, with regular and frequent steamship communication with all ports in the region, and with good telegraph and wireless facilities. Singapore, he argued, was ideal due to 'its geographical position as the gateway to the Far East, in the centre of the arena'.[21]

The League and the Rockefeller Foundation

In early 1922 Wickliffe Rose from the Rockefeller Foundation (RF) and Rajchman from the League entered into correspondence regarding the allocation of Foundation money for institutional strengthening, international collaboration and staff development through the establishment of a health exchange, and the development of a system of epidemiological intelligence. The latter goal was envisaged as being undertaken by specific agencies which might also organise enquiries and conduct epidemiological research, publish regularly and facilitate the rapid exchange of information to ensure timely and appropriate action.[22] Rockefeller was interested primarily in the compilation of available statistics rather than the generation of new data, and this was the task for which the League sought funding.[23]

The establishment in the Far East of a centre to extend the epidemiological intelligence service of the Health Organisation of the League (LNHO) had wide support from interested governments within Asia and the Pacific. The Executive Committee of the Foundation on 12 June 1922 approved a programme in support of League activities to begin on 1 January 1923, with $32,840 p.a. for five years allocated for epidemiological surveillance and $60,080 p.a. for three years for the interchange of health and sanitary personnel.[24] Funds were made available from 1 October 1922 from the Rockefeller Fund, with funding renewed on 1 January 1928 for a further seven years for epidemiological intelligence. From 1925 additional ear-marked funds were allocated for the establishment and operation of the Far Eastern Epidemiological Bureau, with the stated expectation that Rockefeller support would be phased out as countries subscribed to the service;[25] the agreement provided for the allocation of $50,000 for the first year and a total of $125,000 for a five-year period.

White credits Gilbert Brooke, who at the time of the Commission of Enquiry was the Port Health Officer in Singapore, with responsibility for the original scheme.[26] Brooke referred to the Far Eastern Epidemiological Bureau as Rajchman's 'child', although he claims its genesis in a study tour on public health and quarantine conditions, undertaken in 1912 by the Chief Health Officer of the Straits Settlements to Java, Australia, South Africa, Siberia and Japan; the report of this tour, dated 14 February 1914, advocated the establishment of an epidemiological bureau in Singapore.[27] The need for such an organisation had also been foreshadowed in the first meeting of the Health

Committee of the League of Nations, in its acknowledgement of the unsatisfactory system for the compilation of health and medical statistics.[28] Miyajima's lobbying for international action and White's recommendation hence responded to a widely expressed need for the service. White's recommendation was accepted unanimously by the Health Committee at its meeting in February 1924, and by the Council of the League a month later. It was expected that a bureau would be able to maintain close liaison with 'asiatic countries' and to monitor 'plague and cholera, essentially Asiatic diseases', provide better information for other international and regional health services (the American Public Health Service, the OIHP and the Egyptian Quarantine Board) and provide a link between East and West that would increase the role of the Health Organisation in preventive medicine.[29]

In advising Dr Selskar Gunn, the European representative of the International Health Board of the RF, of this decision, Rajchman noted the support of the countries of the region. Rajchman's letter to Gunn formally solicited the Board's interest in the establishment and running costs of an epidemiological intelligence bureau in the Far East, as 'a logical and indispensable corollary to the investigations and work of our service'.[30] A letter was sent to governments in South, Southeast and East Asia, including Australia and New Zealand, to canvass opinions regarding the establishment and location of the bureau. All but two advocated Singapore and agreed to the Terms of Reference negotiated between the secretariat and the RF.[31] These were:

(a)   to collect and transmit at regular intervals, from all Far Eastern countries, information regarding the incidence and spread of infectious diseases, especially in ports and their hinterland;

(b)   to collect and transmit periodical reports of vital statistics, etc., in Far Eastern ports;

(c)   to collect data regarding alterations, additions or amendments to sanitary laws and regulations, and regarding measures taken to combat transmissible diseases and to prevent their propagation;

(d)   to publish, at regular intervals, returns, data, tables and general vital statistics regarding Far East countries;

(e)   to transmit all the above-mentioned information, periodically to the ports and health administrations of all the Far East countries concerned and also to the Health Section of the LN, whose duty it shall be to communicate them to the OIHP and to the various health administrations;

(f)   to render all possible assistance to governments concerned in matters which fall within its competence.[32]

The RF was concerned that the bureau should become self-supporting; White had been pressed on this by Dr Russell of the Foundation in an interview on 4 November 1924, and in response he noted the willingness of governments to send delegates to the preparatory meeting and the fact that the compilation of statistics by a central bureau would effect cost and time savings for governments which already compiled and transmitted such information routinely.[33] It was expected that participating countries would subscribe to the service and that subscriptions would increase over time.

A preliminary conference of government representatives was held in Singapore from 4 to 13 February 1925 to get 'active and intelligent support' for the Bureau in order to assure the RF of their support. Participants at the meeting clarified the nature and amount of information which each government was prepared to send routinely, the means by which this would be done (telegraph, wireless, etc.), the form in which the information would be compiled and the assistance which could be provided to facilitate the operation of the service, for example, special rates for cables.[34]

Discussions at the meeting provided evidence of strong support. As discussed above, the Government of India had been critical of and refused to assist in the Commission of Enquiry, and whilst it supported the establishment of the Bureau, it did so on the understanding that its functions would be 'strictly limited' and would exclude any 'quasi-administrative or executive functions'.[35] To facilitate the work of the Bureau it was 'prepared to place at the disposal of the Bureau all statistical information which it collects for its own purposes', but additional information would be made available subject to cost. It was not prepared to make any commitment of a grant-in-aid or subsidy.

Dr L'Herminier, the delegate from French Indochina, focused on the commercial implications of changes in sanitary regulations and, flowing from this, was nervous that the publication of epidemiological data might impede trade; whilst recognising the value of public health, the government was concerned that 'a too rigorous or inopportune application of sanitary regulations may have a disastrous effect upon commerce and industry and thus tend to defeat its own object by bringing the sanitarian and his profession into disrepute'.[36] Yet L'Herminier also spoke of the need for country contributions to ensure the successful operation of the Bureau, expressed concern that Rockefeller funds might only last three years,[37] and offered free transmission of information weekly, from the wireless station in Saigon. The Dutch East Indies also offered to broadcast from Java free of charge; both the Straits Settlements and Siam agreed to subvent the service.[38] These were the concrete promises of commitment that the Foundation had been seeking.

The RF itself remained aloof from the work of the Bureau, relying on official reports and audits, and occasional high level communication with Geneva, for reassurance that its allocation was well spent. This was somewhat surprising. Drs M. E. Barnes and P. F. Russell of the Foundation had conducted a survey on sanitary conditions, primary health care and hookworm infection in Malaya in 1925, which had resulted in a three-year anti-hookworm campaign from 1926 to

1928; a similar campaign was conducted in Java during the same period.[39] Yet the Foundation was not represented on the Advisory Council, staff visiting or based in the region appear to have had little (if any) contact with the Bureau, and there was no obvious influence on Bureau programmes of Rockefeller interest in the control of venereal disease, water and sanitation, helminthic infections, or maternal and child health. The only evidence of Foundation interest in the Bureau is some correspondence from John Grant, in Peking late in 1926, who wrote and cabled to Rajchman on a number of occasions to encourage Chinese participation in the Advisory Council of the Bureau.[40]

Defining the East

The enterprise drew its metaphors from the army, as was common within medical and public health discourse of the time. The aim of the Bureau, there-fore, was to gather epidemiological intelligence 'to seek out the enemy' and 'to safeguard their territories against invasions of epidemics',[41] to serve as a 'clearing-house' for information on major infections and disease in ports, which would thereby enable the health administrations of the 'East' to 'frame defensive measures' against the introduction of disease from *foreign* countries.[42] In opening the preliminary conference to establish the Bureau, the Governor of the Straits Settlements was to speak of the collection of epidemiological intelligence as a prerequisite to 'effective action against our common enemy', with statistical data and the technology of rapid communication 'weapons unknown to former generations . . . weapons [which] will be used to the best advantage'.[43]

In much of the archival material that relates to the purposes and functions of the Bureau, as well as that describing other activities of the Health Organisation, communicable disease is represented as an external threat: not only by virtue of its infectiousness, but through its introduction from an outside force – a foreign vessel, another port, another country. Hence, whilst the primary enemy in epidemiological surveillance was disease – especially plague, smallpox and cholera – the implicit enemy was the outsider, and tensions of autonomy, empire, and territory were played out literally and metaphorically in the work of the Bureau. In pursuing the metaphor, epidemiological information was represented as the mechanism of reconciliation, hence '[a]s regards epidemiological information, it must serve as an intermediary between all the countries of the world'.[44] France went further, to acknowledge the link between imperialism and medicine, and at the preliminary conference the Governor of Cochin-China stated that 'France [had] adopted as the essential basis of her colonization programme the principle of pacific penetration by public health activity'.[45]

The 'East' or 'Far East' was an imprecise geopolitical term, initially used to refer to North Asia (China, Manchuria, Japan) and later extended to include Southeast and South Asia, parts of Australia and the Southwest Pacific, East Africa, and parts of North Africa – essentially any country of the Pacific and Indian Ocean rims connected by commerce or related maritime activities. Hence the Suez and the Panama Canals, Cairo and Tananarive were drawn into the catchment area of epidemiologic intelligence. The use of 'Far Eastern' adjectively to designate the area was never contended or regarded as problematic, and although the Advisory Council to the Bureau decided that it should officially be known as the Eastern Bureau, Health Section, League of Nations, it was far more commonly referred to as the Far Eastern Bureau. The use of the term 'Eastern', whilst not contentious, was certainly connotative, and drew upon orientalist stereotype.[46] White, who was sensitive to the politics of international agencies and tensions between nations, represented the Far East as 'the endemic home *par excellence* of some of the important scourges of humanity'.[47] This association of place and disease, pursued in more complex ways in the discourse of 'tropical medicine',[48] was sustained in the Bureau's reportage, and little attention was given to the political economic context of the incidence and distribution of disease in many of these countries. M. Velghe, for example, in a meeting of the Health Committee referred to the Far East as 'a breeding ground for cholera and plague';[49] a 1931 Bureau pamphlet began with the statement that 'Eastern countries are the home of those serious epidemic diseases which the world has learnt to fear',[50] implying the natural presence of epidemic diseases in the region.

Whilst the 'Eastern' was not contested, there was some disagreement about the nominal term for the region, field or area of surveillance, and in this issues of sovereignty and control appear to be implicated. The first Director of the Bureau, Gilbert Brooke, in a letter to Rajchman in March 1925 referred to the Bureau as 'your new child in the Far Eastern Arena'[51] and maintained the use of the term 'arena' (as well as the metaphors of paternity) thereafter, although the term 'arena' was certainly used earlier, for example by White throughout his report.[52] Even so, the Health Committee was uneasy about the term, and at its fourth session, in discussing the role and composition of an advisory committee to the Bureau, suggested that 'eastern waters' would be a more appropriate nomenclature.[53] Brooke ignored this recommendation, and continued to use 'arena' in correspondence and published reports, and it was to remain in use by Gautier, Biraud and Park in official publications of the Bureau.

The descriptor 'Far Eastern' was, as already suggested, a wildly inaccurate term. Technically it included all territory between longitudes 20° and 160° East of Greenwich, and latitudes 40°N and 40°S.[54] Brooke divided the arena into western, central, eastern and southern areas, including in the west, the east coast of Africa and the Asiatic coast from Egypt to Burma; in the centre, Malaya, the Dutch East Indies, Borneo and the Philippines; in the eastern area, the Asiatic coast from Siam to Siberia, Japan and Hong Kong, and in the southern area of ports and countries, Australia and 'strategic outposts' of New Zealand, French New Caledonia, Fiji and Honolulu.[55] Brooke's argument for this division was based on prevailing patterns of commerce, whereby the maritime connections within each group tended to be self-contained, with inter-regional links maintained through the larger ports only.[56] Operationally, this meant that the Bureau sent comprehensive telegrams to the large ports, and regional specific information only to the smaller ports. Brooke preferred to opt for inclusiveness rather than exclusivity in terms of the coverage provided by the Bureau, and maintained this position over membership of the Advisory Council.

The appointment of the Director

White recommended to Dr Madsen, President of the Health Committee, the appointment of Gilbert Brooke as director of the Bureau, believing that he would accept a temporary part-time appointment to start it up. Rajchman took this up with the Colonial Office in London, and Brooke's release was approved by the Governor of the Straits Settlements on 8 August 1924. In mid-August 1924 White informed Brooke that funds were available and that Brooke could expect to be offered the post. White asked Brooke to find accommodation, to begin arrangements for an intergovernmental conference, and to explore the possibility of special rates for cables. White also sought Brooke's advice regarding staffing, although he noted that a statistician, Dr S. Deutschman, working in the League of Nations statistics department had been recommended, and that additional British staff were not possible because of national quotas.

At the time of the preliminary conference, Brooke believed that he was already appointed, but was deeply offended by the low honorarium offered, one suggested by the Colonial Office in London.[57] Brooke was finally appointed as Director on a part-time basis in June 1925,[58] although his Bureau duties were such that he had little time for his work as Chief Health Officer in Singapore. He continued until the end of October 1926. Dr Raymond Gautier, and in his absence Dr Y. M. Biraud, took over as temporary Director of the Bureau, while Rajchman discussed with Dr Cumpston, Director General of the Australian Department of Health, nomination of an Australian for the post.[59] Gautier remained temporary Director until Dr C. L. Park, an Australian doctor, was appointed in 1932; Park continued until the suspension of the service in February 1942.

As already noted, the Health Committee of the League of Nations, which was responsible for establishing the Bureau, determining its aims and objectives, securing funding and determining issues of governance, had sought to keep the scope of the Bureau narrow and membership of its Advisory Committee small. Brooke however had argued strongly for collaboration and incorporation to ensure that all interested regimes would have a 'vested interest' in the Bureau and that this was essential to consolidate efforts to date:

> I have now got almost everyone in the Arena interested and working for us, except China . . . *I should consider it a calamity if you don't invite S[outh] Africa, Portuguese E[ast] Africa, Kenya, Tanganyika, Madagascar, Mauritius, Seychelles, Massowa, Djibouti, Egypt, Iraq, Persia, Sarawak, and Portugal (for Macau and Timor Dilly) as well as the others* . . . Very few are likely to accept, but that doesn't matter![60]

Delegates to the Advisory Council were determined at the third session, held in December 1927 in New Delhi, which determined that there be one delegate each from Australia, China, the Dutch East Indies, Indochina or other French colonies, India, Japan, Japanese colonies, Siam and British colonies and dependencies. Provision was made for observers from independent health administrations in the Eastern Bureau's area, but votes at meetings and payment of expenses were to be limited to the designated delegates.[61] At the same time, wide geographic coverage was encouraged; one of the anticipated benefits of the Bureau (from the point of view of the League) was that it would collect epidemiological intelligence on Asiatic Russia, the Near East and the East African coast as well as the ports of Asia and the western Pacific.[62] White was to write to Brooke, late in 1925, that 'I do not know where to stop' regarding the nomination of ports, and the service provided proved so valuable that there was increasing pressure for similar bureaux to be established in other regions.[63]

As with other matters, Geneva maintained its line and Brooke his own opinions and ideas, expressing these to Geneva through either long, passionate and enthusiastic letters or flat, depressed and formal notes. Brooke worked hard to expand the Bureau's areas of interest, leading to countless descriptions of his 'resourcefulness, energy and devotion'.[64] Geneva, through White, responded to Brooke in letters either disarmingly personal and warmly encouraging (since Brooke and White were related by marriage, this was easy enough), or equally cool and formal. Since it received advice from the Health Committee, the Advisory Council reflected Geneva's perceptions of the Bureau and its direction, but White was the main conduit of the Health Organisation policy, financial and managerial concerns. However, he was to acknowledge a year later that:

> In looking over the files of correspondence with you to-day I was struck by the relative absence of any adequate expression of the appreciation which the work you have done for the Singapore Bureau has called forth on all sides . . . I do want to let you know in my private capacity that we are all much more grateful to you than may have appeared from letters received . . . I never in my most sanguine moment expected you to achieve more than half of what you have already accomplished in so short a time.[65]

The collection and dissemination of epidemiological intelligence

The Bureau began operating on 1 March 1925 and had eight staff by late 1926. An office was established at 67 Robinson Road, a bank account opened, free broadcasts secured, auditors and solicitors appointed and codes developed to reduce transmission costs. By June, Egypt and other East African colonies had been approached to participate, monthly reports were being distributed and Brooke was seeking an assistant director, other staff and a house press to hold down printing costs and time spent on proof corrections.

Operations proceeded as follows. At the first occurrence of plague, smallpox or cholera, the country in question cabled a summary of the position of the infection (location of infection, number of cases and number of deaths) and a statement regarding measures taken to control the disease and prevent its spread. The Bureau determined which countries were in direct communication with the infected one and informed them by cable of the infection, its extent and seriousness. All countries provided weekly information up to the previous Saturday on cases and deaths from the three target diseases; the Bureau worked on the imperfect supposition that a nil return indicated nil cases. A summary of this information was broadcast in code the following Friday from Saigon, courtesy of the Government of Indochina. This was received by most health administrations and allowed them to decide on action to prevent disease, long before it was possible for 'such disease to present itself in their harbours' through maritime or air traffic.[66] Ports that could not receive the broadcast messages were sent cables. Information was also transmitted to masters of ships moving between ports, and a daily summary of information was also transmitted in English in clear (i.e. not code) from Malabar, Java and from Tokyo, Shanghai, Hong Kong, Sandakan, Madras, Karachi and Tananarive. Where there was an outbreak of infection on board, the ship would cable the information to the next port to ensure appropriate action on arrival for case treatment and for action to prevent the spread of infection. Finally, information regarding other communicable diseases was sent by cable or by a letter accompanying confirmation copies of cabled information for inclusion in the weekly fasciculus.

In January 1926, 200 weekly fasciculi were being published and distributed; by October this had increased to 375; by 1931, 500 were sent to health administrations in the 'east' and beyond. Over the same period, telegraphic links had been extended from 66 to 135 ports. The annual report for 1926 included testimonies of the value of information provided and 'appreciation of a policy ... that all ports of definite commercial, strategic or national importance should regularly receive information' regarding infectious disease.[67]

Broadcasts were sent in alphabetic code (the AA Code) developed by Brooke to enable maximum condensation of material.[68] The code included phraseology for quarantine work and public health activities as well as disease, hence

enabling its use for inter-port communication and for internal sanitary administration, and consisted of 25 different series of two-letter symbols, each allocated
a specific fixed meaning (e.g. BB = week ending Saturday 17 January 1925 at
midnight; DP = Bangkok; JW = deaths from plague during the week numbered).
Since all sets of letters had pre-assigned meanings, the system was relatively
inflexible, but even so it enabled lengthy epidemiological and public health
reports to be transmitted.[69] Despite the condensation that the code allowed, cable
costs mounted, due to the growth of ports and administrations contributing and
subscribing to information and due to the detail of data being provided. The kind
of information remitted, and its timeliness, 'appeal[ed] to shipping interests' and
to port authorities.[70] Communication costs were also high initially, due to
difficulties in receiving wireless broadcasts. In 1925, when the service was being
established, transmission problems were common. India found it difficult to pick
up broadcasts, Japan initially failed to receive wireless reports, and in October
only British North Borneo and Java were receiving wireless reports despite
expectations that messages would be picked up without difficulty within the
region and in France and Switzerland from the Saigon station.[71] Due to problems
of reception, information was therefore sent to individual ports by cable at
commercial rather than reduced government rates. Costs were also high as a
result of different rates charged for telegrams sent from Singapore to London and
to the Continent.[72]

Problems of reception recurred intermittently for technical reasons relating
to length of radio wave, and due to seasonal interference from monsoons and
typhoons. Technical difficulties were brought before the Advisory and
Technical Committee for Communications and Transit of the League of Nations
in 1931, which resulted in a recommendation that the information should be
classified as a special service, like meteorological information. A recommendation subsequently was made to the Radiotelegraph Convention in Madrid
in 1932 that epidemiological intelligence be sent by wireless to ships on a
600-metre wavelength to ensure reception. In 1933 Saigon changed over from
long to short wave, again improving transmission. Broadcasts were picked up
and rebroadcast by government wireless stations in China, Japan, India; the
station in Tananarive, Madagascar, retransmitted information to East African
coast stations in long wave.[73] Through the 1930s, the Bureau maintained regular
communication through a complex web of stations which both received and
retransmitted information (see figure 6.1). These arrangements remained until
1939.

Singapore began transmission through a Radio-Nations service based in
Singapore in 1939, but there were problems related to weak signals and errors
in transmission. Geneva was able to pick up messages from Singapore and
Saigon, and therefore arranged with Radio-Suisse, at the rate of 50 per cent of
the standard tariff, to relay the Singapore messages to Paris (i.e. OIHP) and to

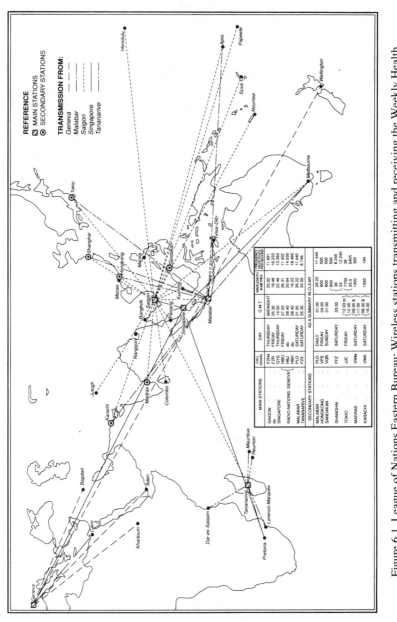

Figure 6.1 League of Nations Eastern Bureau: Wireless stations transmitting and receiving the Weekly Health Bulletin, 1938. *Source*: LN Health Section, Eastern Bureau, *Report of the Work of the Eastern Bureau for 1938* (Singapore: LN, 1939).

Alexandria until confirmation from Alexandria and Paris that they were receiving wireless messages direct either from Singapore or Saigon.[74] However, there was increasing concern about the continuation of existing wireless, tele-graphic and mail services, despite Park's optimism of anticipated continuity from Saigon and Malabar, and correspondence to and from Geneva indicates not only censorship difficulties through the mail but other problems: '[we are] getting some curious sidelights on methods [of transmission]; for example, Indochina will not receive any telegram unless sent in French, but they will transmit code telegrams'.[75] Issues of economy in operating costs and the need to keep airwaves unobstructed became an overriding factor, too; increasingly, security issues were raised with respect to the use of disease-related information; and transmission of information from ports became sporadic and unpredictable. From May 1940 messages were sent only in AA Code, and in December 1941 Park recommended to Geneva that the service be suspended.[76]

Weekly fasciculi included broadcast information and other information cabled or mailed to the Bureau. The earliest fasciculus was a four-page broad-sheet with far more cells empty than with data, and dealing only with plague, smallpox and cholera. Within six years, the reports were disseminating information from 56 health administrations and 147 ports, not only on cases and deaths from plague, smallpox and cholera, but also – depending on the port and its propensity to provide additional data – on typhus, cerebro-spinal meningitis, scarlet fever, choleraic diarrhoea, leprosy, anthrax, psittacosis, recurrent fever and diphtheria; on quarantine provisions operating in various ports and on changes in these requirements depending on the epidemiological picture and on the origin of incoming vessels; details regarding pilgrims and their health; information regarding the organisation of port administration and the equipment held at the port; provisions for the diagnosis and treatment of VD in infected seamen; and numbers of rats caught and rates of infected fleas on rats. Such information was summarised in monthly, six-monthly and annual reports.

Surveillance and sovereignty

Most countries, port administrations and ships were compliant with Bureau requests for information and remitted such information regularly, and the original government agreements to broadcast free of charge or at a reduced rate pertained. Yet there were some continued sensitivities relating to the Bureau's mandate of surveillance.

Early responses relating to the Commission of Enquiry and the role of inter-national agencies in disease surveillance predicted continued tensions, although India, the primary early critic, co-operated with the Bureau. Lieutenant-Colonel J. D. Graham was a member of the advisory committee from its first meeting,[77] and for four years was its Chairman; a civil servant, Dakshinamurthi, was seconded on full salary as Deputy Director from 30 June 1940 until 1 July 1942.[78] Free broadcasts were provided from Bombay, Madras, Calcutta and Karachi. Information required under Articles 1, 2, 4, 6, 12 and 16 of the International Sanitary Convention was remitted to the Bureau, although the government held to its belief that other information should be communicated direct to the OIHP, and remained concerned that the Bureau replicated, rather than functioned on behalf of the Office.[79] It remained rather ambivalent to the Bureau, hence Park's rather racy and hurt account of the breakdown of communication and the discontinuation of the weekly cables in 1940.[80]

Other administrations were sometimes also prickly about their role in the Bureau, though not with regard to its legitimacy. Hong Kong, for example, was sensitive that the representative of the British possessions was always the head of the Health Services of the Straits Settlements.[81] There was some sensitivity, too, over the domination of the British due to its imperial strength in the region and White noted that 'it might be better' if a Deputy Director were appointed who was not British.[82] Bureau relations with China, on the other hand, related to its civil disorder rather than to the politics of the Bureau or suspicion of the effect of its operation on commerce. The Bureau faced considerable difficulty gathering timely and reliable information. Brooke instituted a system of postcard questionnaires which were distributed to doctors, but they were returned by mail and so were of limited use other than for six-monthly and annual reports.[83] Both Brooke and Gautier enjoyed the co-operation of Tsefang Huang of the National Epidemic Prevention Bureau (NEPB) in Peking, but he was hindered by political instability in the countryside and within the central government, communication problems and a lack of resources:

> The repeated failures in most of our efforts towards the improvement of the NEPB administration and the stimulation of public health activities in Peking have developed in one's mentality a sort of passive resistance – so that now one is forced by habit, when a job is on hand, to jump at opportunities like a bulldog ... We have been hanging on and around the Ministry so much since the port survey problem was brought up that now they probably would miss me when I failed to get there for a day or two.[84]

Individuals located in various Chinese ports contributed to the Bureau's work whenever and however possible. Dr C. H. Brangwin, the Customs' doctor in Swatow, wrote in 1927 of the fact that 'the Chinese put all obstacles they can in my way, as they openly say they don't want business interfered with!' and that '[a]ll cables from Swatow to Singapore are in Chinese hands, and though they accept all messages and fees for sending the same, they usually hold them up and forward "By Post", a healthy way of increasing their incomes. The Reds are again in possession of the port.'[85] A month later, Brangwin wrote that he had no code book, he lacked reliable statistics and reports, there was no functioning health department and civil unrest had affected food supplies, movement, communications and disease control:

> The number of cases [of cholera] reported to me by the Mission Doctors was about 100 in three months, the average being one per day which is not up to the 3-per-day of an epidemic. Most of the cases are in outlying villages. The Chinese 'authorities' won't allow any foreign doctor to treat the cases and the Mission Doctors must send all cases seen by them to the Chinese for treatment.[86]

Gautier visited a number of ports in China in 1928, as well as visiting Saigon and Phnom Penh, in an attempt to increase interest in the Bureau and encourage the timely provision of statistical returns, but reported subsequently to Rajchman that 'little progress has been achieved in the matter of quick information from Chinese ports, although the Port Health Officer, Swatow, agreed to resume the sending of regular returns by post, telegraphic transmission being at present out of the question. Tientsin and Tsingtao having been remaining entirely silent since last year'.[87]

Problems existed with respect to a number of other administrations, including Iraq, and here Gautier felt that little could be done to redress 'a somewhat less favourable appreciation of our intelligence service'.[88] In addition, whilst broad-cast information was intended to reach receiving ports in advance of infected ships, in the Gulf ports information tended to arrive too late for precautions to be taken; and the delay in receipt of information similarly affected Syria and Egypt, underlying the need for a Near East regional bureau.

In contrast, Japan provided firm support and, despite its deteriorating relations with the League in the 1930s, it contributed to operating costs on an annual basis through subscriptions and through the subvention of the salary of the statistician and later the Deputy Director of the Bureau, participated in the exchange and training programmes, invited the Advisory Council to meet in Japan and continued to remit information until the outbreak of the Pacific war proper. Japan was arguably motivated by strategic and diplomatic considerations, and was cognisant of the value of epidemiological information to military operations and the effect of infectious disease on occupying troops and colonised populations to meet political economic needs of the militarised states.

The Bureau and the Office internationale d'hygiène publique

I have noted the Government of India's ambivalence towards the Bureau, related to confusion of the respective roles of the Bureau (and the Health Organisation) and the OIHP. At this point, I elaborate on these issues.

The League and its Health Committee were concerned to involve the OIHP and to clarify the activities of the agencies in order to avoid tensions and jealousy, particularly in the light of opposition within the OIHP and the French Foreign Office.[89] The League stressed that the proposal to establish an International Health Organisation was based on the expectation of a formal union of the League and the OIHP. The League envisaged its role as a central agency that collected and transmitted statistics according to the provisions of the Convention, in addition to undertaking other activities such as linking health administrations, co-ordinating international medical and public health research, and collaborating with the Red Cross, the International Labour Organisation and other health agencies. The Office already collected statistical information and published this in its monthly bulletins, but the League argued that delays in distribution meant that the information was of little practical use, that OIHP revenue was insufficient to enable the expansion and upgrading of this service, and that it was limited under the Rome Convention (1906) and could not easily be increased. In sum, the League argued that political, legal and technical reasons prevented the OIHP from collecting and disseminating the information required to ensure adherence to the International Sanitary Convention, whilst the League was well positioned to take on this role and hence support the Office.[90] The League saw the regional bureaux as contributing to this exercise.

Concern about the Bureau and its functions therefore centred on activities which appeared to replicate those of the OIHP, relating to the provision of health information in accordance with the International Sanitary Convention (1912). The Convention was intended to protect and provide sanitary 'defence' of ports, but it was widely accepted to be in need of modification and revision. Meetings to revise the Convention were convened by the OIHP in October 1922, hence India's opposition to the Commission of Enquiry which it felt undercut OIHP initiatives.[91] However, the introduction of a Pan-American Sanitary Code in 1924 further paved the way for a special Far East Convention. Delegates to the Health Committee (and later the Advisory Council to the Bureau) noted provisions under the Convention for special regional agreements,[92] and a sub-committee of the Health Committee was established in May 1924 to modify the Convention to ensure that the Articles were 'efficacious and less burdensome', safeguarding people's health without affecting commercial relations.[93] At the same time, discussions were held between the League and the OIHP concerning ways in which the Bureau might fulfil Conventional functions.[94] Article 7 of the International Sanitary Convention of 21 June 1926 explicitly stated that the Bureau will function as a regional bureau to provide the OIHP with specified information, to be transmitted on a weekly basis to the OIHP and the health administrations of participating countries.[95] The International Sanitary Convention of 1926 came into force on 31 May 1928 after ratification, and the Bureau then began to function as a reporting agency for the Far East to the OIHP by virtue of a number of Articles of the Convention; the bureaux in Washington and Alexandria also functioned as reporting agencies under the Convention.[96]

The implementation of the agreement to remit information to the OIHP was not without difficulty, due to technical problems resulting in delays in receipt of information from the Bureau, which arrived too late for inclusion in the OIHP's weekly communiqué, and to procedural problems such as advice of 'first cases' – where immediate notification rather than inclusion in the weekly transmission would be advisable – and the route of cables and telegrams (through Geneva or direct to the OIHP).[97] There was tension too regarding the transmission of information to participating countries and ports, leading to a formal objection by the OIHP to the revision of the International Radiotelegraphic Convention of 1927 by the League (see p. 121), which reflected League and OIHP notions of confidentiality.[98] In this instance, the OIHP objected to transmission of information by wireless since the 'central office of epidemiological intelligence would incur serious administrative responsibility in the selection of particular items of news regarding epidemics for world-wide distribution and publicity'. The League in response noted the inconsistency between this stance and OIHP moves to improve facilities of the already established wireless service.[99]

The OIHP was also sensitive to the Bureau's answerability both to Geneva (by virtue of its status as part of the League) and to Paris (through carrying out Conventional duties for the OIHP), and to Bureau compliance under the Convention. The Permanent Committee of the OIHP at its session in April to May 1939 reviewed the system of notification of epidemic diseases, and requested that telegrams from Singapore be sent to Paris rather than through Geneva, in pursuance of Articles 1–4 and 7 of the Convention 'in order to facilitate the fulfilment of its duties under this Convention'.[100] In a lengthy letter explaining this, the OIHP emphasised its desire for the Bureau to continue to act as its agent, but stressed that there were delays when cables were sent to Geneva 'of several hours . . . [which] sometimes makes it impossible to prepare the communiqué in time . . . and introduces an extra complication and an element of uncertainty which hampers the smooth working of the services concerned'.[101] Geneva agreed that the Bureau would transmit information to Paris as well as to collaborating governments.[102]

The fall of Singapore and the fate of the Bureau

As hostilities in both Europe and Asia increased, there was a steady decline in the regularity and quality of information being remitted to the Bureau, and wireless dissemination ceased to be possible. From early 1940 French Indochina suspended communication with Singapore. India and other British colonies followed later in the year, primarily for military reasons, for fear that any intelligence might be used by enemy forces. This situation was exacerbated with the Pacific war. On 20 December 1941, therefore, Park cabled the Secretary-

General of the League with advice to close the Bureau, or to transfer it temporarily to Australia.[103] Geneva's draft reply of 22 December advised Park to take with him current accounts, to arrange to store other documentation and to organise appropriate severance for local staff. Park did not receive this advice. The next communication to Geneva, dated 11 March 1942, advised that Park and his wife had arrived safely in Australia.

In an explanatory letter dated 19 March, Park filled in the events of the intervening months. According to him (though not the League's officers), the cabled reply of 22 December had not been received until mid-January and there had been delays in replies to other cables; Park maintained that he had been operating largely in the dark. He had booked accommodation and freight space to allow departure in early January 1942, but cancelled in the absence of instructions from Geneva. That vessel was the last to sail to Australia, and the situation deteriorated rapidly thereafter, with increasingly frequent air raids over Singapore. Park's departure took place at 1 a.m. on 4 February, taking advantage of floor space on a seaplane to Batavia. All personal and Bureau effects were left behind, although archives and equipment had been stored in a room in a government building. Park had also arranged the transfer of $74,000 of Bureau funds to be transferred to an Australian bank; a small amount of Bureau money and Park's own money remained in a Singapore account.

Another chapter would be needed to give a full account of Park's departure from Singapore and the extraordinary recriminations against him, that begin with a note on file questioning his 'very disappointing' behaviour and his irresponsibility in delaying the removal of Bureau files and equipment. The League believed that Park had not done all he should have as head of the Singapore Office, and that he should have acted on his own initiative to safeguard 'vital archives and take measures regarding his staff and his personal belongings, even if he personally had felt it was his duty to remain'.[104] It regarded Park as responsible for the loss of finances, archival material and equipment, and did not accept that he had lacked information to assess the military situation properly. He was badgered to provide an acquittal of money expended from April 1941, under threat of suspension from service and withholding an indemnity and pension benefits. After the war, some of the missing archives and library were recovered,[105] but then and still later, Park was pursued to account for a missing typewriter, various League books, and to say whether he had been refunded $85.55 from the Singapore municipality; and for details of where he had left his car in February 1942, so that it might be relocated![106] Whilst the League continued to chase up such missing items and debate the merits of opening the Bureau, Park chose to stay in Australia and took up appointment as Director of Public Health in the state of Tasmania. His fuller vindication came later, when it emerged that senior British military officers were as surprised as he by the fall of Singapore.

Notes

1 League of Nations Archives (LNA) 12B/18252/11346, Second session of the Health Committee, Minutes of the meetings held in Paris, 20–2 October 1921, p. 21.
2 LNA 12B/26253/11346, M. Miyajima. Memorandum on the need of epidemic intelligence in Far East. Paper submitted to members of the Health Committee of the League of Nations, May 1922.
3 League of Nations (LN), Provisional Health Committee, Minutes of meetings of the Third Session, Paris, 11–16 May 1922 (Geneva: LN, 1922), p. 66.
4 LN Provisional Health Committee. Minutes of meetings of the Fourth Session, Geneva, 14–21 August 1922 (Geneva: LN, 1922), p. 75.
5 *Ibid.* 32.
6 LNA 12B/26210/11346, Health Committee of the League, Various correspondence with Prof. Calmette; LNA 12B/34665/34275 (Jacket 2) LN Provisional Health Committee. Minutes of the meetings of the Fourth Session, Geneva, 14–21 August 1922, p. 32.
7 LNA 12B/26210/11346, Various correspondence with Prof. Calmette; LNA 12B/25549/11346, Minutes of the Fifth Session of the Health Committee of the League (Geneva, 8 January 1923), 7; Report of Enquiry in the Far East, by Dr Calmette – Annex 4, pp. 58–9.
8 LNA 12B/25734/23230, Miscellaneous correspondence respecting the Commission of Enquiry in the Far East (Dr N. White), White to Major General Sir W. R. Edwards, 11 November 1922.
9 LNA 12B/24285/23230, Turner to the Secretary General, 1 November 1922.
10 LNA 12B/25734/23230, White to Major General MacWatt, 27 December 1922.
11 LNA 12B/25734/23230, White to Rajchman, 28 December 1922.
12 LNA 12B/31957/23230, F. N. White, The prevalence of epidemic disease and port health. Organisation and procedure in the Far East. Report presented to the Health Committee of the League of Nations (Geneva: LN, 1923).
13 LNA 12B/25734/23230.
14 LNA 12B/31959/23230, 3040.
15 *Ibid.* 31.
16 *Ibid.* 30.
17 *Ibid.* 31, 36.
18 LNA 12B/35026/34275, Turner to Secretary General, 15 August 1925.
19 LNA 12B/35029/30818, L. Atkinson, 28 August 1924.
20 LNA 12B/35019/30818, Matsuda to Drummond, 15 April 1925.
21 *Ibid.* 41.
22 LNA 12B/22575/11346. Minutes of the Fourth Session of the Health Committee, 14–21 August 1922, esp. 54–9.
23 LNA 12B/26222/21836, Negotiations with the Rockefeller Foundation, Buchanan to Rose, 18 July 1922.
24 LNA 12B/21836/21836, Correspondence between the Rockefeller Foundation and the Health Section, League of Nations.
25 LNA 12B/57957/21836; LNA 12B/41164/21836.
26 LNA 12B/30087/30087.

27 LN Health Section, Eastern Bureau, *Director's Report on the Singapore Bureau and its Work for the Year 1925* (Singapore: LN, 1926), p. 1. White's report (LNA 12B/31959/23230, 34) refers to discussions between Brooke, representing the Straits Settlements, and Dr de Vogel of the Dutch East Indies in 1912 concerning the need for uniform quarantine procedures, in which context routine exchange of epidemiological information would have been required.

28 LN Temporary Health Committee, *Minutes of the First and Second Meetings of the Committee, Paris, 5–6 May 1921* (Geneva: LN, 1921), p. 30.

29 LNA 12B/41502/34275, Stouman to White, 22 December 1924.

30 *Ibid.*

31 The Governments of the Dutch East Indies and French Indochina had promoted Batavia and Cape St Jacques respectively, LNA 12B/42212/34275, Proceedings of the Singapore Conference, 4 February 1925, 4.

32 LNA 12B/34665/34275.

33 LNA 12B/34665/34275, White to Russell, 20 November 1924.

34 LNA 12B/34665/34275; LNA 12B/42212/34275.

35 LNA 12B/42212/34275, 9.

36 *Ibid.* 12.

37 The Advisory Council regularly recorded its concern about the financial status of the Bureau and its desire that financial liabilities be met out of the Health budget of the League without prejudice to subventions made by countries within the region, see e.g. LN Health Section, Eastern Bureau, Annual Report of 1926 and Advisory Council Meetings (Singapore: LN, 1927), 57 (Resolution 6).

38 *Ibid.* 35. The original offer from the Netherlands East Indies was to broadcast throughout Asia and to Australia at the rate of one gold franc per word; it was revised in the light of the offer from French Indochina, see LNA 12B/42212/34275, Brooke to Rajchman, 17 February 1925.

39 L. Manderson, 'Race, Colonial Mentality and Public Health in Early Twentieth Century Malaya', in P. J. Rimmer and L. M. Allen (eds.), *The Underside of Malaysian History. Pullers, Prostitutes, Plantation Workers . . .* (Singapore: Singapore University Press, 1990), pp. 193–213.

40 LNA 12B/53944/34275, Grant to Rajchman, 27 November 1926 and 23 December 1926. However, there may well have been more extensive local contact that was not reported to Geneva, and the documentation of this may have been lost with other Bureau files during the Pacific war.

41 LNA 12B/22575/11346, Health Committee, Minutes of the 4th session of the League of Nations Health Committee, 14–21 August 1922, 10.

42 LN Health Organisation, Eastern Bureau. *The Eastern Bureau of the League of Nations' Health Organisation; A Brief Account of its Functions* (Singapore: LN, 1931), p. 1.

43 LNA 12B/42212/34275, Proceedings of the Singapore Conference, 1.

44 LNA 12B/23519/11346, League of Nations, Health Committee, Report presented by the Second Committee on the work of the Health Organisation, 15 September 1922, 3.

45 LNA 12B/42212/34275, Proceedings of the Singapore Conference, 11.

46 E. Said, *Orientalism* (London: Routledge and Kegan Paul, 1978), remains the seminal work in this respect; and see papers in D. Arnold (ed.), *Imperial Medicine*

and Indigenous Societies (Manchester: University of Manchester Press, 1988) and R. MacLeod and M. Lewis (eds.), *Disease, Medicine, and Empire. Perspectives on Western Medicine and the Experience of European Expansion* (London and New York, 1988).

47 LNA 12B/31959/23230, 43.
48 M. Worboys, 'The Emergence of Tropical Medicine: A Study in the Establishment of a Scientific Specialty', in G. Lemain, R. MacLeod, M. Mulkay and P. Weingart (eds.), *Perspectives on the Emergence of Scientific Disciplines* (The Hague, Mouton, 1976), pp. 75–98.
49 LNA 12B/22575/11346, Minutes of the seventh meeting of the fourth session of the Health Committee, 19 August 1922, 33.
50 LN Health Organisation, Eastern Bureau. *The Eastern Bureau of the League of Nations' Health Organisation*, 1.
51 LNA 12B/41502/34275, Brooke to Rajchman, 13 March 1925.
52 LNA 12B/31959/23230.
53 LNA 12B/43674/34276, Fourth session of the Health Committee, 25 April 1925.
54 LNA 12B/42212/334275, Proceedings of the Singapore Conference, February 1925, 29.
55 LNA 12B/50856/34725.
56 *Ibid.*
57 LNA 12B/42212/34275, White to Rajchman, 17 February 1925. Brooke thought that the honorarium was the League's estimate of the value of his services, and he responded by insisting that he work for nothing or not at all. At the time of this negotiation, however, White was ill, and his house had burnt down and had not been insured. He was therefore under considerable stress and his behaviour was, according to White, 'queer'. Brooke's health remained poor; in June, due to sprue, he weighed only 8 st 13 lb. By early September, however, he was 10½ stone, which he attributed to Marmite!! LNA 12B/45195/34275, Brooke to White, 4 September 1925.
58 LNA 12B/34665/34275, Brooke to Rajchman, 13 August 1925, acknowledges the letter of appointment dated 18 June 1925.
59 LNA 12B/55281/34275, Rajchman to Hoops, 17 November 1926.
60 LNA 12B/45195/34275, Brooke to White, 4 September 1925, italics and abbreviations in the original.
61 LNA 8D/4266/882.
62 LNA 12B/41502/34275, Stouman to White, 22 December 1924.
63 LNA 12B/34665/34275, White to Brooke, 6 November 1925.
64 LNA 12B/34275/34275, Rajchman to Brooke, 18 June 1925; Hoops, Principal Civil Medical Officer in the Straits Settlements, similarly described him as 'energetic and cheery', 14 August 1925.
65 LNA 12B/43209/34275, White to Brooke, 6 October 1926.
66 LN Health Organisation, Eastern Bureau, *The Eastern Bureau of the League of Nations' Health Organisation*, 3.
67 LNA 12B/56751/34275; League of Nations, Health Organisation, Eastern Bureau, Annual Report for 1926 and Minutes of the Advisory Council Meeting held in Singapore, 6–10 January 1927 (Singapore: LN, 1927).

68 G. E. Brooke (comp.), *The AA Cable Code* (Singapore: League of Nations, Health Organisation, Eastern Bureau, 1925).

69 See LNA 8D/1026/430. For example, cabled information transmitted for the week ending 27 August 1932, would be decoded as follows:

RH	Quarantine restrictions against
EF	Calcutta and
IF	Rangoon had been withdrawn
ID	by the Federated Malay States
KY	as regards smallpox
VD	on the 27th
RGRG	Quarantine restrictions have
FL	been declared against Hoihow
ID	(Hainan) by the Federated
KF	Malay States on account of
VD	cholera on the 27th

70 LNA 12B/34665/34275, White to Brooke, 6 November 1925.

71 LNA 12B/42212/34275, White to Rajchman, 17 February 1925.

72 LNA 12B/42212/34275, White to Rajchman, 17 February 1925.

73 League of Nations, Health Section, Eastern Bureau, *Annual Report for the Year 1934* (Singapore: LN, 1935), 2.

74 LNA 8D/38994/341.

75 LNA 8D/38994/341.

76 LNA 8D/41370/341, Eastern Bureau, Singapore. Temporary Closing of the Bureau, 1942, Park to Secretary-General, 20 December 1941.

77 His attendance was sporadic due to other commitments. However, this was true for all members, and attendance at the Advisory Committee meetings, held minimally a year apart and often less frequently to take advantage of other serendipitous travel, did not reflect government commitment to the Bureau or readiness to supply epidemiological intelligence.

78 LNA 8D/41060/341. Dakshinamurthi returned to India in December 1941, on leave, and the fall of Singapore soon afterwards meant that he did not complete the final six months of secondment.

79 LNA 12B/58864/58670.

80 LN Health Section, Eastern Bureau, *Director's Report on the Work of the Eastern Bureau, Singapore, for the Year 1940* (Singapore: LN, 1941), p. 1.

81 LNA 8D/882/882, Park to Boudreau, 23 March 1933.

82 LNA 12B/42212/34275, White to Rajchman, 17 February 1925.

83 LNA 12B/34665/34275 (Jacket 2).

84 LNA 12B/53994/34275, Huang to Director, Eastern Bureau, 21 November 1926.

85 LNA 8D/751/430, Brangwin to Biraud, 27 September 1927.

86 *Ibid.* Brangwin to Biraud, 25 October 1927.

87 LNA 8D/2165/430.

88 LNA 8D/2165/430.

89 LNA 12B/11463/11346, Temporary Health Committee of the League, Report on the conference between M. Velghe and Dr Pottwin, 7 March 1921; LNA 12B/12458/12458.

90 League of Nations, Temporary Health Committee, Minutes of the first and second meetings of the Committee, Paris, 5–6 May 1921 (Geneva: LN, 1921), 29–30.

91 LNA 12B/25594/22235, Revision of the International Sanitary Convention of 1912.

92 Article 80 of the 1912 Convention, see LNA 12B/42212/34275, 11.

93 LNA 12B/36055/27633, White to Granville, 17 May 1924.

94 LN Health Section, Eastern Bureau, *Report on the work of the Eastern Bureau for 1927* (Singapore: LN, 1928), p. 49; LNA 12B/53944/34275, Rajchman to Biraud, 12 November 1926 and Rajchman to Hoops, 17 November 1926.

95 LN Health Section, Eastern Bureau, *Annual Report for 1927* (Singapore: LN, 1928), 20 (Annex VIII, Agreement concluded between the Office international d'hygiène publique and the Health Committee) and 57–9 (Appendix 6, Replies received from administrations associated with the Eastern Bureau regarding duties under the International Sanitary Convention).

96 The relevant articles were 1, 2, 3, 6, 9, 12, 14, 16, 21, 28, 50 and 57 of the Convention, see LN Health Section, Eastern Bureau, *Minutes of the fourth session of the Advisory Council of the Eastern Bureau, Singapore 14–16 February 1929* (Singapore: LN, 1929), p. 30.

97 LN Health Section, Eastern Bureau, *Annual Report for 1929* (Singapore: LN, 1930), pp. 8–9, 27–9.

98 LNA 12B/56751/34275, 67–74, Proceedings of a Sub-committee on Item 4 of the Agenda: 'Consideration of suggestions transmitted by the Permanent Committee of the Office International d'Hygiène publique'.

99 LN Health Section, Eastern Bureau, *Annual Report for 1931* (Singapore: LN, 1932), p. 7.

100 LNA 8D/348/341, Bureau de Singapour, Correspondance avec l'Office international d'hygiène publique, Paris, T. Morgan to Secretary-General, 1 August 1939 (official translation from French original).

101 *Ibid.*

102 Park had not been sending the cabled information to Paris and thought the imperative was to get it to the eastern ports; but he had also not thought about this in terms of the obligations under the Convention and was happy to cable rather than airmail the information to Paris.

103 LNA 8D/41370/341, Temporary Closing of the Bureau, 1942, Park to Secretary-General, 20 December 1941.

104 LNA 8D/41370/341, Temporary Closing of the Bureau, 1942, Memo (unsigned) to Stencek, 5 June 1942.

105 *Ibid.* J. G. Ward, Foreign Office, London to Secretary-General, 19 August 1942.

106 *Ibid.*

7

Social medicine at the League of Nations Health Organisation and the International Labour Office compared

PAUL WEINDLING

The problem of social medicine: radical reform or authoritarian interventionism?

The aftermath of the First World War saw a transition from the control of epidemic, infectious diseases to international endeavours promoting social medicine. It was hoped that international peace could be underpinned by alleviation of social deprivation and injustice: effective health and welfare services were intended to stabilise the existence of new states and modernise administrative structures. State administrations adopted ambitious plans to extend social welfare provisions; and a private sector that had been heavily engaged in war relief work attempted to shift the basis of voluntary care away from philanthropic aid, and towards tackling the scientific roots of poverty and disease. The new priority given to maternal and child health, and to the prevention of chronic degenerative diseases (notably tuberculosis and certain sexually transmitted diseases) was linked to a range of demographic and social issues. Visionary schemes promoted innovative concepts of positive health and diverse concepts of 'social hygiene', 'social medicine' and of a healthy 'human economy'.[1] Clinical medicine was to be 'reconstructed through social science', and the organisation of medical care was to be collectivised by state and municipal public health physicians superintending polyclinics and public hospitals.

Whatever the prevailing political system, there was an international consensus among public health experts that the collectivisation of health care should look to advances in biological and social sciences. The most radical schemes were the Soviet polyclinics that had many admirers among Western advocates of social medicine.[2] Yet social medicine under communism was as heterogeneous as in the West: the Health Commissar Semashko drew extensively on the biologically based German theories of 'social hygiene' as formulated by theoreticians like the newly appointed professor of social hygiene in Berlin, Alfred Grotjahn, or as used in shaping the development of state and municipal clinics under the

Prussian Welfare Ministry official, Adolf Gottstein. The centre and right were as interested in the new social medicine as reformers on the left. In Britain the Dawson Report of 1920 introduced the terminology of 'primary' and 'secondary' health care, based on model health centres and district general hospitals.[3] In France a National Office of Social Hygiene was organised in 1925 in the Ministry of Labour, Hygiene and Public Welfare.[4] US Foundations promoted socialised models on an international basis.[5] The Rockefeller Foundation (RF) supported innovative research and public health schemes through its International Health Board, in order to build up an internationally minded cadre of public health experts;[6] the Russell Sage Foundation funded 'clinical sociology' at Yale; the Milbank Memorial Fund developed total health indicators; and the Commonwealth Fund promoted child-guidance clinics.[7] Voluntary initiatives were launched that would form the basis for a new international health organisation on a voluntaristic model.

Medical experts in international organisations regarded themselves as in the vanguard of the advance to social medicine: monitoring health conditions, facilitating interchange of expertise, and setting optimum standards of health and welfare provision. Despite divergent starting points, there was to be a remarkable convergence in the policies of the International Labour Office (ILO) which set out to tackle ill-health as arising from working conditions and poverty and the more scientific approach of the League of Nations Health Organisation (LNHO).

The articulation of a co-operative and intellectually innovative programme of social medicine had to overcome obstacles arising from narrower conceptions of the LN's health work. While the mid-1920s programmes based on physiology, bacteriology and setting biological standards allowed these two organisations to build up networks of communication among medical experts, conflicts of interest arose. Member governments wished to see the technical agencies of the League of Nations acting in a subordinate role, essentially servicing their public health administrations. This worked as long as the agencies were content with simply tabulating information and minimum standards. But in the late 1920s in response to the deteriorating international economic and political situation, the technical staff of the ILO and LNHO began to promote ambitious programmes of optimum standards. Co-operation between these two agencies led to attempts to solve socio-economic and medical problems in highly innovative ways that enraged certain governmental representatives.

The history of social medicine has recently undergone a major shift of perspective. Protagonists of social medicine were often historically minded, and sought to convey the impression that they were an enlightened elite struggling against vested state, professional and economic interests. Social medicine was considered as intellectually coherent, objectively based in social or biomedical science, and benignly reformist.[8] For example, social medicine in Weimar

Germany with its array of health centres and polyclinics was interpreted as a 'shattered alternative' suppressed by right-wing political and professional interests.[9] Soviet social medicine was held to be an internationally recognised radical model. More recent historical work has identified a range of political interests operating within social medicine, and a prominent concern with eugenics that ranged from providing a rationale for positive welfare measures like maternity benefits to 'negative eugenic' measures such as compulsory sterilisation. Instead of being seen as placing medicine on a socio-economic and humanistic basis, social medicine, particularly its biologistic formulations, is seen as intrusive in invading spheres of civic society and subordinating them to medicalised control. In creating new career opportunities in polyclinics and social administration, social medicine thus spearheaded professional imperialism.

Hitherto the major testing ground of interpretations of international medical schemes has been the activities of the RF, which attempted to internationalise American models of public health as enshrined in such leading academic centres as the Johns Hopkins School of Public Health.[10] The confluence of the diplomatic interests of the United States with RF activism in strategically important areas like the Far East and South America has fuelled interpretations that the RF was an informal agency in the extension of US imperialism. It was consistent with the RF's oriental interests that from 1925 it gave substantial funds to the Far Eastern Bureau of the LNHO. Within the United States the RF has been accused – by Richard Brown and Howard Berliner – of using its scientific priorities to promote an elitist (and incidentally gender-biased) professional imperialism in medicine consistent with corporate capitalism. Moreover, in backing programmes of human biology the RF has been seen as covertly supporting modernised forms of eugenics. Against these interpretations are views of the RF as philanthropically disengaged from national politics and as visionary in promoting social surveys and scientifically based strategies to tackle the causes of sickness. RF innovations ranged from new vaccines, as for yellow fever, to virtually religious evangelising for cleanliness that accompanied the hookworm prevention programmes.[11]

These interpretative divergences can be extended to social medicine. Systems of social medicine may be seen as flawed in that they were overly geared to serving the interests of public health professionals: the medicalisation of what had hitherto been conceptualised in moralistic or socio-economic terms expanded career openings for professional elites, while augmenting their social status and powers. (In 1933 the LNHO had a staff of 53, 25 of whom were paid by the RF.)[12] But social medicine was often tainted by eugenics with biologically based concepts of the poor and sick as an hereditarily degenerate and (so-called) 'social problem group'.[13] Moreover, the type of laboratory or statistically based studies supported by the RF masked immense socio-economic and gender inequalities. Much research was merely applied physiology rather than analysing health as a complex result of living and working conditions, and of income in association with patterns of consumption. By the 1940s counter-currents in social medicine emphasised holistic and psychological dimensions, as exemplified by the innovative director of the RF's medical programme, Alan Gregg, or by John Ryle (Oxford's first – and last – professor of social medicine), or by leading Nazi experts in hygiene like Heinrich Zeiss, the Berlin professor of hygiene who had worked under Semashko in the Soviet Union.[14]

The emerging interpretation of the LN technical agencies is that their achievements were more durable than the diplomatic failures of the League that were based on flawed principles of collective security. I will apply some of the more critical interpretations developed for the RF to appraise the medical work of the ILO and LNHO. These two organisations approached social medicine from divergent socio-economic and biological starting points. It may be objected that the relations between the ILO and RF were minimal in the medical field: although the ILO hoped that the RF might fund an interchange of medical inspectors of factories, this was only achieved on an irregular basis, and support for the ILO's encyclopaedia of occupational health was not forthcoming. Contacts were greater regarding social science projects, and this included vital statistics and surveys of social insurance provisions.[15] By way of contrast, the LNHO drew between a third and half of its budget from the RF, and formulated policies in conjunction with some of the more innovative RF field officers.[16] Between 1922 and 1927 $350,000 was granted by the RF to the LNHO for epidemiological intelligence, between 1922 and 1929 $500,000 was spent on the interchange of medical officers, and between 1930 and 1934 a further $700,000 was granted.[17] Moreover, the RF contributed $2 million to the League of Nations library.

RF support was essential in giving the LNHO autonomy from the subservient role envisaged by governmental representatives. The Director of the RF's International Health Board commented in 1928: 'Most students of government will, I believe, hold that the health organisation should not in any way be independent of the League.'[18] But by 1940 the head of the Epidemiological Section was planning an autonomous health organisation free from the by then discredited LN.[19] The ILO was even more successful in maintaining its autonomy: by 1935 it made a determined contribution to furthering independent policy initiatives in the fields of health and welfare.

It is worth considering whether the LNHO's policies were conceptually flawed because these placed excessive emphasis on training public health administrators requiring elaborate institutional structures, in order to dispense what were essentially medical solutions to social problems of chronic diseases associated with poor diet and poverty. The ILO may also be scrutinised regarding whether it realised its potential of developing a system of social medicine sensitive to economic conditions, technical hazards and the needs of working populations.

Industrial health and the ILO

The ILO, established in 1919 with a British Treasury loan, was very much a product of concern with industrial welfare in First World War Britain and France.[20] The British view was that the ILO was to function rather like the civil service in gathering information for a governing body. Early in 1920 both the ILO's industrial health section and the planned LN health organisation had the appearance of being offshoots of Whitehall ministries, as Christopher Addison (the first Minister of Health), Eric Drummond (a former Foreign Office official who was appointed Secretary-General of the LN), Rachel Crowdy (Chief of the Social and Health Sections of the LN from 1919) and Harold Butler (a former Home Office official, appointed to the ILO) set out to demarcate between the spheres of the two health organisations.[21] British expectations of the ILO were upset by the withdrawal of the United States, and by Jean Monnet securing the appointment as Director of a French socialist, Albert Thomas, who had previously organised munitions production and a medical inspectorate.[22] The constitution of the ILO was tripartite with representation from employers and workers in addition to state representatives. French trade unionists had a more dynamic vision of the ILO as not subservient to member-states, but as 'the instrument of international social reform' to secure the socio-economic reconstruction of Europe. As 'a scientific and impartial body' it was to further the claims of international labour on governments, and its tripartite structure avoided the governmental ethos of the LN that rendered it vulnerable to the criticism that it was nothing but a meeting of government delegates with no popular mandate.[23] The ILO had a broader membership than the LN, including Austria and Germany from 1920, and there were considerable informal contacts with the Soviet Union (which ceased to co-operate during the 1930s, paradoxically when it was admitted to the League of Nations) and the United States (which joined the ILO in 1934, but was never a member of the League).

As Director-General, Thomas had a dynamic conception of the Labour Office. He argued that it should take the initiative in approaching governments for the ratification of conventions to protect labour. Although his plan for an interventive international inspectorate was not realised, he established a network of regional offices. The ILO placed much effort into collecting economic and labour statistics, in order to provide a basis for conventions that could shape industrial-welfare legislation.[24]

The initial concerns of the ILO were the protection of women and children, and the securing of an eight-hour day. It hoped to secure six weeks of paid maternity leave before and after birth, and a further three months' paid leave in the case of illness. Women were to be excluded from work dangerous in the event of maternity. The ILO attempted to extend international conventions, such as banning the use of white phosphorus in the manufacturing of matches and pottery.

Once the International Labour Conference agreed to a convention, member-states were obliged to consider action on any issue within one year. The aim was that all states should have standard labour legislation, and that this would ensure that there was no unfair competition. The successor states of Central/Eastern Europe required guidelines for their social legislation, although the ILO's policies were at this time largely inappropriate for non-European and non-industrial states. By 1939, there were 67 ILO conventions and 66 recommendations. But the difficulties of ratification and implementation were profound. Britain refused to ratify the eight-hour working day (using the excuse of Sunday railway work) so holding up the ratification by other countries (such as Italy and Latvia) which was conditional on British action. Britain also declined to ratify the Maternity Convention on the grounds of the different position of married women under the National Health Insurance Act.[25]

The ILO's overall premiss was that welfare was determined by socio-economic conditions. Pay and social security benefits were the keys to good health. Yet although the ILO initially made an expansive bid for a key role in international health (legitimated by the Treaty of Versailles which assigned to the ILO 'the protection of the worker against sickness, disease and injury arising from his employment'), it rapidly restricted its medical programme. In the controversially thorny field of sexually transmitted diseases it limited its role to securing improved medical facilities for merchant seamen.[26] The ILO was restricted by the politics of expediency in having to maintain cordial relations with other international bodies like the LNHO. In return for limiting its role in international health, the ILO gained representation on the LN's Health Council.

There was a fundamental dilemma inherent in the scientific universalism of the ILO's reformist policies. For in seeking to justify its reformist demands in the universalist terms of science, it had to devolve initiatives to scientific experts whose empirically based approaches were necessarily limited to what could be proven in the laboratory. The industrial hygiene section was established in 1920 under the Italian physician Luigi Carozzi. His physiological approach meant that even within the ILO his department was peripheralised.[27] Although there were initially political tensions over the establishing of an industrial hygiene committee – it was denounced in the House of Lords in April 1921, Carozzi created a virtually autonomous sphere by establishing an advisory committee on industrial hygiene, and he devoted his main energies to liaising with inter-national experts and government medical inspectors of factories.[28] One of Carozzi's staff in 1934 complained in a moment of embittered frustration about how the physiological approach excluded study of workers' psychology and of the social and political context of work.[29] Whereas major policy concerns of the ILO were to advance the causes of maternity benefits and pensions, and to advance curative medicine in the shape of sickness insurance, by the mid-1920s preventive medicine for occupational diseases became a highly technical and narrowly focused area of activity.[30]

The ILO studies and reports (series F) on industrial health show that in the early 1920s the ILO was prepared to allow groups of workers vulnerable to accidents or sickness an individual voice.[31] By 1927 the tone of these reports had become strictly technical. It should be noted that certain experts had radical sympathies: there was contact with progressive spirits in occupational health such as Ludwig Teleky, the Austrian pioneer of an economically based social medicine, or Thomas Legge, the British medical inspector of factories who moved from the Home Office to the Trades Union Congress in 1929. Yet the need for consensus crippled dynamic initiatives since overwhelming scientific proof was a prerequisite for any measure. The ILO secured widespread compliance with existing conventions on phosphorus and white lead. Anthrax prevention required nearly a decade of gathering information about laboratory investigations carried out elsewhere (for as with the LNHO there was no in-house laboratory) before a series of recommendations were issued. Technical difficulties were such that when a convention for workmen's compensation for occupational diseases was drafted in 1925, it included only lead and mercury poisoning, and anthrax infection. The Standard Code of Industrial Hygiene was drafted in 1930, and concentrated on technical procedures. Studies were also made of silicosis (from 1924) and of certain occupational cancers, although the ILO was slow to respond to newly identified occupational diseases like asbestosis.[32] Difficulties arose in collecting scientific evidence so that it could be conclusively proved that a specific hazard was the cause of a disease. The ILO's occupational hygiene programme had neither the advantages of the broader socio-economic perspectives of nineteenth-century writings on occupational hygiene, nor of the interwar interest in industrial psychology and in the elimination of fatigue and stress at work. The ILO's contributions to industrial hygiene, geared to rigid and demanding scientific criteria, thus came to appear to be haphazard and lacking an overall policy. Moreover, the ILO was Eurocentric until 1935, preoccupied with social problems in industrialised societies. But there were certain achievements. The need to provide an accessible compendium of technical information meant that Carozzi concentrated his efforts on producing an impressive *Encyclopaedia of Occupational Health*, that became – and has remained – an international standard work of reference.[33]

A further defect of the ILO was the lack of advance on the statistics of occupational diseases. From 1930 the ILO *Yearbook of Labour Statistics* contained sections on unemployment and employment, hours of work, wages, the cost of living and retail prices, workers' family budgets, emigration and immigration, and industrial relations. Accident statistics in thirty countries were published separately in the *International Labour Review*, and were included in the *Yearbook* from 1940. These statistics excluded deaths from occupational diseases and no attempt was made to correlate mortality or morbidity with economic trends. This was a major failing given that the Depression forced crucial problems concerning poverty, unemployment and sickness onto the agenda of international organisations.[34]

The LNHO's advance to social medicine

By the mid-1920s the LNHO like the ILO's industrial health section adopted a narrowly technical approach, rejecting broader concerns with welfare. This transition was illustrated by the separation of the Health Organisation from the Social Section in 1920. After concern with epidemic infectious diseases, the LNHO came to concentrate on standard setting by the mid-1920s. It achieved this by designating certain laboratories, notably the National Institute of Medical Research of the Medical Research Council (MRC) in London and the State Serum Institute at Copenhagen. The programme was rapidly enlarged, as the LNHO achieved a degree of financial autonomy with funds from the RF. Whereas the RF initially refused funds for the Epidemic Commission, arguing that tuberculosis as a social disease in Eastern Europe caused a higher mortality than an infectious, epidemic disease like typhus, the Foundation was attracted to a programme oriented to social diseases and the scientific universalism of standard setting.[35] The RF supported the Health Organisation's weekly, monthly and annual epidemiological reports. The LNHO's monthly reports included a section on general mortality rates, the incidence of plague, cholera, yellow fever, smallpox and syphilis, infant mortality and indicators of health of other age groups such as deaths from puerperal fever. Mortality trends in large towns were given, including mortality from infant and children's diseases. Co-operation with the Paris-based International Office of Public Hygiene and the setting up of a Far Eastern Office in 1924 meant that by 1937 72 per cent of the world's population was covered by the LNHO's medical statistics. The *Yearbook* issued from 1925 provided a useful overview of national public health and industrial health services.

Efforts were made regarding international standardisation of mortality statistics. When the Ministry of Health attempted to introduce a standard record card devised by the LNHO, *The Times* opposed this as bureaucratic and unnecessary in forcing doctors to replace the listing of symptoms with the diagnosis of a particular disease.[36] Major Greenwood, the medical statistician at the London School of Hygiene, argued against the League's quest for global statistics and instead demanded detailed studies of particular industries in co-operation with the ILO.[37] Although it was hoped that sickness insurance funds would enforce the development of standard diagnoses, a report on tuberculosis statistics doubted this, and pointed out that information for rural areas was also likely to be less accurate.[38] In 1928 the German medical statistician Emil Eugen Roesle of the Reichsgesundheitsamt (Reich Health Office) proposed a scheme for morbidity (as opposed to mortality) statistics. Roesle argued that these could reveal gender inequalities, for example the greater levels of sickness suffered as a result of childbearing. But his proposal was not realised. It was feared that those countries with more advanced administrative systems for the notification of diseases like tuberculosis would register higher rates of disease.[39]

During the 1920s the Health Organisation was primarily concerned with the standardisation of mortality statistics, or providing a quantified basis for chemotherapeutic drugs and vaccines. Social deprivation, diet, the overall health conditions of a population, and the factors affecting the incidence of diseases were initially not considered. Diseases such as syphilis received attention from the point of view of developing standard testing procedures, as for the diagnostic Wassermann and flocculation tests for syphilis, and standard regimes for treatment, as for salvarsan. The case of syphilis, with widely varying forms and human sensitivity to the causal spirochaete, well illustrates the defects of an approach geared primarily to European countries: for in Africa laboratory facilities were lacking and patients could not be relied on to undergo protracted courses of treatment with drugs that might in any case not be available.[40] When the League took up the question of malaria it concentrated on malaria in South-East Europe.

The circumstances of the Depression revealed the social potential of international standards. Nutritional standards, particularly the individual food factors that make up a healthy diet, were scrutinised and the quantity of food factors required was calculated. Conferences on vitamin standards, held in London during June 1931 and June 1934, publicised how the National Institute of Medical Research recommended standard units for vitamins A, B1, C and D.[41] The Tuberculosis Committee shows a shift from technical issues during the 1920s to social issues by the 1930s. Its initial concern was the efficacy of the French BCG vaccination, which it considered in the light of British Ministry of Health statistics. In 1932 the committee acknowledged the importance of higher earnings, shorter working hours, better diet and improved living standards in accounting for the decline of TB.[42]

The LNHO initially did little to advance social medicine on an economic basis. On its panels of experts were advisors – Grotjahn, Charles Newman of the British Ministry of Health and René Sand, the Belgian working for the League of Red Cross Societies – who supported preventive programmes based on forms of social biology. There were pressures from feminists and socialists for improved conditions of diet and housing during the mid-1920s. But the LNHO was concerned with professional training in public health, and a technical approach was consistent with the internationalist ethos cultivated by Ludwik Rajchman as Director.[43]

By the late 1920s Rajchman's political opinions became increasingly forthright, at the same time as greater effort was put into socially oriented programmes. A programme for social medicine was a positive response to the world's economic ills. Rajchman blended RF, German and Soviet initiatives into a new programme for rural social medicine, and could draw on the organisational flair of the by then exiled Yugoslav public health planner, Andrija Štampar. Symptomatic of this change was that in 1929 a report was issued on 'Health Centres in Europe'. The League particularly supported their development in Poland, Czechoslovakia, Yugoslavia and Turkey. The 1931 congress on rural hygiene recommended that health centres should be the basis of all new health care systems.[44]

Co-operative programmes

During the 1920s the ILO and LNHO co-operated on a few limited schemes: the Anthrax Commission (1925–9), the Cancer Commission (1928–30), and study tours by industrial medical officers in 1925 and 1929. Sir George Buchanan, the British representative to the Health Organisation and one of its Vice-Presidents, doggedly opposed 'mixed committees', as part of the British policy of preventing independent research initiatives. He denounced any pretensions of the LNHO to 'constitute itself a super-health authority which supervises or criticises the public health administrations of the world'.[45]

The Great Depression prompted both organisations to challenge the view that they were to have a minimalist role, such as co-ordinating the statistical information of member countries. As a result of pressure from the workers' delegation to the ILO, the League of Nations organised a world monetary and economic conference in June 1933. Despite its failure, the economic and technical organisations of the League pursued policies oriented to ameliorating the rapidly worsening living conditions. The new dynamism was facilitated by Harold Butler becoming Director of the ILO in 1932. Co-operation between the ILO and the LNHO marked a new and highly innovative phase of developing social medicine on an economic basis. There was a series of studies and conferences dealing with how health was shaped by diet, housing and economic conditions. The LNHO joined forces with the ILO in organising surveys of rural hygiene, and in analysing the relations between public health and sickness insurance. Nutrition was a major common focus. The International Institute of Agriculture (founded in Rome in 1905) was also involved. The LNHO's change in policy was signalled in September 1932 by a report on 'the Economic Depression and Public Health'. The defects of national aggregate statistics in concealing poverty were pointed out, and the report called for studies of morbidity, nutrition, the psychological effects of unemployment, and the effects of poverty on children and youth. Mixed committees of various League organisations correlated socio-economic and medical data. Amongst the most innovative work was that on malnutrition of such vulnerable groups as mothers and children. Nutritionists like John Boyd Orr pointed out that the vicious circle of agricultural depression and urban malnutrition could be remedied by increasing the production of healthy foods. By the early 1930s Rajchman was sponsoring programmes on a broad range of social factors affecting health like diet, occupation, unemployment and housing.[46]

The LNHO's nutrition research was the product of scientific experts frustrated with the fundamental irrationality of the prevailing social order. Nutrition exemplifies how scientists were keen to extend their expertise in support of radical reforms. The take-off of nutrition research in the early 1930s coincided with the high point of tensions between the perennially mean British Ministry of Health and nutrition experts of the MRC.[47] For the innovative leaders of British nutritionists, Edward Mellanby (Secretary of the MRC) and John Boyd Orr, were prominent members of the LNHO nutrition committees. British nutritionists could criticise the British government by invoking the new standards and perspectives on nutrition endorsed by the LN, but which they themselves had formulated.[48] The ILO stressed the inadequacy of the nutritional standards used in the Unemployment Act of 1934, and it fuelled widespread criticism of the government such as that by the Children's Minimum Committee. The ILO report on nutrition and health was published at a time when the government had still not decided on new scales. As a result the international nutritional standards forced governments to raise minimum standards used in calculating unemployment and maternity benefits.[49]

Significantly, in view of the deteriorating political situation in Germany, a conference on nutrition of children and the unemployed was held in Berlin in December 1932. The conference correlated national studies of the impact of the depression on nutrition, and the need to link social and medical evidence was emphasised. Evidence was cited for a 'hidden famine' among the unemployed, as exemplified by the German experience when the unemployed subsisted largely on bread, margarine or jam, and potatoes, whereas eggs, butter, and the vital protective foods, notably milk and green vegetables, were lacking. With inadequate vitamins and calcium such a diet was incompatible with 'optimum health and physique'.[50] The conference defined methods whereby malnutrition among the unemployed might be measured: the method of von Pirquet in Vienna was regarded as pioneering, whereby the colour of the skin, subcutaneous fat, weight of the body and conditions of the muscles were recorded.[51] On the basis of the clinical methods the state of nutrition in families suffering total or partial unemployment was compared with those in full-time employment.[52] In November 1935 the first internationally agreed dietary requirements were formulated.[53] Additional amounts of vitamins, minerals and proteins were deemed necessary, and extra calories were required by those engaged in manual labour. In-depth analysis of diets showed that there was substantial malnutrition even in advanced industrial states – something that the British government had been anxious to deny. (The dietary scales were the basis for a minimum emergency diet for the feeding of refugees in Spain.) The ILO also emphasised the need for maternity allowances and insurance schemes, and generally attacked low incomes. The League argued that nutrition improved with income. This went with a general effort to promote consumer-led industrial recovery. The ILO viewed sound diet as basic to health and to a functioning economy. The *Nutrition Report of the League of Nations* of 1937 was a considerable public success.[54]

The Mixed Committee supported the move away from bulk quantity of fats, protein and carbohydrates. The concept of dietary standards included a number of elements: the definition of vitamins, the establishing of human requirements as regards calories, protein, fat, vitamins, etc., and in what proportion these ought to be combined, the assessing of an individual's nutritional state, and the definition of malnutrition. The need for a varied diet was emphasised with an intake of cod-liver oil as rich in vitamin D (for children and pregnant women), vitamin C in the form of fresh fruit or raw vegetables, and plenty of milk; potatoes were praised and milled white flour was condemned. Requirements for pregnant and lactating women were stressed as the population group requiring greatest physical protection, and the US nutritionist, Mary Swartz Rose, prescribed that each child should receive a quart of milk each day.[55] The report represented a crucial turning point, and the Assembly invited the LNHO to continue its work in this sphere.[56] Eleven governments (including Britain, the USA and USSR) set up national nutrition committees to study its recommendations and the ILO conducted inquiries into family budgets.[57]

The LNHO took a lead in promoting a housing committee to study the benefits of sunlight, warmth, water-supply, sewage disposal and reduction of smoke and noise. A programme of co-operation between the ILO and the Health Organisation was drawn up in 1937. This was to encompass rural hygiene, nutrition, physical fitness, leisure, and maternal and child welfare.[58] The programme remained a disjointed torso with fragmentary achievements, and yet its overall rationale deserves appreciation. In endeavouring to prevent the spread of political and economic ills, the LN prescribed brave and innovative remedies, although these would rapidly fall prey to the disorders that they were meant to cure.

Non-eugenic social medicine?

The intellectual rationales of the LN's foray into social medicine need to be placed firmly in the context of their time. It would be tempting to suggest that the political polarisation of the 1930s resulted in a clearly articulated scheme of social medicine on an economic basis. As eugenics came to be increasingly associated with Nazi racial policies, there was a need for clarifying the political ramifications of different forms of public health organisation. Yet the reasons why the ILO and LNHO did not go down the eugenics road were complex.

The nutrition programme was essentially an environmentalist refutation of eugenics. In this sense vitamins as the key to growth and wellbeing were pitted against hereditary determinism of genes. Nutritionists were certainly supporters of welfare improvement: yet their approach was akin to those of the eugenicists in being based on positivistic notions of scientific expertise and of an elite of biologically trained experts dictating social policy. The nutritionists were fixated on milk consumption as a panacea for social ills rather than entering into broader discussion of the causes of poverty and disease: thus the confrontation over nature and nurture meant that enthusiasts for sterile milk clashed with eugenic sterilisation.

The environmentalist rejection of eugenics went with an effort to evade all types of social medicine that focused on intervention concerning the birth rate. Here relations between Rajchman and Grotjahn are instructive. After successfully engineering an apparently liberal appointment of a German staff member to the LNHO secretariat in 1925 (in contrast to the nationalist Heinz Zeiss), Grotjahn hoped that the appointee, Otto Olsen, would move the LNHO towards social hygiene, so representing an antithetical approach to the laboratory based approaches. Rajchman also wished to move away from control of infectious diseases and technical questions towards social medicine. Grotjahn availed himself of the opportunity to obtain RF funding for a planned Center of Public Health Documentation in Geneva, but by 1927 Grotjahn withdrew from the scheme.[59] This withdrawal may be interpreted as marking a break between Grotjahn's social hygiene that centred on fertility control, and Rajchman's more environmentalist outlook.

In seeking to establish the ILO position on population politics, it is worth noting that Albert Thomas took a prominent role at the World Population Congress held in Geneva in 1927, inaugurating the International Union on Population. Yet even this gathering was unable to endorse birth control, instead prescribing selective welfare benefits and immigration controls. By way of contrast Rajchman, who was normally outspoken to the point of outraging the more conservative LN representatives, was enigmatically silent on birth-control issues. Rachel Crowdy of the Social Section was more sympathetic but recognised that participation in any conference on world population was impossible as long as member states had not endorsed birth control. When Janet Campbell as chair of the LNHO Committee on Maternal and Child Welfare raised the issue of medical indications for birth control and abortion in 1932, she encountered stiff opposition. The prevailing climate of opinion in the LN was unsympathetic. Although Roman Catholics were only beginning to formulate a condemnatory policy towards birth control in the early 1930s, the conversion to Catholicism of the LN Secretary-General Drummond, the conservative sympathies of his successor Joseph Avenol, the increasingly important influence of Latin American members of the LN all acted as a break to tackling even the notion whether condoms might be a barrier to the spread of sexually transmitted diseases.[60] The approach to social medicine was more in line with the pronatalist ethos of France than of other North American and European Protestant countries where eugenics had a greater impact.

Such a notion of a medicalised pronatalism would explain the rationales of the LNHO's comparative study of still births and infant mortality in the first year of life. The investigations focused on selected urban and rural districts in Austria, France, Germany, Italy, the Netherlands and Norway. Climatic, geographical, social and health conditions were taken into account. The League sought to solve the problem of why infant mortality was steadily falling, whereas still births and deaths of the newborn were preventable, and required increased antenatal supervision. It endorsed the value of breast feeding, milk hygiene and education in bringing down infant mortality rates (it was also emphasised that infant mortality increased with the order of births). The report attempted to correlate infant mortality with economic and housing conditions, arguing that poor housing went with infectious diseases and digestive problems after birth; in areas of better housing (notably Oxfordshire) still births and congenital abnormalities were of a greater relative importance. The League hoped that the analysis would enable the respective role of medical, hygienic and social factors to be understood.[61]

A range of measures was prescribed for ameliorating maternal health such as improving midwifery, equal benefits for illegitimate children, and medical supervision of women in industry, improved education and housing. These suggest that welfare measures could be consistent with pronatalism. In 1937 the LNHO began to study the problem of persistently high maternal mortality, and the associated problem of the organisation of maternity services. In the mid-1930s the LNHO established a demographic committee, which dealt with the question of whether there was an optimum size for a population. Crucial factors affecting women's health, such as the availability of contraception and the incidence of abortion, were ignored by the LN. While the LN kept itself free from eugenics, it failed to respond to the birth-control question and to the transition to lower fertility rates that were characteristic of the more developed economies. The paucity of women experts on LNHO committees (with the

Anglo-American exceptions of Alice Hamilton – expert in occupational health but an absentee – and Janet Campbell contributing to discussions of child health) and their total absence from senior positions on the LNHO technical staff – in marked contrast to the Social Section – should be noted. There was a pronounced gender divide between medical science and the caring social sphere.[62]

The LNHO recognised that morbidity and mortality statistics gave a very inadequate idea of health conditions. Taking a cue from the Milbank Memorial Fund a new concept of 'health indices' based on demographic, medical, cultural, environmental indices was suggested; attention was paid to factors in restricted geographical localities like population density, morbidity, insanity and alcoholism, and to expenditure and availability of health services. The first of such total surveys was of New Haven, Connecticut, in 1936 and the second was of the rural district of Mezökövesd in Hungary. Trials were initiated in European cities, and there was an ambitious study of Brussels overseen by René Sand.[63] The Organisation was feeling its way towards a new concept of 'positive health' just as Europe was about to plunge into total war.

In assessing the ILO and LN programme of social medicine, it is important to recognise that given the financial and political constraints, a broad-ranging and innovative programme to develop social medicine on a socio-economic basis was successfully launched. The programme contrasted to the biologistic premises of Nazi racism. However, pronatalist priorities that were characteristic of the period were in evidence, and provided a coherent rationale for maternal and infant welfare, nutritional and housing reform, and indeed total environments whether urban or rural. Both the LN and the ILO were much concerned with the living conditions and diets of adult workers, who were hard hit by the mass unemployment of the Depression. Given the vital function of income for the welfare of family dependants, concern with wage-earners was strategically important for pronatalism. It is necessary to take account of what was absent from the ILO/LN programme. In contrast to eugenicists, mental health and the inheritance of mental defect were not studied, just as the ILO gave scant attention to industrial psychology. This was consistent with a neglect of non-productive sectors of the population. Other conspicuous absences were concerns with the elderly, and the disabled. While the LNHO/ILO programme was pioneering, it was very much of its period with the response to the economic malaise of the Great Depression being crucial.

The agenda of the LNHO/ILO programme indicated a renewed sense of concern with the socio-economic bases of health. It was unfortunate that the very economic problems that spurred the LNHO into action also curtailed its resources.[64] The co-operative programmes of social medicine united a heterogeneous alliance of socially engaged medical experts. Yet the approach remained driven by the scientific preoccupations of the laboratory. Although innovative, it cannot be taken as a precursor of more populist programmes, notably the 'health for all by the year 2000' agenda of the WHO forty years on. The physiological and biochemical concerns of the nutritionists, and the ethos of pronatalism suggest that here was social medicine in a technocratic and elitist mode.

Notes

1 For traditionalist overviews of social medicine: R. Sand, *Health and Human Progress. An Essay in Sociological Medicine* (London: Kegan Paul, 1935). G. Rosen, *From Medical Police to Social Medicine* (New York: Science History Publications, 1974). E. Lesky, *Sozialmedizin. Entwicklung und Selbstverständnis* (Darmstadt: Wissenschaftliche Buchgesellschaft, 1977). For historical correctives: D. Porter and R. Porter, 'What was Social Medicine? An Historiographical Essay', *Journal of Historical Sociology*, 1 (1989), 90–106. M. Hubenstorf, 'Sozialhygiene und industrielle Pathologie im späten deutschen Kaiserreich', R. Müller, D. Milles (eds.), *Industrielle Pathologie in historischer Sicht* (Bremen: Universität Bremen, 1985), pp. 82–107. M. Hubenstorf, 'Die Genese der Sozialen Medizin als universitäres Lehrfach in Österreich bis 1914', medizinische Dissertation, FU Berlin, 1992. P. J. Weindling, *Health, Race and German Politics between National Unification and Nazism, 1870–1945* (Cambridge: Cambridge University Press, 1989).

2 S. G. Solomon, 'Social Hygiene and Soviet Public Health, 1921–1930', S. G. Solomon and J. F. Hutchinson (eds.), *Health and Society in Revolutionary Russia* (Bloomington and Indianapolis: Indiana University Press, 1990), pp. 175–99.

3 C. Webster, 'The Metamorphosis of Dawson of Penn', in D. and R. Porter (eds.), *Doctors, Politics and Society: Historical Essays* (Amsterdam: Rodopi, 1993), pp. 212–28.

4 L. Murard and P. Zylbermann, 'La Mission Rockefeller en France et la création du comité national de défense contre la tuberculose (1917–1923)', *Revue d'histoire moderne et contemporaine*, 34 (1987), 257–81.

5 See chapter 15 by Martin Bulmer in this volume.

6 See chapter 10 by John Farley in this volume.

7 See chapter 14 by Mathew Thomson in this volume.

8 E.g. Rosen, *From Medical Police to Social Medicine*.

9 E. Hansen, Michael Heisig, Stephan Leibfried, Florian Tennstedt in association with Paul Klein, Lothar Machtan, Dietrich Milles, Rainer Müller, *Seit über einem Jahrhundert . . . : Verschüttete Alternativen in der Sozialpolitik* (Cologne: Bund Verlag, 1981). P. J. Weindling, 'Shattered Alternatives in Medicine', *History Workshop Journal*, 16 (1983), 152–7.

10 E. Fee, 'Designing Schools for Health in the United States', in E. Fee and R. Acheson (eds.), *A History of Education in Public Health* (Oxford: Oxford University Press, 1991), pp. 155–94.

11 Howard Berliner, *A System of Scientific Medicine: Philanthropic Foundations in the Flexner Era* (New York: Tavistock, 1985). E. Richard Brown, *Rockefeller Medicine Men: Medicine and Capitalism in America* (Berkeley: California University Press, 1975). J. Ettling, *The Germ of Laziness. Rockefeller Philanthropy and Public Health*

in the New South (Cambridge, Mass.: Harvard University Press, 1981). D. Fisher, *Fundamental Development of the Social Sciences. Rockefeller Philanthropy and the US Social Science Research Council* (Ann Arbor: University of Michigan Press, 1993). D. Fisher, 'The Impact of American Foundations and the Development of British University Education', PhD dissertation, University of California, Berkeley, 1977. R. E. Kohler, *Partners in Science. Foundations and Natural Scientists 1900–1945* (Chicago: Chicago University Press, 1991).

12 RAC RF 1.1/100/21/176 Boudreau to Strode 8 November 1933.

13 P. M. H. Mazumdar, *Eugenics, Human Genetics and Human Failings* (London: Routledge, 1992), pp. 182, 203.

14 T. M. Brown, 'Alan Gregg and the Rockefeller Foundation's Support of Franz Alexander's Psychosomatic Research', *Bulletin of the History of Medicine*, 61 (1987), 155–82; D. Porter, 'Changing Disciplines: John Ryle and the Making of Social Medicine in Britain in the 1940s', *History of Science*, 30 (1992), 137–64. D. Porter, 'John Ryle: Doctor of Revolution?', Porter, *Doctors*, pp. 247–76. P. J. Weindling, 'Heinrich Zeiss, Hygiene and the Holocaust', Porter, *Doctors*, pp. 174–87.

15 The RF turned down an application to fund the new encyclopaedia in 1924; see ILO archives Geneva (hereafter ILO) HY 104 Relations with the RF. For social science proposals see RAC RF 6.1/1.1/38/465 S. H. Walker memo August–September 1935.

16 The RF's policy was that the LNHO should draw on no more than 25 per cent of its budget from the RF, RAC RF 1.1/100/21/173 letter of Russell to Morgan, 8 June 1928.

17 RAC RF 1.1/100/20/164 memo of 1/3/1929.

18 RAC RF 1.1/100/21/173 letter of Russell to Strode, 13 June 1928.

19 RAC RF 1.1/100/22/181 Biraud to Sawyer, 1 September 1940.

20 Its chief architects were G. N. Barnes – Secretary of the Amalgamated Society of Engineers, a Labour MP and wartime Minister of Pensions; Harold Butler (1883–1951), a senior civil servant at the Ministry of Labour (a Fellow of All Souls and later the first Warden of Nuffield College); Sir Malcolm Delevigne, a civil servant in charge of the Industrial Division of the Home Office, who had been British representative at the international conference on labour regulations in 1905, 1906 and 1913.

21 ILO L 6/1 Permanent International Health Organisation. Preparatory Documents. L 6/3 Health Organisation. G. N. Barnes, *History of the International Labour Office* (London: Williams and Norgate, 1926).

22 On the history of the ILO see J. T. Shotwell, *The Origins of the International Labour Organization* (New York: Columbia University Press, 1934), 2 vols.; D. A. Morse, *The Origin and Evolution of the ILO and its Role in the World Community* (Ithaca: Cornell University Press, 1969); G. A. Johnston, *The International Labour Organisation. Its Work for Social and Economic Progress* (London: Europa, 1970).

23 J. N. Horne, *Labour at War. France and Britain, 1914–1918* (Oxford: Oxford University Press, 1991), pp. 336–7, 344–5.

24 E. J. Phelan, *Yes and Albert Thomas* (London: Cresset Press, 1936). A. Thomas, *International Social Policy* (Geneva: ILO, 1948).

25 N. Valticos, 'Fifty Years of Standard-setting Activities by the International Labour
   Organisation', *International Labour Review*, 100 (1969), 201–37. M. Stewart,
   Britain and the ILO: The Story of Fifty Years (London: HMSO, 1969).

26 P. J. Weindling, 'The Politics of International Co-ordination to Combat Sexually
   Transmitted Diseases, 1900–1980s', in V. Berridge and P. Strong (eds.), *AIDS
   and Contemporary History* (Cambridge: Cambridge University Press, 1993),
   pp. 93–107, especially pp. 95–6.

27 ILO archives, P 506 personal file on Luigi Carozzi (1880–1963).

28 ILO Hy 103/1 Delevigne to Phelan 22 April 1921. Hy 1001/0 Advisory Committee
   on Industrial Hygiene. Provisional meeting 22 October 1921. Hy 603/1 Circular to
   Government Health Services of Medical Inspection.

29 ILO archives P 1407 file of Arnold Stocker.

30 M. Robert and L. Parmeggiani, 'Fifty Years of International Collaboration in
   Occupational Safety and Health', *International Labour Review*, vol. 100 (1969),
   85–136. For the sociological implications of scientisation of industrial medicine see
   D. Milles, 'From Workmen's Diseases to Occupational Diseases: the Impact of
   Experts' Concepts on Workers' Attitudes', in P. J. Weindling (ed.), *The Social
   History of Occupational Health* (London: Routledge, 1985), pp. 55–77.

31 E.g. *International Labour Office Studies and Reports Series F (Industrial Hygiene)*,
   no. 3 (The Union of Painters, Varnishers, Decorators, Colour Workers and White-
   washers of Germany, *Prohibition of the Use of White Lead in Painting*) (Geneva:
   ILO, 1921).

32 P. J. Weindling, 'Asbestose als Ergebnis institutioneller Entschädigung und
   Steuerung', in D. Milles (ed.), *Gesundheitsrisiken, Industriegesellschaft und
   soziale Sicherungen in der Geschichte* (Bremerhaven: Wirtschaftsverlag NW,
   1993), pp. 351–61.

33 *Occupation and Health. Encyclopaedia of Industrial Hygiene*, 2 vols. (Geneva: ILO,
   1930–2).

34 *Bibliography on the International Labour Organisation* (Geneva: ILO, 1954).

35 RAC RF 1.1/789/2/11 Newman to Vincent, 21 August 1920.

36 *The Times* (5 January 1921). Reference from B. Towers, 'The Politics of
   Tuberculosis in Western Europe 1914–40. A Study in the Sociology of Policy-
   making', PhD dissertation, Birkbeck College, University of London, 1987,
   p. 166.

37 M. Greenwood, *Some Observations on Methods of Statistical Research and upon the
   Interpretation of Statistical Data* (Geneva: LN, 1926). Reference from Towers,
   'Politics of Tuberculosis', pp. 169, 284.

38 Towers, 'Politics of Tuberculosis', p. 170. S. Rosenfeld, *Die Tuberkulosestatistik*
   (Geneva: LN, 1925).

39 E. Marcusson and D. Tutzke, 'Die Bedeutung des Lebenswerkes von Emil
   Eugen Roesle (1875–1982) und die Entwicklung der medizinischen Statistik in
   Deutschland', *Zeitschrift für die gesamte Hygiene*, 21 (1975), 649–52. E. Roesle,
   *Essai d'une statistique comparative de la morbidité devant servir à établir les listes
   spéciales des causes de morbidité* (Geneva: LN, 1928).

40 I. Löwy, 'Testing for a Sexually Transmissible Disease 1907–1970: The History
   of the Wassermann Reaction', in V. Berridge and P. Strong (eds.), *AIDS and
   Contemporary History* (Cambridge: Cambridge University Press, 1993), pp. 74–92.

Weindling, 'The Politics of International Co-ordination', in Berridge and Strong, *AIDS*, pp. 93–107.

41 'Report of the Inter-governmental Conference on Biological Standardisation', *Quarterly Bulletin of the Health Organisation of the League of Nations*, 4 (1935). LNA R 6078–9 concerning standardisation of vitamins.

42 E. Burnet, 'General Principles Governing the Prevention of Tuberculosis', *Quarterly Bulletin of the Health Organisation*, 1 (1932), 489–663.

43 M. Balińska, 'Ludwik W. Rajchman (1881–1965): Précurseur de la Santé publique moderne', PhD thesis, Institut d'Etudes Politiques, Paris, 1992.

44 P. J. Weindling, 'Public Health and Political Stabilisation: The Rockefeller Foundation in Central and Eastern Europe Between the Two World Wars', *Minerva*, 31 (1993), 253–67, cf. pp. 260–2.

45 G. S. Buchanan, *International Coöperation in Public Health. Its Achievements and Prospects* (London, 1934), p. 29.

46 Research Publications LN Documents, spool 3: 9, 'Work of the Health Committee at its 19th Session, Geneva, October 10–15, 1932'. ILO Hy 200, Hy 200/2/2 Collaboration of the ILO and League of Nations.

47 C. Petty, 'Primary Research and Public Health: The Prioritization of Nutrition Research in Inter-War Britain', in J. Austoker and L. Bryder (eds.), *Historical Perspectives on the Role of the MRC* (Oxford: Oxford University Press, 1989), pp. 83–108. M. Warboys, 'The Discovery of Colonial Malnutrition between the Wars', in D. Arnold (ed.), *Imperial Medicine and Indigenous Societies* (Manchester: Manchester University Press, 1988), pp. 208–25.

48 C. Webster, 'Healthy or Hungry Thirties?', *History Workshop Journal*, 13 (1982), 110–29. Compare J. Beinart, 'The Inner World of Imperial Sickness: the MRC and Research in Tropical Medicine', in Austoker and Bryder, *Historical Perspectives*, pp. 119, 124–5, for the complexities of the situation.

49 P. J. Weindling, 'The Role of International Organisations in Setting Nutritional Standards in the 1920s and 30s', in H. Kamminga and A. Cunningham (eds.), *The Science and Culture of Nutrition 1840–1940* (Amsterdam: Rodopi, in press).

50 'The Economic Depression and Public Health', *Quarterly Bulletin of the Health Organisation*, 1 (1932), 425–76. LNA R 6074–7 concerning nutrition.

51 *Report of the Health Organisation for the Period October 1932 to December 1933* (Geneva: LN, 1933), pp. 39–43. 'Conference of Experts for the Standardisation of Certain Methods Used in Making Dietary Studies', *Quarterly Bulletin of the Health Organisation*, 1, 3 (September 1932). 'The Most Suitable Methods of Detecting Malnutrition due to the Economic Depression', *Quarterly Bulletin of the Health Organisation*, 2, 1 (March 1933).

52 *Report of the Health Organisation between the Fourteenth and Fifteenth Ordinary Sessions of the Assembly* (Geneva: LN, 1933). In June 1935 Burnet and Ayckroyd argued in the *Quarterly Bulletin of the Health Organisation* that deficiencies in important nutrients were a common feature of modern diets.

53 The diet based on 24,000 calories was produced by the League's Health Committee meeting in London in a *Report on the Physiological Basis of Nutrition* (London: LN, 1935).

54 See also LN, *The Problem of Nutrition. Interim Report of the Mixed Committee on*

the Problem of Nutrition, 3 vols. (Geneva: LN, 1936). ILO, *Workers' Nutrition and Social Policy* (Geneva: LN, 1936).

55 J. A. Eagles, O. F. Pye and C. M. Taylor, *Mary Swartz Rose, Pioneer in Nutrition* (New York: Teachers College Press, 1979), pp. 98–100.

56 LN circular letter, 'Problem of Nutrition', 30 November 1936.

57 Goodman, *International Health Organisations*, pp. 121–2. *Methods of Conducting Family Budget Enquiries* (International Labour Office Studies and Reports, Series N).

58 ILO Hy 200/0 Co-operation between the Health Organisation and the International Labour Organisation. Certain tensions emerged over topics and approaches, especially in relation to the rural life conference.

59 Grotjahn was annoyed at Rajchman's refusal to appoint a German archivist for the Center. LNA R 985 doss. 52707 International Public Health Archives. Letters of Gunn to White 27 May 1927, Grotjahn to Rajchman 5 and 9 May 1927. RAC RF 1.1/100/20/171 Grotjahn, Memorandum with regard to the establishment of International Public Health Archives, 16 May 1926. C. Kaspari, 'Alfred Grotjahn (1869–1931) – Leben und Werk', medizinische Dissertation, Bonn 1989, pp. 285–7. A. Grotjahn, *Erlebtes und Erstrebtes. Erinnerungen eines sozialistischen Arztes* (Berlin: F. A. Herbig, 1932), pp. 257–71.

60 Weindling, 'Politics of International Co-ordination', pp. 100–1.

61 LNHO, *Memorandum Relating to the Inquiries into the Causes and Prevention of Still-births and Mortality during the First Year of Life* (Geneva: LN, 1930). J. Campbell, *Infant Mortality; International Enquiry of the Health Organisation of the League of Nations* (London: LN, 1929).

62 See chapter 8, by Carol Miller. In 1928 the Council for the Representation of Women in the League of Nations petitioned that women should be able to collaborate with the Health Organisation. ILO regulations insisted on there being women representatives for the discussion of women's issues, which were central to the ILO's programme from its inception. It demanded that women take a greater role in industrial health matters in member countries by insisting that there be adequate numbers of women factory inspectors. But apart from a few women trade unionists, women were absent from ILO delegations and commissions, except from those dealing with women's issues.

63 K. Stouman and I. S. Falk, 'Health Indices. A Study of Objective Indices of Health in Relation to Environment and Sanitation', *Quarterly Bulletin of the Health Organisation*, 5 (1936), 901–96. K. Stouman, 'Health Indices Established in an Experimental Study of the City of Brussels', *Quarterly Bulletin of the Health Organisation*, 7 (1938), 122–67.

64 RAC RF 1.1/100/22/182 R. Gautier, 'International Health of the Future', London, 15 March 1943.

8

The Social Section and Advisory Committee on Social Questions of the League of Nations

CAROL MILLER

The underlying aim of much of the work of the Social Section of the League of Nations was to improve the quality of life of women and children. Proposals put forward to reach this goal reflected assumptions about gender roles and relations as well as changing ideas about the role of the state in sustaining them. Recent comparative research on social welfare policies and programmes of western European countries and the United States between the 1880s and the end of the Second World War has demonstrated the importance of considering both the role of women in social welfare movements and the visions of gender embodied in the state-sponsored social policies that emerged.[1] Popular notions about women's special capacity as actors in the social field also led to women's extensive participation in the social committees of the League of Nations (LN). The decision to appoint a woman, Dame Rachel Crowdy, as Chief of the Social Section was a conscious one. Unlike all other LN permanent advisory committees, women usually enjoyed equal representation on the social committees. In the same way, many government delegations to the LN Assembly included women who were then appointed to the Fifth Committee (Social Questions). The Social Section actively solicited the support of women's organisations in connection with the work of the social committees and many of their proposals were taken up by the League.[2]

While one aim of this chapter is to give due recognition to the role of women in the League's social activities, it also suggests that their contribution was mediated through the particular social welfare approach adopted by individual women and their male colleagues. The social committees brought together a wide range of players and interests – politicians, civil servants, lawyers, medical experts, social workers, moral reformers and feminists – thus providing an interesting case study of the dynamics influencing interwar developments in the field of social welfare; these included the shift from voluntaryism to professionalism, the change from repressive policing policies for social problems to more positive approaches, and finally, the new interest in human rights.[3] The League's social committees served as a forum for the expression of intellectual rationales linking social welfare to the international protection of human rights of women and children, thus preparing the ground for the human rights work of the United Nations (UN) after 1945.

The Social Section

The Social Section was one part of the specialised services of the LN secretariat. Its major role was to co-ordinate and provide administrative support for the work of the permanent advisory committees on social questions. The advisory committees investigated specified subjects and made recommendations to the LN Council on action to be taken by the LN Assembly in these areas. The greatest institutional constraint imposed on the Section was the narrow field of activities which fell under its mandate. In 1919 the Section was entrusted with the responsibility for issues concerning the traffic in women and children, the traffic in opium and other dangerous drugs and health questions dealt with by the LN Assembly and Council. The International Labour Organisation (ILO) had responsibility for the broad range of issues connected with 'fair and humane conditions of labour for men, women and children' (Article 23a, LN Covenant) including pensions, child labour, family allowances, maternity benefits, and protective legislation for working women. The LN Health Organisation (LNHO), created in the early 1920s, dealt with issues of public health and social medicine including infant and maternal mortality, nutrition, rural hygiene and various diseases. The Opium Section, originally part of the Social Section, was in 1930 established as a separate section of the LN secretariat. Although collaborative efforts with other bodies were in principle provided for, the Social Section effectively retained responsibility over only two areas, the problems connected with trafficking in women and children and, from 1924, the residual aspects of child welfare not covered by the ILO or the LNHO.

The work of the Section was further limited by budgetary and staffing constraints. Dame Rachel Crowdy often referred to the disadvantaged position of her section in comparison with the LNHO. As table 8.1 shows, the Social Section operated with a fraction of the LNHO budget. In 1930 the LNHO comprised twenty-eight officials under the LN budget and sixteen officials sponsored by a Rockefeller Foundation (RF) grant, whereas the Social Questions and Opium Traffic Section (prior to its split into two separate sections) employed just twelve officials. After 1930 the Social Section comprised on average three professional staff members and three administrative and clerical assistants.

Crowdy regretted that, unlike the LNHO, her section was unable to contract experts on subjects examined by the social committees. She admitted that 'all we can do in the Social Section is to endeavour to obtain the services of persons having the best "all round" knowledge of the subjects with which we have to deal'.[4] A brief investigation of the background of the professional members of

Table 8.1. *Budget (Swiss francs) of the Social Section and the Health Organisation compared*

Year	Social Section[a]	Health Organisation
1921	150,000	400,000
1922	96,250	392,125
1923	*217,500*	700,500
1924	*167,413*	641,120
1925	*241,921*	809,764
1926	*356,914*	988,165
1927	*275,181*	996,700
1928	*286,817*	992,638
1929	161,155	1,012,957
1930	166,270	1,148,897
1931	164,575	1,319,976
1932	114,838	1,003,084
1933	124,793	980,000
1934	123,136	900,000
1935	126,416	1,176,624
1936	137,381	1,180,533
1937	218,374	1,179,170
1938	202,894	1,000,000
1939	191,126	985,000

[a]Except for items in italics all figures are for the traffic in women and child welfare work of the Social Section. Figures in italics are combined with the opium work.
Source: LN, *Official Journal* 1921–39.

staff confirms Crowdy's statement. Crowdy made her reputation as a dispenser with the British VADs, a detachment of women volunteers who served in the field as nurses and ambulance drivers during the First World War. Two others, Princess Gabrielle Radziwill (Lithuania) and M. de Steller (Hungary), a nurse, had previously worked for national branches of the Red Cross. Professional training of other members included journalism, legal research and archival work. Only A. M. Colin (Belgium) had any direct expertise in the subjects treated by the Social Section. Prior to joining the secretariat, she had been the Secretary of the International Association for the Promotion of Child Welfare (IAPCW) in Brussels. The absence of professional social workers and trained social scientists within the Social Section undermined the ability of the Section to rein in the competing interests represented on the social committees.

The unique structure of the two main advisory committees serviced by the Social Section, the Committee on the Traffic in Women and Children and the Child Welfare Committee, brought together liaison officers from the ILO and the LNHO, between nine and twenty-one government delegates,[5] and 'assessors' (experts) representing as many as twelve transnational voluntary organisations active in the social field. These included, for example, the Jewish

Association for the Protection of Girls and Women, the League of Red Cross Societies (LRCS), the International Association for the Promotion of Child Welfare (IAPCW), the International Save the Children Fund (SCF), and the Women's International Organisations (a group of ten transnational women's groups). Apart from the occasional high-ranking civil servant, most of the male government delegates were diplomats. By contrast, the majority of the women government delegates had some experience in the field of social welfare. Among the women who came to Geneva as delegates and assessors to the social committees or as government delegates to the Assembly's Fifth Committee (Social Questions), were many prominent feminists and social reformers: these included Grace Abbott (USA),[6] Dr Gertrud Bäumer (Germany), Clara Campoamor (Spain), Kerstin Hesselgren (Sweden), Alexandra Kollantai (USSR), Eglantyne Jebb (Britain), Julia Lathrop (USA), Germaine Malaterre-Sellier (France), Frantiska Plaminková (Czechoslovakia), Eleanor Rathbone (Britain), Avril de Sainte Croix (France) and Charlotte Whitton (Canada). The Social Section's contact with representatives of ministries of social welfare and major voluntary organisations active in the social field contrasted with the diplomatic detachment of most other League bodies. The variety of interests represented on the committees ensured that they would become the sites of debate on the role of voluntary or private associations, social work professionals and the state in meeting the needs of women and children.

The Advisory Committee on the Traffic in Women and Children

The LN Covenant entrusted the League with 'the general supervision over the execution of agreements with regard to the traffic in women and children' (Article 23c). Before the war, two international agreements to suppress the traffic had been concluded, the first in 1904 and the second in 1910. These agreements provided for the establishment of national machinery to co-ordinate and exchange information on trafficking in women. In addition, participant states agreed to punish the traffickers if the victim was under twenty years of age, even if she had consented. The efforts of the League resulted in two additional international treaties.[7] The International Convention for the Suppression of the Traffic in Women and Children (1921) raised the age of consent to twenty-one and provided new methods for the protection of women and child emigrants and for the supervision of employment agencies recruiting foreign women. In 1922, the Advisory Committee on the Traffic in Women and Children was set up by the LN Council to monitor the progress of ratifi-cations to the 1921 Convention and to investigate problems connected with the traffic.

Trafficking in women and prostitution are complex problems interwoven into broader patterns of gender relations. Often legislation and social policies have discriminated against women in the name of public order and health as well as in the name of protecting women.[8] The Advisory Committee on the Traffic in Women and Children had little interest in public health arguments for controlling prostitution and the trafficking in women. Instead, it took up the humanitarian work of protecting women and children. The broad composition of the Committee meant that a number of perspectives on prostitution were represented including 'social purity' and social welfare reform. In later years, the participation of experts also introduced mental hygiene and psychoanalytical perspectives. While moralistic, social scientific and socio-medical approaches competed for influence on the Committee, consensus was organised around the protection of human rights.

Initially, many of the policies promoted by the Advisory Committee and the character of investigations undertaken under its auspices reflected the 'social purity' campaigners' preoccupation with 'protection' of innocent girls and women and the need to 'reclaim fallen women'.[9] The 'social purity' element of the moral reform campaign was represented most forcefully on the Committee by the International Bureau for the Suppression of the White Slave Traffic. 'Social purity' campaigners had distinct ideas about gender roles and relations and the way in which they shaped sexuality, marriage and motherhood – ideas which were challenged by the existence of the prostitute. An interconnected chain of issues reflecting a preoccupation with public morals appeared on the agenda of meetings of the Committee on the Traffic in Women and Children: raising the age of consent and marriage, censorship of obscene publications, the social impact of the cinema, protection of young women emigrants and travellers, and control over certain types of employment contracts for women in the entertainment business. Implicit in the 'social purity' approach was the important role to be played by the state in regulating morality. In practice, many of the proposals revealed an underlying agenda linked to defining the boundaries of acceptable employment for and behaviour of young women. Although the 'social purity' campaigners saw prostitution as an 'infringement of the liberty of the subject', they were prepared to curtail women's rights in order to protect or restore their 'virtue'.

The more substantive contributions of the Committee drew on a related element of the moral reform movement inspired in part by the work and ideas of Josephine Butler but also by broader international movements concerned with the rights of individuals.[10] In this sense, trafficking in women was perceived to be a human rights problem involving the violation of the basic rights of the individual. There was a demand by many Committee members for laws which protected women from abuse and exploitation by the trafficker as well as from 'protective' practices that restricted their rights. Women's groups represented on the Committee were aware that protection could easily become 'a hidden form of slavery': '[w]hen the protection which is afforded affects the dignity or the freedom of the individual, the remedy is worse than the evil'.[11] The general legal principle being upheld in the execution of the LN conventions on the traffic in women was the right of a woman to the inviolability of her person and the protection of her individual rights.[12]

One important role of the women Committee members was that of monitoring policy proposals made by the Committee to ensure that women's rights were not infringed upon by over-zealous 'protectionists'. Long before the League adopted the 1933 Convention for the Suppression of the Traffic in Women of Full Age making the procurement of a woman of any age a punishable offence, women's groups had urged that procurers for the traffic should be punished regardless of the age and moral character of the women involved, thus taking the emphasis off the 'fallen woman' and placing it on the exploitative nature of her relationship with the procurer. On numerous occasions women members spearheaded protests against measures proposed by their colleagues which unduly restricted the rights of women and prostitutes. Proposals included the following: certificates of good conduct and moral character for girls under age travelling alone; legislation restricting the travel of women alone; and an international convention for the forcible repatriation of foreign prostitutes.[13] There was broader support, however, for other recommendations by members of the Committee aimed at eliminating the possible financial and sexual exploitation of young women who took up contracts as entertainers in clubs and cabarets abroad. While women Committee members were anxious to establish methods by which women and children would be protected from exploitation they opposed measures which, by discriminating unfairly against women, indicated the continued existence of a double standard. Less repressive in character than some of the manifestations of the 'social purity' approach, the humanitarian concern with the protection of human rights was still conceptually linked to moral reform.

There were also early attempts to place the work of the Committee on a social scientific basis. In 1923, one member of the Committee, Grace Abbott of the US Children's Bureau, formally suggested that an investigation be undertaken with the aim of getting a factual basis concerning the sources and conditions of the traffic upon which to make recommendations. Up until this point the Committee had little idea of the extent of the traffic and the information that did exist often came from sources prone to sensationalism. The sum of $75,000 was provided for the investigation by the RF through the American Bureau of Social Hygiene. In 1927, the expert committee appointed by the Bureau to carry out the investigation presented the results of several years' research by agents working undercover in various countries. Although perhaps less widespread than suggested by some anti-traffic campaigners, the inquiry provided evidence of traffic between Europe and Latin America (and to a lesser extent, North Africa). Because the traffic was primarily between countries in which state regulation of prostitution existed, the report drew conclusive links between the traffic and regulation of prostitution: licensed brothels increased the demand for foreign prostitutes. In contrast to popular notions of innocent girls being abducted from city streets, the report showed that many of the 'trafficked' women were either prostitutes or contracted entertainers who had entered into the situation of their own free will. However, the study also indicated the extent of economic deprivation, physical abuse and marginalisation in their new environment – in part a result of their complete lack of legal rights.[14] The LN enquiry was later extended to the Far East and offered further evidence that licensed houses provided a source and a market for the traffic. In 1937, a LN Bureau was established to improve collaboration between central authorities in Asia on issues concerning trafficking in women. This work represented one of the few attempts of the Committee to move beyond a Eurocentric approach to what had long been seen as 'the *white* slave traffic'.

The Committee's investigations provided the essential data on which further standard setting in this area depended. Earlier, in response to demands by voluntary organisations that the League take up the issue of regulation of prostitution, the Secretary-General, Sir Eric Drummond, had stated, 'it would appear quite impossible for the League of Nations to concern itself with these questions at all' given that they were national rather than international concerns.[15] Many of the League member states were regulationists and the League was reluctant to enter into such a controversial area. In the 1920s there was some tension owing to the fact that several countries represented on the Advisory Committee were regulationists, including France. According to Crowdy, government delegates were often either hostile to or only lukewarm about the Committee's activities. Only the delegate from Britain, Home Office official S. W. Harris, and the assessors had, in her view, 'any wish for progress'.[16]

On the basis of the investigation, however, the Assembly was soon openly pressing for the abolition of state regulation of prostitution in those member states in which it was still being practised. In the late 1930s the Committee drafted a convention for the punishment of persons who exploit the prostitution of others (Suppression of Exploitation of Prostitution) which would have been concluded by the LN in 1940 had not war broken out. Using the principles of the legislation in force in abolitionist states, the League hoped to set new international standards in the area. The draft convention was particularly important, for it marked the legal shift from control of traffic across borders to punitive measures against those exploiting prostitutes in their own countries. Despite initial resistance, the Committee had drawn the League into national concerns, thus helping to re-define the role of intergovernmental institutions in shaping national policy.

New approaches were also being taken to the problem of prostitution in general. A Home Office brief sent to the Social Section in 1919 had indicated that, while governments could police the international traffic, the prevention of prostitution was a matter for voluntary effort. However, led by the government delegate from Uruguay, Dr Paulina Luisi, women committee members drew attention to what they saw as the root causes of prostitution: unsatisfactory working and family conditions, which could only be improved with political, economic and social equality for women. Luisi also advocated free medical treatment for all venereal disease patients and sex education in primary and secondary schools.[17]

The impact of Luisi and like-minded reformers can be seen in the kinds of issues that gradually made their way onto the agenda. In 1927, the women members persuaded the Committee to adopt a resolution making a connection between the traffic and the low wages paid to women in certain branches of employment, in particular, domestic servants. The question came under the jurisdiction of the ILO, which was requested to study the problem.[18] Women government delegates to the Assembly's Fifth Committee, including Helena Swanick (Great Britain), also linked the traffic in women to the low status of women, and thereby re-enforced the demand for a broader analysis of factors leading to prostitution.[19] Such arguments lent force to calls by women's organisations for a League-sponsored inquiry into the status of women throughout the world.[20] As will be shown below, these developments signalled an increased awareness of the impact of a broad range of social, political and economic factors on prostitution and the trafficking in women.

The Child Welfare Committee

Formed in 1924, the Child Welfare Committee[21] experienced more difficulty than the Committee on the Traffic in Women and Children in establishing its political legitimacy as an intergovernmental body. One of the greatest obstacles to the effective work of the Committee in the 1920s was the restricted conception of 'child welfare' adopted by influential British Foreign and Home Office officials in their dealings with the League. The British government had encouraged the transfer to the League of the international work of the Brussels-based IAPCW. This move was in compliance with Article 24 of the Covenant which sought to consolidate intergovernmental organisations under the direction of the League. Once the transfer had been effected, however, the British resisted involving the League in much of the work proposed by the Committee.[22]

There was strong disagreement over the question of what matters related to child welfare could be properly construed as international. The IAPCW had begun to adopt an integrative approach to child welfare. Evidence of this was the division of the Association into three sections: legal (juvenile courts, adoption, probation, etc.); hygiene (clinics, prenatal and post-natal care of infants); and morality (moral and intellectual development).[23] The LNHO took over the medical issues, thus leaving the Social Section to work out the international aspects of what remained.

In launching the League's work in the field in 1924, the LN Assembly resolved that 'the League can most usefully concern itself with the study of those problems on which the comparison of the methods and experience of different countries, consultation and interchange of views between the officials and experts of different countries and international cooperation may be likely to assist the Governments in dealing with such problems'. At the same time, it adopted the International SCF's Declaration of the Rights of the Child, commonly known as 'The Declaration of Geneva', whereupon member states were invited to follow its principles in their child welfare work. The Declaration represented an early attempt to outline the rights of the child to normal development materially and spiritually. No substantive obligations were attached to its acceptance.[24]

At its first session in 1925 the Committee on Child Welfare adopted a wide definition of its terms of reference:

> The Advisory Committee thinks it right to take the normal child as the basis of its study, and to emphasise the constructive side of child welfare as much as the more limited though vital question, of protecting the child from adverse influences or wilful exploitation. There is also the difficult problem of the abnormal child whose free development is hampered by physical, mental or moral defectiveness, and whose lot calls for special care and sympathy.[25]

It also delineated three categories of work: documentation, research and discussion.[26] This approach reflected, in part, the influence of representatives of the US Children's Bureau. At the time the Committee was being formed Crowdy offered Grace Abbott, Director of the Children's Bureau, a free hand in shaping the direction of the Committee's work.[27] Abbott urged that the Committee should follow the methods adopted by her own organisation of using detailed social research following scientific principles as a basis for defining broad social welfare policy. She suggested a range of specific tasks including summaries and analyses of laws, methods of administering laws and public provision for children, and studies of private and public undertakings to promote child welfare. At the same time, she hoped that the Committee would focus on the 'normal' child, not just the needy child, and advocate an increased role for state-sponsored social provisioning.[28] The fact that many of Abbott's suggestions were adopted at the Committee's first session implies that many members were receptive to her ideas.

Early sessions of the Committee produced a loaded agenda including such subjects as sex education, the effects of the cinema, physical recreation, blind children, illegitimacy and family allowances. Under pressure from Committee members each with his or her own special 'cause', the Committee tended to pass resolutions for circulation to governments on the basis of short discussions. Reaction soon set in.

The British Foreign Secretary, Austen Chamberlain, bluntly stated to the LN Council in 1926 that 'child welfare is not primarily a matter for international action, and . . . the purposes which the League can serve in this direction are limited'. He pointedly referred to recreation and sex education as matters that did not call for international regulation. Indeed, he argued that there was 'a danger for the League in thus invading the purely national sphere of its Member States lest those states should be indisposed by the interference and the real purpose of the League be obscured'.[29] It is perhaps worth noting one example of the susceptibilities of governments. The British Council member was much concerned by the appointment in 1925 of feminist and social reformer Eleanor Rathbone as an assessor to the Child Welfare Committee representing the Women's International Organisations. The reason for his consternation is hinted at in correspondence over the matter between the Home Office and the Foreign Office: 'The prospect of having to sit in conference with this lady in the presence of representatives of other States who are always ready to make capital out of our domestic differences is, to put it mildly, disconcerting.'[30] The sensitive nature of the 'non-political' work of the social committees should not be underestimated.

As a result of Chamberlain's comments in 1926, the report of the work of the second session of the Committee was not adopted by the Council. The British stance was particularly criticised because the British had opposed the creation of the IAPCW after the war on the grounds that the international aspects of child welfare should be considered by the LN.[31] The event led to efforts by S. W. Harris to establish more firmly the parameters of the Committee's work. He identified two areas of child welfare work. The first included the properly international aspects, that is, activities in which the action of one country depended either wholly or partially on the steps taken in another. In these (rare) cases, the role of the Committee was to prepare conferences and conventions. The second, wider area, was that primarily of domestic concern. In this area, according to Harris, the Committee could engage in interchange of information and discussion and prepare on a scientific basis specialist reports that would help governments in their own work.[32] Also concerned to improve the functioning of the Committee, Julia Lathrop, an American social worker associated with the Children's Bureau, proposed that a clear statement of its scope, rights and duties be prepared.[33]

Under pressure to define more clearly the actual scope of the Committee, Crowdy resisted both Harris' attempts to limit the work and Lathrop's efforts to keep the Committee's range as wide as possible so as to enable the study of the 'normal' child. While she was sympathetic to Lathrop's concerns, she was afraid that such a statement would prove limiting. Experience with the Committee on Traffic in Women and Children had shown that the Committee was able to broaden the scope of its work to areas of domestic jurisdiction because it had not attempted to stick to a narrow definition of issues. With characteristic optimism, Crowdy countered another of Lathrop's concerns, namely that the 'whole child' had been sacrificed by the Assembly's decision that all labour and health issues concerning children be dealt with by the ILO and LNHO. She argued that the Child Welfare Committee could influence activities in such areas through pressure on the liaison officers from these organisations.[34]

Although Crowdy's failure to discipline the Committee was in part a matter of strategy, there is no doubt that her approach undermined the effectiveness of the Committee's work. The Committee covered a wide range of subjects which, though often interrelated, were not dealt with as a whole. Her approach, however, was perhaps less short-sighted than that of S. W. Harris, whose correspondence with Crowdy over the years shows a strong inclination to attempt to control the direction of the Section's work. In 1930, Harris warned the British Foreign Office of the tendency of women's organisations to regard the Committee 'as a useful vehicle for bringing up questions of special interest to women but not directly connected with Child Welfare'.[35] Harris was unable to position the welfare of the child within the context of broader socio-economic factors affecting women and the family. He shared the Home Office's preoccupation with one aspect of child welfare during this period – juvenile delinquency.[36] By 1930, his relations with Crowdy had completely broken down, and Crowdy's replacement in 1931 by diplomat Eric Estrand was unlikely to have been regretted by Harris.

Despite Crowdy's optimism the Committee found it difficult to move into the constructive side of child welfare. Instead, like the Committee on the Traffic in Women and Children, the Child Welfare Committee continued to focus on problems associated with the rights and protection of vulnerable groups. Through its comparison of child welfare legislation the Committee sought to establish the social and legal rights of the illegitimate child and to improve the legal position of unmarried mothers and their children.[37] Various studies were undertaken concerning guardianship, boarding out (fostering) and juvenile offenders. Funds came from the American Social Hygiene Association for a study on the role of environmental factors in child neglect and juvenile delinquency.[38] This enquiry led to a further study on the organisation of juvenile courts and institutions for erring and delinquent minors.[39] The focus on delinquents and children at risk was in part a continuation of 'childsaving' which had its origins in the moral reform movement of the nineteenth century. The double-edged nature of 'childsaving' has been well documented.[40] While the motivation of the Child Welfare Committee appears to have been a humanitarian concern with ending legal practices that victimised children, the possible influence of the threat to 'the race, law and order' posed by neglected and delinquent children deserves more attention than can be given here.[41]

Through its links with the ILO, and at the instigation of Eleanor Rathbone, the Child Welfare Committee was able to promote investigations into the connection between family allowances and the birth rate, the child mortality rate and the physical and moral well-being of children. The Committee also came out in support of family allowances, both private and state sponsored, as a means of making 'it possible for parents adequately to discharge their responsibilities towards their families'.[42] Women's organisations raised the issue of family desertion and Crowdy urged them to pressure governments for an international convention on maintenance payments.[43] With the aid of the Child Welfare Information Centre set up in the secretariat in 1933, the Committee produced an array of publications surveying comparative legislation concerning child welfare and special studies of topics mentioned above.

One subject not taken up by the social committees, despite efforts on the part of several committee members, was sex education.[44] The American Social Hygiene Association made $5,000 available to the Social Section in 1926 for an investigation on the subject, but the money was later diverted to a study on neglected children.[45] Because sex education was dangerously close to birth control – a forbidden topic at the League on the grounds that it roused national and religious feelings – the Social Section was forced to steer clear of controversy. The League's concern with human rights did not extend to reproductive rights of women to control their own fertility.[46] It is worth noting, however, that Crowdy, in a letter to Margaret Sanger, described herself as 'strongly in favour of the birth control movement'.[47]

In many ways the loaded agenda of the Child Welfare Committee reflected the pronatalist concerns of the period. The preoccupation with producing healthy, well-adjusted citizens rests uneasily alongside the humanitarian concern of alleviating suffering through the protection of human rights. This tension was equally pronounced in the 1930s when the social work of the LN was looked at by governments with a new enthusiasm.

The League's social programmes in the 1930s

It was only in response to the economic depression that, influenced by the unprecedented domestic measures to ameliorate hunger, poor living conditions and other social problems, the League's programmes were recast to deal with broader social welfare concerns. Beginning in 1934, various committees were established by the Council to investigate the structure and efficiency of the League's technical organs, including the social committees.[48] One illustration of the development of a social welfare ethic is the changed attitude of the British government. Whereas Chamberlain had observed in 1926 that child welfare was not primarily a subject for international consideration, in 1935 the British government urged that the work of the Child Welfare Committee should be redefined in such a way as to give more attention to the constructive aspects of child welfare.[49]

In response to growing demands for integrative welfare programmes, a new Advisory Committee on Social Questions replaced the Traffic in Women and Child Welfare Committees in 1936. Provisions were made for more regular collaboration with the ILO and the LNHO. A small sub-committee was formed to deal with the repressive character of the work in connection with the traffic in women, while the broader social aspects were dealt with by the Advisory Committee as a whole. As table 8.1 (p. 156) indicates, the budget of the Social Section grew in the late 1930s. However, apart from 25,000 Swiss francs for a new publication, *Review of Social Questions*, most of the increase was intended to cover the expenses of the bureau investigating the traffic in women in the Far East.

One casualty of the heightened political salience of social questions at the League was the 'assessor'. The new Committee on Social Questions was composed entirely of government representatives (twenty-one in total). This development reflected two dynamics: the gradual shift from voluntaryism to government intervention and the reduced role of lay persons in view of the professionalisation of social work. Given the increased interest of governments in social questions, the representation of lay personnel on the social committees was not always such as to facilitate the most effective intergovernmental action. The women's organisations which had long urged the expansion of the League's social activities were eased out precisely when such a change took place. The new Committee was empowered to nominate experts for the study of specific subjects. Former assessors from the social committees were retained as corresponding members. This enabled the Social Section to keep in touch with voluntary organisations for mobilising public opinion in favour of the League's activities – another indication that voluntary organisations were no longer seen as major players in the social field.

Changing ideas about social welfare were also evident in recommendations made from 1935 onwards by the Fifth Committee of the LN Assembly. The Fifth Committee claimed to be guided in its recommendations by a new awareness among governments 'that social conditions are closely related to economic factors and peace in the political sphere'.[50] The Advisory Committee on Social Questions was advised to take as its focus the needs of the 'normal child'. Possible lines of enquiry suggested were the comparative study of the organisation and conduct of child welfare work with reference to the competence of public authorities and voluntary organisations and to the extension of child welfare work to non-urban populations.

In defining the mandate of the new Advisory Committee on Social Questions the Assembly stipulated that it should be: (1) a centre of international documentation, in order to facilitate the exchange of experiences, methods and results between governments and voluntary organisations; (2) a centre of study which would conduct, direct or simply provoke international or national enquiries on social questions; (3) a centre of action, to organise co-operation between governments, prepare conventions, agreements, international conferences, etc., and establish co-operation between private organisations dealing with international social questions. In addition, the Advisory Committee was advised to 'take into account and follow the new tendencies of social work', including 'the professional character of certain forms of social work' and to consider the work of voluntary organisations 'as a complement to the official social service'.[51]

Given that the Child Welfare Committee had attempted to take a broad view of the term 'child welfare' from the very beginning, it agreed that more attention should be devoted to the study of subjects concerning 'the majority of children', not only needy children.[52] The Committee further noted the 'marked tendency for States to assume even wider and more generalised responsibilities for the health and welfare of the population as a whole' as a result of which '[g]overnments . . . are endeavouring to correlate health, social, economic, and educational services'.[53] In view of such developments, the Committee observed in 1938 that 'all questions of social service, health, labour and economic conditions are closely inter-connected'. It concluded that 'if . . . any real practical and fruitful action is to be undertaken, it is imperative that these questions and the problems they raise should be treated as a whole'.[54] It was recognised that one of the main weaknesses of the Child Welfare Committee had been the weak lines of communication with other League technical committees. Mixed committees on special subjects such as nutrition were thus established comprising members of the ILO, the LNHO and the Advisory Committee on Social Questions. By 1938, the Assembly had mandated the three bodies to develop joint programmes.[55]

A new consensus on the importance of broader social welfare approaches was evident at the LN after 1936 in the range of subjects investigated. In 1937, the mixed committee on the problem of nutrition reported on the assessment of the nutritional state of children, nutritive food requirements during the first year of life, the optimum amounts of milk required at different ages and the social aspects of malnutrition among children both in urban and in rural communities. Similar investigations were being undertaken into the minimum standards of living conditions, wages, occupational safeguards and their links with minimum standards of nutrition. The Social Questions Committee took the view that where income 'falls below reasonable minimum living standards, the problem [of nutrition] becomes one of social assistance'.[56] Similarly, comparative studies on the organisation and administration of welfare work among the young and on the training of social workers pointed to a growing role of social assistance in League member states.[57]

The Committee also continued investigation into many of the subjects on the agenda prior to its reorganisation in 1936. The new role played by social scientists and medical experts was reflected in the character of Committee reports and publications. Whereas earlier reports had stressed the role of voluntary organisations in the prevention of prostitution and rehabilitation of prostitutes, there was an increased commitment to the involvement of government social services. If, as its research seemed to indicate, factors such as education, illegitimacy, employment, and family and living conditions influenced prostitution, wider solutions needed to be found. Included were proposals for the provision of adequate systems of social assistance so that destitute women would not be forced into prostitution for economic reasons. According to the Committee, the aim of social assistance should be to ensure good health, vocational training, employment services, and after-care support. Studies carried out by the Committee in collaboration with medical experts and ILO officials concluded that rehabilitation services depended on the foundation of wider social and health measures. Efforts to combine social assistance with medical treatment for venereal disease were advocated. Other experts, including Dr Tage Kemp, Director of the University Institute for Human Genetics, Copenhagen, advised further research into the possible influence of the mental state of prostitutes, including feeble-mindedness and psychiatric problems.[58] Such suggestions were unlikely to have been welcomed by those who had long seen the Committee as a means of emphasising the economic and social causes of prostitution and its fundamental link to the low status of women.

A similar tendency towards a broad range of approaches was also evident in discussions on illegitimacy. A Committee report on children born out of wedlock raised the issue of the legal rights of the child as well as the mother's right to maintenance, and concluded that social assistance would enable the child to remain with the mother.[59] The stigma attached to unmarried motherhood was somewhat challenged by the growing emphasis on the need to eliminate its perceived causes through the provision of better housing and working conditions, marriage endowments, and family allowances to facilitate early marriage. Continued fears of population decline may also have lessened the marginalisation of unmarried mothers.[60] In a new departure reflecting the collaboration of medical experts, sterilisation of the feeble-minded was also raised as an option to reduce illegitimate births.[61]

A report in 1937 on the causes of juvenile delinquency advocated prevention 'through the development of constructive measures of social protection and the utilisation of all that modern science can offer in understanding the child and the prevention of his delinquency'.[62] Research connected with the child study movement and the child guidance movement introduced new methods to deal with 'problem' children. Developments in the interwar period reflected new alliances between social welfare and developmental psychology.[63] If the main concern of the Committee remained the protection of the rights of marginalised groups of mothers and children, there was evidence of a growing interest in identifying environmental and developmental factors which placed children at risk and undermined normal child development.[64]

It is difficult to balance the evident intergovernmental co-operation with the themes of pronatalism and nationalism implicit in much of the child welfare work that pre-occupied Committee members during the period. 'National efficiency' remained an important theme in the build-up to another world war. Concerns about the physical and emotional health of children were informed partly by governments' perceptions of children as national resources.[65] In the context of the League's work, however, other influences were equally important. The unprecedented participation of women politicians, social workers and feminists on the bodies here considered brought to the fore maternalist and feminist concerns. If their policy demands sometimes co-incided with those of pronatalists as, for example, in the case of family allowances, their major concern was to improve the lives of women and children.[66] At the same time, the participation of delegates from governments and transnational organisations ensured that the committees served to facilitate international co-operation on social issues, thus diffusing the nationalist concerns implicit in some of the topics under discussion. Of the major powers, only the USSR was not at some point represented on the social committees, although from 1935 to 1938 Alexandra Kollantai represented her government on the Fifth Committee (Social Questions) of the LN Assembly.[67]

While providing an intergovernmental forum for discussion and exchange of information, the League made only a limited contribution to policy-making in the social field. For many years it was guided by voluntaryism rather than a professional ethic; this effectively meant that its ability to transform humanitarian concerns into social policy was greatly undermined. As such, it was slow to respond to demands for integrative social welfare programmes. The publication by the League of comparative studies of social legislation and policies adopted by different countries may have provided models for those governments seeking new approaches. However, given its financial and staffing constraints, the Social Section remained unable to provide direct technical assistance to member states. Only in the 1930s, when the economic crisis forced governments into an unprecedented degree of social and economic intervention, did the restructuring of the League's technical organisations provide the institutional framework for the design of health and social welfare programmes to benefit the majority of the population and not only vulnerable or disadvantaged people.

Nonetheless, it was in connection with such vulnerable groups that the work of the League's social committees had a lasting impact. Despite the newly elaborated mandate of the Advisory Committee on Social Questions in the late 1930s and the increasingly expert character of its work, the spirit of the discussions remained guided by the principle of the protection of human rights. The substance of the draft convention on trafficking in women prepared by the Committee in 1937 provided the basis of the Convention for the Suppression of the Traffic in Persons and of the Exploitation of the Prostitution of Others approved by the UN General Assembly in 1949 which remains the principal instrument guiding the work in this field of the UN Commission on Human Rights. The 1949 Convention declared that prostitution and the traffic in persons are 'incompatible with the dignity and worth of the human person and endanger the welfare of the individual, the family and the community'. Embodied in the Convention is a provision by which states 'agree to take or encourage, through their public and private educational, health, social, economic and other related services, measures for the prevention of prostitution and for the rehabilitation and social adjustment of the victims of prostitution'.[68] If the League ultimately did little to combat the economic and social causes of prostitution, it helped to provide a legal framework for the international protection of individuals against exploitation for the purposes of prostitution.

The failure of the League to produce any conventions in the field of child welfare must be linked to the resistance of governments to interference in matters considered to be primarily of domestic concern. Discussion and exchange of information represented the limits of action in this area. The only proposals that emerged for standard setting in the field by way of international conventions concerned the age of consent and marriage and the execution of maintenance orders abroad in cases of family desertion. It is worth noting, however, that the UN Convention on the Rights of the Child (1989), which provides the framework for UNICEF's work, recognises the Geneva Declaration of the Rights of the Child (1924) as its historical antecedent. Similarly, many of the topics treated by the LN social committees including treatment of juvenile offenders, age of consent and marriage, and foster placement have all become subjects of human rights conventions, declarations and recommendations.[69] In summary, the League's activities in the social field, by focusing as they did on human rights and the alleviation of human suffering, provided little in the way of social scientific *solutions* to problems experienced by women and children. The outbreak of the Second World War in 1939 brought a halt to most of the League's activities leaving open to conjecture whether the re-structuring of the social committees would have led to greater international advances in the social field.

Notes

1 Gisela Bock and Pat Thane, *Maternity and Gender Policies. Women and the Rise of the European Welfare States, 1880s–1950s* (London: Routledge, 1991); Theda Skocpol, *Protecting Soldiers and Mothers. The Political Origins of Social Policy in*

the United States (Cambridge, Mass.: Belknap Press, 1992); Valerie Fildes, Lara Marks and Hilary Marland, *Women and Children First. International Maternal and Infant Welfare 1870–1945* (London: Routledge, 1992); and Seth Koven and Sonya Michel, *Mothers of a New World. Maternalist Politics and the Origins of Welfare States* (London: Routledge, 1993).

2 For a discussion of the participation of women in the League secretariat, Assembly delegations and League advisory committees see C. Miller, 'Lobbying the League: Women's International Organizations and the League of Nations', unpub. DPhil thesis, University of Oxford, 1992, and C. Miller, 'Women in International Relations? The Debate in Inter-war Britain', in R. Grant and K. Newland (eds.), *Gender and International Relations* (Milton Keynes: Open University Press, 1991). The committee on the Traffic in Women and Children and the Child Welfare Committee discussed here were grouped together first as the Advisory Commission for the Protection and Welfare of Children and later as the Advisory Committee on Social Questions.

3 The term 'human rights' came into usage at the League only in the late 1930s but a concern with the respect and protection of the inherent dignity and worth of each human being was implicit in its humanitarian work from 1919 onwards. See chapter 10, 'The Contribution of the League of Nations to the Evolution of International Law', in J. G. Starke, *Studies in International Law* (London: Butterworth, 1965); and A. H. Robertson, *Human Rights in the World* (Manchester: University of Manchester Press, 1972).

4 League of Nations Archives (LNA), Geneva, R. Crowdy to Dr Hein, 10 October 1928, S158 Outgoing letters October 1928.

5 Nine governments had representatives on the first Advisory Committee on the Traffic in Women and Children: Denmark, France, Great Britain, Italy, Japan, Poland, Romania, Spain and Uruguay. By 1936 a total of twenty-one governments were represented including the above-mentioned countries and Argentina, Belgium, Canada, Chile, China, Hungary, India, Mexico, Netherlands, Turkey, Switzerland and the USA.

6 Early efforts to draw the US into the League through collaborative work in the social and humanitarian field resulted in the presence of officials from the US Children's Bureau in the capacity of assessors and, later, government delegates, to the social committees. See T. L. Diebel, 'Struggle for Cooperation: The League of Nations Secretariat and Pro-League Internationalism in the United States, 1919–1924', unpublished memoir, Graduate Institute of International Studies, Geneva, 1970.

7 Laura Reanda, 'Prostitution as a Human Rights Question: Problems and Prospects of United Nations Action', in *Human Rights Quarterly*, 13 (1991), esp. 207–9.

8 See Kathleen Barry, *Female Sexual Slavery* (London: New York University Press, 1984), pp. 30–7; Paul Weindling, 'The Politics of International Co-ordination to Combat Sexually Transmitted Diseases, 1900–1980s', in Virginia Berridge and Philip Strong (eds.), *AIDS and Contemporary History* (Cambridge: Cambridge University Press, 1993), pp. 93–107; Edward J. Bristow, *Vice and Vigilance: Purity Movements in Britain Since 1700* (Dublin: Gill and MacMillan, 1977); and Frances Newman and Elizabeth Cohen, 'Historical Perspectives on the Study of Female Prostitution', *International Journal of Women's Studies*, 8, 1 (January–February 1985), 80–5.

9 Minutes of the 25th Annual Meeting of the National Vigilance Association and the International Bureau in *The Vigilance Record*, 10 (November 1921).

10 See Robertson, *Human Rights*, for a description of humanitarian movements concerned with human rights.

11 LNA, Statement by the Women's International Organisations, C.T.F.E./40, 3 July 1921.

12 LNA, 'Proposals Attached to the Letter of Chairman of the Special Body of Experts on Traffic in Women and Children Addressed to Mr. S. W. Harris', 22 February 1927, 12/58966/647 R637; see also Ki-Tcheng, *La femme et la Société des Nations* (Paris: Les Presses Modernes, 1928), p. 36.

13 See LNA, C.T.F.E./195, March 1924; LNA, R. Crowdy to A. Neilans, 1 February 1924, S156 Outgoing letters February 1924; LNA, C.T.F.E./Experts/P.V.2, 1 April 1924; LNA, C.T.F.E./502, 3 March 1931.

14 See LN, Advisory Commission for the Protection and Welfare of Children and Young People, Traffic in Women and Children Committee, Report of Special Body of Experts, Part I (C.52.M52.1927.IV.) and Part II (C.52(2).M.52(1).1927.IV.).

15 LNA, N. Stack to E. Drummond, 19 March 1920 and R. Crowdy, memo to Captain Walters, 1 April 1920, 12/3628/x R636.

16 LNA, R. Crowdy to S. W. Harris, 31 January 1924, S156 Outgoing letters January 1924; LNA, R. Crowdy to Mr. Tufton, Foreign Office, 7 June 1923, S156 Outgoing letters June 1923.

17 Donna J. Guy, *Sex and Danger in Buenos Aires: Prostitution, Family and Nation in Argentina* (Lincoln, Nebr.: University of Nebraska Press, 1991), pp. 96–7. LNA, memo to M. Delevigne, Home Office, 17 July 1919, 12/647/647 R636.

18 LNA, C.T.F.E./351, 30 April 1927, p. 8; LN, Minutes of the Seventh Session of the Traffic in Women and Children Committee, First Meeting, 19 March 1928 (IV.Social.1928.IV.15.), p. 8.

19 LN, Records of the Tenth Ordinary Session of the Assembly, Minutes of the Fifth Committee, Third Meeting, 12 September 1929, *Official Journal Special Supplement* (hereafter cited as *OJSS*), No. 80,.p. 18.

20 In 1937 the LN Assembly voted in favour of an enquiry into the legal status of women. See Carol Miller, '"Geneva – The Key to Equality": Inter-war Feminists and the League of Nations', *Women's History Review*, 3, 2 (1994), 219–45.

21 The Committee was originally conceived as part of the Committee on the Traffic in Women and Children. For an indication of the various transformations of the social committees see E. R. Ranshofen-Wertheimer, *The International Secretariat: A Great Experiment in International Administration* (Washington, DC: Carnegie Endowment for International Peace, 1945).

22 LNA, R. Crowdy to G. Abbott, 16 January 1927, S157 Outgoing letters January 1925. See article by P. Rooke and R. Schnell in this collection.

23 LNA, memo from R. Crowdy to E. Drummond, 14 March 1924, S152 Child Welfare.

24 LNA, C.P.E./131, Child Welfare, Resolutions of the Assembly, the Council and the Child Welfare Committee, 19 December 1927.

25 LNA, C.T.F.E. 273, Draft Report of the Fourth Session, 27 May 1925.

26 Julia Lathrop, 'International Child Welfare Problems', in *Proceedings of the Academy of Political Science*, 12 (June 1931), pp. 418–23.

27 LNA, R. Crowdy to G. Abbott, 16 January 1925, S157 Outgoing letters January 1925.

28 LNA, C.P.E. 9 [June?] 1925.

29 LN, Minutes of the Fortieth Session of the Council, Second Meeting, 9 June 1926, *Official Journal* (hereafter cited as *OJ*), 7th Year, No. 7, July 1926, p. 865.

30 Public Records Office, London (PRO) FO/371/11070, J. Anderson to Sir Eyre A. Crowe, 1 April 1925, 2963/300/98.

31 A flourish of letters emanated from the Social Section as Crowdy tried to change the approach of the British Government and to placate offended parties, in particular American social workers on whom she was depending to push forward the work of the Committee. LNA, R. Crowdy to the Hon. A. Cadogan, 18 August 1926, S157 Outgoing letters 1926. See also S157 Outgoing letters September 1926–December 1926.

32 LNA, C.P.E./88, Memorandum by the British Delegate, 3 March 1927.

33 LNA, R. Crowdy to J. Lathrop, 31 January 1927, S158 Outgoing letters January 1927.

34 LNA, R. Crowdy to J. Lathrop, 31 January 1927, S158 Outgoing letters January 1927.

35 PRO FO/371/14945, Confidential letter from Mr Harris (Home Office) to Mr Cadogan (Foreign Office), 7 May 1930, W5575/9/98.

36 The ideas influencing the Children's Branch of the British Home Office are explored in Harry Hendrick, *Child Welfare: England 1872–1989* (London: Routledge, 1994), pp. 169–86.

37 LN, Study of the Position of the Illegitimate Child (L.o.N.P.1929.IV.5); LN, Official Guardianship of Illegitimate Children (C.265.M.153.1932.IV.); LN, Study on the Legal Position of the Illegitimate Child (C.70.M.24.1939.IV.).

38 LN, Enquiry into the Question of Children in Moral and Social Danger, 2 April 1934 (C.285.M.123.1934.IV.).

39 LN, Organisation of Juvenile Courts and the Results Attained Hitherto (C.975.M.540.1931.IV.); LN, Institutions for Erring and Delinquent Minors (C.I.M.I.1934.IV.).

40 Hendrick, *Child Welfare*.

41 See Cathy Urwin and Elaine Sharland, 'From Bodies to Minds in Childcare Literature', in Roger Cooter (ed.), *In the Name of the Child: Health and Welfare 1880–1940* (London: Routledge, 1992); Theresa Richardson, *The Century of the Child: The Mental Hygiene Movement and Social Policy in the United States and Canada* (New York: State University of New York Press, 1989); and Hendrick, *Child Welfare*.

42 See LNA, C.P.E./150; C.P.E./38, 4 March 1926; and C.P.E./131 19 December 1927, p. 6.

43 Resolutions adopted by the Executive Committee of the International Council of Women, June 1927, No. 24 in LNA 13/56903x/43088 R1022; LNA, R. Crowdy to E. Zimmern, 30 August 1928, S158 Outgoing letters August 1928.

44 LNA, Joint Meeting of the Traffic in Women and Children Committee and the Child Welfare Committee, 19 March 1928, C.T.F.E./7th Session/Mixed, C.P.E./4th Session/P.V.2.

45 LNA, C.P.E./132, Note by the Secretary, 11 January 1928.

46 For a picture of the European context see Felicia Gordon, 'Reproductive Rights: The Early Twentieth Century European Debate', *Gender and History*, 4, 3 (Autumn 1992), 387–99.

47 LNA, R. Crowdy to M. Sanger, 20 October 1925, S157 Outgoing letters October 1925; see also LNA, C.P.E./63 on biological education and Confidential Circular 15, 1927 regarding the position to be adopted by the League on birth control.

48 See Martin David Dubin, 'Toward the Bruce Report: The Economic and Social Programs of the League of Nations in the Avenol Era', in *The League of Nations in Retrospect*, Proceedings of the Symposium organised by the United Nations Library and the Graduate Institute of International Studies, 6–9 November 1980 (Berlin and New York: Walter de Gruyter, 1983), pp. 42–73, for an account of the work of these committees; Elsa Castendyck, 'Social Questions', in *World Organization: a Balance Sheet of the First Great Experiment*, Symposium of the Institute on World Organization (Washington, DC: American Council on Public Affairs, 1942), pp. 112–20.

49 LNA, C.C.F.C.2, Reply from the Government of the United Kingdom to Circular Letter 170.1934, quoted in Dubin, 'Toward the Bruce Report', p. 49.

50 LN, Records of the Seventeenth Ordinary Session of the Assembly, Meeting of the Fifth Committee, Annex 3, *OJ* Special Supplement, no. 160, p. 58.

51 LN, *OJ* Special Supplement, no. 160, pp. 57–9.

52 LN, Advisory Committee on Social Questions, Report on the Work of the Committee in 1937, First Session, 15 May 1937 (C.235.M.169.1937.IV.).

53 LN, Records of the Nineteenth Ordinary Session of the Assembly, Minutes of the Fifth Committee, 1938, *OJ* Special Supplement, no. 188, p. 48.

54 *Ibid.*

55 See Dubin, 'Toward the Bruce Report'.

56 LN, Advisory Committee on Social Questions, Report of the Work of the Committee in 1937, First Session, 15 May 1937 (C.235.M.169.1937.IV.), Part 3: Social Aspects of Health and Nutrition.

57 See LN, Child Welfare Councils (Denmark, Norway, Sweden), (C.8.M.7.1937.IV.).

58 This shift in approach was a result of an investigation into the prevention of prostitution carried out by the Committee with the collaboration of the ILO and two experts – Dr Cavaillon, Technical Inspector-General of the Ministry of Health, France, and Dr T. Kemp, author of *Prostitution: An Investigation of Its Causes, Especially with Regard to Hereditary Factors* (Copenhagen: Levin and Munksgaard, 1936). LN, Advisory Committee on Social Questions, Report of the Work of the Committee in 1938, 6 May 1938 (C.147.M.88.1938.IV.).

59 LN, Advisory Committee on Social Questions, Report of the Work of the Committee in 1938, 6 May 1938 (C.147.M.88.1938.IV.), p. 10.

60 The influence of the decline of the birth rate on the treatment of illegitimate children is hinted at in LNA, C.Q.S./Section Session/P.V.11, 28 April 1938, p. 11.

61 LN, Advisory Committee on Social Questions, Report on the Work of the Committee in 1939, Third Session, 15 July 1939 (C.214.M.142.1939.IV.), pp. 13–14.

62 LN, Advisory Committee on Social Questions, Report on the Work of the Committee in 1937, First Session, 15 May 1937 (C.235.M.169.1937.IV.); LN,

Principles Applicable to the Functioning of Juvenile Courts and Similar Bodies, Auxiliary Services and Institutions (C.375.M.252.1937.IV.).

63 See Urwin and Sharland, 'From Bodies to Minds'; Richardson, *The Century of the Child*; and Hendrick, *Child Welfare*.

64 See LN, Enquiry into the Question of Children in Moral and Social Danger, 2 April 1934 (C.285.M.123.1934.IV.). This document summarises the main trends in child protection in Germany, Italy, France, England, Canada and the USA, including a discussion of the impact of the child guidance movement.

65 See Urwin and Sharland, 'From Bodies to Minds' and Hendrick, *Child Welfare*, 'Part III. Minds and Bodies: Contradiction, Tension and Integration, 1918–45', pp. 131–210.

66 This tension between feminism and pronatalism is examined in Sondra R. Herman, 'Dialogue: Children, Feminism, and Power: Alva Myrdal and Swedish Reform, 1929–1956', *Journal of Women's History*, 4, 2 (Fall 1992), pp. 82–112.

67 While this deserves further investigation, evidence suggests that it may have been a result of the reluctance of the USSR to participate in the League's 'palliative' social efforts. K. W. Davis, 'The Soviet Union and the League of Nations, 1919–1933', *Geneva Special Studies*, 5, 1 (1934).

68 Centre for Human Rights, *Human Rights: A Compilation of International Instruments* (New York: United Nations, 1988), pp. 181–9; Reanda, 'Prostitution as a Human Rights Question", p. 209.

69 Centre for Human Rights, *Human Rights*.

9

'Uncramping child life': international children's organisations, 1914–1939

PATRICIA T. ROOKE AND RUDY L. SCHNELL

The normal child is the most valuable member of the community, and whereas welfare work flourishes in most countries, and has everywhere aroused popular imagination and generosity, there remain the great questions of education and training, mental and moral, of the young . . . We want to protect and develop the normal child as well as the abnormal, weakly, or poverty stricken . . . We may point out that many women's organizations considered and passed in 1922 a children's charter setting forth the right of every child to have opportunities of full development. (*The Times*, 5 February 1925)

Developing a discourse

The present preoccupation with child abuse and the discussion on the best means of protecting child life merely elaborate a rhetoric whose antecedents are in the nineteenth-century child-saving movement which flourished in industrialised nations. A study of international child protection organisations illustrates the continuity of such rhetoric which moved from a sentimental depiction of victims to a medico-social scientific discourse of children at risk that expanded the concepts of victimisation, exploitation and abuse.

It is through discourse that social claims become persuasively defined and social conditions are identified and transformed into social problems whose advocates lobby for recognition of the priority of their claims.[1] Discourse can be taken to mean:

a public discussion that is neither independent of, nor strictly determined by, the sociocultural and political setting in which it takes place, and that is primarily among but not limited to a definable group of activists who agree that a certain condition represents a problem, share a general conception of its nature, are committed to its remedy and are actively engaged, through research, argument, experimentation, and the implementation of policies and programs in defining its general and particular cases and in promoting and initiating general and specific courses of remedial action.[2]

176

Discourse, in this sense, is central to the claims that were made by inter-national child-protection organisations such as the International Association for the Promotion of Child Welfare (IAPCW), the Save the Children International Union (SCIU), and to a lesser extent the League of Red Cross Societies (LRCS). The League of Nations Child Welfare Committee and the Traffic in Women and Children Committee brought together representatives of states and international voluntary associations. These child-protection organisations did not pioneer the new analyses which emerged in the 1920s and 1930s in the international arena but rather incorporated an established, ongoing wave of child reform activism which had transformed public understanding of social problems with regard to child and family life. In short, they provide us with interesting sites of contestation and arenas of discourse in which layers of ideological practices in child protection met.

At the League committees and in the forums of the other international bodies, different generations of social reformers worked side by side to establish emerging frames of reference based on progressive social philosophies and centralist planned social organisation. Subsequently a dominant discourse replacing the former rhetoric was articulated by the latest wave of social reformers, a core of professionals who were convinced that state intervention was necessary to replace unsophisticated forms of co-ordinated services or discrete charitable efforts.

The three decades prior to 1914 saw the culmination of the nineteenth-century campaigns to rescue dependent, neglected and delinquent children. What had started as largely religiously inspired efforts to remove children from dangerous conditions slowly transformed into a social movement for children that would burst the limits commonly associated with child saving. Early attempts to define a role for the state are seen in the British Children Act of 1908 and the first White House Conference of 1909 in the United States. In the latter case the Conference, unable to reconcile different viewpoints, had called for both a federal initiative in the form of a Children's Bureau and a national voluntary organisation, what was to be the Child Welfare League of America, to complement any federal agency.[3]

The emerging discourse represented in these examples depicted a new type of child; indeed the ideology of childhood itself. The old typification argued for protection on the assumption of the 'abnormal child' – such casualties of urban industrial society as the abandoned, dependent and delinquent, or such products of social dislocation as the orphaned or refugee. This typification reinforced a social class analysis that, while no longer claiming that the poor were 'the dangerous and perishing classes', nevertheless saw dependence as a form of dysfunctionality. Operating under this typification organisations such as the Red Cross and the Save the Children Fund (SCF) provided relief for extreme cases of 'abnormal' child life whereas earlier, at least by the First World War, the

IAPCW was arguing for a new typification of child welfare which required a broader definition. The belief behind this new typification was that the children of the middle classes and of the stable working classes were the foundation of the well-being of the State.

Former child-saving practices were transformed by concepts concerning the 'normal child'. In turn programmes for the normal child were shaped by progressive terminologies constructed around a more expansive and inclusive concept – 'the whole child' – which encompassed ideas of 'process', 'growth' and 'development'. Thus the theories of medicos and psychologists in the Child Development Movement and those of pedagogues and practitioners of the New Education Movement were appropriated by the growing corps of social workers who legitimated their claims to domain expansion through 'professional' personae.

International initiatives during the interwar years are best understood in the context of such a discourse in which national voluntary and public organisations operated. In principle, organised concern for child life divided into (1) saving children by either removing them from inadequate guardianship or shoring up the family unit; and (2) preventing infant mortality by the provision of scientific health care and the education of mothers in the practice of maternal and child hygiene. Consequently infant mortality and childhood morbidity were increasingly the domain of medical practitioners who by the early twentieth century could claim substantial victories over major diseases. The medical side of child saving would in general move from success to success and consequently any campaign that identified itself with medical expertise received a respectful hearing.[4]

The issue of infant mortality was part of the larger public health campaigns to control or prevent the epidemics which occurred regularly throughout the world. The growing success of medical research in identifying the causes of illnesses and in providing reliable measures of prevention, if not treatment, promised that many of the diseases threatening pre-school children could be controlled. We have already noted that medical practitioners soon asserted that expertise in advising parents – and particularly mothers – as to the proper sanitary and hygiene precautions necessary for healthy child life. Leading advocates of infant and maternal hygiene shaped that message to fit the social classes being instructed. Moreover, governments frequently separated their propaganda along class lines. In France, for example, with its concern with a low fertility rate, the attempt to conserve infant life recognised that for working-class mothers material assistance in all its forms was needed to ensure proper care, while in middle-class homes advice about improved mothering was essential.[5]

Non-medical child saving gradually developed sophisticated methods of case work and expanded its domain under the impetus of charity organisation to include family welfare, community organisation and the administration and co-ordination of social services. Much of the contestation among children's advocates turned on the scientific nature of the claims or on efforts to convert child welfare into a social utility similar in scope to public schooling. In the 1920s a third contender for the ownership of ideas appeared in the child-development movement which was heavily underwritten by major foundations in the United States. The Laura Spelman Rockefeller Memorial established university-based child research centres and supplied the academic infrastructure for a new specialty; and the Commonwealth Fund helped create another complementary specialisation, child guidance. Both child-development and guidance experts took the normal middle-class child as the standard for comparing individual development and social adjustment.[6]

The theme of the normal child runs through the interwar discourse of the children's organisations; however, as either slogan or concept, its meaning varied significantly. The most comprehensive statement came from the exponents of progressive child welfare in the United States who envisioned a social utility serving all children. Grace Abbott, second chief of the Children's Bureau, was a recognised spokesperson for such views as is demonstrated in her invitation to be Rapporteur-Général at the International Congress of Childhood, Paris, 1924, for the session, 'The Guiding Principles of Social Service in Child Welfare Work'. This conference had been called by the LRCS, the SCIU, the International Union for Infant Welfare, and the IAPCW. Later Abbott succinctly described the institutional expression of progressive child welfare in 1932, when she said that the Children's Bureau:

> was to serve and correlate the experiences of all the agencies interested in some special aspect of children and child life. The bureau was to be a research organization, and the whole child was to be the subject of its study . . . Pediatricians, lawyers, statisticians, psychiatrists, and psychologists, as well as specialists in social research and social work for children, were to work together on studies of the individual child and in evaluation of community provision for children or community neglect of children.[7]

According to this view, child welfare was a comprehensive co-ordinated set of services directed by a central agency that was concerned with the whole child and every child and not any one particular speciality. It was a model either admired or emulated by international child welfare bodies.[8] For example, the League of Red Cross Societies praised the United States Children's Bureau's (USCB) innovation: a heated mobile child welfare centre for rural communities staffed by a female physician, a public health nurse, and an advice agent.[9] At the same time the Red Cross unfailingly admired and advertised the USCB's infant mortality work and agreed with its first chief, Julia Lathrop, that a solution to infant deaths would be the 'best and most valuable indication which we possess for determining the material and moral condition of a nation'. As early as 1921 the LRCS *Bulletin* asserted that the USCB was a 'model' for other government agencies and when Grace Abbott took over as chief the *Bulletin* enthused about her youth, training and expertise.[10] Although a national agency, the USCB provided the LRCS with a successful example by which to describe objectives which were implemented through funded research, pilot projects, co-ordination of government agencies, protective services, university course work, medical input, and professional training. The LRCS, however, could not replicate such a model because of its limited carrying capacity for the number of social problems it could handle at any one time.

Respect for training and expertise based on scientific models motivated the Red Cross to be more supportive of the USCB than, say, the SCIU whose methods – it believed – reflected the more traditional approaches to child protection. For much the same reasons the Red Cross closely followed the proceedings of the Pan-American Conferences on Child Welfare.

When it came to emergency relief the Red Cross, and all similar international bodies such as the Save the Children Fund, resorted to the rhetoric of the old typification using stock forms of sensationalism, for example, the anti-typhus campaigns in Poland and Eastern Europe or the colonies of Russian children abandoned in Siberia who required family reunion. The Red Cross was as adept at publicising its work as the commercial press – through the use of headlines such as 'APPALLING PLIGHT OF 5 MILLION EUROPEAN CHILDREN' in 'deadly peril of disease', little babies 'racked by famine', and 'heart rending scenes of dying infants'. Its encouragement by the use of photographic footage of the 'adoption' of babies supported in their families or institutions at a cost of two shillings a week was compelling.[11]

Nonetheless the LRCS tended towards the new typifications of *child welfare* promotion as can be seen as the opening session of its 1919 Cannes conference when Henry P. Davison, Chairman of the War Council of the American Red Cross (ARC), said, 'We wish to throw the light of science upon every corner of the world. *We want you to know about child welfare.*' Consequently in this spirit a resolution was passed 'that the promotion of a wide development of child welfare work be selected as the first important constructive [peacetime] activity'.[12] This particular thrust was in keeping with the Red Cross' commitment to a scientific 'universal health campaign', out of which developed a department of child welfare.[13] From the Cannes conference to the 1924 meeting of the General Council of the LRCS Secretariat in Geneva this interest is evident. Infant mortality, scientific feeding, tuberculosis and the education of women (particularly the dangers of artificial feeding, wetnursing and infant hygiene) filled the records of the LRCS from its foundation in 1920. Its underlying principle was that there should be added to the national Red Cross' '*temporary* and *remedial* activities a *permanent* mission of prevention of which child welfare was to play an integral part'.[14]

Collecting statistical information about infant mortality, linking the nursing section with the dissemination of popular propaganda (especially the public health visitor with women's work programmes), became a major preoccupation. Maternal and child welfare were seen to be part of an organic whole in keeping with progressive views of social organisation with child welfare 'the principal regeneration of the race'.[15] By claiming a 'fifty percent wastage of human life among various European nations' the *Bulletin* explicitly connected artificial feeding to natural selection, economic waste and a decline in productivity.[16] Consequently *mothers* were to assume the awesome burden of 'safeguarding the race', because it was believed that women were 'easier to convince' than men in these matters.[17] Campaigns to educate women promoted the cinema as didactic entertainment just as baby exhibitions were popularised.[18]

This eugenic thrust was disclosed as early as 1920 by Dr Leonard Findlay, chief of the Child Welfare Department, when he observed that Rousseau had been among the first seriously to consider 'puericulture' in the eighteenth century; however, this social issue had broadened in the twentieth century to incorporate 'the subject of eugenics'. Therefore a consideration of the mother before and after confinement, social hygiene, home visiting, consultation centres, crèches and day nurseries, as well as universal health programmes for mothers and children, became imperative.[19] While targeting of women and mothers was scarcely a new strategy, the 1920s saw an extension of its importance by couching it in pseudo-scientific and eugenic theory.[20] The Junior Red Cross may have adopted an apparently innocuous motto – 'Happy Childhood the World Over' – but its international parent maintained an ideology of much sterner stuff.[21]

The ARC had conducted successful courses on puericulture for the medical staff in Lyons, in March 1918, by providing four months of practical training. As breastfeeding was seen as the only 'true remedy' for decreasing infant mortality the Red Cross promoted the Strauss Law – payments by an infant welfare visitor to mothers before and after confinement to encourage breast feeding.[22] Nonetheless the eugenic assumption was bolstered by other considerations because, as Julia Lathrop observed in 1921, child welfare was above all 'an economic problem'.[23]

Thus we see in the LRCS within a brief temporal space the evolution from one typification of child protection as a social problem to the legitimation of another kind of discourse. By comparing the language of the original LRCS campaigns after the war and the language that followed we see a radical move from sentiment to science. The LRCS did not stand alone in this embrace of the new typification and scientific discourse, as the SCF serves to remind us of the universalisation of these new child-protection criteria. Moreover a rivalry between the Child Welfare Department and the SCIU over claims to the international work of child protection reflects a radical new site of contestation over ideas and practices.

Indeed the early history of the SCIU proved to be a chequered one because of this rivalry. The work of the LRCS with relief and children frequently overlapped despite the different images they projected. The style adopted by the Red Cross was scientific and medical, whereas Eglantyne Jebb admitted that it was in the SCIU's appeal to emotion that an outpouring of sentiment and monies occurred. The tensions between these two popular organisations were exacerbated because the SCIU simultaneously enjoyed patronage from the International Committee of the Red Cross. The tension was already apparent by its second Congress in 1924. Indeed, the 'continual bickering' between them intensified the SCIU's perception that the LRCS was an empire-builder monopolised by unsympathetic medicos and in 1921 its director Donald Brown agreed. He remarked that 'the League of Red Cross Societies was in a position to undertake the building up of a large organization and was not willing to waive its rights to be the co-ordinating authority of international relief'.[24]

The Save the Children Fund/Save the Children International Union

The SCF was launched at a public meeting in May 1919 with the objective of raising funds for the relief of distress among children and their families in postwar Europe. Immensely successful in raising funds during its first years, the SCF supported institutions mainly in Vienna and Budapest, but also in other parts of Austria and Hungary as well as in Germany, France and Serbia.

The principal force behind the SCF was Eglantyne Jebb (1876–1928), who with her sister Dorothy Buxton (1881–1962) founded the agency. Jebb exhibited throughout her brief career a potent mixture of child-saving enthusiasm and commitment to scientific child welfare. Although Edward Fuller quotes Jebb to the effect that 'the new charity . . . must have the same clear conception of its objects and seek to compass them with the same care, the same intelligence as is to be found in the best commercial and industrial enterprises',[25] what distinguished Jebb was a powerful grasp of the ideals that undergird her practical work. One of her basic ideas was the need for international co-operation which she saw expressed in the SCIU. Both the SCF and the SCIU were 'to undertake child rescue and to promote child welfare, and to provide an organization by which the best technical means can be made universally available for the purpose of raising the standard of child care and protection throughout the world'.[26]

Additionally the SCF promoted the establishment of national SCF societies around the world which would advance the cause of children without regard to race, nationality or creed. In keeping with its origins, the SCF quickly became noted for its work with refugee and famine crises, for example, feeding centres in Russia in 1921–2 and in Greece in 1923–4 and the settlement of refugees in Bulgaria and Albania in the 1920s.

However, Jebb's interest in child life extended beyond relief work and practical development. She encouraged the SCF to undertake the study of child welfare around the world with the aim of influencing individuals and governments to promote scientific child welfare. The SCF's magazine, *The World's Children*, under the editorship of Edward Fuller, carried many articles on topics relating to child welfare. Holding transnational views of human society, which were embodied in the International Committee of the Red Cross, she thought its 'founders were the first people in history to base an organisation on the axiom that in relief of suffering neither national nor political distinctions are to be taken into account'.[27]

In October 1920, the Council of the SCF approved a constitution that was to make clearer the competence of the Fund, that is, '(1) to put a certain proportion of the international work on a more constructive basis and (2) to help British Children in time of need . . . [by working] through existing societies'.[28] Despite the establishment of the SCIU, the SCF continued its international work. Not surprisingly it did not readily give up prior claims to the international social problems marketplace. In theory the Geneva bureau and the various national committees, including the SCF, were to have distinctive functions, that is, propaganda and practical work, respectively. Nevertheless, the SCIU Executive wanted to do the first piece of practical work 'in order to emphasize the international character of the undertaking'.[29]

The feast day of the Holy Innocents, 28 December 1920, was a red-letter day for the SCIU. At an audience with Pope Benedict XV it was agreed that a special collection would support the Fund's relief work. Forty countries complied following the encyclical letter on 'behalf of the Suffering and Starving Children' wherein it was emphasised: 'In this matter we cannot desist from offering a public tribute of praise to the society entitled SCF which has exerted all possible care and diligence in the collection of money, clothing and food.'[30] Such patronage placed an indelible seal of approval on an organisation which, second only to that of the Red Cross, had already captured the imaginations of child savers and philanthropists worldwide.

Jebb was among the architects behind the formulation of a Children's Charter beginning in 1922. Working on two fronts as it were – with the SCF Council in London and the SCIU Office in Geneva – she proposed three separate documents: (1) a declaration of rights; (2) a legislative code to be embodied in a future Convention from Geneva; and (3) a charter summing up the work to be done for children both by private organisations and the State. The Council considered a draft children's charter at a special meeting in January 1923. Although two members objected both to the consideration of the draft and to specific items in it, the Council justified its action on the grounds that the charter would help 'to establish a minimum standard of child well-being throughout the world'.[31]

The Declaration of the Rights of the Child as approved by the Fifth General Council of the SCIU and then by the Fifth Assembly of the League of Nations (LN) in 1924 was a much briefer document than that originally proposed by the SCF or by Lady Aberdeen's International Council of Women in 1922. Touted by the President of the Assembly as 'the Charter of Child Welfare of the League of Nations', the five articles of the Declaration of Geneva were divided between concerns for *normal* development and for children in need of special care, that is, the hungry, ill, backward, delinquent, dependent or those in distress.

Although going beyond old child-saving concepts in its emphasis on the normal child, it still fell short of the view of North American child welfare espoused by Grace Abbott and the Canadian Charlotte Whitton at the LN in the interwar years, which promoted child welfare as a set of social services, paralleling public education, which would have as their object the whole child and every child.[32] In brief, scientific child welfare was to 'uncramp child life', not just to ensure normal development, as Jebb advocated, by fostering the fullest intellectual, moral, emotional and physical development of the 'whole child'. Although neither Jebb and the SCF nor the International Council of Women shared quite this expansive view of child welfare, the North American philosophy suggested that the Declaration of Geneva was formulated to encourage states to undertake constructive as well as remedial work on behalf of all children.[33]

A special sub-committee was appointed to consider the SCF's relationship with the SCIU in light of the LN Assembly's action in adopting the Declaration. It argued that the SCIU's sponsorship of the Charter obliged it to further the principles of the Charter. However because of the inclusiveness of the Declaration, the sub-committee recommended that the SCIU focus on the issues of child labour; the protection of infant life; alien, deserted and delinquent children; and education. The SCIU was to continue its practical or relief work to encourage national societies in developed countries to assist less developed countries to adopt higher standards. Next, the sub-committee recommended that the SCIU become a major centre for documentation and publishing by merging *The World's Children* and the SCIU's publications and by transferring some of the SCF's administrative expenses to Geneva.

Despite accepting the report in principle the Council was reluctant either to shift its overseas relief to Geneva or to transfer its major publishing efforts to the SCIU. Moreover an Italian proposal to establish a society under the aegis of the LN to raise relief funds to be administered by the Red Cross was seen as a threat to the SCF's role as the major European society dedicated to large-scale relief work. The scope of the sub-committee report and the limited practical considerations discussed indicated that the SCF was not ready to transfer its international work to the SCIU even while Eglantyne Jebb played a leading role in the work at Geneva. This tension was compounded by those competing interests all claiming ownership over the child-protection domain: the national SCF branches (especially the British) and the international arm; the SCIU and the IAPCW; and all groups which felt under siege as the League of Nations took up claims to child protection.

Discussions with leading representatives of the SCIU regarding the possibility of transferring field work and publications to Geneva resulted in another agreement in principle for better co-ordination of common work, for example, management of relief work, propaganda and fund-raising, and publications, should be pursued.[34]

Because Jebb sat as a representative of the SCIU on the Child Welfare Committee of the LN, the relationship between the League and the SCIU was a concern to the SCF. Jebb judged the Committee's 1926 programme to be 'much overcharged' and that the Fifth Committee's report was 'so worded that it could be made to cover any subject which anyone might wish to bring *forward*'. She also identified as 'practical work' all international conventions and matters that might be the subject of national legislation.[35] Working tirelessly as an assessor in the 1920s, Jebb was replaced by Dr Wilhelm Polligkeit who took over the SCIU at her death in 1928. The SCIU's publication, *Revue Internationale*, regularly reported the work of the League committee, paying particular attention to the repatriation of, and relief for, alien and blind children. In one instance the SCIU provided the Child Welfare Committee with comparative data, believing that such a practical gesture ultimately rendered 'more useful service than by the occasional relief'. It provided similar data to the Health Organisation and ILO; for example, details about the Pirquet System of 'scientifically based feeding' which recommended 666 calories a day and a balanced diet of proteid calories, fat and carbohydrates for refugee children. By May 1927 the *Revue Internationale* commented enthusiastically on the *scientific* research into child life:

> It will be of little value for the League to undertake investigations and to accumulate information if the results obtained are to remain of mere academic interest. The scientific collection of data is the only possible basis for a scientific world policy of child saving.[36]

Jebb saw the SCIU as fulfilling several functions at the League of Nations. First, it represented the interests of poorer and less developed countries. Secondly, it could supply information based on its field work and affiliated societies to the Social Section. Thirdly, it could follow up the work of the Advisory Commission by establishing its own parallel committees, for example, one on education in relation to employment that would meet with representatives of the Child Welfare Committee and the International Labour Office. Finally, the SCIU could publicise the work of the Advisory Commission.[37]

By 1926 Jebb was proposing a SCIU-sponsored conference on children of non-European races. As early as November 1926, a preparatory meeting in Geneva began the work for the conference which would include such topics as infant mortality, child marriage, and child labour in relation to education.[38] European missionary societies figured prominently, American organisations were solicited, and a questionnaire was completed and vetted by the ILO.[39]

Although the theme of the conference was limited to African Children, the SCF meeting of experts was closely involved in steps leading to its convening. The International Conference on African Children held in June 1931 was the first world meeting to focus its attention on children of the developing world. The Conference conferred future work on the SCIU, which subsequently considered four lines of action: (1) documentation, (2) propaganda, (3) practical work in Africa and (4) organisation of regional, national and international conferences. Practical work was ruled out because of the expense.[40]

Inspired by the Conference, the SCF established a child-protection committee which would study such issues as infant mortality, child labour and education, and child slavery. The committee's formation was also stimulated by the requests from John Harris of the Anti-Slavery and Aborigines Protective Society that the SCIU prepare a memorandum on the effects of slavery on children for submission to the Temporary Slavery Expert Committee of the LN. The Mandates Commission was also involved.[41] The Child Protection Committee suggested the formation of an African committee composed of the organising committee of the 1931 Conference and representatives of the SCIU for the purpose of setting up an African Bureau, which would further the work of the 1931 conference.[42] The long-term goal was the creation of the Eglantyne Jebb Office which would eventually take over the work of the Africa Committee. In the meantime the Committee might be a means of arousing interest in and securing financial support for the SCIU from America and other sources. Earlier the Child Protection Committee argued that no further activities should be undertaken until the African work was further advanced; however the Africa committee would keep an eye on conditions of children in other countries, with a view to forming panels of advisors later.[43]

In November 1933, the SCF Council adopted a resolution deploring the failure of governments – in the face of economic distress and nationalism – to undertake disarmament. It claimed that there were 'no better means of securing and preserving civilization than by safeguarding the rights and interests of children and teaching them to be lovers of peace and brotherhood and good citizens not only of their own country but also of the world'. Two years later Geneva hosted a World Youth Congress which propagated similar ideas about peace. To further their peace work, the Council pledged to undertake a campaign in 'the form of meetings, . . . press publicity, the education of children in ideas of international understanding, the encouragement of correspondence and contact between them and the children of other lands and any other measures likely to promote the ends in view'. Later the Council would justify what it termed political action, for example, the Westminster enquiry into child life, the Conference on African Children, the Unemployment Enquiry, agitation in favour of school meals, and issues of medical and child welfare work in Grenada, Sierra Leone, etc., on the grounds that they were appropriate for the times.[44]

During the 1930s the Child Protection Committee struggled to define its purpose and scope and to work out how best to keep abreast with the new discourse that underplayed family welfare. In 1937 when broaching this issue it decided to limit its work 'to children up to the beginning of adolescence as recognized by the country concerned' as a first step. In a formal statement of its revised policy the Child Protection Committee acknowledged that its purpose was not only to continue the research and propaganda of the Conference on African children but to help carry forward the last wishes of Eglantyne Jebb to further the interests of non-European children. It also recognised that the initial concern for the care of young children and of expectant and nursing mothers was too narrow and that the principles of the Declaration of Geneva should guide its work. In brief, the scope of the Committee should include 'All things closely related to the "normal development" of children of non-European race, and their preparation for life.' As understood by the Committee, such an approach included the following topics: health, education and training, employment and family life. The Committee would undertake research and propaganda, make representations to governments and co-operate with other organisations having similar aims. The new typification – that of the normal child and the whole child – had won the day. A paper by Edward Fuller praising the USCB reveals this enthusiasm for progressive and scientific methods.[45]

Although the Second World War put an end to the SCF's work outside Great Britain it began to plan for post-war reconstruction. In April 1942 at an Inter-Allied Conference in London, the National Council of Women and the SCF agreed to revise the Children's Charter. Using the Declaration of Geneva as the preamble, the Charter would be brought into line with contemporary needs so that it might 'serve as a guide to child-welfare work in Great Britain after the war'.[46] A redefinition of the activities of the SCF and Red Cross was published in a survey, *Children in Bondage: A Survey of Child Life in the Occupied Countries of Europe and in Finland*, in 1942.

In summary the combined efforts of the SCF and the SCIU reflected during her life and into the next decades Jebb's commitment to two projects: the Declaration of the Rights of the Child which would be adopted by the League of Nations in 1924, thereby setting the precedent for United Nations action in the form of the Declaration of the Rights of the Child in 1959 and of the Convention on the Rights of the Child in 1989; and the Conference on African Children that would be held in June 1931. In this initiative Eglantyne Jebb demonstrated the peculiar mixture of practical work and constructive programmes that would advance the interests and needs of children in what is now called the developing world. She also exhibited a commitment to pragmatic adoption of the new social scientific methods.

Apart from the sequence of events and contributions that make up the combined efforts of the SCF and SCIU, the latter body constitutes a dynamic case study of the evolving discourse that adapted to concepts of the normal child and the whole child in the 1920s and 1930s. At the same time as the LN committee was engaging in questions of scientific research and social-work training the SCIU was also moving towards the new typifications of social problem discourse by emphasising professional expertise. Not that this is coincidental given that international conferences on child welfare throughout the 1920s and 1930s uniformly revolved around such concerns. The professionally identified corps of child-care workers and social-policy planners that emerged during these years eagerly transmitted 'progressive' theories and social science methods while frequently aligning these arguments to state-supported family welfare and education. Such broader social philosophies effectively subverted a 'band-aid' approach to relief which the SCIU appeared to represent but which in reality it no longer represented, indeed had only briefly represented.

A study of the SCIU reveals its commitment to a progressive philosophy that saw 'life as a continuous process ever seeking to develop and express itself more fully'. By the 1930s it had become an apparatus that fully incorporated what it had only discussed a decade before, namely:

> Child welfare has grown to be a science and an art whose work is to see that this life cycle is carried on under the best possible conditions and not damaged through carelessness or ignorance. The various' phases of the cycle are cared for in different forms of child welfare.[47]

Under the broader umbrella of the child-study movement which articulated the concept of the normal child an even more expansive concept had evolved – that of *the whole child* – whose language included terms such as 'life-cycle' and all aspects of development – physical, psychological, educational, recreational, spiritual – from the prenatal to the adolescent. Thus child-welfare advocacy adopted slogans such as 'rejuvenating life cycle' which led to further growth and according to the progressive philosophy espoused by the chief of child welfare in the LRCS expanded 'to overcome the adverse elements in an ever-changing environment'.[48]

The SCIU accepted the broadening of its scope at the same time as it pursued its traditional interest – that of 'simple relief work' in times of distress. However, by the 1930s progressive philosophies and educational programmes pervaded child welfare, including that of relief organisations such as the SCIU, whose willingness to adopt them was evident at its 1921 conference.

> In times when the acute need for relief work does not exist, educational child welfare can be found substantially to reduce the amount of relief required, as need frequently arises from ignorance and abuse rather than from actual want.[49]

The proceedings of this Congress included an optimistic belief in the power of education. Indeed in some quarters education as a 'panacea' had held a sway over professional child welfare groups much earlier. Such beliefs were reinforced by the attendance of child-welfare interest groups at the International League for New Education conferences. In 1927 over 1,200 delegates from fifty countries and governments – many of whom were child welfare advocates – met in Locarno, including members of the SCIU who organised educational sessions there as they had previously in Calais in 1921, Territet in 1923, and Heidelberg in 1925.[50]

International Association for the Promotion of Child Welfare

The origins of the IAPCW in the European conferences on aftercare and the international conferences on infant hygiene linked it to the two major concerns of late nineteenth-century child saving: the care of dependent, neglected and delinquent children and the prevention of infant mortality. In that sense, within the developing child-welfare discourse of the interwar years, the IAPCW was ambiguously located.

If nineteenth-century child saving's major concern had been the care and rehabilitation of the dependent, neglected and delinquent, the fundamental assumptions shaping its rhetoric and practice were: first, that the chief cause of wayward youth and all its social consequences was the lack of adequate guardianship; and secondly, that the line separating adequate and inadequate guardianship was the one which separated the poor from the rest of society.

The three decades prior to the First World War were marked by growing international concern for the well-being of infants and children, expressed in numerous congresses, beginning in Paris (1883) and culminating in Brussels (1913). Although much of this work was limited in scope, focusing, for example, on infant mortality, and offered little in on-going activities, its episodic and uncoordinated character was not out of keeping with the slow development of national policies and programmes.[51] Nevertheless, there was a general convergence of interests in child life in 1913 when the International Congress for the Promotion of Child Welfare approved a resolution calling for an International Office to be set up in Brussels. Although the war put all initiatives on hold, the Belgian government had been authorised to establish an international centre for child welfare.[52]

At this point it is necessary to take a cursory look at the links between the IAPCW and the LN. The founding of the League in 1919 promised greater co-ordination of social and health initiatives internationally. Article 23 of the League Covenant committed certain concerns covered by international agreements to League supervision: clause (a) 'fair and humane conditions of labour for men, women, and children'; clause (b) 'matters of international concern for the prevention and control of disease'; and clause (c) 'the general supervision over the execution of agreements with respect to the traffic in women and children, and the traffic in opium and other dangerous drugs'.[53] Duties under 23(a) were assigned to the International Labour Organisation; while responsibilities under (b) and (c) were incorporated into the League secretariat as the Health and Social Questions Section, which was reconstituted in 1922 as the Social Questions Section with the establishment of the permanent Health Organisation.

In 1921, an LN-sponsored international conference on the Traffic in Women and Children called upon the League to appoint an international standing committee to advise the Council on all matters relating to this problem. The Advisory Committee on the Traffic in Women and Children would consist of nine delegates or representatives of states (members) and five assessors (experts) drawn from international organisations concerned with the suppression of the traffic. It was to become part of the Social Section.[54]

Child welfare, apart from protecting children from exploitation in the form of slavery, child labour, or prostitution, was clearly not understood to be a proper concern of the LN; however, the efforts of the Government of Belgium to realise the 1913 promise of an international child-life office in Brussels in the form of the IAPCW eventually forced child welfare on to the agenda of the League. Immediately the Belgian proposal for an International Association which would hold regular congresses, publish a journal of international child-welfare activities and maintain an International Office in Brussels, met British opposition both in the Foreign and Home Offices and in the new Ministry of Health. At first the British government refused to participate in the 1921 Congress on the grounds that it was not international in character and that, in any case, 'future international congresses on this and other health matters should presumably be organised or at any rate supported by the League of Nations'. Nonetheless, the Home Office and the Ministry of Health sent delegates to the Congress to express British opposition to the creation of the IAPCW and the International Office on the grounds that 'the establishment of a new International Association and Bureau independent of the League to deal with the protection of childhood appears to involve a breach of the spirit, if not the letter of Article 24'.[55]

Despite British opposition, the Belgians pushed ahead with plans for an International Office which would 'serve to stimulate and co-ordinate different lines of study, to test by statistics and carefully verified experiments the progress of various methods, to bring to the knowledge of all the efforts made by all, and thus converge them to a focus'.[56] The Belgian Government's request for American participation in the form of an American section or committee received a favourable response from the Children's Bureau, whose new chief, Grace Abbott, saw the IAPCW as an international counterpart of her agency.[57] However, the IAPCW eventually found the project beyond its resources and by June 1922 its executive was pressing the Secretary-General to be placed under the direction of the League.[58]

British opposition to any recognition of or support for the IAPCW continued. The Home Office contended that if the IAPCW were to continue it

> should be placed on an entirely unofficial basis, should be organised on lines similar . . . to the International Bureau for the Suppression of the Traffic in Women [a non-governmental organisation established in 1899 to spearhead the suppression of the traffic in persons]. An association so constituted would carry on its work in the same way as any other unofficial Association which has for its aims the formation of international public opinion and the promotion of international action.

Earlier the Home Office had pressed the Cabinet to instruct the British representatives on the League Council to 'oppose the proposal . . . both on the grounds of the expense involved and of the defects in the constitution of the Association'.[59]

The above defects referred to its comprehensive mandate (neglected children in institutions or boarded out, juvenile courts and delinquency, child protection, and adoption and guardianship as well as infant hygiene and physical and mental defect) and the role of non-governmental members in its governance. Nevertheless, in 1924, the intergovernmental aspects of the IAPCW were entrusted either to the Advisory Committee on the Traffic in Women and Children or to the Health Organisation.[60] Although Dame Rachel Crowdy, Chief of the Social Section, and others thought that the transfer meant that the IAPCW would be closed down, its executive clearly had no intention of committing organisational suicide.[61]

The reaction of the American delegate to the reorganisation of the Social Section is instructive because it made clear the fault-line dividing European and North American conceptions of child welfare. In her correspondence with Dame Rachel, Abbott claimed that it would 'retard the development of a comprehensive child welfare program in the United States . . . a real forward looking program covering the entire field of child care'.[62]

Prompted by Abbott, Raymond B. Fosdick, closely associated with the RF interests, wrote that the 'combination [of the traffic and child welfare] represents an idea that was prevalent perhaps twenty-five or more years ago when child welfare was conceived to be exclusively a business of protecting children from external assault'. In the United States, child welfare meant 'more positive and affirmative terms – not only health, but in the general release of those forces in childhood which make for happiness and a balanced life. The emphasis . . . not so much to protect . . . from external situations as to develop a child and remove the inhibitions which might cramp and narrow its life.'[63] The last point on the uncramping of child life hammered home the positive aspects of modern, scientific child health and welfare subsumed under the slogan of 'the normal child'.

Abbott prepared a detailed memorandum on the child-welfare programme, which spelled out the North American view and initiated a spirited controversy within the League Section.[64] Pointing out that the 'trial and error method' was 'giving way to a scientific determination of [children's] needs by means of a careful study of accumulated experiences . . . , and by carefully conducted experiments along lines indicated by experience', Abbott claimed that 'the most useful function which the League can perform . . . would seem to be to assemble and make available to experts in child welfare the facts about the present conditions of children and what has been found possible and practical under given conditions in different countries'.

Indeed, Abbott argued that the IAPCW, by considering the whole field of child welfare, had made a 'peculiar and special contribution as distinguished from other international child welfare organizations and conferences'. Although the IAPCW had started with a concern for dependent and delinquent children, the 'inter-related character of the problems' associated with child life had forced it to be inclusive; now the reconstituted Advisory Committee threatened to undo the pioneering work started at Brussels. On the other hand the division of the work among the Social Section, the LNHO, and the International Labour Office (ILO) had already destroyed the whole child/ every child approach advocated by Abbott and her professional colleagues.

At an extraordinary meeting on 14 June 1924, the governing committee decided that rather than disbanding the International Association it should be transformed into an international voluntary organisation which could serve as an international centre for all those interested in child welfare. The reconstituted International Association continued to operate during the remainder of the interwar years by holding regular international congresses and publishing the *Bulletin International de la Protection de l'Enfance*. However, the high hopes espoused at the 1921 Congress were never fulfilled. In becoming the organis-ation that the British delegates at the Congress had proposed, moreover one that was subsidised by the Belgian Oeuvre nationale de l'Enfance, the IAPCW became, even more than the SCIU, a Eurocentric agency with little capacity for encouraging research and publications.

League of Nations

The LN was the prism through which evolving attitudes and approaches to protecting child life during the interwar period can be identified. As the League was only constituted by its member states it is scarcely surprising that little unanimity could be reached on the Child Welfare committee with regard to executing its recommendations or in the Assembly through multilateral agreements. Even before annual reports were submitted to the Assembly, discussion reflected intricate geo-cultural diversities as well as trans-Atlantic differences and social philosophies. Nonetheless a common understanding had emerged out of previous discourses whose main principles were incorporated into social welfare policies. Indeed, as we have argued elsewhere, an internationalising of the discourse on child life occurred during these years with a professional group of claims-makers becoming the advocates of children's rights to protection.[65]

The new claims-makers emerged out of a union of case-work methods and modern psychological knowledge which had marked the beginnings of the shift from voluntarist forms of child saving to a systematic rationale for child-welfare programmes. Instead of working with children in isolation from their network of experiences and emotional connections, child-welfare promoters sought to treat them within the context of families and communities. Since providential and hereditarian theories of behaviour were generally eschewed by child savers, children with problems were seen as the products of their environments, which included most significantly their families and neighbourhoods. In this sense eugenic theories were more readily applied to the medical side of child protection. Consequently, the stress on keeping children with their natural families led logically to the need for investigating and counselling families, the compilation of dossiers on other family members, co-operation with community agencies, the promotion of social worker both as 'friend' and agent of government authority, and finally, the expansion of auxiliary services to support family structures if these broke down at any point.

Protecting children and ensuring their dependence meant eliminating the conditions within the family and community that were endangering and, more positively, creating the conditions that would ensure proper child development. Moreover one national document on mothers' allowances observed:

> If we fail to intervene we cost the state much more. With our increasing knowledge of human behavior and the increasing facilities for dealing with family problems our successes should become more numerous and our failures fewer.[66]

These sentiments were echoed at the international level as we have seen in the cases of the LRCS child welfare department, the SCF/SCIU and the IAPCW.

By the 1930s, in the face of universal economic crises the new discourse on the normal child in family settings required redefinition so as to take into account broader parameters and the economic rationale which is demonstrated in the document cited above. The discourse on child life now argued that young persons and infants were a national resource whose future could be calculated on a social abacus measuring the young in terms of future productivity and a cash return. Metaphoric terms such as the 'wastage of children' and 'the ultimate cost to the community' became common usage among a network of international protection organisations. Malthusian tenets about worthless and excess children were replaced by a rhetoric that commodified and sentimentalised children at one and the same time. As one historian argues, in a relatively short time children metamorphosed from useless to priceless sentimental beings. In brief, formerly represented by romantic imagery children were now 'blameless' victims.[67] Not coincidentally, protective legislation for women in industry reinforced the preciousness of child life in a language of reproduction rather than of production.[68] While the League of Nations embarked on internationalising the discourse on child life its industrial arm – the International Labour Organisation – expanded the boundaries of protective legislation for women as mothers, or at the very least potential mothers, as the body-politic took on the politics of the body.[69]

Thus we see several themes emerging at the League in the shift from protection of dependent, neglected, refugee or deviant children, to an emphasis on preventative and educational programmes for the normal child; and much more than this, on the *normalising* of all children. In this light we might better understand the child welfare committee's preoccupation with the question of illegitimacy.[70] By stressing the desirability of abridging birth certificates so as not to denote parental marital status, the League's Child Welfare Committee implicitly recognised the enduring relationship between stigma and poverty of mother and child in these circumstances. Thus the illegitimate child was to be *normalised* by legitimation and recognised in mothers' or family allowances.

Given the dislocation of populations during a war whose aftermath witnessed famines and refugee movements, the committee supported conventions to enable alien and refugee children to return to their countries and families of origin and to enforce maintenance orders abroad in times of parental desertion. Therefore in the face of seemingly insurmountable economic and political obstacles the Child Welfare Committee in Geneva worked in close liaison with the ILO, LNHO, the International Institute for Intellectual Co-operation and the Institute for Unification of Private Law with regard to dispossessed children.

Infant and maternal mortality, public health and infant epidemic diseases, housing, working conditions, child-rearing practices, nutrition, feeding of infants, child-care centres – all spilled over from the Health Organisation into the purview of the League's Child Welfare Committee just as they appeared on the agenda of the SCIU, LRCS and IAPCW as well as at the Pan-American Child Welfare Conferences.[71] The uniformity of the discourse is evident in the proceedings of national or international child-protection conferences or in the preambles to the reports of any of the leading international organisations. The repetition and duplication of the same themes represents a consensus of opinion if not practice.

A particularly interesting regional development was the holding of the first Pan-American Child Congress in Buenos Aires in 1916 on the initiative of South Americans interested in child health and welfare. That Congress and the second in Montevideo in 1919, which had very limited American participation, nevertheless demonstrated a fairly comprehensive conception of child life. The second Congress resolved that 'child welfare work should begin before the child is conceived, . . . [and] ought to continue until the close of the period of adolescence' and a committee reported favourably on the proposal of Dr Luis Morquio to create an American International Bureau for the Protection of Childhood that would 'serve as a centre of studies, activities, and propaganda in America, in regard to all questions pertaining to children'. Established in 1927 at Montevideo, the Inter-American Children's Institute, as it came to be known, served the functions that the Brussels International Association had envisioned and would eventually become a specialised agency within the Organization of American States.[72]

For the tenth anniversary of the League's child-welfare committee, in 1934, a report was circulated to the Assembly summarising a decade of work and listing a number of comparative studies the League Committee had conducted. The comparative studies conducted by the Committee during its first decade covered legislation on age of marriage and consent; systems of family allowances; collaborations with the ILO; children's cinema; the legal position of the illegitimate child (including questions of guardianship, social insurance and birth registration); and the standardisation of juvenile justice systems. This document comprised its most comprehensive study, consisting of a weighty three-part analysis of the new sociological and psychological theories on dependence and delinquency (often conflating the two), the necessity for expanding child study and observation centres as well as specialised educational facilities, the importance of social work training and the co-ordination of auxiliary support services.

During its first decade the Committee had a drafted convention which had been transmitted to governments as a model for bilateral agreements on the return of young people and children to their homes. The SCIU praised this convention although it recognised the complex web of legal problems in its application.[73]

The following year, 1935, saw the child-welfare committee explore the boarding-out of young people into foster families, a topic publicised at the Balkan Conference on Child Welfare, Athens, and again at the Pan-American Union of Child Welfare, Mexico City, within the year. Arguments for de-institutionalising dependent and even delinquent children mirrored ideas about the socialisation of the normal child within the normal family.[74] The language of the child-study movement (which was shorthand for normal child) insisted that coercive and congregate institutions be replaced by educational establishments. Reflecting such sentiments, the Committee's 1935 report agreed in as much as it reinforced the belief that family life ought not to be broken cavalierly.[75]

Nonetheless despite assumptions of both normal family life and normal children, the vexed question of delinquency remained. It was an issue which was framed in theories on socio-psychological dysfunctionality within 'socially depressed milieux' that produced youngsters who were placed in 'moral isolation or contact with harmful influences if returned to their former environment'. The 1935 Report of the Fifth Committee impressed a conviction that auxiliary services were therefore imperative.

> Institutions can serve the community well, provided they have firmly in mind that they are not an end in themselves and that the value of their work will be judged not on the basis of whether the establishment runs smoothly, but on the far harder test of the behaviour and social adjustment of the young people after leaving the shelter of the institution.[76]

A year later three major documents on the boarding-out of children in families were completed and submitted to the Social Questions Section. These were accompanied by a similar recommendation by the SCIU.[77]

In effect the re-organisation of the Child Welfare Committee and Traffic in Women and Children Committee into the Advisory Committee on Social Questions reflected the new approaches to welfare, social work and child care which now predominated the discourse on child protection. The stress on expertise, scientific study, and the overlapping and inter-relationship of social programmes, was replacing *ad hoc* measures as many member-states of the industrialised world were attracted by arguments for centralised state inter-ventions and a bureaucratised control of child-care services. Katharine Lenroot, third chief of the USCB, represents this growing belief. Writing to a Hungarian delegate about the placement of children in foster homes she observed, 'One of the great difficulties that we have found here is the tendency often encountered to view a particular, specialised subject apart from its setting in the whole social program and thereby to gain a distorted idea of it.'[78]

Concomitant with the emphasis on retaining children in their natural families, the rise of family case work and the need for community-based programmes – all of which ultimately required massive state funding and control – was an emphasis on residual classes of dependent children, who increasingly became the object of state responsibility and institutional care. Among these categories were the delinquent, the feeble-minded, and developmentally handicapped, who had been identified in the nineteenth century as deviant groups in need of special care. Indeed, one of the refinements in child saving had been the distinction and separation of the neglected and abandoned from the delinquent and the separation of both categories from the mentally and developmentally handicapped, as well as the separation of these categories from normal children.[79]

The unbelievable dislocation of the 1930s had extended social work and social service as a profession to deal not merely with society's losers but with the victims of an appalling economic disaster; subsequently social workers would find their value in counselling and aiding family life by keeping children within this social unit whenever possible. Consequently the surveillance of normal child life in a supposedly normal family setting was deployed more subtly than through cruder methods of intervention by counselling and the new psychological theories of child development and social group dynamics. Despite the dreadful pressures and distress, the new demand on the profession created a new sense of purpose and relevance that would flower in the 1950s in the confident expansion of social work.

These shifts pressured the League committee to expand its scope. Youth unemployment and the effects of the economic depression upon children and family life were brought to the forefront of its studies and discussion in the mid-1930s. Regrettably such expansion of direction occurred during its tenth session, at the very time when the child welfare budget was cut from 53,000 Swiss francs in 1930 to 24,000 Swiss francs in 1934. Compare this to the 1 million and ¾ million made available to the Finance and Economic Committees respectively or even to the 316,000 Swiss francs to the Mandates Commission and one can see how unconvinced the secretariat remained as to the importance of child welfare. The budget cuts rendered the committee so ineffectual that S. W. Harris, the frustrated British member, expressed the view that he would rather see the work stopped totally than continuing under such circumstances.[80]

Conclusion

If there is any one instance demonstrating the growing paralysis of the Child Welfare Committee by the late 1930s, it can be seen at its 1938 meeting. During the second session in May, Princess Cantacuzena of Romania called for a resolution to establish 'neutral zones for the protection of children in times of war'. This was largely a symbolic gesture similar to that of the nuclear-free zone concept later in the century but because the Declaration of Geneva stated that the child was to be the first to receive help in times of distress she argued that neutral zones should be called 'lieux de Genève' and that the International Committee of Red Cross Societies address the matter at its June conference. The arguments for and against the proposal were framed in stirring but sterile rhetoric. No agreement – not even a 'pious' one – could be realised, as the delegates were gagged by their governments' claims to sovereignty. Waxing indignant, Madame Huica of Spain concluded the session with the comment that she could not congratulate the Committee on this particular morning's work. Insisting that delegates had consciences and hearts of their own, she retorted to the self-justifying protestations that flew across the table, 'Surely they could have declared that they condemned the massacre of children?'[81] Eglantyne Jebb would have agreed, given her belief that 'all wars, just or unjust, disastrous or victorious, are waged against the child'.[82]

Acknowledgements

We wish to acknowledge an SSHRC/Killam Fellowship (1990–2) for assisting our research for this chapter and an SSHRC Research Grant (1991–4). We owe a special debt to the archivists at the League of Nations Historical Collections, the International Federation of Red Cross and Red Crescent Societies, and the Archives d'Etat, Geneva; to the National Archives, Washington; and to Rodney Breen of the Save the Children Fund, London.

Notes

1 Joel Best, *Threatened Children – The Rhetoric and Concern About Child Abuse* (Chicago: University of Chicago Press, 1990).

2 Richard A. Meckel, *Save the Babies: American Public Health Reform and the Prevention of Infant Mortality* (Baltimore: Johns Hopkins University Press, 1990), p. 8.

3 Ivy Pinchbeck and Margaret Hewitt, *Children in English Society*, vol. II: *From the Eighteenth Century to the Children Act 1948* (London: Routledge & Kegan Paul, 1973); and Nancy Pottishman Weiss, 'Save the Children: A History of the Children's Bureau, 1903–1928' (PhD dissertation, University of California, Los Angeles, 1974.)

4 Meckel, *Save the Babies*; Samuel H. Preston and Michael R. Haines, *Fatal Years: Child Mortality in Late Nineteenth-Century America* (Princeton: Princeton University Press, 1991); and Ellen Ross, *Love and Toil: Motherhood in Outcast London, 1870–1918* (New York: Oxford University Press, 1993).

5 Alisa Klaus, *Every Child a Lion: The Origins of Maternal and Infant Health Policy in the United States and France, 1890–1920* (Ithaca: Cornell University Press, 1993).

6 Hamilton Cravens, *Before Head Start: The Iowa Station and America's Children* (Chapel Hill, NC: University of North Carolina Press, 1993); and Margo Horn, *Before It's Too Late: The Child Guidance Movement in the United States, 1922–1945* (Philadelphia: Temple University Press, 1989).

7 Grace Abbott, 'Address', *Proceedings of the National Conference of Social Work, 1932* (Chicago: University of Chicago Press, 1932), p. 48; and File: 0-1-0-4[1] International Child Welfare Congress, Children's Bureau, RG 102, Box 347, Central File 1921–24, National Archives, Washington, DC (hereafter NA).

8 Robyn Muncy, *Creating a Female Dominion in American Reform, 1890–1935* (New York: Oxford University Press, 1991).

9 International Federation of Red Cross and Red Crescent Societies Archives, Geneva (hereafter IFRC), *Bulletin*, 2, 2 (November 1920): 95.

10 IFRC, *Bulletin*, 2, 12 (September 1921): 529–33.

11 IFRC, for example, *Daily Telegraph* 21/05/1920, 11/06/1920; *Daily Graphic* 21/07/1920; and 'Appeal from League of Nations', 21/08/1920, *Bulletin* (1920–1): 5.

12 IRFC, *Bulletin*, 1, 2 (June 1919): 4–5, and 6–7 (March–April 1921): 230–2; the commitment to child welfare and its programmes is repeated in Reports of the Secretariat, vol. I, Third Meeting of the General Council, Paris, 28 April to 1 May 1924.

13 IRFC, *Bulletin*, 2, nos. 13–14 (October–November 1921): 499–500; and Reports of the Secretariat, vol. I, Third Meeting of the General Council, Paris, 28 April to 1 May 1924.

14 IFRC, The Cannes Medical Conference, 1/04/1919, in documents First General Council in Geneva, 2/03/1920, pp. 2–6; and *Bulletin*, 1, 1 (May 1919): 95–8.

15 IFRC, Reports of the Secretariat, vol. I, Third Meeting of the General Council, Paris, 28 April–1 May 1924; and *Bulletin*, 2, 6–7 (March–April 1921): 232.

16 IFRC, *Bulletin*, 2, 13–14 (October–November 1921): 499–500.

17 IFRC, Proceedings of the Fourth Meeting of the General Council, Geneva, 30 March 1922, pp. 86–7; and *Bulletin*, 2 (September 1921): 456–8.

18 IFRC, 'The Beginnings and Growth of Popular Health Instruction', Proceedings of the General Council, Geneva, 28–31 March 1922, pp. 51–3.

19 IFRC, 'Description of a Child Welfare Unit for Pioneer Work', in Department of Organisation, 'An Outline . . . March 1920', pp. 1–2, 27–32.

20 IFRC, *Bulletin*, 2, 6–7 (March–April 1921): 199–200; 'Courses on Hygiene for Women', *The Polish Red Cross*, 19, 176–8; 'An Outline for Discussing Its Program and Organization for Peacetime Activities', Meeting of the General Council of the LRCS March 1920, pp. 1-2.

21 Pan American Conference of Women, Baltimore and Washington, DC, 20–9 April, 1922, in *Information Circular*, 1, 6 (June 1922): 8.

22 IFRC, *Bulletin*, 2, 9 (June 1921): 417, 441–5, 490–1, 499, and 530; and Resolution XXXIV, vol. I, Reports of Secretariat, Third Meeting of the General Council, Paris, 28 April to 1 May 1924, p. 198.

23 IFRC, *Bulletin*, 2, 2 (September 1921): 532.

24 Their co-operative work is documented in the SCIU's *Revue Internationale* (1921–40).

25 Edmund Fuller, *The Rights of the Child: A Chapter in Social History* (London: Victor Gollancz, 1951), p. 17.

26 *Ibid*. p. 87.

27 *Ibid*. p. 39.

28 SCF, London, Council Minutes, 7/10/1920; Archives de l'Etat de Genève, Records of the International Union for Child Welfare, Foundation File 1920 [Save the Children International Union]; and Correspondence File 20/10/1919–4/04/1920, Jebb to Susanne Ferriere, 29/01/1920, 24/06/1921, 17/06/1921; Jebb, 'Future of Union', 10/06/1921; and Memo from British Red Cross Society and the Order of St John of Jerusalem, 26/06/1921.

29 SCF, Council Minutes, 1/09/1922.
30 IFRC, Box, Réunion relative à la situation des réfugiés russes, Geneva, 17/02/1921, 6–7.
31 SCF, Council Minutes, 26/01/1923.
32 P. T. Rooke and R. L. Schnell, *No Bleeding Heart: Charlotte Whitton, A Feminist on the Right* (Vancouver: University of British Columbia Press, 1987).
33 SCF, Council Minutes, 21/06/1925.
34 SCF, Council Minutes, 14/10/1925; and Council Minutes, 16/06/1927.
35 SCF, Council Minutes, 20/05/1926.
36 SCIU, Box: International Congress; 'What the League Can Do For Children', *Revue Internationale* (May 1927): 323–30, and LNA, Eric Drummond to W. A. MacKenzie, 22/02/1929, 11C/10396/322.
37 SCF, Council Minutes, 20/05/1926.
38 SCF, Council Minutes, 3/01/1929.
39 SCF, Council Minutes, 6/06/1929.
40 SCF, Council Minutes, 4/02/1930, 8/07/1930, 5/12/1930, and 9/07/1931.
41 SCF, Council Minutes, 3/03/1932; and LNA, Mentie to M. V. Catoseni, Mandates, 19/04/1932. 6B/36731/2053. For details of 1928 conference and African questionnaire by SCIU see 11C/7745/7745, and Report on International Conference on African Children, Geneva, 22–5 June, 1932, to Child Welfare Committee, Eighth Session, 9/04/1932, Africa, C.395.M.221.1932.IV.
42 SCF, Child Protection Committee (hereafter CPC) Minutes, March 1932; and Council Minutes, 19/05/1932.
43 SCF, CPC Minutes, 3/05/1932.
44 SCF, Council Minutes, 16/11/1933 and 15/02/1934.
45 SCF, CPC Minutes, 28/11/1937, 15/03/1938, and 22/02/1939; NA, Children's Bureau, Edmund Fuller to Katharine Lenroot, 8/02/1937, File 0-1-0-7[2], Box 666, Central File 1939–40.
46 SCF, *23rd Annual Report 1941–42*, p. 19.
47 SCIU, File: UISE 1922–3, Second Congrès International des Oeuvres pour le Secours Aux Enfants, Geneva, 1921.
48 IFRC, *International Journal of Public Health 2* (July–August 1921), quoting W. O. Pitt, Chief of Division of Child Welfare.
49 SCIU, File: UISE 1922–3, Second Congrès International des Oeuvres pour le Secours Aux Enfants, Geneva, 1921.
50 SCIU, Box: Foundation 1919–20, File, Correspondence 20/10/1919–4/02/1920 and 'Notes of Meeting', 21 Jan 1921 in Oscar Bosshart/Jebb Correspondence; LNA, Conference on Child Welfare, Brussels, July 1921, 13B/13896/11316 and Rachel Crowdy's and Eric Drummond's observations, 1/04/1922, 6/04/1922 in *Minutes*, 13B19641/19641. Also see SCIU *Bulletin*, 3rd Year, 9, 30/03/1922, 123.
51 Recent national studies with comparative aspects are Deborah Dwork, *War is Good for Babies and Other Young Children: A History of the Infant and Child Welfare Movement in England, 1898–1918* (London and New York: Tavistock, 1987); Meckel, *Save the Babies*; Preston and Haines, *Fatal Years*; R. Cooter (ed.), *In the Name of the Child* (London: Routledge, 1992).
52 IAPCW, Brussels, *International Record of Child Welfare Work*, 1 (Oct.–Nov. 1921). The idea of a permanent international bureau was first proposed at the 2nd

International Congress of Protection (Congrès de Patronage) in 1894, LNA, Memorandum, Secretary-General, League of Nations, C.564.1922.XII. 4 August 1922.

53 F. A. Walters, *A History of the League of Nations* (London: Oxford University Press, 1960), pp. 58–9.

54 LNA, Traffic in Women and Children – Report by M. da Cunha, 12 Sept. 1921, 14th Meeting of Council, 12/18533/13720.

55 PRO, London, Foreign Office (hereafter FO) 371/6962, S. W. Harris to Under-Secretary of State, 17/06/1921, Edward Troup to Under-Secretary of State; and LNA, S. W. Harris to Sir Eric Drummond, Secretary-General, 12/07/1921, 13B/15391/1136; and International Conference for the Protection of Children (1921), 13B/14047/11316.

56 'Essentially a Work of Peace', *International Record of Child Welfare Work*, 1 (Oct./Nov. 1921): 7.

57 NA, Children's Bureau, Central File 1921–24, Box 160, File 0-1-3-1 International.

58 PRO. Henri Velge, IAPCW Secretary-General, to Sir Eric Drummond, 9/06/1922; and Secretary-General, memorandum, C.564.1922.XII, 4/08/1922.

59 PRO, FO 371/8241, Minutes, 2/10/1922; and Malcolm Delevigne to Lord Curzon, 14/11/1922; and FO 371/8241, Delevigne to Secretary, Cabinet Office, 17/08/1922; and LNA, 12/40793/34652.

60 LNA, Memorandum by the Secretary-General, IAPCW A.33.1924.IV, 22/08/1924; and Report of the Fifth Committee to the Fifth Assembly Protection of Children, A.107.1924.IV, 24/09/1924.

61 SCIU, 'Session extraordinaire du comité de l'association internationale pour la protection de la "favie" Bruxelles, 14 juin 1924', *International Record of Child Welfare Work*, 28 (July 1924), 694–719.

62 NA, Children's Bureau, Abbott to Crowdy, 13/04/1925, File 0-1-3-1.

63 LNA. 12/42399/34652, extract, 9/02/1925.

64 LNA, 12/44514/34652, [10/06/1925], Memo re proposed child welfare programme, submitted by Miss Abbott . . . in response to the request of the Secretary of the Committee.

65 P. T. Rooke and R. L. Schnell, 'Internationalizing a Discourse: Children at Risk, the Child Welfare Committee, and the League of Nations', *New Education*, 14 (1992), 61–72.

66 National Archives of Canada, Ottawa (hereafter NAC), Records of the Canadian Council of Social Development, Box 2, 'Aid to Dependent Mothers and Children in Canada: Social Policy Behind Our Legislation' (1931), 14.

67 Vivian Zelizer, *Pricing the Priceless Child: The Changing Social Value of Children* (New York: Basic Books, 1985); and SCIU, *Revue Internationale de l'Enfant* (July/August 1924), 489–502.

68 SCIU, 'The Protection of Women in Industry Before and After Childbirth', *Revue Internationale*, pp. 571–7; and Susan Lehrer, *Origins of Protective Labor Legislation for Women 1905–25* (Albany: State University of New York Press, 1987).

69 Carol Riegelman Lubin and Ann Winslow, *Social Justice for Women: The International Labor Organization and Women* (Durham, NC: Duke University Press, 1990).

70 LNA, see 'Argument for the Normal Child', Appendix II, pp. 26–8, in *Report of Liaison Officer with ILO*, C.P.E. 528 and C.235.M.169.1937(IV), 15/05/1937.
71 LNA, an example of these items is found in the Child Welfare Report on Work of the Tenth Session, 12–17April 1934. C.P.W. 476(1).
72 NA, Children's Bureau, Central File, 1937–40, Box 644, folder Pan-American Child Congress.
73 One of the more comprehensive reports expressing international perspectives submitted by the SCIU was 'An Enquiry into the Auxiliary Services of Children's Courts' (March 1930). Professor Thomas D. Eliot, University of Washington, conducted the enquiry and wrote articles for the *Revue Internationale* on juvenile courts. See LNA, Child Welfare Committee, Sixth Session, 9/04/1930, C.P.E. 251 and also W. A. MacKenzie, Secretary-General SCIU to Rachel Crowdy, 3/04/1930, 11C/19040/407.
74 LNA, see the following documents: C.P.E. 90(2), C.P.E. 134, C.P.E. 141(1), C.P.E. 283, C.P.E. 322, C.P.E. 394(1), C.P.E. 238(1), C.P.E. 325, C.P.E. 430, C.P.E. 445(1) and C. 264.M.119. 1931. IV. The Balkan Conference, October 1935, is discussed in 11C/16645/16645. Also see *International Labour Review*, 21, 3 (March 1930) for collaborative efforts with ILO.
75 LNA, report of the work of the Committee, 3/05/1935, C.187.M.194.1935(IV), pp. 9–10.
76 LNA, report of the Fifth Committee to Assembly, 24/09/1935, A.54.1935(IV).
77 LNA, report on the Work of the Commission, 1936, C.204.M.127. 1936. IV. See also SCIU, Julia Vajkai of the Hungarian SCF, 'The Anti-Social Family and the Maladjusted Child', *Revue Internationale* (June 1928).
78 LNA, Lenroot to Vajkai, 8/09/1936, 11C/18651/10854; see Roy Lubove, *The Professional Altruist* (Cambridge, Mass.: Harvard University Press, 1965); Kathleen Woodroofe, *From Charity to Social Work* (Toronto: University of Toronto Press, 1971).
79 Harvey G. Simmons, *From Asylum to Welfare State* (Downsview: National Institute on Mental Retardation, 1982); Patricia Rooke and R. L. Schnell, *Discarding the Asylum: From Child Rescue to the Welfare State in English Canada 1800–1950* (Lanham: University Press of America, 1983).
80 LNA, Progress Report, 24/04/1936, C.P.E. 539, and correspondence in 11C/23685/2994; Unemployment and Child Welfare – Enquiry by Social Section: Reports by European Nations and Japan, October 1933, 11C/7619/3424; and Julia Eva Vajkai (Hungary) to E. E. Ekstrand, Secretariat, 30/10/1931, 11C/8508/547; and Budget (1934), 11C/2946/2927.
81 LNA, Social Questions/2nd Session/P.V.17, 3/05/1938, p. 79.
82 SCIU, File: Fonds Commemoir, Box UISE, Correspondence (1919–30).

10

The International Health Division of the Rockefeller Foundation: the Russell years, 1920–1934

JOHN FARLEY

In 1928 Dr Frederick Russell, recently appointed Director of the International Health Division, reminded Dr Michael Connor, Director of the Health Division's Brazilian Yellow Fever Commission, of the Division's real objectives. 'What we want to do', he elaborated, 'is to help each country establish a health organization suitable to the needs of the country . . . and we hope that the yellow fever work will lead to a better health organization in the states and in the nation of Brazil.'[1]

That indeed was the original goal of the organisation founded in 1913 as a mirror of the older Rockefeller Sanitary Commission for the Eradication of Hookworm Disease from the south. Using hookworm as their weapon, both organisations hoped to awaken public interest in (1) hygiene and sanitation by which hookworm could, it was hoped, be prevented and in (2) scientific medicine, which had revealed the cause and cure of the disease. By such means both Rockefeller organisations were then prepared to follow up their hookworm demonstration work by helping to set up local health agencies to promote health, hygiene and public sanitation. 'The purpose of our work in any country is not to bring hookworm disease under control', Wickliffe Rose, the organisation's first Director, noted in 1917, 'but to make demonstrations which will lead ultimately to the enlistment of local agencies in the work.'[2] To Rose there was an administrative gap between knowledge and the application of that knowledge for public welfare; the hookworm campaign was a means to bridge that gap.

But in 1929, eighteen months after he had written to Connor, Russell was anticipating a very different organisation. 'It is probable', he wrote, 'that our organization can make a greater contribution to public health by pursuing scientific studies in the field than by further developing health organizations on the basis of existing knowledge.'[3] To Russell, there was also a gap, but it existed at the level of knowledge. In the words of Raymond Fosdick, 'the margin between what men know and what they use is much too thin'.[4]

However, both of Russell's statements were somewhat disingenuous. By 1929 the Health Division was no longer using hookworm simply as a means to build up national and local health organisations; it had entered the business of controlling or even eliminating it and other diseases. Furthermore, by then, it had already helped to set up field laboratories, in which research as well as routine testing and diagnostic work were well under way. More significantly, in 1928, Russell had taken another decisive step away from the original concept of the organisation by pressing for a centralised laboratory in New York, controlled by the Health Division, where fundamental problems of disease rather than applied field problems could be addressed.

In this chapter I shall examine this apparent change of emphasis. How and why did it come about and what impact did it have on the organisation? Was the organisation in 1934, the year of Russell's retirement, so very different from the organisation he had taken over from Rose in 1924? As a background I begin with a brief account of the organisation as it existed before Russell appeared on the scene.

The background

The early years

When the International Health Division, or Health Commission as it was originally called, began its programme in 1913, the initial plans called for the Rockefeller Sanitary Commission to continue its work in the south, while the Health Commission would extend the hookworm work into Latin America, the Orient and the empires of Britain, France and the Netherlands.[5] But the Sanitary Commission closed down in December 1914 and its work in the South was handed over to the Health Commission. Also, after Rose had been wined and dined in London during his 1913 visit, the Health Commission opted to concentrate its activities on the British empire, as well as the South, the Orient and Latin America. In addition, after becoming involved with war relief, the Commission moved into Europe, where it concentrated on tuberculosis.[6]

In the 1920s, after successful hookworm demonstration campaigns in the British West Indies and in Wilson County, North Carolina, the Health Commission (now called the International Health Board) entered the second stage of its operations when it co-operated with the US Public Health Service to open county health units across the breadth of the United States and collaborated also with governments to establish similar agencies in foreign countries.[7] By 1925 such agencies had been set up in twenty-five of the American States, three countries of Europe and in Brazil.[8] In the early years these units, one of the earliest of which opened in Northampton County in North Carolina, existed primarily to bring improved sanitation and hygiene to the area in order to eliminate hookworm.

The Northampton County Health Department, North Carolina

In August 1917, the Northampton County Health Department, on the northern boundary of the State, opened its doors. Even though, in those early years, it dealt primarily with hookworm, soil pollution and typhoid vaccinations, the Department was divided into various units which became responsible also for the control of contagious diseases, including the post-war flu, for school health inspections and for infant hygiene. They even formed a so-called life-extension unit, which promised every adult a physical examination in order to 'prolong life, and to make the quality of living better'.[9]

Most of these units focused on the schools. The Hookworm Unit, for example, emphasised the discovery and cure of hookworm in the school population. Empty labelled specimen boxes were left in the schools and returned the next morning with faecal contents wrapped in paper. This material was then mailed (!) to the central laboratory in Raleigh and the parents of those found to be infected notified and asked to permit their children to be treated with oil of Chenopodium – one drop for every year of age.

But the education of students into the benefits of hygiene was always a priority item. The hookworm unit ran sanitary contests in which points were accumulated for the best essays on sanitation, for the use of toothbrushes, for vaccinations and for the schools and homes that made the greatest sanitary improvements. On 18 April 1917 the Governor of North Carolina and numerous other officials gathered to honour the prize winners at a ceremony advertised as 'WAR PROGRAM on GERMS and GERMANS (Our Two Greatest Enemies)' where they heard Miss Ella Outland and Miss Bettie Long (boys, of course, wouldn't be seen dead in such a situation!) read their prize essays on 'Sanitation in Home and School', and the Governor address the crowd on 'War Savings and Sanitation'.

The Soil Pollution Unit, set up to stop contamination of the soil and drinking water, worked hand-in-hand with the Hookworm Unit. Like their cousins in the Hookwork Unit education became their main emphasis. Public and school lectures and newspaper articles generated political pressure in favour of sanitary legislation. They seem to have been successful. By June 1918 a Northampton County Ordinance requiring each house to have a sewage closet or a 'decent, properly located and fly proof sanitary privy' had been proclaimed, with the threat of a minimum $5 dollar fine for the first offence and up to $50 or 30 days' imprisonment for repeated violations. Once built, of course, these privies had to have a government seal of approval.

The location and remedy of such handicaps as hookworm, poor eyesight and hearing, enlarged tonsils, and dental problems became the mission of the School Inspection Unit, and once again the onus fell on the poor teacher who was required to complete yet another health questionnaire after a physical examination of each child in the class. The schoolteacher was also an important element in the Quarantine Unit, also originally set up at the beginning to protect the community against contagious diseases. Apart from teaching her pupils about such diseases, she was asked to select health officers and health captains from each of her classes to write reports and complete questionnaires for the Health Department. The parents of those discovered to be carrying a contagious disease would receive a set of state rules and regulations, including a covering letter from the local quarantine officer. 'I wish to appeal to you as a law-abiding citizen and as one who has due consideration for the health and possibly lives of your neighbors and your community', this letter warned, 'to give the County and the State . . . your full cooperation.' Then, in the final flourish, the officer reminded them, 'Whatsoever ye would that men should do unto you, do ye even so to them: for this is the law." All the while the good people of Northampton County were bombarded by weekly newspaper articles endorsing the healthy life: 'Little Journeys along the Byways and Highways of Disease and Health', as the County Health Officer called his series of articles.

What this and other departments did in the early 1920s was repeated elsewhere as the number of health units mushroomed throughout the South. Beginning with hookworm and the prevention of soil pollution, each, including the one in Northampton County, gradually broadened its scope to form, eventually, a well-rounded county health department. Each of these organisations shared the same campaigns, filled in the same forms, collected the same statistics, took similar photographs, and above all compiled the same quarterly and annual reports.[10]

During the 1920s these county health units began to take on another health problem, malaria. By the end of the First World War, the International Health Board had moved beyond the single focal disease of hookworm to take on malaria and yellow fever and was shortly to attack the tuberculosis problem in France. All these diseases turned out to be very different from hookworm and could not be easily fitted into the original model of the organisation. None of them could be used to dramatise the miracles of modern medicine, because there were no theatrical cures, no masses of expelled worms to amaze the population, the politicians and the medical profession; none were diseases of poor sanitation that could be prevented by building sanitary privies; with tuberculosis they were taking on huge social problems which they were ill-equipped to handle; and with malaria and yellow fever they were taking on two diseases about which a great deal was still unknown. Thus without cures and simple means of prevention and with so much unknown they were forced to change the focus of the organisation. They could not mount dramatically successful demonstration campaigns against either malaria or yellow fever in the hope of awakening interest in health and scientific medicine, without first investigating how such campaigns were to be organised and what methods were to be used and without initiating research into the epidemiology of both diseases. Thus, inevitably, as they expanded to take on diseases surrounded by so much mystery, the diseases themselves became the focal issue; the control or even elimination of malaria and yellow fever were no longer means to an end, as hookworm had been, but ends in themselves.

Malaria

The decision to take on malaria presented the Health Board with a host of difficulties. Unlike hookworm there was no universally recognised way by which the disease could be controlled or eliminated; many favoured attacks against mosquito vectors, while others looked to quinine. There were also doubts as to whether any of the methods were affordable. Thus, in 1915, the Health Board set up experiments in the Mississippi Delta (the flood plain between the Mississippi and Yazoo rivers whose rich alluvial soils had become the site of a booming cotton plantation system in which white planters gathered large profits at the expense of disenfranchised black sharecroppers living lives of hopeless poverty) and across the Mississippi in Arkansas. These experiments involving quinine therapy, screening of houses against mosquitoes and anti-mosquito measures, were designed to determine if and by what means malaria could best be controlled, and at what cost.[11]

By the end of 1916, despite the total absence of controls, *all* these experiments were reported to have been successful and malaria to have declined at a cost that such communities could afford. Although the validity of some of these claims was later undermined by a very critical report by Frederick Hoffman, statistician to the Prudential Insurance Company,[12] the officers of the Health Board were nothing if not enthusiastic. In a report entitled 'Cheaper to Get Rid of Malaria than to Have it', George Vincent, President of the Rockefeller Foundation (RF), spoke, not of control, but of elimination. 'These demonstrations have left no room for doubt', he proclaimed, 'malaria elimination is feasible, scientifically and economically, it represents a striking contribution to community progress and human happiness.'[13]

The destruction of mosquito larvae and elimination of their breeding sites in towns and the use of screens and quinine in more rural areas became the chosen method of malaria control. With such apparent successes now at hand, malaria control was soon added to the list of duties of many county health units in the South. In 1922, for example, an anti-malarial campaign involving anti-mosquito work, publicity, school education, screening and quinine distribution was added to the duties of many county health units in Mississippi. Also during the 1920s, the Health Board co-operated with state officials in Rio de Janeiro to drain, clear and oil potential breeding sites in ten municipalities, and reported 'striking results' in the reduction of malaria.[14]

The same pattern repeated itself wherever one looks, whether in the South or in countries like Brazil. County Health units began by emphasising hookworm, and soil pollution. They then took on such problems as child hygiene and soon added malaria control and often tuberculosis to the list. In the mid-1920s the Health Board encouraged further expansion and sophistication by establishing Bureaux of Sanitary Engineering, Bureaux of Epidemiology to monitor and control other communicable diseases such as typhoid and Bureaux of Vital Statistics to produce necessary health statistics. Growing numbers of laboratories were included and in many states and countries training stations for health officers were developed to train personnel in public health administration, hookworm control and malaria control. These county health units, developed in the South, were then exported with very little change to other countries and remained in the front line of the Health Division's activities.

Shortly after these malarial campaigns began, however, a new weapon appeared on the malaria scene, Paris green. This mixture of copper and arsenious oxide when mixed with road dust and spread by a hand blower was discovered in 1921 to kill selectively *Anopheles* larvae. Up until then oil larvicides had killed mosquito larvae belonging to every genera by blocking their respiratory systems. But Paris green killed only particulate-feeding larvae; larvae of *Culex* and *Aedes*, being predators, were left unharmed. This new chemical made it easier to direct attacks only on the breeding sites of the anopheline vector, and seemed to render 'species sanitation' that much easier. In other words application of Paris green on selected breeding sites of the malarial vector could reduce the density of the vector to such a degree that transmission would be broken and malaria could be eliminated. As a result any control problem now needed to be preceded by an extensive survey to discover the loci of malaria in the community, the identity of the malarial vector and its place of breeding. But often the local mosquito fauna was unknown or at other times the identity of anopheline larval stages could not be ascertained unless they were allowed to develop into the identifiable adult form – a tedious process to say the least. Thus, every Paris green campaign, and the first ones began in the Philippines in 1924 and in Sardinia and Southern Italy a year later, carried a commitment to field research, and a laboratory in which to do it. Thus the link to Russell: the setting up of public health laboratories a few years before these events had led Rose to bring Russell into the organisation.

The laboratory service

By 1918, the necessity of having public health laboratories associated with the health units had become clear to Rose after correspondence with Hermann Biggs, Commissioner of the New York State Health Department. They were necessary, he was told, to assist local physicians in their diagnoses, to produce and distribute various antitoxins and vaccines, and to test water, milk and foodstuffs.[15] Convinced as to their potential value, Rose enquired whether anyone would be willing to direct a laboratory service within his organisation, and discovered Brigadier-General Frederick Russell of the US Army Medical Corps.

A native of Auburn, New York, and a medical graduate of Columbia, Russell joined the International Health Division in 1920 after a 22-year distinguished military career. He had been put in charge of the Army Laboratory Service in the First World War and it was as Director of the Health Board's Public Health Laboratory Service that he accepted his new position immediately after retiring from the army. In 1924 he was to become Director of the International Health Board where he remained until his retirement in 1934.

In the documentary record, Russell comes across as an impressive, tough, authoritarian, militaristic figure who did not suffer fools gladly, intimidated many people, and, at one time or another, clashed with most of the officials within the organisation. He also, it seems, respected those who stood up to him and was willing to listen to others whose opinions he respected.[16]

Under his direction the laboratory services grew rapidly, becoming part of many health units in the South and abroad. He informed Rose, shortly after taking office, that each region needed a central public health laboratory in order to educate local physicians and in which staff could be given practical training. Physicians, Russell wrote, needed reliable diagnostic service in order to improve their own practices and to learn which diseases were prevalent in each area and which were not. 'It is', he told Rose, 'quite as important to educate physicians as the public.'[17] But, as Russell noted in a 1926 memorandum on the objectives of the laboratory service, the important routine diagnostic tests should only be one of the laboratory functions; they should also participate in 'public health investigations'.[18]

Three years earlier Leesburg, Georgia, had been chosen as a site for a malaria station to investigate the epidemiological problems of malaria in the South, knowledge of which was required for an 'intelligent and economic attack' on the disease wherever it occurred. Its first director, Samuel Darling, showed *Anopheles quadrimaculatus* to be the major malarial vector in that area and a young trainee, Paul Russell, produced the first key to malaria-transmitting *Anopheles* larvae in the USA.[19] But malaria was not the only disease where similar knowledge gaps existed. As Dr Howard, Director of the West Indian programme, noted in a 1920 report pertaining to hookworm, 'we must venture into the field of research'.[20] Again, as in the malarial story, a hookworm field research unit was opened in 1922, this one in Andalusia, Alabama, which acted as a training base for health officers and in which field research on hookworm was carried out. As Russell pointed out in his first report as Director of the International Health Board, 'when a specific work is undertaken, as in the control of hookworm disease or malaria, it is soon found that there are serious gaps in the knowledge essential to successful control'.[21] To plug these gaps many of the field laboratories began to move into areas of applied field-centred research.

But in 1928 Russell's interest in research seemed to take a new direction which brought him into conflict with many scientific directors of what was now the International Health Division. He argued, as a result of the Health Board's experiences with yellow fever, that a central research laboratory was needed in New York. Russell believed that such a laboratory should provide the scientific underpinning of the Health Division's work. But whereas the existing laboratories provided obvious support for the field work and were geared primarily for epidemiological investigations, Russell now proposed a laboratory which seemed destined to become independent of the field and to threaten the field-centred nature of the organisation. To understand why Russell turned in this direction, a brief look at the Health Board's work with yellow fever is necessary.[22]

Yellow fever

In 1918, when the Health Board's first campaign against yellow fever began in the port of Guayaquil, Ecuador, the etiology of the disease was still in doubt. Known to be transmitted by *Aedes aegypti* mosquitoes, it was usually thought to have a bacterial or a protozoan cause. But not in doubt was the assumed urban nature of the disease. Only in urban centres, the so-called 'key-centres', would there be a sufficient immigration of non-immunes to keep the disease-causing 'virus' in circulation and from where the virus could be carried to other locations. Thus the essence of a yellow fever campaign lay in decreasing the number of *Aedes* mosquitoes in these key-centres below a 'critical number' (assumed to be less than 5 per cent; that is to say, the mosquito could be found in less than 5 per cent of the households examined) at which point transmission would be broken and the disease would die out.[23] Reducing the numbers of such a house-loving insect proved to be comparatively easy for any well-oiled campaign; it was necessary only for householders to eliminate potential breeding sites around their houses.

By such means the mosquito population of Guayaquil was reduced so significantly that the city seemed free of disease. Indeed, by early 1923, when the Health Board was invited by the Brazilian Government to assist in the Federal Comissao de Febre Amarela, only the ports of Northeast Brazil were considered important key centres in South America, and any outbreaks of the disease outside these cities were considered 'merely the sparks from a big fire'.

But news of these successes in Guayaquil was overshadowed by Hideyo Noguchi's surprising discovery that what he believed to be yellow fever could be transmitted through guinea-pigs and was caused by a minute spirochete bacteria, *Leptospira icteroides*, which Noguchi claimed to be filterable and similar to but immunologically distinct from *L. icterohaemorrhagiae*, causal agent of infectious jaundice or Weil's disease.[24] The validity of these claims was accepted without too much unease by most members of the Health Board, including Simon Flexner and Russell – Noguchi was, after all, an esteemed member of the Rockefeller Institute, and campaigns against the mosquito vector were not affected by Noguchi's discovery.

But the question was important to the Health Board's Yellow Fever Commission which in 1926 began working in the Lagos laboratory in Nigeria. Before their control programme could begin it was necessary to determine whether the nature, etiology and mode of transmission of yellow fever in West Africa was the same as in South America. But to their consternation, not only were they unable to locate any *Leptospira*, but guinea-pigs proved to be refractory to infection. Indeed all tests, based on the assumption that *Leptospira* was the causal organism, proved negative.

Members of the Commission, some of whom had been trained by Noguchi, naturally concluded that two different diseases existed. 'With this identity disproven', they reported, referring to the South American and West African diseases, 'the whole structure built as it is on this supposition falls to the ground and we are faced by the fact that there are many gaps in our knowledge of the West African disease.'[25] What was to be done? The answer, according to Dr I. G. Kligler, lay in the laboratory. Until now, he argued, the Commission had emphasised surveys and field work. But with these negative findings, he continued, a reversal in policy, a change in organisation and a change in personnel is required. Henceforth laboratory-based scientific research must take first priority; the Survey Commission must be replaced by a Scientific Commission. Flexner agreed. After hearing the news from West Africa he told Russell that the Health Board had no alternative but to stay in West Africa and unravel the situation. And that would mean building up the Lagos yellow fever laboratory.[26]

In April 1927, Dr Henry Beeuwkes, Director of the West African programme, travelled to Europe where he heard some highly critical remarks directed towards Noguchi's work including the rumour that *Leptospira icteroides* could not be differentiated from *L. icterohaemorrhagiae*, the cause of Weil's disease. Realising that the issue would never be resolved without a susceptible laboratory animal, Beeuwkes visited Hamburg where he contracted to have some chimpanzees, Brazilian marmosets and Indian rhesus and crown monkeys delivered to Nigeria.

In May, the chimpanzees and crown monkeys arrived, but none proved susceptible to yellow fever. On 30 June, however, blood from a 28-year-old male from Togoland, Asibi, suffering the second day of a heavy fever, was injected into a rhesus monkey. Four days later the monkey developed a fever and died but

not before its blood was injected into another monkey and before a hungry
swarm of female *Aedes* was allowed to feed on the wretched monkey, strapped
to a board and placed in a cage with the mosquitoes.[27]

By December 1927, the Asibi strain of 'virus' had been passed by direct
inoculation or mosquitoes through twenty-six monkeys, all but two of which
developed a high fever and died. Furthermore post-mortem examinations of
these monkeys by Oskar Klotz of the University of Toronto generally revealed
jaundice, haemorrhaging and pathological changes in the liver, spleen and
kidneys, typical of human yellow fever. 'This is the first experimental animal
that I have seen inoculated with blood from a yellow fever case, in which the
lesions bore resemblances to human yellow fever', he told Russell, which 'leads
me to believe that the virus of yellow fever has been successfully implanted into
these animals'.[28]

But the nature of the so-called virus still remained a mystery. It could pass
through a Berkefeld filter and was clearly not *Leptospira*. That organism was
never found in post-mortems of any of the monkeys and while monkeys given
an inoculation of convalescent serum (serum from a recovered yellow fever
patient) before being challenged with a dose of virulent blood remained free of
the disease, those given *Leptospira* antiserum quickly developed the fever and
died. In addition a single monkey inoculated with a virulent *Leptospira* culture
showed no reaction but later died after inoculation with blood from a yellow
fever patient. To those in Lagos the implications of these discoveries were all too
clear: *Leptospira icteroides* bore no relationship to yellow fever, at least in West
Africa.[29]

Wilbur Sawyer, who, on Russell's promotion, had replaced him as Director of
the Division's Laboratory Service, realising that the problem would be resolved
by ascertaining whether immune serum from South America could protect
against the West African 'virus', ordered the American antiserum to be trans-
ported to Africa. Meanwhile Russell, who still retained much of his original faith
in Noguchi's work, informed Connor that the etiology of yellow fever in Brazil
needed to be re-examined. Either *Leptospira* was not linked to the disease in
Brazil or there were two different diseases with the same pathology transmitted
by the same mosquito.[30] To do this, Russell decided to establish a small yellow
fever laboratory in São Salvador, the capital of Bahia State, where, he hoped,
experiments on imported monkeys would clear up the *Leptospira* mystery once
and for all. However, results from West Africa made any further work on
Leptospira redundant. Convalescent serum from South America protected
rhesus monkeys from fatal attacks of West African yellow fever, showing that
the two diseases were 'immunologically identical'.[31]

What the Bahia laboratory did show, however, was a disturbing number of
unexpected yellow fever cases throughout Brazil. This discovery was based on
the 'liver-punch' or 'viscerotome', a device which could be used to puncture a

corpse and snip off a small piece of liver without the necessity of an autopsy. Routine microscopic examinations of such pieces taken from the bodies of those dying of a fever within ten days of its onset, had revealed the existence of the disease in areas of Brazil where no yellow fever was assumed to exist.[32] By the end of 1931 nearly 14,000 liver sections had been examined in the Bahia laboratory, and yellow fever cases had been shown to exist in seven states and twenty-five municipalities. Eventually, a few years later, these events led to the discovery of jungle yellow fever.

At this point Russell could have accepted the status quo, and continued with control work against the yellow fever vector in Brazil and West Africa, backed up now by two important field laboratories. But that was not to be. Impressed by the work of these laboratories Russell began to press for a central yellow fever laboratory in North America where more fundamental work could be carried out. 'We have never had a laboratory of our own', he told Connor, 'a condition which I now regret, because having had our laboratory in Lagos has made all the difference in the world in the value of our work.'[33] Russell's eventual success in acquiring this laboratory was described by Lewis Hackett as a 'major turning point in the history of the International Health Division'.[34]

The yellow fever laboratory

Russell began quietly in June 1928 by acquiring two rooms from Simon Flexner on the top floor of the Rockefeller Institute's animal house in Manhattan, east of Central Park, and converting them into a yellow fever laboratory under the direction of Wilbur Sawyer. But clearly he desired to go beyond that. In November 1928 a special committee presented a set of recommendations on the future of the Health Division to which Russell added his comments.[35] The present emphasis on administrative control, Russell argued, was not ideal; too many were engaged in administration and far too many of those working directly with diseases in the field were too greatly concerned with control problems and had 'lost contact with scientific aspects'. Unfortunately, he continued, even those 'who had retained the inquiring mind', had been provided with inadequate facilities. In the future, he urged, the Health Division must be permeated with the 'scientific attitude of mind, that is, with the spirit of inquiry and desire to increase knowledge'. In order to prevent diseases, he continued, they must be investigated 'with the best modern scientific methods'. The International Health Division must behave like the American Telegraph and Telephone Company, he argued, which went beyond building lines and renting phones to support research which may or may not have any obvious practical application. It was not enough, he went on, to offer research grants to university-based scientists. We need to develop the research outlook in our own staff by hiring scientific men who would be able to work in the field and in our own research laboratories. 'The staff of the International Health Division', he warned, 'is supposed to be composed of scientific men. Every effort must be made to keep them such.'

This hard-hitting memo naturally generated a heated response, most of it negative. George Vincent, Victor Heiser and C.-E. A. Winslow were all adamantly opposed, arguing that there was no need to change the existing programme when it had worked in the past and when more needed to be done. As Heiser noted, 'there is still a tremendous amount of needless suffering and death because existing scientific knowledge has not found its way into the lives of the people', reminding the Trustees that the Foundation had been created to promote the welfare of mankind.[36] Naturally, Simon Flexner, Director of the Rockefeller Institute, felt threatened. The Institute, he informed Rufus Cole, one of the scientific directors, must retain its research emphasis, 'unimpaired'. In Flexner's opinion the introduction of 'field workers of quite ordinary capacity and training' would harm the Institute and convert it into 'a kind of graduate school of instruction for field workers'. Unhampered, fundamental research was the job of the Institute, Flexner claimed, and any field worker of the Health Division could, as in the past, be sent to Johns Hopkins, Harvard, London or Toronto universities; there was absolutely no need for a 'home station'.[37]

But there was some support for Russell's proposals. Wade Hampton Frost, Professor of Epidemiology at Johns Hopkins School of Hygiene and a scientific director of the Health Division, was in sympathy but not totally enthusiastic. To him the Rockefeller Institute remained the agency of fundamental research, whereas, in the past, any research of the Health Division should be directly linked to problems of disease control. A central laboratory for general research, he told Russell, would be acceptable if it were directly geared to the problems in the field, but workers in such laboratories, he warned, have a tendency to initiate studies from 'the standpoint of their attractiveness as intramural laboratory investigations'.[38]

Russell needed to tread carefully. In an additional memo he stressed that the Health Division would seek only practical knowledge pointing out, with obvious reference to yellow fever, that 'many public health measures are now based upon observations which urgently need restudy'. But in addition to field laboratories, with which all were in agreement, he argued again for a 'home station' to study the problems being investigated in the field. Again yellow fever lay at the core of his argument; with dangerous viral diseases like yellow fever, work could be done more safely and better in their own well-endowed laboratory in the United States.[39]

According to Vincent the crucial meeting of the scientific directors of the Health Division held on 14 October 1929 resulted in Russell's defeat. The policy of the Division was to remain unchanged, he informed Flexner, and 'the question of setting up even a very modest center of research for the

International Health Division has either been abandoned or is held indefinitely in suspension'. However, he noted, the yellow fever work was to go on, and even if successful Vincent thought 'it unlikely that the other plan will be urged, at least for the present'.[40] In other words the Trustees rejected Russell's request for a central research laboratory in which fundamental research would be carried out, but allowed him to retain a central yellow fever laboratory where, presumably, they imagined only research of an applied nature linked to the field would go on. Russell may have lost the battle, but he certainly had not lost the war!

Initially the yellow fever laboratory must have been a scary place to work. The monkey room on the top floor of the Institute's animal house was the largest of the two rooms, 'they, in a sense, being more important than the men who merely worked on them', one of the workers remembered:

> It was called the 'dirty' room. It was here that monkeys died of the virulent Asibi virus, and here that the danger lay of infectious blood unknowingly being sprayed or splattered about from some sick monkey with bleeding gums or bloody stools. No one touched anything unless he were dressed for it – white trousers, long white coat, rubber gloves, and rubber apron. Just one object in the monkey room was regarded as 'clean' – the doorknob on the screen door leading to the inner room. No person working in the 'dirty' room ever touched it. If it became necessary to go out while still in working clothes, some 'clean' person had to open the door from the other side, or else rubber gloves had to be taken off, disposed of, and fresh ones put on. This procedure was time-consuming and often irritating, but it was vital inasmuch as a way had to be left for a caller to enter and pass through into the inner room without the danger of touching a contaminated door. Workers on finishing tasks in the monkey room would immediately strip off their gloves and coats and drop them into a container of lysol. Later the garments were boiled.[41]

Clearly two issues needed to be addressed. They needed to discover an experimental animal less expensive and less dangerous to handle than the monkey and a yellow fever vaccine was needed to protect laboratory workers from the often fatal disease. They were successful on both these counts and by the use of mice were even able to develop a vaccine for mass vaccinations made necessary by the discovery of jungle yellow fever. In June 1937 satisfactory field trials in Minas Geraes with a new vaccine, virus 17D, led to the first mass vaccinations of over 36,000 later in the year. As Soper enthused, 'a definite step forward has been made and . . . efficient protection of populations exposed to jungle yellow fever is in sight'.[42]

From 1928 until Russell's retirement in 1934 the laboratory within the Rockefeller Institute kept almost entirely to yellow fever. But Russell and Sawyer made sure that the laboratory space continually grew over the years, and continued to hint, at least, that research on other diseases also needed to be done. As early as 1930 Russell had mentioned to Flexner that when the occasion arose it would carry out investigations on other diseases which were being dealt with in the field.[43] He continued to press for 'more scientific studies of public health problems' both in the field and at a home station, and urged often that they should 'search for new knowledge' and gradually relinquish their support of health departments.[44]

In 1930 such an opportunity to investigate some fundamental problems of malaria presented itself to Russell. In that year he received a plan for new malaria investigations from Mark Boyd, Director of the North Carolina Station for Malarial Field Studies in Edenton, which had replaced the original malarial station in Leesburg, Georgia, in 1926. Boyd had recognised the enormous possibilities for carrying out fundamental malarial research in mental hospitals where patients with general paralysis of the insane, brought on by tertiary syphilis, were believed to undergo remission if subject to high fever and, for that reason, were often inoculated with the malarial parasite. Encouraged by Russell, Boyd decided that Tallahassee, Florida, with a reported 57 per cent splenic index would be an ideal site for a malaria station and gained permission to use the Chattahoochee State Hospital for experiments on 'induced malaria'.[45]

The Tallahassee research laboratory, which opened in 1931, was clearly the model that Russell was looking for. The laboratory was not built to deal simply with the local problems of malaria as Leesburg and Edenton had been. With its own supply of anopheline mosquitoes reared in the insectary, 'as large, vigorous and blood thirsty as the best wild mosquitoes', with a supply of humans available for infection with both *Plasmodium vivax* and *falciparum*, Boyd enthused over 'the apparently inexhaustible opportunities for research afforded by the malaria therapy service'.[46]

The work done at the station appears to have been precisely the kind found objectionable by many of the field officers. By the time it closed in 1946, Boyd and others had published 123 papers mostly in the *American Journal of Hygiene* and the *American Journal of Tropical Medicine*. They dealt chiefly with acquired immunity and comparative susceptibility of various anopheline species and varieties to *Plasmodium*. He also published material gathered in the more than 1,500 files on induced malaria which had 'thrown light on obscure aspects of the disease'. But, curiously, as far as I can tell, none of the scientific directors who had been suspicious of any attempt to separate the field and the laboratory complained about this work going on in Florida.

Meanwhile, the huge success of the yellow fever programme convinced many in the organisation that Russell had been correct. The problems that remained to be solved, he informed the scientific directors in 1933, are those where insufficient knowledge existed. What had been done for yellow fever now needed to be done for malaria, he urged, and as a result his 'home station' finally opened on 1 January 1934 as a separate wing of the Rockefeller Institute, investigating both yellow fever and now malaria. It received its own separate budget which grew to average over 8 per cent of the Health Division's total budget and its title changed from the 'Yellow Fever Laboratory' to the 'Labora-tory of the International Health Division'. The nearby Institute hospital, Sawyer told Russell, offered an opportunity to study induced malaria in arthritic patients, and investigations on monkey malaria offered 'a set of practically limitless opportunities'.[47] Russell's victory was now complete. At the end of the year he stepped down, to be replaced by Sawyer; the Directorship of the Health Division had passed again to a laboratory man.

Despite Russell's enthusiasm for research, field work in county health units still remained central to the work of the International Health Division during the early 1930s. But, as planned and obviously with Russell's approval, the Health Division started to withdraw support from these units in the mid-1930s and passed on the responsibility to the states themselves. In 1934 thirteen states received support but a year later only four states remained. However, abroad the numbers of county health units had grown. They could be found in seventeen countries of Central and South America, the Caribbean, Europe and the Far East. A few years later they even moved into my own Canadian Province of Nova Scotia, where tuberculosis and enteritis rather than hookworm and malaria provided the major problems.

But many in the organisation felt unease over what Russell and now Sawyer meant by field research. 'The Scientific Directors wondered', Hackett wrote, 'whether by "field research" [Russell] did not mean lab research in the field rather than their concept of public health and statistical investigation.'[48] Many expressed concern at whether any close collaboration could continue between those sweating and toiling in the primitive conditions of most field postings and those working in glamorous laboratories of the bigger cities where careers could be built by publishing articles in prestigious journals. When, in 1935, after ten years of field campaigns, the experimental malaria stations in Italy were transferred to the new Institute of Public Health in Rome, Lewis Hackett, one of the Health Division's most successful field generals, pointed out that the absence of field stations seemed to have changed the entire character of malarial work in Italy. Field stations, he believed, were 'the life of a malaria laboratory', and without them the new Laboratory for the Study and Prevention of Malaria would be preoccupied with the study of bird and monkey malaria, to the exclusion of the practical and applied.[49]

But in the long run Russell was victorious, winning many over to his point of view. Support for 'the advancement of knowledge' led the Health Division and other divisions of the Rockefeller Foundation to endow and support institutes of teaching and research at university schools of hygiene at Harvard, Johns Hopkins, Toronto and the London School of Hygiene and Tropical Medicine, particularly in the late 1920s and early 1930s. In the process the International Health Division began to offer, in the words of Lewis Hackett, more support to the 'advanced, cultured and prosperous nations' of the north than to the 'poorer, ignorant and backward countries' of the south.[50] He even approved of this new emphasis. In a 1946 address to the Instituto de Conferencias Populares in Buenos Aires, Hackett acknowledged that the advancement of knowledge had now become more important than bringing up to date 'backward sections of human thought and action'. As if throwing away all his years in South America, Sardinia, the Pontine Marshes and along the toe of Southern Italy, he revealed the new thinking:

> It seems now quite clear that the sums invested in equipment for Fleming . . . or in the 200 inch lens for the observatory on Mount Palomar . . . have been more productive than similar amounts applied to stimulating research, improving the training and supplying instruments of precision where there has been no indication of profound scholarship or inventive genius, or where the Governments and the Universities have little appreciation of the value of their men of scientific and cultural ability.[51]

This transition began during the Russell years. The Rockefeller flag became thereby firmly planted in the camp of those who argued for the wholesale transfer of technologically driven western medicine to the Third World, irrespective of the social conditions and health needs of these countries. The medical elite in these countries as well in the West, believed that Western models were applicable anywhere at any time and continually stressed that the quality and type of health care provided by the Western trained or influenced physicians, must become the model and replace any broader based notions of health delivered by less formally educated health workers. With a few notable exceptions, members of the International Health Division before the Second World War believed in the necessity of high medical standards and rarely questioned the maxim of many Western-trained African physicians that 'our people deserve nothing but the best', irrespective of how many were denied access to any health care because of this policy.[52]

Acknowledgements

This is part of an on-going study of the history of the International Health Division, supported by grants from The Rockefeller Archive Center and the Social Sciences and Humanities Research Council of Canada. I thank both for their support.

Notes

1 Russell to Connor, 14 February 1928. RFA. RG 1.1. S. 305. B.20, f. 158.
2 Rose to L. Hackett, 25 April 1917. RFA. RG 1.1. S.305. B.15, f. 133.
3 Russell, 'The Program for Future Work of the International Health Division', 9 September 1929. RFA. RG 3. S.908. B.11, f. 124.

4 R. Fosdick, *The Story of the Rockefeller Foundation* (New York: Harper, 1952), p. 140.

5 Rose, 'Outline plan for cooperating in the work of relief and control of uncinariasis'. RFA. RG. 3. S.908. B.12, f. 128. The original resolutions setting up the International Health Commission were approved at the meeting of the trustees of the Rockefeller Foundation (RF) on 27 June 1913.

6 John Ettling's *The Germ of Laziness* (Cambridge, Mass.: Harvard University Press, 1981) gives the definitive history of the Sanitary Commission, but the story of the International Health Commission and its successors has had a very chequered past. On his death in 1962, Lewis Hackett left behind a very valuable ten-chapter MS. dealing with the history of the Health Division which he had been commissioned to write twelve years previously, and which formed the basis of his Presidential Address to the American Society of Tropical Medicine in 1960. (L. Hackett, 'Once upon a Time', *American Journal of Tropical Medicine*, 9 (1960), 105–15.) Anxious to see the work completed, the Rockefeller Foundation turned to Greer Williams. But his 200,000 word, eight-part, 63-chapter, MS. entitled 'The Friendly Americans: The Story of the Rockefeller Foundation in World Health' (RFA. RF 3. S.908) was rejected by Little, Brown and Company, as being fit only for the specialist reader. The author then agreed 'to take the choice cuts . . . and throw the carcass away', and a much shortened popular version *The Plague Killers* (New York: Scribner, 1967) eventually appeared. But restricted to a popular account of campaigns against hookworm, yellow fever and malaria, it no longer bore much resemblance to a history of the Division. Indeed the chapters on hookworm were savaged by Scribner with the comment that the original version had 'too many references to privies and to the Rockefeller Foundation'. Roy Acheson, *Wickliffe Rose of the Rockefeller Foundation: 1862–1914* (Cambridge, UK: Killycarn Press, 1992) also provides a useful introduction to the work of the International Health Commission and is the first part of a full biography of Rose now in preparation.

7 Information from J. A. Ferrell, *History of County Health Organizations in the United States, 1908–1933* (Washington: US Government Printing Office, 1936).

8 This was also part of the International Health Board's agenda to encourage the power of intrusive centralised governments. In Brazil this took the form of supporting the National Government over State and municipal governments (see chapter 11 in this volume); in the American South support of State governments over local municipalities (see W. Link, *The Paradox of Southern Progressivism, 1880–1930* (Chapel Hill, NC: University of North Carolina Press, 1992)).

9 'A General History and Summary of 17 months of Health Work in Northampton County, North Carolina. August 1, 1917 to January 1, 1919'. RFA. RG 5.1.2. S.236. B.43, f. 654. I could have chosen many other such units in other States as an illustration, but the report of Northampton County so excels others in its richness, that I had no difficulty in selecting it for discussion. The over-zealousness of the report and my own rendering of it should not be allowed to override my own feeling that such campaigns must have had very positive results.

10 Such plans were outlined by John Ferrell in 'Memorandum in Reference to Proposition from the North Carolina State Board of Health for the Control of Hookworm and other Soil-pollution Diseases', 17 April 1917. RFA. RG 5.1.2 S.236. B.43, f. 654.

11 Reports of these experiments in RFA. RG 5.3. S.227. B.46 and RG 5.3. S.204. B.12.

12 F. Hoffman to Rose, 19 December 1917. RFA. RG 5.1.1. B.22, f. 386.

13 RF, Annual Report 1918.

14 These campaigns are described in 'Annual Reports of the work of the IHB in Brazil for 1924 and 1926'. RFA. RG 5.3. S.305 B.108 and 109.

15 Biggs to Rose, 21 February 1918. RFA. RG 3. S.908. B.15, f. 174.

16 The Greer Williams notes (RFA. RG 3.1. S.908. B.7H, f. 8694) contain details of interviews about Russell conducted by Lewis Hackett.

17 F. Russell, 'Suggestions for a Modification of the Plan of the I.H.B. in New Countries', 25 October 1921. RFA. RG 3. S.908. B.15, f. 174.

18 F. Russell, 'Principles and Policies of the International Health Board with regard to Public Health Laboratories in the United States', 1926 memo. RFA. RG 5.3. S.908. B.15, f. 174.

19 S. T. Darling to F. Russell, 31 December 1924. 'Report of Year's Work, 1924, in Malarial Control in Lee County, Georgia'. RFA. RG 5.2. S.212. B.8, f. 46.

20 H. Howard. Report of Itinerary and Observations of H. H. Howard, Director for the West Indies. 8 January to 18 March 1920. RFA. RG 5.2. S.420. B.41, f. 248.

21 Annual Report of the International Health Board, 1925, p. 3.

22 G. Strode, *Yellow Fever* (New York: McGraw Hill, 1951) provides the best account of the Health Division's work on the disease.

23 For details of the key-centre theory, see H. R. Carter, *Yellow Fever. An Epidemiological and Historical Study of its Place and Origin* (Baltimore: Williams and Wilkins, 1931).

24 Noguchi published these findings in a series of papers published in the *Journal of Experimental Medicine*, 29 and 30 (1919). His work is discussed in Greer Williams, *The Plague Killers* (New York: Scribner, 1967). The life and work of this fascinating and complex figure is discussed more fully in Isabel Plesset, *Noguchi and His Patrons* (New York: Fairleigh Dickinson University Press, 1980).

25 I. Kligler, 'Discussion of the Studies on the West Africa yellow fever', RFA. RG 5.2. B.52, f. 332.

26 Meeting between Flexner and Russell, 12 October 1926. RFA. Russell Diaries, vol. 2.

27 A. Stokes, J. Bauer and N. Hudson, 'Experimental Transmission of Yellow Fever to Laboratory Animals', *American Journal of Tropical Medicine*, 8 (1928), 103–64.

28 O. Klotz to Russell, 3 October 1927. RFA. RG 5. S.1.2. B.305, f. 3881.

29 Beeuwkes to Russell, 17 September 1927. RFA. RG 5. S.1.2. B.306, f. 3887.

30 Russell to Connor, 23 April 1928. RFA. RG 1.1. S.305. B.20, f. 158.

31 West African Yellow Fever Commission. 4th Annual Report, 1928. RFA. RG 5.3. B.215.

32 Soper to Russell, 24 August 1930. RFA. RG 1.1. S.305. B.21, f. 165.

33 Russell to Connor, 11 May 1928. RFA. RG 1.1. S.305. B.20, f.158.

34 L. Hackett, 'History of the International Health Division', chap. 10, 'The Laboratory and the Field'. Typed MS. RFA. RG 3. S.908. B.5, f. 37.

35 Russell, 'Memo concerning Future Developments of the IHD', RFA. RG 1. S.100. B.11, f. 91.

36 Heiser's reply. 16 September 1929. RFA. RG 3. S.908. B.12, f. 129.

37 Flexner to Cole, 3 and 12 July 1929. RFA. RG 1. S.100. B.11, f. 91.

38 W. Frost to Russell, 19 June 1929. RFA. RG 1. S.100. B.11, f. 91.
39 Russell, 'The Program for Future Work of the International Health Division'. 9 September 1929. RFA. RG 3. S.908. B.11, f. 124.
40 Vincent to Flexner, 22 October 1929. RFA. RG 1. S.100. B.11, f. 91. Other than allocating $40,000 for studies at the Rockefeller Institute, the minutes of the 14 October meeting make no mention of the laboratory crisis.
41 T. Norton, 'Recollections of the Yellow Fever Laboratory', October 1946. RFA. RG 1. S.100. B.11, f. 92. Thomas Norton was engaged as a technician shortly after the lab opened.
42 Soper to Fosdick, 17 January 1938. RFA. RG 1.1. S.305. B.23, f. 184.
43 Russell to Flexner, 28 October 1930. RFA. RG 1. S.100. B.11, f. 91.
44 Russell to Fosdick, 9 July 1931. RFA. RG 1. S.100. B.11, f. 91.
45 Details in RFA. RG 1.1. S.211. B.1, f. 2.
46 Details of the work done there can be found in the Annual Reports of the Florida Malaria Research Station. RFA. RG 5. S.211. B.19.
47 Sawyer to Russell, 12 July 1934. RFA. RG 5.4. B.25, f. 284.
48 L. Hackett, 'History of the International Health Division'. Lab. and Field. Rough Outline. Typed MS. RFA. RG 3. S.908. B.5, f. 37.
49 'Second Quarterly Report of the Work of the International Health Division in Italy. April 1–June 30, 1935'. RFA. RG 5.3. S.751. B.249.
50 In 1924, about 20 per cent of the budget was allocated to projects in North America. By 1935 that percentage had climbed to 35 per cent and by 1950, when the Health Division closed, it had reached 55 per cent. By 1950, also, 80 per cent of the total budget was spent in North America and Europe, far from the tropics where it had started out.
51 L. Hackett, 'The Rockefeller Foundation and the Modern Concepts of Public Health', Paper to Instituto de Conferencias Populares, Buenos Aires, 2 August 1946. RFA. Hackett Papers. S.3. B.14, f. 167.
52 These issues are discussed in M. King (ed.), *Medical Care in Developing Countries: A Primer on the Medicine of Poverty* (Nairobi: Oxford University Press, 1966); Brian Maegraith, *One World* (London: Athlone Press, 1973); John Farley, *Bilharzia: A History of Imperial Tropical Medicine* (New York: Cambridge University Press, 1991), chap. 17, and many other recent publications.

11

The cycles of eradication: the Rockefeller Foundation and Latin American public health, 1918–1940

MARCOS CUETO

Between 1918 and 1940 Latin America became a testing ground for one of the most ambitious and controversial concepts in modern public health: disease eradication. The eradication of infectious diseases in Latin America became a popular endeavour among many US public health authorities of the early twentieth century. This concern arose for a complex combination of technical and political reasons which included the success of local eradication efforts earlier in the century (e.g., those carried out in Havana and Panama at the turn of the century), the fear of Latin America infecting or reinfecting the US, and the perceived need to protect those areas of the world which the US considered under its economic influence.[1]

Partially because of the absence during the 1920s and 1930s of an effective international framework through which Latin American countries could act on common health problems, the Rockefeller Foundation (RF) played an active role in the emergence and application of the eradication concept (the Pan American Sanitary Bureau, created in 1902, functioned until the early 1930s with a small staff and as a virtual branch of the US Public Health Service).[2] The RF's eradication campaigns had several by-products such as the reorganisation of Latin American public health institutions, the expansion of public health services to rural areas, and the shift of the academic and technical centre of influence from France to the US.

Three diseases in Latin America captured the attention of the RF and became the focus of eradication: hookworm, yellow fever and malaria. These diseases were considered technically susceptible for elimination through short-term and well-organised campaigns. The campaigns in turn were considered as a means for initiating public health reforms in a number of countries. Because the disease, sanitary and social realities of Latin America were more complex than the Foundation expected, the campaigns and reform efforts met with mixed results. As a result, during the interwar period optimism about eradication went through cycles of boom and slump and the concept changed its meaning.

Hookworm

In 1914, the RF created the International Health Commission (changed to Board in 1915 and to Division in 1927) (IHD) for the purpose of extending the work of the Rockefeller Sanitary Commission for Eradication of Hookworm Disease to countries other than the United States. The disease attacked primarily young men working in rural areas in the most productive period of their lives and was characterised by anaemia and fatigue. Because of these features the disease was perceived as an explanation of the low productivity of rural workers and considered an obstacle for the expansion and intensification of US commerce and industry abroad.

Technically the control of the disease appeared simple by 1919. The cycle of the parasite (*Ascaris* worms), the main mode of transmission (the hookworms enter the body through the toes and are expelled with human faeces infecting barefoot people), and two drugs of potent anthelmintic value and easy administration were all well known.[3] In addition to the administration of weekly doses of drugs it was hoped that the construction of latrines and educative work (lectures, microscopical demonstrations and distribution of literature) would suffice to curb the disease.

The first attempts at complete eradication of hookworm infection in Latin America occurred during the First World War in the Guianas, the Caribbean and Central America. During these campaigns, Wickliffe Rose, the Director of the IHD, considered public health reform and American prestige as the main goals of their work:

> The work for the relief and control of uncinariasis [another word for hookworm] which we are organizing in these Latin American countries is to be regarded merely as an entering wedge toward a larger and more permanent service in the medical field. It will lead inevitably to the consideration of the whole question of medical education, the organization of systems of public health and the training of men for the public health service . . . the South American people have come to know us mainly as a people interested in our own business advancement. Such service as the Foundation has to render will tend to counteract the effect of the purely mercenary spirit and to establish a basis of real cooperation.[4]

The first contact of the RF with hookworm in South America occurred as part of a survey made in Brazil in 1916.[5] The survey included dispensary demonstrations on hookworm in several rural localities. The dispensary consisted of a travelling tent and a staff of a physician and lay assistants, which visited towns examining, treating and educating people free of charge, and teaching how to construct latrines.[6] The task of constructing latrines was considered crucial since barefoot peasants who walked on ground infested with contaminated human faeces usually acquired the disease. As a result of these demonstrations as well as another visit by an RF officer in 1917, the Foundation initiated a two-fold programme in Brazil: the teaching of hygiene and pathology at the University of São Paulo and a hookworm campaign. The agreement of the RF with the Brazilian government included the appointment of an RF officer as Director of a new Department of Uncinariasis.

An important by-product of the campaign in Brazil was the organisation in 1920 of the Federal Health Service into a more centralistic National Department of Health, which included a Division of Rural Public Health devoted to three principal endemic diseases: hookworm, malaria and Chagas disease.[7] Another important outgrowth of the hookworm campaign was the organisation of rural sanitary services in four states and later the IHD transferred its funds from hookworm demonstrations to the organisation of rural posts which resembled US county health units.[8]

In an effort to overcome the typical part-time appointments in Latin American public health organisations, the posts were to be organised with well-qualified, full-time and well-paid salaried health officers. The units developed general sanitary works such as laboratory examinations, hookworm treatments, vaccinations against smallpox and some sanitary engineering work. In 1924, the RF terminated an eight-year period of co-operation leaving 122 Federal-state rural posts in operation in 17 of the 20 states of Brazil.[9] The case of Brazil suggested the growing tendency of the Foundation's hookworm work in Latin America in leaving the domain of simple demonstration and in taking on something of the attributes of a state-directed rural health service.[10] The trend was clearly illustrated by the RF's hookworm campaign in Colombia.

With the co-operation of Colombia's President, the IHD began to work in hookworm control in that country in 1920. A preliminary survey was organised not only to provide valuable information but also as a device to convince reluctant authorities about the need for reform in public health. To begin with a survey was considered crucial for presenting hookworm as a separate and dramatic disease and for convincing everybody of the urgency of treatment. The results of the survey were partially utilised in popular lectures to secure co-operation among people who considered anaemia to be a fact of life. The survey found an average infection rate of about 75 per cent for the population of the country (labourers working in coffee plantations showed the highest infection rate).[11]

After the survey the RF appropriated US $40,000 to organise a Department of Uncinariasis which was placed under the direction of a Foundation representative. In addition, the RF provided a fellowship in public health to study in the US. The new Department was composed of two parts: a section of cures with the duty of making examinations and giving treatments and a section of soil sanitation to supervise the construction of sanitary privies. During the first six months the number of workers in the campaign grew from 11 to 85. Their task seemed monumental since over 95 per cent of the rural homes were without latrines.

Between June 1920 and June 1926, 334,041 Colombians of six provinces were examined, of whom 307,456 were found to be infested with hookworm.[12] Some of them were treated with the newly introduced mixture of carbon tetrachloride and oil of Chenopodium. The treatment met some opposition, since there were a number of deaths after treatment. This occurred because treatment had toxic effects and was counterindicated with alcoholism, severe malnutrition, malaria, heart disease, pulmonary tuberculosis, among other conditions. In rural areas, it was difficult if not impossible for sanitary inspectors to administer safe dosages and to determine the condition of the patients before treatment.

When the period of work stipulated in the agreement with Colombia was about to end, the RF considered that the work had not progressed to a point at which its direction could be satisfactorily handed over to local personnel. Consequently, the Foundation proposed a new agreement to achieve a closer relationship between hookworm control operations and the reform of the government's public health service. Under the agreement the RF provided 50 per cent of a US $75,000 budget for five years, exclusive of the salary of a representative, plus two or more public health fellowships for Colombians.[13] Fellowships were considered an important means for reformulating public health in Colombia and in other Latin American countries.

Since 1917, the IHD offered to advanced Latin American students a number of public health fellowships to study at Johns Hopkins University and other North American institutions. These fellowships were part of the RF's efforts to attract the Latin American medical and public health personnel who sought training abroad on American lines. A result of these fellowships was that the traditional Latin American preference for graduate medical training in Paris was discouraged. Between 1917 and 1942, the RF awarded 316 fellowships in public health to Latin Americans, especially to Brazilians.[14] These fellowships were awarded to members of what the RF considered to be the strategic centres of higher education, which turned out to be those institutions most closely resembling the American model of medical education. Two important conditions of the grant were that fellows had to be assured of a definite post upon their return and no grant was awarded to people unattached to an institution. Some of the former fellows of the RF participated in the additional surveys and campaigns against hookworm organised by the RF. As an outgrowth of these campaigns, rural county health units were established and supported by the Foundation in a number of countries. Some of the most important campaigns were carried out in Paraguay (1923–7); Venezuela (1927–8); and Mexico (1923–8).[15]

The RF found it difficult to develop these campaigns to a self-perpetuating stage partially because the number of native physicians was insufficient. The lack of 'appropriate personnel' to perpetuate the campaigns was considered serious, since during the 1920s the number of doctors in most Latin American countries was far below the estimated 'need' (though not far below the actual demand). The ratio of physicians to population was often fairly favourable in the larger cities where medical services were concentrated but very unfavourable in rural districts.[16] In addition, even in the fifties it was difficult to find a sufficient number of 'properly trained' public health officials, according to American standards. Latin American education was considered by Foundation officers as emphasising clinical instruction, neglecting laboratory work in the basic sciences and being detrimentally influenced by the French model.[17]

Partially because of the lack of public health personnel the majority of people living in rural areas took care of themselves through self-medication and consulted healers, herbalists and so-called quacks. Both the RF and native physicians condemned native healers and domestic medicine as primitive. The refusal to understand and engage with popular beliefs or to enlist non-Western practitioners contributed to the typical cultural resistance to public health modernisation. During the hookworm campaign in Colombia, for example, the RF confronted some opposition since there was an extended belief among the population that it was better to deposit excreta in the ground where 'they would be dried by the sun', and not in the 'dark, evil-smelly holes [latrines]' which breed mosquitoes.[18] In a related development, during the hookworm campaign in Brazil an RF officer narrated that when testing people's blood a native healer: 'told them that we were selling the blood . . . to the Devil. So all the people ran home and we had nobody left to work with in that town.'[19]

Another difficulty confronted by the Foundation was the economic roots of hookworm, which ultimately required raising the living standards of the people. For example, the installation and use of latrines in Colombia met with considerable opposition since the popular opinion was that they were a luxury. Many people also believed that anaemia was due to starvation and therefore the money spent in erecting latrines would be better used in providing food.[20] In rural Brazil, where the population went unshod or wore sandals with wooden soles, it was difficult for RF doctors to promote the use of shoes since they were considered a luxury (the cheapest pair was equivalent to three-weeks' wages). In addition, during the wet season, shoes and even sandals were considered an inconvenience since they gathered up the sticky mud, increasing the weight on each foot. As a result, adults working in the field rarely and children never used shoes.[21]

Despite cases of popular resistance, however, the majority of the Latin American governments welcomed and supported the RF's hookworm campaigns. The main reason for this support has to do with the state of development of public health institutions in Latin America during the early twentieth century. By the late 1910s, a number of infectious diseases were already controlled in the major cities of Latin America, which with their improvements in water supply, sewage systems and garbage disposal became more salubrious than the countryside. Hookworm, a rural disease, afforded the opportunity to concentrate on an area of importance for economies based on the exportation of agricultural products and where – with the exception of Brazil – little work had been done. Since 1916, the Brazilian Belisario Pena had headed an important local movement of rural sanitation which proposed the reform of public health services (his efforts resulted in the creation of a Service of Rural Prophylaxis).[22]

In addition, the campaign against hookworm was perceived by the Latin American governments as an opportunity to end the duality in the administration of health services – between the state and the municipalities – that characterised the public health organisation of many Latin American countries of the 1910s.

Until the late nineteenth century most Latin American governments practised a non-interventive policy in matters relating to public health which were usually in the charge of municipal or state councils. This policy was altered in extreme cases, such as the menace of an extensive epidemic when committees of sanitation were organised whose duration was ephemeral. Around the turn of the twentieth century public sanitation began to be organised as a branch of the national government and most of the Latin American countries formed national departments of *sanidad* or *salubridad publica*.[23] These institutes lacked autonomy and resources and were usually under a joint Ministry responsible for Development, Assistance or Education. With the exception of Chile – which created a Ministry of Health and a Welfare system as early as 1924 – there were no ministries of health nor compulsory health insurance until the 1930s.

The Pan American Sanitary Bureau contributed to the efforts of the state-organised public health institutions in the late 1920s when it was empowered by the International Sanitary Conference in Paris to act as the 'regional' organisation of the Office international d'hygiène publique (OIHP) and collect health statistics and epidemiological information from the Americas.[24] The decision led to the creation by the Bureau of a small staff of American travelling representatives. The field staff began to offer a consultative service for advising on control of epidemics in Latin American countries and on the organisation and improvement of health services, especially in Peru, Chile, Ecuador, the Central American countries and Mexico.[25]

The consolidation of national health institutions in the Latin American countries of the interwar period was part of a process of the state taking control of public health as part of the general expansion of the nation-state's powers.[26] In rural areas the conflict between state and municipal health services was part of the skirmishes between the state apparatus and agrarian elites. The campaigns of the RF took sides in these struggles and favoured the efforts of the central government to extend its authority to the rest of the country. Rather than sympathising with the Foundation's goals of eradication as an international endeavour or sharing its promotion of public health reform, it appears that the governments were interested in reinforcing state authority by an association with a wealthy ally and a source of technological know-how.

By the late 1920s, hookworm campaigns everywhere in Latin America failed to eliminate entirely hookworm infestation (it was discovered that in areas where public health infrastructure was not built the incidence of hookworm infection returned after two years). With the exception of Brazil, the county health units which emerged with the hookworm campaigns became disorganised. According to Birn, Mexican RF-sponsored county health units encountered the opposition of traditional practitioners and provincial physicians who resented their displacement.[27]

During the 1930s, the RF re-evaluated its hookworm goals in Latin America because of newly perceived difficulties not considered, such as the gigantic dimension of hookworm infestation in some countries, the problems in administering safe doses, the high cost of the campaigns, the resistance of native healers and some physicians, the tension between foreign experts and local inspectors, the temporary nature of the majority of the latrines constructed, the disturbed political conditions of some countries which discontinued services and the fact that despite the surveys hookworm disease was never fully considered a problem of primary importance in many countries.[28]

As a result of these factors, the elimination of hookworm, the original goal of the RF, was progressively soft-pedalled and the eradication concept was partially discredited. However, another disease kept alive, at least for a while, the hope of eradication.

Yellow fever

Since 1916 the IHD of the RF was convinced that the first worldwide sanitary task which might be undertaken with promise of lasting results was the eradication of yellow fever.[29] Material interests in controlling the fever were strong because it was considered a disease of ports and big cities of the Americas. Since the First World War, imports and capital from the US flowed into the larger Latin American countries, helping to consolidate an export economy based on raw materials. These economies depended a great deal on the salubriousness of a country's ports and coastal regions where many products were stored and loaded aboard ships. There was also a great fear that yellow fever would return to subtropical regions of the US, and, with the opening of the Panama Canal in 1914, would extend to tropical Asia, until then free of the disease.

In addition to the commercial reasons the promise of academic prestige played a role in the quest for eliminating the fever because until the late 1920s the etiology of yellow fever remained a mystery (and therefore a race to identify the microorganism and to develop a serum and a vaccine existed). Eventually, research on yellow fever became one of the few areas in tropical medicine where Americans overcame the early lead of Europeans in the field. Competition and some nationalism led an anonymous officer of the RF to affirm that the 'glory' of the elimination of yellow fever would have to go to 'North American . . . executors'.[30]

Optimism about yellow fever eradication was sustained on two scientific beliefs that proved to be mistakes. First, the so-called key-centre theory, which considered yellow fever to be a human disease of big urban centres transmitted only by the mosquito *Aedes aegypti*, a domestic species which breeds in artificial water containers. During the 1910s and 1920s, the key-centre theory also sustained the idea that small communities did not maintain endemicity (and therefore need not be treated and should not be taken care of) and that the disease was self-liquidating through the exhaustion of the non-immunes (because an attack of yellow fever usually produced permanent immunity). The hope for the elimination of the fever lay in the fact that key-urban-centres with a steady supply of non-immunes were few in number in the Americas.

By the early 1930s, some new facts were established that contradicted the key-centre theory on yellow fever. These facts included: that the disease could be transmitted by mosquitoes other than the *Aedes*, that small communities do maintain endemicity and that there was a permanent reservoir of infection in the jungles. This led to the denomination of jungle yellow fever, although clinically and immunologically there is no difference between jungle and urban yellow fever, the only difference being epidemiological.

The second mistake, which inspired many yellow fever eradication efforts of the late 1910s and 1920s, was Hideyo Noguchi's vaccine and sera. In July 1918 a commission of the Rockefeller Institute of Medical Research carried out scientific studies on yellow fever in the Ecuadorian port of Guayaquil. A spectacular result of this work was Noguchi's announcement of a spirochetal agent, called *Leptospira icteroides*, which in guinea-pigs produced lesions suggestive of yellow fever. On returning to the US Noguchi produced both a serum and a vaccine for yellow fever.[31] Although the vaccine never came to be relied upon as the primary preventive measure, it was widely distributed by the RF to thousands of people and permitted persons with certificates to travel freely during yellow fever campaigns.[32]

Noguchi, however, was completely wrong on yellow fever (as explained by John Farley in chapter 10) and his vaccine was proved to be useless. The acceptance of *L. icteroides* and of Noguchi's vaccine for so many years by the clinicians who treated cases and by experienced laboratory workers suggests the power and prestige of the Rockefeller Institute during the 1920s.

Because of the key-centre theory and Noguchi's findings, by 1918 the epidemiological and scientific aspects of yellow fever seemed to be completely understood. For many, including the RF, it was just a matter of enforcing certain technical measures which a few experts were familiar with. The key-centre theory shaped the first RF campaign against yellow fever, which began in November 1918 in Guayaquil. The port-city was considered one of the main pest-holes of the Pacific and was usually blamed for reinfecting towns in Ecuador, Colombia, Peru and Chile. It was hoped that freeing Guayaquil would eliminate the disease from the remaining towns of the Pacific coast of South America. Instead of isolating cases and fumigating houses as the Ecuadorian authorities were doing, Michael E. Connor of the IHD, in charge of the Guayaquil campaign, concentrated on the larvae which grew in the large quantities of water that people stored in cans, wooden barrels and earthenware vessels. Connor emptied or destroyed small water containers, used mosquito-proof tanks and stocked large containers with fish. It was observed that several local river fish were very active as larvivores. After six weeks the results were spectacular. There had been more than 250 cases a year between 1910 and 1917, and 460 cases in 1918 alone.[33] By June 1919 the last case that ever occurred in Guayaquil was recorded. The next year the IHD withdrew its yellow fever representative and the local authorities assumed sole responsibility for inspection of larvae in domestic water containers. The RF experience in Ecuador was extended to the other Latin American country considered as a major endemic centre of yellow fever, namely, Brazil.

In 1923 the RF took charge of the administration of the state-organised Yellow Fever Service of northern Brazil.[34] The RF set up their activities entirely independently of any other Brazilian public health services in order to set an example of an American service and because of lack of confidence in local institutions. Following the belief that cleaning the major urban centres would end the infection, eleven control posts were established in the port cities and at Manaus, key to the Amazon region. The incidence of reported yellow fever declined so satisfactorily that by 1925 all but four of the stations had been closed.

Using massive distribution of fish and Noguchi's vaccine and serum the RF organised yellow fever surveys, campaigns and services in Guatemala (1919); Peru (1920–2); Colombia (1923); Central America (1921–2); Brazil (1923–40); and Mexico (1921–3).[35] As table 11.1 shows, the most significant amount of money spent by the IHD of the RF in Latin America between 1913 and 1940 was used in yellow fever. As in the agreements signed for hookworm, the RF requested that the Latin American governments contribute part of the campaign budgets on a decreasing basis but demanded technical and administrative control. In these campaigns Americans directed operations with an unlimited confidence in the capacity of technological resources, little community awareness and limited assistance of locals in directive positions. These campaigns

Table 11.1. *Appropriations of the International Health Division of the Rockefeller Foundation in Latin America, 1913–1940 (in US dollars)*

Country	Hookworm[a]	Yellow fever	Malaria	Public health services and education[c]	Miscellaneous expenses[d]
Argentina	—	—	61,459	15,000	30,000
Bolivia	—	22,877	—	—	—
Brazil	782,283	4,484,799	443,238	721,208	2,000
Colombia	178,929	245,276	19,353	68,280	4,000
Costa Rica	122,104	—	16,276	36,077	20,000
Cuba	—	—	76,800	41,896	—
Ecuador	—	92,647	3,252	—	—
Guatemala	129,153	—	539	20,865	
Guianas	134,032	2,000	10,000	—	—
Honduras	14,465	—	—	2,699	—
Jamaica	188,083	—	5,639	37,946	285,239
Mexico	60,539	432,482[b]	19,980	147,327	166
Nicaragua	109,780	—	9,975	42,559	—
Panama	219,553	1,000	22,267	59,503	996
Paraguay	66,157	13,514	—	60	—
Peru	—	131,941	—	—	—
Puerto Rico	115,645	—	130,753	129,334	44,503
Salvador	45,367	—	13,996	6,282	—
Venezuala	3,863	36,865	8,754	2,560	—
Other Caribbean islands	382,273	—	7,715	39,370	—
General expenses	12,648	239,127	—	680	—
Total	2,565,054	5,702,528	849,896	1,371,646	386,904

Source: International Health Division, Appropriations for work in Latin America from 1 July 1913 to 11 December 1940. Rockefeller Foundation Archives. R.G. 1.2. Series 300. Box 2. Folder 14. Rockefeller Archive Center.
[a]Hookworm includes control and investigation of internal parasites.
[b]Includes small expenditure for Central America.
[c]Includes administrations, laboratories, nursing, training stations, buildings and equipment.
[d]Includes respiratory diseases, and the collection of wild animals.

were largely devoted to the reduction of mosquito breeding in previously endemic centres and were instrumental in the disappearance of urban yellow fever from the Americas and in the eradication of *Aedes aegypti* from many South American cities.

By 1925 it was concluded that no yellow fever existed in the Americas with the exception of a small corner in northern Brazil.[36] Optimism increased because despite a 1927 search in Brazil only one case was found. The RF was already celebrating the event as a confirmation of the key-centre belief 'that cleaning the big-port cities would automatically end the infection in the interior'.[37] Reflecting the trend, the federal government shifted 400 men from yellow fever mosquito eradication to killing rats in response to a bubonic plague epidemic.[38]

However, in 1928 Rio de Janeiro was suddenly attacked by a severe epidemic of yellow fever. Yellow fever returned to Rio after an absence of twenty years, without *Aedes aegypti* and when the closest endemic region was a thousand miles away. By 1929, the epidemic was brought to a close, after a total of more than 800 cases and 436 deaths. The Brazilian director of health blamed the reappearance of yellow fever on the RF, charging that it had let the disease slip through from northern Brazil.[39] For lack of a better explanation the RF attributed the epidemic to movements of troops from the northeast to Rio but could not avoid the impression that some of its assumptions on yellow fever were wrong. At about the same time, outbreaks of yellow fever were reported elsewhere in Brazil (Bahia, Recife and Belém). By 1929, the disease appeared on ships as far south as the Rio de la Plata, Argentina, and as far up as Manaus, Brazil. Yellow fever, which was supposed to be on the verge of extinction, appeared to be distributed over a coastal distance of 4,500 miles. In addition, the disease appeared in a number of rural locations in Latin America, including Socorro in Colombia and Guaspati in Venezuela, both small centres far from any foci of infection and isolated from large cities. These events were a serious blow to the Foundation's confidence, questioned the validity of the key-centre theory, made evident that yellow fever also had a jungle variety and a reservoir in the jungles and demonstrated that urban sanitation reduced but not eliminated the incidence of the disease.[40]

From these events, the RF and some Brazilians concluded that more power to enforce sanitary measures was needed. This led to the renegotiation of the yellow fever agreement between the RF and the Brazilian government. Following the revolution of 1930 which raised Getulio Vargas into power, the RF was asked to take full responsibility for the eradication of yellow fever in all of Brazil with the single exception of Rio. Vargas presided over a heterogeneous coalition that included technocrats and the urban bourgeoisie who favoured the consolidation of a strong state. There was some opposition from several states to the new agreement with the RF because it disregarded the question of state rights. For example, the Secretary of Health of the State of Bahia, Antonio Luiz de Barros Barreto, protested against the agreement with the RF insisting that the RF could not eradicate yellow fever from South America without eradicating it from Brazil, could not eradicate it from Brazil without eradicating it from Bahia and could not come to Bahia without negotiating directly with him.[41] As a result, for several months it was difficult for the RF to work in Bahia. Eventually, the situation required the intervention of the National Department of Public Health and of the Governor of Bahia.

By 1938, Vargas dissolved the Congress, assumed dictatorial powers and baptised his regime as the *Estado Novo* (New State), resembling methods of fascist rulers.[42] The situation, however, was considered as an advantage by RF field-officers. The alliance between the RF and the populist dictator Vargas was not surprising, since it was a continuation of the association between the need of the Foundation for obtaining rapid legal backing for its sanitary work and the local efforts to expand interventionist state policies which based their legitimacy partially on offering public health and other services. According to an influential RF field officer: 'From the point of view of yellow fever control, [Vargas'] concentration of power was most helpful. By decree, the mosquito control service had been empowered to enter all premises and to enforce their control measures upon any recalcitrant householder'.[43]

Remnants of the key-centre theory led to the decision that the campaign should include smaller towns and villages of 2,000 population and over. However, due to the new technique of viscerotomy, it was discovered that a considerable number of deaths were occurring in smaller towns located in rural areas. In 1934 came another great outbreak of jungle yellow fever in Matto Grosso, Brazil, initiating an epidemic that in the next five years engulfed most of southern Brazil, Paraguay and Argentina. It finally retreated towards the northeast passing through the states of São Paulo and Rio de Janeiro and disappeared in 1938. The unexpectedly widespread distribution of jungle yellow fever, especially between 1937 and 1939, and the very extensive use of the 17D vaccine to combat it (by 1939 1,600,000 were vaccinated in Brazil) put a heavy strain on the resources of the Yellow Fever Service.[44] Work on yellow fever was complicated since it was found that due to an over-attenuation of some batches of the virus some of those vaccinated had not been protected from yellow fever and indeed had died from it. In addition, the production of the vaccine in Brazil became contaminated with hepatitis. As a result the RF suspended the local production of vaccine.[45] Another source of tension was the popular resistance to viscerotomy. It consisted of the routine post-mortem collection and examination of liver tissue from all persons dying after brief febrile illnesses and it was considered a more accurate method than clinical diagnosis for establishing the distribution of yellow fever. Introduced by the Foundation in 1930, by 1939 over 175,000 liver specimens had been examined. Many in the rural population simply considered viscerotomy as an 'abominable profanation' of corpses.[46]

After many delays, in 1939–40 arrangements were made to transfer the Yellow Fever Service, which had been under the control of the RF for sixteen years (1923–40), to the government, an important exception to its policy of avoiding active participation in the administration of government services for a prolonged period of time. Most of the sections of the Yellow Fever Service were incorporated into a National Yellow Fever Service subordinated to the Ministry of Education and Health.

The discovery of jungle yellow fever in Brazil and in other parts of South America invalidated previous optimism about eradication and suggested that the goal was not feasible. The goal of yellow fever eradication, which began as a device to create modern administrative structures considered necessary to apply established technology, turned into the enforcement of techniques which proved useless for eliminating the disease. In the late 1930s the RF began to lose its interest in yellow fever as an administrative public health problem. According to one of the main actors of the story, the yellow fever eradication programme was the most 'magnificent failure in public health history'.[47] However, hopes of success in eradication reappeared with malaria.

Malaria

The third Latin American disease that attracted the RF's attention and revived the eradication concept was malaria, a major cause of morbidity and mortality in the region.[48] During the 1910s, when the RF began to work against malaria, there was an agreement among world authorities on identifying the plasmodia and the *Anopheles* as the causative organism and the vector of malaria. In addition, it was clear that the only malaria drug of value was quinine and that mosquito reduction was one of the few techniques available. However, there were many unresolved puzzles, such as which were the *Anopheles* typical to specific Latin American regions.

In Latin America, very little malaria control was being done until the 1930s. Trained personnel were scarce, training facilities almost non-existent, and malaria services in national public health departments almost unknown. The majority of the rural population considered, as with anaemia for hookworm, that the intermittent fevers characteristic of malaria were facts of life. Since the 1920s, the work of the RF concentrated on assistance to local authorities in organising practical demonstrations to prove the feasibility of malaria control; some field studies to improve prophylaxis of drugs such as chloroquine and the training of personnel for malaria programmes.

Before DDT and related modern residual insecticides became available (only after the Second World War) Paris green (a larvicide made from copper arsenic for control of *Anopheles* breeding) was used successfully by the RF in several Latin American countries. The new technique conflicted with the more traditional approach of some local physicians who advocated a system of detecting parasite carriers and treating them with quinine to curb the disease.[49] The approach revealed the clinical background of many local public health personnel who tried to match an ideal clinical picture with every sick individual.

One of the first RF campaigns against malaria took place in 1925 in Tucumán and Jujuy, both locations in northern Argentina. A five-year agreement was signed between the Foundation and the National Department of Hygiene of Argentina to operate a Bureau of Studies and Demonstrations in Malaria. Because of the expense of employing full-time medical men, the RF broke its rule and placed greater responsibility upon non-medical personnel for subsoil drainage operations. Lay assistants were selected as chief inspectors from the regular staff, given intensive training in basic epidemiology and placed in charge of individual posts to fight against *Anopheles pesudopunctipennis*, the main vector of malaria in the region.[50] More than eradicating malaria from northern Argentina, the Foundation's emphasis was on control, that is, on reducing the density of the main vector in the belief that it would hamper the transmission of the disease.

Additional important malaria surveys and campaigns were done in Brazil (1919–28) and Venezuela (1927–8).[51] As in the case of hookworm and of yellow fever, the RF thought that knowledge and techniques were already well developed and at their disposal; what was lacking was a method of enforcing its application. The neglect of the social and cultural dimensions of the campaigns was exemplified in 1928 by George Vincent, the President of the Foundation, with the statement: 'a good malaria fighter must learn to think like a mosquito'.[52]

The RF campaigns against malaria in Latin America experienced a major turn in 1938 when the African *Anopheles gambiae*, the most dangerous mosquito of its family (first detected in Brazil in 1930 by a member of the Foundation's staff), was responsible for the greatest epidemic of malaria ever to hit the Americas. The epidemic encompassed some 200 miles from Natal to the Jaguaribe valley in the state of Ceara producing 100,000 cases and 14,000 to 20,000 deaths. The area was one which had been free of malaria so there were no natural immunities. The invasion of Brazil by the African mosquito stimulated the fear of the Americas being struck by the devastation caused by malaria in Africa.

A special Anti-Malaria Service was established by a decree of President Vargas, and in January 1939 the campaign was placed under the sole direction of Fred L. Soper, who had since 1927 been the regional director of the IHD in the Rio de Janeiro Office and the chief Foundation representative in Brazil. Soper transferred much of the staff and resources of the Yellow Fever Service to the new Malaria Service, because of its experience, its discipline and the liberty of action it enjoyed – a freedom not normally accorded to government agencies – and organised a staff which at its peak of activity had some 4,000 employees.[53]

The selection and training of personnel was an overwhelming task since the members of the Yellow Fever Service had no experience in working with *Anopheles*. In addition, the requirement of a certificate of at least one year of military service (required for employment in any Brazilian agency using federal funds) was difficult to fulfil and initially prevented the malaria service from recruiting the number of people needed. A major difference from the campaigns against hookworm and yellow fever was the non-existence of a concrete technique believed to eradicate *A. gambiae*, since no practical system had ever been worked out for the eradication of this species. Another difference from other campaigns was that the RF made no effort to establish the microorganism (what specific kind of plasmodium) they were fighting. The new Service thus began operations without a definite preformulated plan.

The strategy that finally proved useful to the anti-*gambiae* campaign was to reduce the size of the infected area, working from the periphery to the centre, in order to destroy all larvae and adult mosquitoes in the infested territories and adjacent areas with Paris green and spraying of kerosene and diesel oil, and to disinfect all vehicles for the destruction of adult mosquitoes leaving the *A. gambiae* zone. The meticulous mapping and zoning of rural areas, the individual responsibility for a specific zone, and the careful recording and checking of all field work resembled yellow fever operations. Traditional anti-malaria measures such as ditching, oiling and the distribution of fish to eat the larvae contained in ponds played little part in the campaign.[54] In addition, contemporary methods for identifying the intensity of infection such as spleen rates, blood parasite rates, etc., were irrelevant.

In the rural areas the squad, consisting of an inspector and three assistants, equipped with two hand-powered pressure pumps and two spray pistols, made the round weekly, spraying all houses in assigned zones. All rooms were sprayed, leaving a thin oily film on furniture and other household articles. The massive use of Paris green created some problems of poisoning of the skin and ulcers and caused the death of cattle and other domestic animals. However, no human deaths were attributed to the technique.

By the end of 1940, malaria was infrequent in the previously infected area and no trace of the insect was reported in Brazil. The success appeared to be due to a simple technique, the use of massive financial and human resources and the complete coverage of the infested area. In 1940, the RF withdrew from anti-malaria work in Brazil leaving the programme to the Brazilians. The eradication of *A. gambiae* in Brazil was instrumental in rehabilitating the eradication concept after the failed experiences with hookworm and yellow fever.

Despite the fact that the campaign in Brazil was unique (because of the introduction of a new mosquito), the RF concluded that the eradication concept was still valid since at least one species of *Anopheles* could be surrounded, blocked and eventually cleared from an infested zone.[55] The knowledge gained from the experience in Brazil was used in eradicating *Anopheles gambiae* from upper Egypt, a campaign that Fred L. Soper and the RF carried out with the Egyptian Government and Allied Military Forces between 1943 and 1945. Following this campaign and another one against malaria in Sardinia between 1945 and 1950, many in the international public health field truly believed that optimism about eradication was well founded and should be accomplished on a world scale.[56]

Conclusions

Despite their mixed results, the campaigns developed by the RF in Latin America during the interwar period were a major factor for consolidating United States' influence in the emergent Latin American public health institutions and in shaping the content of the eradication concept. The organisation of independent services by disease, the extension of public health to rural areas where county health units appeared, and the centralisation of sanitary authority to the government, were expressions of the new American influence in the region. The aid of the RF facilitated the trend of wresting public health authority from municipalities and placing it under national supervision. The trend was part of a political change that was characterised by an increased governmental regulation in public services.

Just before and during the Second World War, American influence in Latin America was strengthened by an increased number of fellowships and grants offered by US agencies, such as the Office of the Coordinator of Inter-American Affairs, the Institute of International Education, and the Pan American Sanitary Bureau; and by US private philanthropies, which included the Kellogg Foundation, the John Simon Guggenheim Memorial Foundation, the Commonwealth Fund; the W. R. Grace Company and certain US universities. These institutions were offering so many public health and medical fellowships that Latin Americans could 'shop around' to determine which fellowship would suit them best and many in the US considered that the supply of good candidate material from Latin America was being exhausted.[57]

An outcome of this aid – and of the prior work of the RF – was that since the 1940s the ties of Latin American public health organisations with US institutions and models were evident. In contrast, French influence remained strong in Latin American medical education, at least until the 1950s. This was partially because medical schools which were organised following French lines existed before the arrival of the Foundation, whereas the organisation of national public health apparatuses coincided with the arrival of the RF.

It is interesting to note that the RF tended to associate eradication with diseases believed to be easy to identify, treat and control and with projects that required short-term campaigns with little investment in environmental and living conditions. Illnesses that would have required long-term work or a more complex approach, such as tuberculosis or gastrointestinal diseases, were avoided. Even those structural sanitation aspects of the diseases selected for eradication were neglected. For example, the main sources of hookworm and yellow fever recurrence were the scarce and inadequate systems of sewerage and water supply. However, the infrastructure solutions of these problems were very expensive and beyond what the Foundation considered its sphere of action.

Eradication went through cycles of boom, bust and boom which meant a continuous reformulation of the concept. From the elimination of a disease, the concept changed to the reduction in the incidence of a disease and finally it ended as the elimination of one of the vectors that transmitted a disease. Initially, launching eradication and control campaigns were considered as means for the reorganisation of public health organisations. However, beginning with the campaigns against yellow fever and later during the campaign against the *Anopheles gambiae*, eradication became an object in itself and RF officers defended the autonomy and independence of the services they directed as the best means of achieving the elimination of the mosquito and paid less attention to the reorganisation of public health services.

Changes in the content of the concept of eradication were partially stimulated by the discovery of mistakes, little knowledge of local epidemiological characteristics and unanticipated difficulties of an environmental, financial, cultural and political nature. The transformation of what eradication meant for the RF was instrumental in maintaining some continuities such as keeping alive some hopes of rapid results, ignoring failure, denying other more dramatic health needs and maintaining a trend that favoured technical interventions over social and educational measures. These continuities partially explain the persistence of the eradication concept and of American influence. The arrival of DDT and other techniques after the Second World War not only kept alive in many Latin American public health organisations the goal of eradicating some endemic diseases such as malaria but also encouraged the reductionist and technical self-contained trend that characterised the eradication efforts of the interwar period.[58]

Notes

1 For a history of the eradication concept, see Fred L. Soper, 'Rehabilitation of the Eradication Concept in Prevention of Communicable Disease', *Public Health Reports*, 80 (1965), 855–69; and E. Harold Hinman, *World Eradication of Infectious Disease* (Springfield, Ill.: Charles C. Thomas, 1966).

2 In 1920, Hugh Smith Cumming was appointed US Surgeon-General and also Director of the Bureau. He was to be repeatedly re-elected and to act in this dual capacity until 1936, when he retired from the US Public Health Service, continuing as the Bureau's Director until 1947. During most of the interwar period the Bureau was not an organisation but a board of changing composition, whose members were elected at each Pan American Sanitary Conference and continued to reside and be employed in their own countries. See N. Howard-Jones, 'The Pan American Health Organization: Origins and Evolution', *WHO Chronicle*, 34 (1980), 419–26.

3 See H. H. Howard, *The Control of Hookworm Disease by the Intensive Method* (New York: Rockefeller Publication no. 8, 1919); and John Ettling, *The Germ of Laziness: Rockefeller Philanthropy and Public Health in the New South* (Cambridge, Mass.: Harvard University Press, 1981).

4 Rose to Greene, 30 September 1915. Rockefeller Archive Center (RAC). Rockefeller Foundation Archives (RFA). RG 1.2, Series 300, Box 2, Folder 16.

5 The visit followed the rule of the RF to develop programmes only where local conditions were known. 'Medical Education in Brazil, Diaries, Memoranda, Notes, Reports by the Medical Commission to Brazil 1916, Lewis W. Hackett 1919, Dr Robert A. Lambert 1923–25, George K. Strode 1925–26', RAC. RFA. RG 1.1, Series 305, Box 2, Folder 15.

6 A member of the commission was Bailey K. Ashford who had used the dispensary in Puerto Rico in 1904. The dispensary became very popular in the US during the nineteenth century as an alternative to the hospital in providing medical care for the urban poor. See Charles E. Rosenberg, 'Social Class and Medicine in Nineteenth Century America: The Rise and Fall of the Dispensary System', *Journal of the History of Medicine and Allied Sciences*, 24 (1974), 32–54.

7 See Nilson do Rosario Costa, *Lutas Urbanas e Controle Sanitario Origens das Políticas de Saúde no Brasil* (Petropolis: Vozes & Abrasco, 1985), pp. 99–105.

8 Lewis Hackett, 'Relief and Control of Hookworm Disease in Brazil, From November 22, 1916, to December 31, 1919'. RAC. RFA. RG 5, Series 2, Box 24, Folder 148. For a description of the original county health units and the role played by the RF in their formation, see John Farley's contribution to this volume.

9 'Summary of International Health Division – South America', p. 38, RAC. RFA. RG 3.1, Series 908, Sub-series Pro-11, Box 12, Folder 129.

10 This was partially due to the decline of the dispensary system in the US, Rosenberg, 'Social Class'.

11 The population was estimated at the time to be approximately 3,250,000. The rate in the tropical areas was approximately 84 per cent as compared to 9.6 per cent in the temperate zone. W. A. Sawyer, 'Public Health in Colombia', RAC. RFA. RG 5, Series 2, Box 27, p. 34.

12 These provinces were Antioquia, Santander, Boyaca, Cundinamarca, Tolima and Huila. Pablo García Medina, 'The Sanitary Organization in Colombia [1926]', RAC. RFA. RG 5, Series 2, Box 27, p. 13.

13 Frederick A. Miller, 'Relief and Control of Hookworm Disease in Colombia from 14 June to 31 December 1920', RAC. RFA. RG 5, Series 2, Box 27.

14 Pan American Sanitary Bureau, Proceedings Latin American Fellowship Conference, 12 February 1943, Washington, DC, Pan American Sanitary Bureau 1943, mimeo.

15 The campaigns in Mexico and Venezuela have been the topic of two remarkable theses: by Anne-Emmanuelle Birn, 'Local Health and Foreign Wealth: The Rockefeller Foundation's Public Health Programs in Mexico, 1924–1951' (unpublished doctoral dissertation, The Johns Hopkins University, 1993); and by Julia Emilia Rodriguez, 'The Failure of Public Health Philanthropy: The Rockefeller Foundation in Venezuela, 1926–1934' (Master's thesis, Columbia University, 1993).

16 Some backward countries with a large rural population such as Guatemala had in 1922 a population of 2,500,000 with only 132 doctors, 74 of whom worked in Guatemala City. Robert A. Lambert, 'Medical Education in Guatemala: Report on the Guatemala Medical School, 1922', RAC. RFA. RG 1.1, Series 319, Box 1, Folder 1.

17 For a study of how the RF assessed Latin American medical schools of the 1920s, see Marcos Cueto, 'Visions of Science and Development: Rockefeller Foundation's Latin American Surveys of the 1920s', in Marcos Cueto (ed.), *Missionaries of Science: The Rockefeller Foundation and Latin America* (Bloomington: Indiana University Press, 1994).

18 See Rafael Martinez-Briceño, 'Importancia Social de la Campaña contra la Anemia Tropical', *Repertorio de Medicina y Cirugía*, 15 (1924), 227–41.

19 National Library of Medicine, Bethesda, Maryland. History of Medicine Division. Alan Gregg, Brazil Diary, 1919. Alan Gregg Papers. MS. C 190, Box 5.

20 For a description of these beliefs and practices, see Martinez-Briceño, 'Importancia Social'.

21 See the description of this problem by the RF officer who worked at the Institute of Hygiene at São Paulo, Wilson G. Smillie, *Studies on Hookworm Infection in Brazil: 1918–1920* (New York: Rockefeller Institute for Medical Research, 1922).

22 See Nara Britto and Nísia Trinidade Lima, *Saúde e Naçáo, A Proposta do Saneamento Rural: Um Estudo da Revista Saúde (1918–1919)* (Rio de Janeiro: Estudios de Historia e Saude, Fiocruz, 1991).

23 As early as 1897 Brazil had a federal department of public health which initially was responsible for the control of the sanitary conditions in the important ports of the country. On public health institutions in Latin America during the early twentieth century and the interwar period, see Emerson Elias Merhy, *A Saude Pública como Política; Um Estudo de Formuladores de Políticas* (São Paulo: Editora Hucitec, 1992); Ronn F. Pinneo, 'Misery and Death in the Pearl of the Pacific: Health Care in Guayaquil, Ecuador, 1870–1925', *Hispanic American Historical Review*, 70 (1990), 609–38; José Alvarez Amézquita, Miguel E. Bustamante, Antonio L. Picaźos and F. Fernandez del Castille, *Historia de la Salubridad y de la Asistencia en México* (Mexico, D.F.: Secretaría de Salubridad y Asistencia, 1960); Maria Eliana Labra, 'O Movimiento Sanitarista Nos Anos 20; Da Conexao sanitaria Internacional a Especializaçao em Saude Pública no Brazil' (unpublished Master's thesis, Escola Brasileira de Administraçao Pública, Fundaçao Getulio Vargas, 1985); and Wilbur A. Sawyer, 'Public Health in Venezuela', 1925. RAC. RFA. RG 5, Series 2, Box 37, Folder 224.

24 See Howard-Jones, 'The Pan American Health Organization', p. 419.

25 The first trip of the Bureau's US officer who travelled to Latin America in an advisory capacity is described in: 'El Dr. John D. Long entra en el Servicio del Gobierno de Chile como asesor sanitario', *Boletín de la Oficina Sanitaria Panamericana*, 8 (1925), 283–4.

26 Santos analysed this characteristic for the Brazil of the 1920s. See his illuminating work, Luiz Antonio de Castro Santos, 'Power, Ideology and Public Health in Brazil 1889–1930' (unpublished doctoral dissertation, Harvard University, 1987).

27 Anne-Emanuelle Birn, 'High Influence in a Low Key: The Rockefeller Foundation and Public Health in Mexico', paper presented at the Conference on Disease and Society in the Developing World: Exploring New Perspectives, College of Physicians of Philadelphia, 24–6 September 1992.

28 According to Rodriguez it was difficult for the Foundation 'to elicit enthusiasm [for the campaign] from the [Venezuelan] people because hookworm . . . was not a

deadly disease and its victims could not see the immediate benefits of eradicating it'. Rodriguez, 'The Failure of Public Health Philanthropy', p. 35.

29 Wickliffe Rose, 'Memorandum on Yellow Fever: Feasibility of its Eradication, 7 October 1914'. RAC. RFA. RG 5, International Health Board/Division, Series 300, Box 22, Folder 135.

30 'Yellow Fever' (nd). RAC. RFA. RG 3, Series 908, Box 8, Folder 86.

31 See Hideyo Noguchi, 'Yellow Fever Research, 1918–1924: A Summary', *Journal of Tropical Medicine and Hygiene*, 28 (1925), 185–93.

32 Heiser to Flexner, New York, 12 July 1920. RAC. RFA. RG 5, International Health Board/Division, Series 1.1, Box 47, Folder 713.

33 See Michael E. Connor, 'El Dominio de la Fiebre Amarilla en el Ecuador', in Archivo Histórico de Guayas, *La Fiebre Amarilla y los Médicos de Guayaquil* (Guayaquil: Publicaciones del Banco Central del Ecuador, 1987), pp. 105–13; and Michael E. Connor, 'Yellow Fever Control in Ecuador, Preliminary Report', *Journal of the American Medical Association*, 74 (1920), 650–1.

34 The Federal Department of Health took responsibility for the Federal capital, Rio de Janeiro; and the states of Espirito Santo, Rio de Janeiro, Minas Gerais and São Paulo operated their own services. Instructions Approved by the Minister of Interior Affairs and Laid down by the National Department of Public Health, Concerning the Execution of the Services of Yellow Fever, 11 September 1932. RAC. RFA. RG 5, Series 2, Box 24, Folder 142.

35 Some of these campaigns are analysed in Armando Solorzano, 'Sowing the Seeds of Neo-Imperialism: The Rockefeller Foundation's Yellow Fever Campaign in Mexico', *International Journal of Health Services*, 22, 3 (1992), 529–54; Marcos Cueto, 'Sanitation from Above: Yellow Fever and Foreign Intervention in Perú, 1919–1922', *Hispanic American Historical Review*, 72 (1992), 1–22; Steve Williams, 'Nationalism and Public Health: The Convergence of Rockefeller Foundation Technique and Brazilian Federal Authority During the Time of Yellow Fever, 1925–1930', in Cueto, *Missionaries of Science*; and Augusto Gast Galvis, *Historia de la Fiebre Amarilla en Colombia* (Bogotá: Ministerio de Salud, 1982). See also Henry Hanson, 'General Report on Yellow Fever Campaigns in Colombia, Period May 1923 to December 31, 1924', RAC. RFA. RG 5, Series 5, Box 27, Folder 163; and Henry Hanson, 'The Yellow Fever Survey in Venezuela, 1925', RFA. RG 5, Series 2, Box 37, Folder 223.

36 In 1928 the RF installed a yellow fever laboratory in Salvador Bahia and put it under the direction of D. C. Davis. The laboratory was financed entirely by the RF from 1928 to 1934 and then transferred to Rio where it functioned until 1940.

37 The Rockefeller Foundation, *Annual Report, 1925* (New York: The Rockefeller Foundation, 1925), p. 199.

38 Interview with Fred Lowe Soper, Washington, DC, 14 October 1963. RAC. RFA. RG 3, Series 908, Box 7-h, Folder 86.102.

39 Interview with Fred Lowe Soper.

40 The RF had been working in the northeast of Brazil since 1914. Fred L. Soper, *Ventures in World Health, The Memoirs of Fred Lowe Soper* (Washington, DC: Pan American Health Organization, Scientific Publication no. 355, 1977), p. 95.

41 Soper, *Ventures*, p. 97.

42 See Robert M. Levine, *The Vargas Regime: The Critical Years, 1938–1940* (New York: Columbia University Press, 1970).

43 Hugh H. Smith, *Life's a Pleasant Institution: The Peregrinations of a Rockefeller Doctor* (Tucson, Ariz.: Smith, 1978), p. 120.

44 Between 1932 and 1937 the RF contributed about US $630,000 for yellow fever work in Brazil and it appeared that the expenses would increase. South America Yellow Fever Control and Investigations. RAC. RFA. RG 1.1, Series 305, Box 23, Folder 185.

45 Interview with Fred Lowe Soper, 14 October 1963. RAC. RFA. RG 3, Series 908, Box 7-H, Folder 86.102, p. 12.

46 'Yellow Fever', *The Rockefeller Foundation Annual Report 1939* (New York: The Rockefeller Foundation, 1940), p. 25. The information on popular rejection of viscerotomy was given to me by the Brazilian historian Jaime Bechimol. Letter to Marcos Cueto, 29 July 1993.

47 Fred L. Soper made this statement in 1960. Fred L. Soper, *Building the Health Bridge, Selections from the Works of Fred L. Soper*, edited by J. Austin Kerr (Bloomington and London: Indiana University Press, 1970), p. xiv.

48 For an account of the importance of malaria in Latin America before and after Rockefeller's intervention in the region, see Saul Franco Agudelo, *El Paludismo en América Latina* (Guadalajara: Editorial Universidad de Guadalajara, 1990).

49 Paul F. Russell, 'Memorandum: The Influence of the Rockefeller Foundation on Modern Malariology', RAC. RFA. RG 3, Series 908, Box 15, Folder 159.

50 See The Rockefeller Foundation, *The Rockefeller Foundation Annual Report, 1928* (New York: The Rockefeller Foundation, 1928), pp. 95–8. The campaign had only a temporary success. According to a report by the Argentine's President of the Department of National Hygiene, by the 1920s malaria was endemic in the northern region of the country. Miguel Sussini, 'La Sanidad en Argentina', *Boletín de la Oficina Sanitaria Panamericana*, 16 (1937), 509.

51 The campaign in Venezuela is partially analysed in Ana Teresa Gutierrez, 'La Busqueda de una Ilusión: La Investigación sobre Malaria en Venezuela', *Quipu*, 8 (1991), 171–200.

52 As cited by Robert Shalpen, *Toward the Well-Being of Mankind: Fifty Years of the Rockefeller Foundation* (New York: Doubleday and Company, Inc., 1964), p. 32.

53 Between 1938 and 1940 the RF appropriated a little more than US $330,000 for control measures of malaria in Brazil. 'Brazil *Anopheles Gambiae* Control'. RAC. RFA. RG 1.1, Series 305, Box 16, Folder 14.

54 The role of Paris green is analysed in Gastao Cesar de Andrade, 'O Verde-Paris na Campanha contra o *Anopheles Gambiae* no Nordeste Brasilero', *Boletín de la Oficina Sanitaria Panamericana*, 23 (1944), 210–23.

55 After the Second World War Soper became one of the main advocates of the concept of eradication in the Americas and in the world, see Agudelo, *El Paludismo*, pp. 154–69.

56 Among them was Soper who between 1947 and 1959 was the Director of the Pan American Sanitary Bureau and between 1949 and 1959 the Regional Director of the World Health Organisation for the Americas.

57 For a discussion of this point see the Introduction of Cueto, *Missionaries of Science*.

58 On the use of DDT against malaria in Latin America, see Agudelo, *El Paludismo*,
   pp. 127–52. The revival of eradication with the introduction of DDT against malaria
   during the 1950s in third-world regions of the world is analysed in Randall M.
   Packard, 'Malaria Eradication and Post-War Discourses on "Development" and the
   "Underdeveloped World"', paper presented at the Conference on Disease and
   Society in the Developing World: Exploring New Perspectives, College of
   Physicians of Philadelphia, 24–6 September 1992.

12

The Pasteur Institutes between the two world wars.
The transformation of the international sanitary order

ANNE MARIE MOULIN

Throughout the nineteenth century the international sanitary order had relied on quarantine and the surveillance of travellers and goods. More than half a century of international sanitary conferences, in all twelve meetings from 1850 to 1912, can be summarised as leading to the establishment of sanitary cordons against all pestilences coming from the East and an attempt to control migration, in particular the great pilgrimages.

The First World War fostered a new type of interest in international health with the recognition of the devastating potentialities of epidemic agents on multitudes thrown together in a giant battlefield. The Balkan experience was crucial in that it exposed millions of men, coming from all countries in the world, to a wide range of epidemic hazards, including water-borne diseases, typhus and malaria.[1]

Two kinds of considerations, political and epidemiological, rendered the sanctuarist view pointless:

> the vagaries of battlefields illustrated the similarities of epidemiological conditions across borders and the necessity of co-ordinating national actions in the domain of public health;
> health was posited as an important factor in the planning of a future and, it was hoped, better world in a new geopolitical space.[2]

The pacifist wave after the Treaty of Versailles led to the perception of public health as an ingredient of civilisation and a condition of international peace. Pacifists considered the harmonious co-operation of scientists to be a prerequisite for the development of international health.[3] The alliance between science and medicine, the supremacy of Western medicine and its universality were not questioned. But the idea of redistributing the conquests of Western science on an equal basis through an international scientific network was attractive. The projected League of Nations had to have a daughter-cell organism in the scientific domain of hygiene, an international group of scientists dedicated to an ideal of transcending borders just as epidemics ignored them.

244

Wilson's doctrine embodied the new concern for involving small nations that emerged from the post-war turmoils in the conduct of scientific matters, including medical ones.

In this process, the international drive to establish the League of Nations (LN) clashed with existing organisations. The most difficult encounter was with the Office international d'hygiène publique (OIHP),[4] founded in 1907. Attempts to integrate the OIHP into the planned Health Organisation were a failure in the face of the political nexus created by the presence of non-members of the League in the OIHP and the determination of most Office members to retain their former autonomy. In the years that followed, quarrels representing a dramatic waste of time and energy lasted until the Second World War when, surprisingly, the OIHP outlived the LN.

More interesting is the encounter with the Pasteur Institutes, present on the international field almost since the foundation of the mother house in Paris in 1888. The Pasteur Institutes evolved as a French-centred international institution, although it was clearly not internationalist in spirit.[5] Its members claimed to be active in many domains pertaining to international health, such as collecting epidemiological data from all over the world, training experts, conducting anti-epidemic campaigns, scientific research and producing sera and vaccines.

The Pastorians presented themselves as the apostles of a scientific faith whose tenets were universally applicable. However, this approach has to be understood in the context of the imperialist nation state. Since the mid-nineteenth century, sanitary concerns had converged with the imperialist ideologies of the great powers.[6] Medicine had been considered as a political asset to demonstrate European superiority and also as a means of securing the European settlers' presence in the countries of the 'white man's grave'.[7] For reasons of prestige and in quest of local efficacy, Western countries came to develop a new brand of science, called tropical medicine[8] in Egypt and India, and in the British, Belgian and French parts of Africa.

Internationalists after the First World War put their hopes in experts who would espouse global perspectives before seeing those of their own countries and would intervene in various matters ranging from nutrition to professional education and drug surveillance. But the scarcity of means in men and money at the disposal of the LN hindered the plans for a new international sanitary order. In 1923, the staff of the LNHO consisted of only seven permanent members and four temporary positions.[9] Collaboration with institutions in the field was a necessity.

The Pasteur Institutes could be envisaged as organs of the LNHO. They had helped to establish public health as a profession and emphasised the necessity of research in the spheres of epidemiology and preventive medicine. They constituted a network, active in public health in the six continents. However, the institutes claimed to be supranational and the relationship between the Pasteur Institutes and the LNHO was to involve both co-operation and tensions.[10] The Pastorians chaired or hosted at Paris a number of important meetings organised by the LN: the International Conference for the Standardisation of Sera and Serological Tests in 1922, the first International Conference on rabies (chaired by Paul Remlinger, director of the Tangiers Institute) in 1927, the Laboratory Conference on Blood Groups in 1930, and the Conference which fixed guidelines for BCG utilisation.[11]

The Pasteur Institutes. An international institution

In 1885, news of the scientific miracle, the preventive treatment of rabies, conducted by Pasteur on little Joseph Meister, spread among the public. A sponsoring committee, created in the following months, promoted the building of an institute. Pasteur initially conceived of this institute as an establishment that could shelter patients from the whole world, with the exception of Latin America as supposedly too far away. But by the time bitten patients flocked to Paris from abroad, a centrifuge current had dispersed the Pastorian method towards foreign countries. The administrative board of the new Institute in Paris registered the movement: 'Monsieur Pasteur, convinced of the efficacy of his treatment, has done his best to facilitate the creation of new foci of anti-rabies inoculation'.[12]

In most Western countries, with the exception of Germany, which kept its distance, the initiative came from local doctors who came to Paris and carried away rabbits, inoculated according to Pasteur's own guidelines. In other European countries and in the other continents, the initiative came from governments. In Russia, through the patronage of the Prince of Oldenburg, Governor in Moscow, four stations were founded in Odessa, Moscow, Saint Petersburg[13] and Samara. Similar initiatives (as documented by letters to and from Pasteur) were taken by the Emperor of Brazil, the Prince of Siam and the Ottoman Sultan. Pasteur sent his companions to initiate anti-rabies centres and high-ranking physicians came from Mexico, Rio de Janeiro or Constantinople to receive special training in Paris. This was an echo of the tradition of physicians acting as diplomats, private envoys from their Majesties, often personally attached to the royal person, such as Zoeros Pasha for the Ottoman Sultan or Eduardo Liceaga for Mexican President Porfirio Diaz.

The Saigon Institute, founded in 1891, was the first extension of the Pastorian model to the colonial world. Deputy Etienne, then Under-Secretary for the colonies, asked Emile Roux to appoint a trainee to start a department of bacteriology and vaccinotherapy in Indochina. Initiatives either from the settlers or local governments led to the foundation of similar stations in Tunis, Saint Louis du Sénégal, Madagascar, Algiers, Tangiers and Brazzaville.

The mushrooming of the Pasteur Institutes resulted from local initiatives and from a missionary doctrine. Pasteur was equally persuaded, in his own terms, that science has no homeland and that scientists should be dedicated to their own countries. In fact, he was the first adept and prophet of a new scientific religion and could see no contradiction between the universalist essence of his somewhat private science and his strong link to the national state which sponsored the Institute. Again, no contradiction was felt between the expansion of the French cultural influence through the transfer of Western medicine in the specific Pastorian guise and the universal application of Pastorian science celebrated as humanitarian: 'Never ask from the unfortunate: from which country or which religion art thou? Do tell him: thou doth suffer, it is enough for me, and I will relieve thee.' In a time of religious decline and aggressive secularisation, Pasteur's message, 'Go and Teach all Nations!' (a commandment that was highlighted in hagiographic accounts) officially transformed scientists into missionaries of the new faith.[14] The Pastorian[15] name appeared very quickly to designate men from throughout the world dedicated to a common gospel:[16] the investigation into the cause of diseases and the discovery of a collective and individual mode of prevention. The members of this religious order of a new kind[17] were first of all military doctors who formed half of the cadets at the 'Grand Course' of microbiology taught by Emile Roux and collaborators.[18] They published in the *Annales de l'Institut Pasteur* and in the *Bulletin de la Société de Pathologie Exotique*, created in 1908, around the 'twin gods of parasitology',[19] Laveran and Mesnil.

Before 1914, the Pasteur Institutes, scattered over the world, were hardly an institution. They associated establishments located in the colonies and institutes located in zones of nation states such as the United States or imperial Russia. The Pasteur Institute label functioned as an umbrella term concealing very different situations: it could be viewed as a synonym for modern science, a friendly gesture towards French research, unless it was a gesture of defiance towards a powerful neighbour in the context of negotiations for independence. Each institute struggled to maintain its autonomy, usually ran a journal of its own and finally favoured the distant patronage from Paris over integration into a subnetwork. Programmes were poorly integrated: there was nothing such as a scientific board elaborating a research policy from above.

As time passed, the Pasteur Institutes adopted converging features: a pattern emerged which associated a centre for the preventive treatment of rabies, the distinctive Pastorian trademark, a laboratory for smallpox vaccine production or distribution, and diphtheria serotherapy. Diphtheria had been the second historical signal reinforcing the Institute's legitimacy. If rabies had fascinated the popular audience, diphtheria treatment definitely convinced the medical community. It has been discussed whether rabies (in Indochina, for example) or diphtheria in North Africa was an actual priority in public health. Obviously, the imposition of the new treatment was a symbolic necessity and a mark of the continuity of a doctrine addressed to all contexts. By coining the word vaccination and including under this umbrella term past, present and future methods for disease prevention,[20] Pasteur and his disciples aimed at capturing the promises of the new field of infectious diseases (more or less coextensive with the entire science of pathology).

The policy of the overseas institutes resulted from a combination of entrenched principles and pragmatism. The canonic programme was combined with exploration of 'novel diseases' for which tropical climates offered unique opportunities. Epidemics conditioned both demand and supply. One original feature was the attempt to associate the promotion of the local food industry: fruit juices and preserves in Algeria, wine-making in Tunisia, rice, alcohol and fish condiment (*nuoc-mam*) production and control of the opium quality in Cochinchina, hevea and cinchona plantations in Tonkin.

On the eve of the First World War, and in contrast with the early years, the Pasteur Institutes were mainly composed of institutes located in colonial territories.[21] In the non-French zones of influence, such as the United States, Russia or Brazil, many institutes had disappeared. Most of the anti-rabies centres which had been created by students directly inspired by the Pastorian model had evolved as independent stations, although they sometimes maintained a current of scholarly exchange with Paris, such as the Mexican department.

In the colonies, the institutes formed two main blocs:

the North African group, associating Tunis, Algiers and Tangiers;
the Indochina group,[22] with Saigon and Nha-Trang;

Another pole was located in Black Africa;[23] Brazzaville and Madagascar.

After the war. The Pastorian League

The founder of the Pasteur Institute in Saigon, and later director of the Pasteur Institute in Lille, Albert Calmette,[24] joined Emile Roux at the head of the Institute in Paris in 1919. Roux's official activities were turned inward, while Calmette was responsible for the activities abroad, which took new directions with the post-war reorganisation of alliances.[25] In the house of Pasteur, two mansions have been contrasted: Emile Roux's on one side, 'silent and hardly penetrable', and Calmette's mansion, on the other, 'talkative and entertaining'.[26] Calmette, 'benevolent but wavering', a skilled diplomat, wrote to correspondents from all over the world, travelled abroad, and played an important role in the foundation of new overseas establishments while pursuing his scientific work which culminated with the official development of the BCG antituberculosis vaccine in 1928.

In fact, Roux and Calmette collaborated closely on foreign matters, whose crucial character for the scientific destinies of France was well appreciated.[28] In 1922, Calmette predicted that 'an era will come when each capital, perhaps each population center will possess its Pasteur institute . . . No people can do without it' and adopted Pasteur's words characterising laboratories as 'the temples of the future, wealth and well-being'.[29]

In the aftermath of the war, the French delegations who attended the various international conferences were composed of Pastorians. Calmette, Roux, and Fernand Widal were at the Cannes meeting of 1919,[30] organised by the League of Red Cross Societies (LRCS). Members of the Council of the LRCS included the Pastorians: Roux and Calmette again, and the Belgian Jules Bordet. There was an official shift from metropolitan-centred sanitary policy to a decentralised policy involving small countries in a kind of scientific parliament. In 1920, the LN planned a Committee composed of experts to tackle various sanitary questions in a spirit markedly differing from the old routine of quarantine measures. Issues such as nutrition, epidemic surveillance, the training of specialised staff, popular education, the co-ordination of medical research, and collecting epidemiological data, figured as priorities for the agenda of this committee.

But the victorious French did not display a conciliatory mood towards the old enemy. Following Roux and Calmette's example, the Pastorians declined any collaboration with German colleagues and supported the boycott initiated by the Treaty of Versailles.[31] They wanted to reap the fruits of their victory. They mounted an ambitious scientific offensive. Their military doctors, already on active service, were active on the cultural and diplomatic level. General Dr Arnauld, commanding the expeditionary troops in Greece in the context of the anti-malaria campaign, elaborated plans for an institute in Athens with the philanthropist Basil Zaharoff and Minister Venizelos. In a similar context, when diplomats replaced the army, the representative of the Shah of Persia at the Peace conference, Zoka el Molk, negotiated the opening of a Pasteur Institute in Teheran.

Emile Roux discussed in his correspondence with Charles Nicolle in Tunis the creation of a 'Mediterranean League' which would associate the North African institutes with the newly created stations of Teheran, Athens, Constantinople and Beirut. The name Mediterranean referred to a new sense of heritage, where the French allied with the successive invaders and received the blended heritage. It also referred to a geographical and epidemiological entity, opportunely erasing differences in ethnicity or religion in peoples living on the shores. As a testimony to this spirit of collaboration, the *Archives des Instituts Pasteur d'Afrique du Nord* appeared from 1921 to 1923. From his seat in Tunis, Charles Nicolle speculated: 'I will see with great pleasure the "Greater Archives" expanding our imperialism over the Eastern Mediterranean.'[32]

Only a part of this great project came to fruition. The military doctor Mathis who had been appointed informally for Constantinople never filled his position,[33] as the Kemalists successfully resisted Allied pressure[34] and the dismantling of Turkey. However, the Pastorian heritage remained in evidence with a former pupil of Maurice Nicolle at the head of the Istanbul institute until 1922.[35]

In Lebanon, where the French were struggling against the British to ensure their share of dominion, the idea of an Institute in Beirut would have transformed the modest rabies station, founded by a Jesuit doctor in 1913, into a fully fledged Pasteur Institute. The station was modestly funded by the Haut Commissaire during the French Mandate in the Middle East. Here the scientific lines of descent were rather elusive, since, if the rabies strain came from Paris through Cairo, neither the Director nor his associate had been trained in the mother house. Moreover, the method employed was not the Pastorian type of virus attenuation. In 1934, after some cases of 'laboratory rabies', the Pastorian and rabies expert Paul Remlinger came from Tangiers to investigate. Beirut was banned from the Pastorian realm and blamed for the lack of serious advances in its experimental endeavours.[36]

Only Athens and Teheran were founded. They made a substantial scientific contribution to Pastorian work, although somewhat provincial in tone and scope, between the two world wars.[37] The Greek and Iranian governments supplied funds but the institutes had to find the much-needed extra resources by providing microbiological analyses to local doctors and municipal sanitary authorities, concerned with the purity of milk, water and food.

The great expectations in the wake of the Allied victory were succeeded by retreat on the colonial ground, inside the official zones of influence. Despite Yersin's initial concern for China and his path-breaking discovery of the plague bacillus at Hong Kong in 1893, the Pasteur institutes in China (ChengTu 1911–44 and Shanghai, founded in 1937), remained mediocre in size and prestige.[38] The Indochina institutes preferred to penetrate the Chinese market with their vaccines than to staff laboratories with Pastorian experts.

From an informal aggregate of stations scattered over the world, unified by the reference to a great man and his methods, the Pasteur institutes evolved into a league, or rather a pyramid, divided and hierarchically organised in subsets, centres and subcentres. The Administrative Board in Paris became increasingly concerned with restricting the label to institutes under its control. Two major conditions emerged: first, any institute had to find independent sources of funding; second, the scientific direction had to be approved by Paris. The direction could refuse to endorse its scientific involvement and withhold even a formal agreement. Roux distinctly favoured negotiations with governments and became increasingly cautious with the 'lost children' soliciting recognition.

Roux and Calmette were suspicious of doctors belonging to ethnic 'minorities' in the sphere of the former Ottoman Empire, invoking the French scientific protectorate, alongside a long-established tradition. This happened to be the case with the attempts to create an institute in Alexandria, where local doctors in vain solicited sponsorship in 1928.

The situation was more complex in the case of the Pasteur Institute in Palestine.[39] It had been founded in 1913 in Jerusalem, with the support of the Zionist League, by Dr Beham, who was from Russia and a friend of the Pastorian Marmorek. The laboratory maintained routine microbiological and serological activities despite many difficulties in the political context of British-dominated Palestine; it produced anti-rabies and smallpox vaccines and published a *Bulletin* in Hebrew and French. In 1928, the Institute, which claimed its independence from the official sanitary administration, was progressively starved of resources by the British Department of Health.[40] The Pastorian authorities, who had initially tolerated the use of the Pastorian label, were reluctant to patronise an institution so long as it had no financial support of its own, in spite of the pressure from Zionist organisations[41] and from the Jerusalem consul.

In the overseas establishments two rationales intersected in the scientific organisation. On the one hand, they were miniaturised Pasteur Institutes which reproduced the original structure. On the other, there was an incipient degree of division of labour, according to local abilities and choices.[42] The capacity for research was alternately emphasised and restricted in the affiliated institutes. The Paris authorities frequently recalled that the foreign institutes had been created primarily for practical purposes and that Paris retained the monopoly on pure research. Between the two world wars, a centre was erected in the grounds of the Institute in Paris to house the research of doctors coming from the tropics[43] for short periods, the so-called Pavillon d'Outremer, directed by Emile Marchoux,[44] founder of the Saint Louis du Sénégal laboratory in 1894. However, the frontier was difficult to delineate, since one important tenet of the Pastorian doctrine was the smooth and easy transition from one to the other.[45]

The Pasteur Institute displayed in 1919 an active and bold policy of scientific imperialism,[46] in clear contrast with its impoverished situation due to wartime inflation.[47] The international dimension which had been a consequence of its prosperity inhabited a renewed dream of grandeur. As time went on, the Pastorians became aware of inequalities in the network, and they had to face the contradictions between their nationalistic ideology and the consequences of their international practice. Not only did they have to face these internal contradictions, but they also had to cope with newcomers who interfered with their ideals of co-ordinating public health throughout the world. Among these newcomers was the Rockefeller Foundation (RF).

Training international experts. The Pasteur Institute and the Rockefeller Foundation

The lists of students kept at the archives of the Pasteur Institute illustrate the flow of foreign students attending the microbiological course before 1914. But the student flow had diminished considerably during the war when the RF offered to resuscitate the enterprise.

There were some analogies between the Pasteur Institute and the RF. Both were active in medical and biological research, and considered medicine as the cornerstone of progress in our civilisation. Both refined programmes for the eradication of diseases in the world. Both developed techniques for influencing governments. After 1914, the RF moved towards an emphasis on health and medicine on an international basis. A system of graduate fellowships for students from nearly every country in the world (including France) was established. The officers of the Foundation argued that the Pasteur Institute was very similar in scope and status to the RF and a partner to be preferred in negotiations on hygiene in France.

In March 1921, the Executive Committee of the RF considered giving assistance to the Pasteur Institute, whose 'contribution to humanity they emphasized'. As the RF officers further discussed the possibility of creating in Paris a medical school independent of the University, they deliberately emphasised the aspects of the Institute which appealed to their American philosophy. The Pasteur Institute, at its creation, had adopted a status which has remained the official ideology. The Institute is a private foundation operating for the public good (understood as public health) and consequently dedicated to scientific research. RF officers considered building a school on the premises and with the collaboration of the Institute. The gift would be forwarded through the Rockefeller Institute as 'an exhibition of the sympathy of one guest institute for another'. In an enthusiastic letter addressed to the director of the Rockefeller International Health Board, Calmette suggested that this school would be chaired and supervised by his own Institute and would staff departments of public health all over the world, 'with a special mention for the small countries of Eastern Europe'.[48] In the Tunis Institute, Nicolle fostered suspicion towards President Wilson's diplomatic efforts, and did not approve of Calmette's attempts to 'tie the Pasteur institute to the trail of the American steamer'[49] and 'beg grants' from the RF.[50]

In spite of Calmette's optimistic statements, the project never came to fruition. The impoverished French state did not grant any money, and the Pastorians wanted absolute control. The RF officers did not trust the Pastorian renaissance.[51] The RF went on keeping an eye on the sister institution and in 1926 appointed a missionary in the guise of Harry Plotz, a well-off bacteriologist who went to Paris where he worked on typhus:[52] Plotz sent his report in 1926.[53]

The RF turned to sponsoring multiple activities through its European section located in Paris and created or supported independent agencies for the control of sexually transmitted diseases and tuberculosis.

Nevertheless, the project for an institute of public hygiene which would be at the same time an international school of public health remained an unresolved issue between the two world wars. It was mooted by the LN after the creation of the Provisional Committee of Hygiene and featured as a priority in the agenda of Rajchman's group as early as 1922.

Rajchman encouraged the scientific 'interchange' of scholars in Europe until 1930 to ensure the dissemination of knowledge and specialised skills crucial to the democratisation of public health by the training of local elites.[54] Beyond individual training, Rajchman aimed at the creation of an international school of hygiene. At some point, he envisaged locating the school in Athens, but Blanc, the director of the Athens Institute, did not abandon a disdainful reserve: 'He [Rajchman] dispatches discourses, and that's it.'[55] Léon Bernard,[56] an expert on tuberculosis who was a member of both the OIHP and the LNHO – himself in charge of a poorly endowed laboratory of hygiene since 1922 – when he succeeded Roux as the President of the Superior Council of Health, in 1928, fought to locate the international school of hygiene in Paris.[57] The project was meant to be completed in 1938.

With the rise of fascism and the demise of the LN, these plans were abandoned. War finally buried them. The French National Institute of Hygiene, created at the time of the Liberation, was a remote offshoot of this project.

The international epidemiology of the Pastorians

The germ theory of diseases had been the matrix of the Pastorian doctrine and the Parisian Institute had aimed, above all, at the production of vaccines. The official view had eclipsed consideration of the secondary factors which could amplify or even trigger infection in the individual and account for the explosion of collective evils. Pasteur's brazen statement: 'whatever the poverty, never will it breed disease', signified the mood of the new hygiene.[58]

Military doctors, trained by Pastorians, were sensitised to laboratory-based medicine. A textbook of microbiology, written in 1902 by Maurice Nicolle and Paul Remlinger,[59] who were then operating in Constantinople, was explicitly directed at practitioners working abroad in difficult conditions. It put the stress on microscopes as the heavy-duty equipment central to such work and offered suggestions on how to transform a baker's oven into a steriliser and iron boxes with candles into incubators for cultivating bacteria.

Nevertheless, military doctors also celebrated the distinct ethos of field research. With the shift to tropical countries, the growing importance of vectors in transmission[60] helped them to replace infectious diseases in their geographical and historical contexts. They contrasted the reductionist investigation under the microscope to the investigation of microbes cultivated in the great laboratory of Nature.[61] The complexity of animal reservoirs and the multiplicity of wild species involved, such as in the case of the plague[62] raging in Morocco, Madagascar and Indochina, revived an ecological point of view.

This holistic epidemiology ignored political frontiers. Oceans circled continents and lands where animals and insects carried identical pestilences, and were submitted to crudely identical conditions. Noël Bernard visited the malaria laboratory in Kuala Lumpur in 1923 and found there inspiration for his own laboratory in Saigon. In 1931, he stated that 'in the absence of epidemiological data on Cochinchina, the Malaysian charts are available'.[63] Pastorians worked on malaria, brucellosis and relapsing fevers which formed indistinguishable epidemiological landscapes around the Mediterranean Sea. Before the French historian Braudel identified the Mediterranean as an historical entity, Pastorian Etienne Burnet in Tunis rejected the division of the world along the terrestrial meridians: 'We have to adopt a sea-centered world division. Peoples are living around seas and oceans bring people together more than they separate them. Once the Mediterranean, the Baltic seas were important; now there is the Atlantic world, the Pacific world, the Indian Ocean world. Mankind is more or less sea-bound.'[64]

On several points of the globe, networks of scholars, where Pastorians were active, mapped the world's main pathogens and vector-borne diseases. If pathogens were not identical in each country, they belonged to large families, and the intra-family links and range of hosts were instructive. Typhus, absent from the quarantined diseases of the past,[65] focused the curiosity of scholars on the quest for a vaccine and therapeutic sera. A typhus network brought together Nicolle in Tunis, Hans Zinsser[66] and Sellards at Harvard, Mooser in Mexico, Weigl in Warsaw and Mesnard in Tonkin. They speculated together on the differences in virulence between *Rickettsia* of the different continents, as potentially suggestive for vaccine production, and they pondered over the genealogy of different kinds of typhus all over the world, as bacteria adapted to different vectors.

These networks could not ignore the imperialist antagonisms. Latin America was one of the grounds on which France and Great Britain measured themselves against the United States. Nicolle paid two visits to the New World to assert the French influence in Bolivia, Argentina, Brazil, Uruguay, Mexico and Guatemala. In Argentina, he reported that 'the Kraus' former institute no longer shelters a single German scholar, and portraits of Pasteur, Roux and Laveran have slowly invaded the laboratories or staircases initially reserved for Germans'.[67] At his prompting, his student Durand went to teach in Bogota in 1930.

The LN started its activities in the domain of international health in coping with the disastrous epidemics and starvation in Eastern Europe. In the following years, its work remained limited in the underdeveloped world (then called the 'poor countries'). Most of them belonged to colonial empires or appeared under an ambiguous political identity in scientific debates.[68] Colonies in Africa or Asia remained a 'reserved hunting-ground' where no international officer could directly operate. Significantly, Rajchman's missions in Asia were mainly located in China which was not officially controlled by the great powers. The proposals for a conference in Africa on tropical diseases were considered as trespassing on Pastorian territory. The Singapore branch of the LNHO was created only in 1925. It appears from Yersin's correspondence in Indochina that it aroused anxiety.

In spite of these imperialist and colonialist links to overseas medicine, something like an expert network in the domain of international health began to function. The Pastorians were an important part of this potential reservoir. Etienne Burnet is the prototype of the hybrid role played by the Pastorians.

Etienne Burnet, Pastorian and international expert

Etienne Burnet, trained in philosophy and converted to medicine, member of the vaccine department at the Pasteur Institute, learned on the Eastern front, first in Macedonia and then at Corfu, that 'war is a great school of hygiene and preventive medicine'.[69] At the end of the First World War, he was a member of a scientific mission sent to America to improve scientific collaboration with the United States. Burnet displayed an unusual open-mindedness by quoting the German bacteriologists Emil Behring and Robert Koch when the armistice was not yet signed. He thoroughly agreed with Wilson's fourteen points, although he was somewhat sceptical about the future. In January 1919, he wrote to Olga Metchnikov, his former master's widow: 'I believe . . . that Europe is not capable of founding a novel society. If Wilson fails, I am convinced that we will face other wars.'[70]

Burnet worked at the Pasteur Institute of Tunis and in 1920 was called to direct the hygiene department, created by the French Governor.[71] In Tunis, he was very eclectic and worked on malaria, trachoma, tuberculosis, brucellosis and typhus. He fought with the local administration, which granted meagre funds to equip the city of Tunis, for example, with hammams,[72] built according to modern standards of hygiene. Burnet advocated the fusion of hygiene and the Pastorian doctrine, to the extent that he envied the situation of Morocco, where the military element permeated the whole medical body and resulted in a perfect co-ordination of the executive and the doctrine.[73]

As an old boy of the Ecole Normale Supérieure, Burnet benefited from a network of relationships more extended than the average military Pastorian. His wife and future biographer, Lydia, was Russian.[74] Burnet involved himself in campaigns in favour of the Soviet Union, ridden with epidemics and civil wars, and he collected funds for victims siding with the Russian-born Pastorian Besredka.[75] He visited Russia in 1923 with the LN Epidemics Commission and initiated the collaboration which led him to be recruited by the LNHO.

Burnet became an international officer under Ludwik Rajchman in 1926. He travelled all over the world as an expert on tuberculosis and leprosy. He was a member of the malaria commission,[76] with Sergent, the director of the Algiers Institute. His main focus became that of nutrition,[77] in clear divergence from the traditional Pastorian emphasis on infectious agents. He launched a survey of food in the Chilean population (indeed, he taught in Santiago).[78] When back in Tunis, he resumed a similar study of the Maghrebi diet along with Pastorian Gobert.

He played a central role in the international conference on BCG, and pleaded in favour of its preventive role in children. He conceived guidelines in the struggle against tuberculosis mainly through his information on industrialised countries and their network of dispensaries and social workers.[79] The interest in tropical diseases sometimes obscured the fact that such infections as tuberculosis were cosmopolitan: 'In the tropics, doctors hardly take notice of the disease that is the greatest killer', noted Noël Bernard in 1923.

Burnet embodied the alliance between science and hygiene which had been the rationale for the foundation of the Pasteur Institute. Emile Roux encouraged him: 'As a hygienist, you will be confronted with cases which can be solved only by laboratory studies. Your two halves (the scientist and the administrator) will converge to form the perfect hygienist.'[80] Burnet integrated Pastorian science into the French tradition of humanitarian hygiene.[81]

The relationship of hygiene with Pastorism has been a matter of controversy. For Bruno Latour[82] and Jacques Léonard, hygiene is but one component of Pastorism, and a particularly successful one at that. For Murard and Zylberman, hygiene evolved independently as an experimental approach to social facts in their own right.[83]

Tensions remained between the ideal of a scientifically determined hygiene and its actual applications in human societies. Following Pasteur, most Pastorians had remained ambivalent towards the secular hand of hygiene in the form of the omnipotent, invasive state.[84] They were reluctant to negotiate vital matters with ignorant administrations. Charles Nicolle lamented 'the fossilisation of the Pasteur institute and its fall into experimental hygiene'.[85] But the same Nicolle favoured his disciple Burnet's nomination at the head of the hygiene department. When he distributed free BCG vaccine in Tunisia,[86] in 1928, he declared that he belonged to a state establishment and was consequently responsible for duties of the state.[87]

In fact, only the institutes outside the metropolis approximated to the integration between science and administration. The Pastorians in the overseas institutes exerted a kind of scientific control over all questions of public health:

urbanisation, occupational diseases and farming related to the malaria issue.[88] The Indochina institutes are a perfect example of integration into the programme of the local health departments,[89] and also of the colonial policy associated with railway building and agricultural development.

The Pastorians used the local sanitary organisation as their secular arm. When such collaboration failed,[90] this was considered as the 'death of the nascent work'[91] and of the 'logical application of the guidelines for antituberculosis prophylaxis'.[92] The Pastorians were sensitive to the economic applications of scientific decisions in tropical countries, as in the case of beriberi.[93] In contrast, the interaction with international associations such as the Far Eastern Association for Tropical Medicine (FEATM),[94] or the missionaries from the LN (Norman White of the LNHO visited Indochina in 1923), remained superficial.

Like Nicolle, most directors were not blind to the strategic advantage for their institutes to find material and financial support in the local authorities. In Indochina, Yersin (Nha-Trang)[95] and Noël Bernard[96] (Saigon) negotiated unrelentingly the contracts which associated them with the public health policy[97] but left them a free hand for their scientific initiatives.

In their zeal for modernisation, Pastorians had little consideration for indigenous cultures. Jennerian vaccine, produced by the Pasteur Institutes, in association with the Pastorian vaccines (rabies, anthrax, etc.) removed local preventive methods such as smallpox inoculation, not without encountering resistance fostered by the hazards of vaccines far from being always safe and effective, as well as resistance to mass coercion and foreign invasion.[98] BCG was experimentally tested on a wide scale on newborn babies in Cochinchina and Cambodia in 1925, before being introduced into France.[99] In Africa, the Pastorians matched their yellow fever vaccine (Dakar strain) against the Rockefeller vaccine that threatened their African market.[100]

During the war, the national state had assumed all responsibilities, including anti-epidemic measures. These coercive measures, for so long considered psychologically undesirable by the French bourgeoisie, demonstrated their efficacy. Burnet defined social hygiene as the 'hygiene of the masses', 'a hygiene which, aware of economic inequalities, compensates for them'.[101] The tension between the cure of the individual and the management of large populations appeared as a general feature of modern medicine. What had been accepted for the colonies also applied to the 'civilised' centres. In many ways, the overseas institutes appeared as a model and suggested that the periphery could compete for scientific hegemony.

The moving centre. A view from the periphery

In the interwar period, the Paris Institute underwent financial difficulties. Stricken by inflation that diminished the patrimony of the foundation, the mother house faced two difficult problems: recruiting staff and funding research. Facing Emile Roux, Nobel Prize-winner,[102] Nicolle emerged as a possible candidate for the Directorship of the Pasteur Institutes and embodied the possible transfer from the centre to the periphery. Directors Blanc in Athens and Mesnard in Teheran were former pupils of Nicolle. When Blanc left Athens in 1926, he moved to Casablanca where an institute was opened. In Athens, the new director Lepine acknowledged: 'You are clearly the boss.'[103]

'Exotic Pastorian' as he called himself, between pride and humiliation, Nicolle was with Yersin one of the two main figures of the Pastorian diaspora. He used to mock the sedentary style of 'the handicapped of the metropolis':[104] 'The people in Paris hate travelling and those who could not escape from parading the Pastorian banner through Europe have come back home so exhausted that they do not want to hear about new journeys.'[105] Nicolle was featured as the spokesman for overseas Pasteur Institutes: 'It seems to me that I am more and more doomed to take care of the Pasteur Institutes out of the metropolis.'[106]

Nicolle was deeply persuaded that the essence of Pastorism was not territorial. A Pasteur Institute consisted of living brain matter. In the true Rabelaisian style, he thought of constructing an institute in 'living stones'.[107] He considered it a big mistake that Sergent had first designed and built up the Casablanca premises before 'naming the men'.[108]

After Roux's death in 1933, Nicolle was, along with Yersin, the heir apparent of the tradition and as Yersin was reluctant to come back to Europe, he found himself in the unique position of representing the empire. He envisaged a Mediterranean network including Algiers, Casablanca, Tangiers, Tunis, Athens and the small institutes in Marseille, Beirut, Suez, Istanbul and Alexandria: 'If decentralisation did occur, Paris no longer would occupy the centre.'[109] He started to call himself 'Tunisian'. In 1928, attending an international conference in Alexandria,[110] he called himself a 'delegate of His Highness the *bey*'.[111] In 1933, when celebrating the centennial of the institute, the Republic of Tunisia was to acknowledge Nicolle's versatile and fertile genius as a token of scientific excellence on the periphery, and as a forerunner of moving hegemony and of a decentralised network of medical innovation.

Conclusion

In 1938, fifteen Pasteur Institutes[112] officially existed: four in North Africa, four in Indochina,[113] four in Black Africa and one in Shanghai, Teheran and Athens respectively. In the speech, rather conservative in tone, which Pasteur Vallery-Radot delivered for the fiftieth anniversary of the Institute, in front of President Lebrun, he emphasised its imperialist quality: 'If French peace reigns over boundless regions, if epidemics are prevented or thwarted, if sanitary reforms can be undertaken, cities built up, and harbours opened to trade, if Europeans can live safely in hostile Africa and the Far East, if morbidity and mortality decrease in a striking way for native populations, all these transformations must be attributed to colonial medicine.'[114] This statement reflects the optimistic and self-satisfied mood of medicine as viewed through the Pastorian lens. Other changes, of which Pasteur's grandson was not aware, were perceptible throughout the history of the interwar generation.

The overseas institutes served as models to solve the two main difficulties in the metropolis: funding and recruitment. They played an important role in the transition between the metropolis-centred conception of health and the internationalist version.

The network of Pastorian researchers illustrates the far-reaching influence of a flamboyant community united by strong ideological links, although its visible territory tended to limit itself to the dimensions of the colonial empire. At the same time, the doctors working in the domain of public health, tended to adopt a more internationalist style of practice, due to the scientific necessities of addressing epidemiological issues across national borders and elaborating common guidelines. Finally, the success of the overseas institutes, compared to the relative stagnation of the mother house, illustrated the shift in the scientific drive away from the centre and raised the issue of the integration of biological research into the economic development of what we now call the third world.

The Pastorian graft had not been a mere transfer of Western institutions. It triggered, although at different times depending on the country, the development of local educational establishments, research agencies and science-industry interfaces. In the generation following independence, Pastorian science was reappropriated in a national tradition and could even function as a basis for counter-hegemony, raising the question of the universality of science and its cultural foundations. Ultimately, Pastorians addressed critically the neutrality of the international organisations.

Although they sometimes figured as simple organs of the French government whose interests framed their public health strategies, the Pasteur Institutes displayed hybrid characteristics which accelerated the transition to the innumerable non-governmental agencies that flourished after the Second World War in the domain of health.

The foundation of World Health Organisation, much more ambitious and more lavishly endowed, initiated a worldwide policy of sending scientific 'missionaries' and training students from many different countries. Networks of researchers were reorganised in a more decentralised and egalitarian way. However, although shaken by wars of independence and political struggles, the overseas Pasteur Institutes[115] managed to adapt to new circumstances. They emphasised the existence of a scientific Pastorian community transcending citizenship and successfully renegotiated the terms of local contracts. They dropped the undesirable components of their image and depending on the context turned into non-governmental agencies. The Pastorian ideology redeployed itself by discovering the virtues of scientific mobility inside an international public health network.[116] Pastorians made the point that the overseas network was a ready-made instrument for a new trend in international co-operation. They retained their position inside this network by arguing that they had taken a crucial role in the historical origins of the concept of international health, and had contributed to its earliest applications.

Acknowledgements

I am very grateful for invaluable information from many friends and colleagues, especially from Kimberley Pelis, Annick Guenel and Mina Kleiche who work respectively on the Pasteur Institutes in Tunisia, Indochina and Morocco, and also from L. Murard and P. Zylberman, M. Osborne, M. Shamay. This work has been conducted through a grant from the French Ministère de la Recherche.

Notes

1 Malaria was a major concern on the Macedonian front, where it preyed upon transplanted troops deprived of what the Sergent brothers in Algiers had called the natives' immunity of premunition.

2 'For the first time in History, those who drew up an important political treaty gave some thought to the health of the nation.' T. Madsen, 'The Scientific Work of the Health Organization of the League of Nations', *Harvey Lectures*, 32 (1937), 145–68.

3 B. Schroeder-Gudehus, *Les scientifiques et la paix* (Montreal, 1978).

4 N. Howard-Jones, *La santé publique internationale entre les deux guerres. Les problèmes d'organisation* (Geneva: WHO, 1979).

5 A. M. Moulin, 'Patriarchal Science: The International Network of the Pasteur Institutes', in P. Petitjean, C. Jami and A. M. Moulin (eds.), *Science and Empires* (Boston: Kluwer Academic Publishers, 1992), pp. 307–22.

6 D. Arnold (ed.), *Imperial Medicine and Indigenous Societies* (Manchester: Manchester University Press, 1988).

7 P. D. Curtin, 'The White Man's Grave: Image and Reality: 1780–1850', *Journal of British Studies*, 1 (1961), 94–110.

8 M. Worboys, 'The Emergence of Tropical Medicine: A Study in the Establishment of a Scientific Specialty', in G. Lemaine, R. MacLeod and M. Mulkay (eds.), *Perspectives on the Emergence of Scientific Disciplines* (The Hague, 1976), pp. 75–98.

9 Besides the staff the Rockefeller Foundation (RF) appointed for the Epidemics Commission.

10 As reported in the Directory of the League of Nations in 1938, the Pastorians constituted half of the French experts in the commissions of the Health Organisation: two in the Malaria Commission (Sergent, Rodhain), one in the Commission for

Biological Standardisation (Louis Martin), *Annuaire de la Société des Nations* (Geneva, 1938).

11 W. C. Cockburn, 'The International Contribution to the Standardisation of Biological Substances. I. Biological Standards and the League of Nations 1921–1946', *Biologicals*, 19 (1991), 161–9.

12 Archives of the Pasteur Institute, Paris (AIPP), Minutes of the Administrative Council, 22 May 1886, p. 2.

13 The Saint Petersburg Institute has in 1993 joined the network of the overseas Pasteur Institutes.

14 'Do you remember Metchnikoff's days in his lecture on immunity and the exciting lessons by Roux? Haven't we been touched by the Holy Spirit's breath?', letter from Charles Nicolle to Calmette, 3 November 1923, AIPP. René Vallery-Radot, Pasteur's son-in-law and biographer, described a Pastorian as like 'somebody who marches toward the temple entrance', Letter to Charles Nicolle, 15 January 1932, Archives départementales de Seine Maritime, Rouen, Fonds Nicolle (ASM).

15 The word was officially coined by the doctor journalist Maurice de Fleury, *Pasteur et les Pastoriens* (Paris, 1895).

16 Charles Nicolle speaks, somewhat ironically, about 'our patron saint Louis Pasteur', Nicolle to Blanc, 27 March 1923, ASM.

17 The analogy of Pastorians with a missionary order has pervaded the hagiographic literature and still occupies an important place in writings dedicated to Pastorians' works. See Lwoff's remarks in 1933, on the ironical mode on the Pastorians as a 'mendicant order' and remarks by Alexis Carrel, obviously inspired by the Pasteur Institute, on scientific congregations, *L'Homme, cet Inconnu*, (Paris: Plon 1936), see *Man the Unknown* Pelican edn (1948), pp. 261–8.

18 M. Faure, 'Cent années d'enseignement à l'institut Pasteur', in M. Morange (ed.), *L'Institut Pasteur. Contribution à son histoire* (Paris, 1991), pp. 62–74.

19 C. Nicolle, Letter to Blanc, 12 January 1915, ASM.

20 A. M. Moulin, 'La métaphore vaccine. De l'inoculation à la vaccinologie', *History and Philosophy of Life Sciences*, 14 (1993), 271–97.

21 A. Calmette, *Les missions scientifiques de l'Institut Pasteur et l'expansion coloniale de la France* (Paris, 1912); *Pasteur et les Instituts Pasteur* (Paris, 1923).

22 N. Bernard, *Les Instituts Pasteur d'Indochine* (Saigon, 1923).

23 C. Mathis, *L'oeuvre des Pastoriens en Afrique noire* (Paris, 1946).

24 N. Bernard, *La vie et l'oeuvre d'Albert Calmette* (Paris, 1961).

25 Rockefeller Archive Center (RAC) RF RG 1.1 Projects, Pasteur Institute, Box 2, Folder 15, 'It is agreed on all sides that Calmette is likely to inaugurate a new era of productivity.' N. Vincent, Rockefeller Foundation officer, to Gates, 13 March 1921.

26 'Silencieuse et impénétrable', 'volubile et expansive', D. Ogilvie, communication at the meeting of the Overseas Pasteur Institutes, directors, Paris, 8 November 1992.

27 C. Nicolle to Blanc, 18 April 1926, ASM.

28 Part of Roux's voluminous handwritten correspondence has been lost or lies unnoticed in private or public archives.

29 A. Calmette, 'L'oeuvre de Pasteur. Son influence sur les progrès de la civilisation', *Bulletin de l'Académie de Médecine*, 68 (1922), 684; see also 'L'institut Pasteur et ses filiales', *Revue d'hygiène*, 45 (1923), 385.

30 Howard-Jones, *La santé publique*, ch. 2.

31 Schroeder-Gudehus, *Les scientifiques*, ch. 5.

32 Nicolle to Blanc, 14 October 1920, ASM.

33 In 1924, he became the first director of the Pasteur Institute in Dakar, which evolved from the Institut de biologie in St Louis du Sénégal.

34 *Istanbul 1914–1923, capitale d'un monde illusoire*, ed. Stéphane Yerassimos (Paris, 1992).

35 A. M. Moulin, 'L'hygiène dans la ville: la médecine ottomane à l'heure pastorienne', in P. Dumont and F. Georgeon (eds.), *Villes ottomanes à la fin de l'empire* (Paris, 1992), pp. 186–209.

36 P. Remlinger, 'Rapport sur le fonctionnement de l'institut Pasteur de Beyrouth', 10 October 1934; Letter from Colonel Dr Martin, director of the Health Department in the Middle East to E. Roux, 24 August 1934, AIPP.

37 Interestingly, the Teheran Institute has survived the difficult period following the Shah's departure in 1978. The scientific relationship, after a period of dormancy, has been revived and some common projects have been launched. Science provides a good basis for reviving diplomatic relations.

38 M. Bastid-Bruguière, 'Les instituts Pasteur de Chine', in Morange, *L'Institut Pasteur*, pp. 253–68.

39 E. Kottek, 'The Pasteur Institute of Palestine', communication to the Congress 'Sciences and Empires', Paris, 1990.

40 Letter from Dr Beham to Colonel Heron, director of the Department of Health, Jerusalem, 20 September 1929, AIPP.

41 A. Alfes and S. Zeitlin, 'Rapport sur l'institut Pasteur de Jérusalem', 1928; 'Rapport sur l'institut Pasteur de Palestine, Société des Amis de l'institut Pasteur palestinien', 1928, AIPP.

42 Madagascar's specific target was plague, as were malaria for Algiers and Saigon, sleeping sickness for Brazzaville, yellow fever for Dakar, and rabies for Tangiers.

43 N. Bernard, 'Formation des microbiologistes coloniaux'. Report to the Minister of Colonies, 1940, Archives du Pharo, Marseille.

44 J.-P. Bado and M. Michel, 'Sur les traces de l'Empire: Marchoux pionnier de l'Institut Pasteur en Afrique noire', Morange, *L'Institut Pasteur*, pp. 296–311.

45 This had been one of the arguments used by Pasteur himself to obtain the patronage of the state and of the industrialists.

46 For a critical appraisal of French scientific imperialism, see L. Pyenson, *Civilising Mission. Exact Sciences and French Overseas Expansion, 1830–1940* (Baltimore: Johns Hopkins University Press, 1993), pp. 340–5.

47 'La ruine s'accentue. Il faudrait à présent une révolution complète', Nicolle to Pasteur Vallery-Radot, 3 January 1920, AIPP.

48 RAC, RF RG 6.1, Series 1.1, IHP, Calmette to S. Gunn, head of the Paris department of the International Health Board for the Foundation.

49 Nicolle to Pasteur Vallery-Radot, 14 February 1921, AIPP.

50 Nicolle to Pasteur Vallery-Radot, Paris, 4 June 1921, AIPP.

51 RAC, RF RG 1.1, Pasteur Institute, memo by Wickliffe Rose, director of the International Health Board of the Rockefeller Foundation, 'Pasteur Institute does not appeal. Better to head Institute under University'.

52 RAC, RF RG 1.1, Projects, Pasteur Institute, Box 2, Folder 16, Embree to Vincent, 28 March 1924.

53 A. M. Moulin, 'Death and Resurrection of Immunology at the Pasteur Institute', in P. A. Cazenave and P. Talwar (ed.), *Pasteur's Inheritance* (New Delhi, 1991), pp. 53–62.

54 M. Balińska, 'Ludwik Rajchman (1881–1965), précurseur de la santé publique moderne' (doctoral thesis, Institut d'Etudes Politiques de Paris, 1992).

55 Blanc to Nicolle, 12 November 1927, ASM.

56 On the ubiquitous Léon Bernard, see L. Murard and P. Zylberman, 'La mission Rockefeller en France et la création du Comité national de défense contre la tuberculose, 1917–1923', *Revue d'histoire moderne et contemporaine*, 34 (1987), 257–81 (258).

57 L. Rajchman, *Eloge funèbre de Léon Bernard* (Paris, 1933).

58 A. M. Moulin, 'Bacteriological Research and Medical Practice in and out of the Pastorian School', in M. Feingold and Ann La Berge (eds.), *Practitioners and Researchers. Aspects of Medical French Culture in the 19th and 20th Centuries* (Oxford: Oxford University Press, 1994), pp. 327–49.

59 M. Nicolle and P. Remlinger, *Traité de microbiologie générale* (Paris, 1902).

60 Simond studied the role of rats in plague; Sergent in Algeria worked on *Anopheles*; the Brazzaville school focused on the tsetse flies (*Glossina*).

61 M. Osborne, 'French Military Epidemiology and the Limits of the Laboratory: The Case of Louis-Félix Achille Kelsch', A. Cunningham and P. Williams (eds.), *The Laboratory Revolution in Medicine* (Cambridge: Cambridge University Press, 1992), pp. 189–208.

62 The role of wild rodents in plague transmission had been well documented by the Russians, especially Tarassevitch. Roubaud in Paris identified the flea species involved in the cycle.

63 *Le Paludisme en Indochine, Exposition coloniale internationale* (Paris, 1931).

64 Quoted by L. Burnet, *Etienne Burnet, un humaniste français de ce temps* (Tunis, 1939), p. 213.

65 An international convention, elaborated by the OIHP and the Health Organisation, was signed in 1926.

66 Unfortunately, the trail of the voluminous correspondence between Zinsser and Nicolle, still extant after the Second World War, has been lost. Zinsser spent a sabbatical year at the Collège de France, in Nicolle's laboratory, in 1933.

67 Nicolle to Pasteur Vallery-Radot, 31 October 1925, AIPP.

68 *25 ans d'activité de l'Office international d'hygiène publique, 1909–1933* (Paris, 1933): Tunisia officially joined the OIHP in 1908, Indochina in 1914, French West Africa, Madagascar and Morocco in 1920, French East Africa in 1929.

69 Burnet, *Burnet*, p. 177.

70 Burnet, *Burnet*, p. 169.

71 On Nicolle's request, Nicolle to Pasteur Vallery-Radot, 3 January 1920, AIPP; Letter from Nicolle to Blanc, 6 January 1921, ASM.

72 Turkish baths.

73 He exclaimed during a banquet: 'Long live Maréchal Lyautey', Burnet, *Burnet*, p. 305.

74 Burnet devoted two novels to the Russian community in Tunisia: *Loin des icônes* and *Porte du Sauveur*.

75 Nicolle to Blanc, 6 October 1923, AIPP.

76 The international congress on malaria took place at Paris in 1928.

77 E. Burnet and W. R. Aykroyd, 'Nutrition and Public Health', *Quarterly Bulletin of the Health Organisation*, 4 (1935), 323–474. Burnet, *Enquête sur l'alimentation au Chili* (Geneva, 1936).

78 C. Dragoni and E. Burnet, 'Rapport sur l'alimentation populaire au Chili', *Bulletin Trimestriel de l'Organisation d'Hygiène*, 6 (1937), 315–67.

79 E. Burnet, 'Principes généraux de la prophylaxie de la tuberculose', *Bulletin Trimestriel de l'Organisation d'Hygiène*, 4 (1932), 511–673.

80 Burnet, *Burnet*, p. 288; elsewhere, Roux comments on the position of director of hygiene: 'c'est un poste intéressant où on peut satisfaire à la fois l'homme de laboratoire et l'homme d'action', Roux to Nicolle, 29 January 1920, AIPP.

81 On this French tradition, see A. La Berge, *Mission and Method. The Early Nineteenth-Century French Public Health Movement* (Cambridge: Cambridge University Press, 1992).

82 B. Latour, *Les Microbes* (Paris, 1979); J. Léonard, 'Comment peut-on être pasteurien?', in *Pasteur et la révolution pastorienne* (Paris, 1986), 143–79.

83 L. Murard and P. Zylberman, 'De l'hygiène comme introduction à la politique expérimentale' (875–925), *Revue de synthèse*, 115 (1984), 313–41; 'La raison de l'expert ou l'hygiène comme science sociale appliquée', *Archives européennes de sociologie*, 26 (1985), 58–9.

84 E. Duclaux, *L'Hygiène sociale* (Paris, 1902).

85 'Impossible, sauf Besredka, de trouver une intelligence', Nicolle to Blanc, 14 April 1925, ASM. AIPP.

86 Nicolle to Calmette, 6 August 1928, Musée Pasteur, Pasteur Institute, Paris.

87 *Ibid.*

88 A. Marcovich, 'French Colonial Medicine and Colonial Rule: Algeria and Indochina', R. McLeod and M. Lewis (eds.), *Disease, Medicine and Empire* (London, 1988), p. 112.

89 'Au moment où [le gouverneur de Cochinchine] se demande comment il va aborder la réalisation [des mesures d'hygiène sociale], nous lui apportons *toute faite* notre organisation pour la lutte contre la tuberculose, nos travaux antérieurs sur le paludisme, des idées précises sur la question des eaux d'alimentation', N. Bernard to Calmette, Saigon, 21 February 1923, Musée, Institut Pasteur, Paris, no. 25338.

90 As was the case when Guérin left the institute in Cochinchina in 1930. Guérin was a close collaborator with Calmette for the vaccine that bears their two names.

91 Noël Bernard to Calmette, 20 July 1930, AIPP.

92 F. H. Guérin, 'Premiers résultats de l'enquête sociale sur la tuberculose dans les écoles de Cholon (Cochinchine)', *Archives de l'institut Pasteur d'Indochine*, 1 (1925), 189–207.

93 On this very important issue of public health, the Pastorians remained faithful to the theory of contagion. N. Bernard, *Rapports sur le béri-béri*, Congrès de médecine tropicale d'Extréme-Orient (Tokyo, 1925).

94 The Association was founded at Manilla in 1908. The Pastorians attended the FEATM congresses in Singapore in 1923, in Calcutta and in Bangkok in 1930.

95 Yersin advises Noël Bernard 'de rendre de tels services à la Cochinchine que le gouvernement ne saurait lui refuser des subsides', Yersin to Calmette, 15 November 1918, AIPP.

96 Noël Bernard was at the head of the two Tonkin institutes in 1923 and chaired the creation of the Hanoi institute.

97 E.g. for the prevention of beriberi through rice consumption.

98 D. Rivet, 'Soigner les Marocains au temps de la décolonisation: la médecine française à l'épreuve', *Mélanges à la mémoire de Charles-André Julien* (Rabat, in press).

99 N. Bernard, 'Le BCG en Indochine', *Annales de l'institut Pasteur* (1927), 284.

100 The production of the Dakar vaccine resulted from a collaboration between Laigret, working at Tunis on the African strain, and Sellards, an American bacteriologist from Harvard: correspondence Laigret–Nicolle, 1933–5, ASM, and C. Mathis, *Les Pastoriens en Afrique noire*.

101 *Société des Nations, Bulletin trimestriel de l'organisation d'hygiène*, 1 (1932), 515.

102 1928.

103 Lépine to Nicolle, 28 November 1932, ASM.

104 Nicolle to Blanc, 24 November 1923, ASM.

105 Nicolle to Blanc, 28 February 1923, ASM.

106 Nicolle to Blanc, 19 January 1926, ASM.

107 Nicolle to Calmette, 12 January 1925, AIPP.

108 'Il n'est pas nécessaire que l'institut Pasteur soit construit ou sur le point de l'être pour que le noyau de son personnel soit constitué. Il faut que ce noyau existe et prouve son existence.' Nicolle to Calmette, 12 January 1925, AIPP.

109 Nicolle to Pasteur Vallery-Radot, 20 May 1934, AIPP.

110 When the creation of a Pasteur institute in Alexandria was discussed.

111 Nicolle to Blanc, 19 April 1928, ASM.

112 A sixteenth was on the point of being added, at Fort-de-France, in the French Indies, see M. Vaucel, 'Les instituts Pasteur outremer et à l'étranger', *Revue de l'enseignement supérieur*, 11 (1964), 109–22.

113 Saigon, Nha-Trang, Hanoï (1926), Dalat (1936).

114 Pasteur Vallery-Radot, *Mémoires d'un non-conformiste, 1886–1966* (Paris, 1966), p. 251.

115 Between the wars, the name 'Overseas Pasteur Institute' strictly referred only to the establishments located in the 'Overseas French departments', cf. Vaucel, 'Les instituts Pasteur', p. 121.

116 For a presentation of the present network, see R. Dedonder, 'Worldwide Impact of Pasteur's Discovery and the Overseas Pasteur Institutes', in S. Plotkin (ed.), *World's Debt to Pasteur* (New York, 1985), pp. 130–9.

13

Internationalising nursing education during the interwar period

ANNE MARIE RAFFERTY

'Without the devoted personal service, the *disinterested* counsel, and the co-operation of experienced nurses who went out from America to the Far East, Continental Europe, and Latin America, public health nursing could not have achieved the relatively high status it now occupies in these areas.'[1] Such was the confident conclusion of Rockefeller officials in 1938, after twenty-four years of Rockefeller interventions in nursing. In this chapter I shall consider the role of the Rockefeller Foundation (RF) in promoting nursing education in England during the interwar period. This episode in RF history was marked by the competitive interplay between a number of international organisations keen to influence the pattern of nursing education. Organisational rivalry and constraints on resources undermined attempts to establish an international infrastructure for nursing education. Moreover the low prestige attached to nursing by the RF circumscribed any investment the Foundation was prepared to make and ultimately the results that could be achieved.

Nevertheless the 'imperial gaze' of the RF ranged far and wide across the realm of nursing, scanning England and certain parts of Central and Eastern Europe for opportunities to invest. Scotland, Wales and Northern Ireland fell outside the RF's immediate scope of nursing vision. In spite of its emblematic status as the centre of the British Empire, England proved disappointingly barren territory for Rockefeller's expansionist ambitions. Economic stagnation, institutional idiosyncracy, professional resistance and organisational complexity conspired against attempts by Rockefeller officials to set new standards for English nursing education and practice.

Foundations for nursing

While the RF's work in medical and scientific research and education has received a great deal of attention from historians, its sponsorship of nursing activities has been relatively neglected.[2] This can be explained by a combination of pragmatics and politics; both in terms of the size of the research communities

266

and investment by Rockefeller itself, nursing has been eclipsed by concentration upon medicine and social science and politics. Between 1913 and 1930 the RF contributed approximately $2.3 million to nursing projects in the USA.[3] Expenditure on one university medical school project alone in Britain (University College and University College Hospital Medical School) amounted to £1.2 million between 1920 and 1923.[4] What little research has been conducted into nursing has focused mainly on the USA. This chapter attempts to put British nursing on the international health organisation map by considering the early attempts to 'internationalise' nursing education during the interwar period.[5]

The RF's interest in nursing was stimulated not by some beneficent desire to promote nurses' autonomy, but by the demands of related programmes in medical education and public health. Its focus on public health nursing can be explained by the increasing reliance of the International Health Board (IHB) upon public health nurses as the 'close bond of contact' between the health staff and the people.[6] Never was it envisaged by Foundation officers that the Foundation would do for nursing what it had done for medical education.[7] Nursing was not considered as an aim in itself. As it was to be described in the report of a conference on nursing education in October 1925, it was regarded purely and simply as an 'ancillary' service.[8] Nursing fitted in well with Wickliffe Rose's hierarchical division of public health labour, which he announced at a conference at the RF in 1914. Rose suggested that there should be three grades of public health workers: the leaders, responsible for the planning, organisation and administration; the specialists, who would be experts in specific disciplines of public health; and the 'foot soldiers' or field workers who would do most of the practical tasks.[9] Nurses were perceived as falling mainly within the category of foot soldiers.

Over a 34-year period the RF assisted in the development of nursing education in forty-four countries. Among its projects were surveys of nurse training; the provision of consultants on nursing and staff members to direct projects during developmental periods; financial support for schools of nursing to facilitate re-organisation and improve teaching; capital support for new buildings, equipment or endowment to schools developing new programmes; fellowship awards for nurses to undertake studies and enable leaders to visit centres in their own or other countries for the observation and discussion of teaching and administrative methods.[10]

The RF was therefore led into nursing education more by accident than design. Modernising medical training depended in part upon modernising bedside nursing, and developing public health nursing was crucial to the success of campaigns for the control of disease and the operation of local health departments that the Foundation was helping government agencies establish for the protection of rural communities.[11] The Foundation's hookworm campaign, for example, had begun in 1909 with the Rockefeller Sanitary Commission from which the development of county health units stimulated the demand for public health nurses. The importance of including a public health nurse in the public health team had been recognised at that time, but the only evidence of any concrete contribution the Foundation made to the project was financial aid to the National Organisation for Public Health Nursing in the USA to set standards for education.[12]

In France the RF's interest in public health nursing derived from the Commission for the Prevention of Tuberculosis (1917–22). Public health nurses were considered as vital collaborators in developing a network of efficient out-patient and dispensary services, although the training of health visitors extended beyond the withdrawal of the Commission in 1923.[13] Work in China began under the auspices of the China Medical Board and Peking Union Medical College, and initial aid consisted mainly in the translation of textbooks and provision of fellowships for Chinese nurses. In 1922 the School of Nursing was established as a division of the Peking Medical College as a step towards introducing the standards of American university nursing education to China.[14]

But the question of standards of training and particularly the place that public health nursing was to occupy within the overall structure of nursing education remained vexatious during the interwar period. One of the greatest impediments to reforming nursing education both in Europe and the USA was the lack of agreement among nurse leaders as to what constituted a proper training. Throughout the interwar period, many organisations were exercised about this question within Europe and on both sides of the Atlantic, including the RF, who set up a committee to investigate the status of and training for public health nursing in the USA in 1918.[15]

The Goldmark report (1922–5), named after its secretary and principal investigator and sponsored by the RF, was the first major initiative to attempt to solve some of those difficulties by allowing opinion to crystallise around some consensual notion of standards as a guide to policy-making.[16] Underlying such concerns were: what should the relationship be between the training of the public health nurse and that of the bedside nurse? Should every public health nurse have undergone a course of bedside nursing first, or was such training not essential to successful public health nursing?

Practice varied in different countries, but in England and the USA it was the norm for most public health nurses to be trained as hospital nurses first.[17] But by the interwar period such practice was being called into question as ill-adapted for the practice of public health nursing. Discussion about the future of public health nursing by international organisations raised a number of more fundamental questions about jurisdiction over standards of education and practice and especially the role that national and international organisations might play in determining these.

The Americanisation of European nursing?

As a result of the various committees sponsored by the RF to investigate American nursing education in the 1920s, a number of sweeping recommendations were made. These included raising the social and intellectual standards of nursing education by establishing university schools of nursing, supporting leadership in practice through practical demonstration sites and promoting a comprehensive curriculum which included public health and social service as an essential element in the educational experience of the student.[18] These developments culminated in the establishment of the School of Nursing at Yale in 1923 under the leadership of Annie Goodrich, who was herself a public health nurse and known to the RF through her involvement with the Peking Union Medical College School of Nursing and the National Association of Public Health Nurses, one of the earliest recipients of Rockefeller funds.

Coincidental with the American programme, the RF was considering carrying on a broader programme of nursing education in Europe. The European programme was initiated mainly through the enthusiasm of Edwin Embree, Director of the Division of Studies, and carried out under his direction as a phase of the work of the Division.[19] But unlike the US programme, it stemmed directly from the war and its related problems of disease and social dislocation. Officers were keen to make a contribution to Europe which went beyond the temporary needs of post-war relief. Nursing however is not mentioned in the classification of projects set before the Foundation Trustees. Nor is there any indication in the informal correspondence between officers that nursing was perceived as a prospective field of co-operation. Embree's recommendation however after his return from a field visit to Europe in 1920 was: 'there are few ways in which America can serve Europe in the field of medicine and public health with such confidence as by giving counsel, direction and personal assistance in the introduction of nursing education'.[20]

Europe provided fertile territory for public health intervention for a number of political and economic reasons; the Red Cross units and hospitals were withdrawing as the emergency receded and the future roles of both the American Red Cross and the newly formed League of Red Cross Societies (LRCS) were uncertain.[21] Governments' economic difficulties made it virtually impossible to embark upon any new enterprises.[22] But they were perceived by the Foundation as being more pliable and receptive to new enterprises than before the war, especially with respect to public health measures given the need to conserve the population's health.[23] New health agencies were springing into existence to combat tuberculosis (TB), malaria and trachoma but the major force inhibiting development was the fundamental need for trained nurses in bedside and public health.[24] Embree's optimism culminated in his effusive claim that:

A definite program of counsel and aid in instituting nurse training might have
almost as important an effect on the application of medical services in Europe as
a similar program in medical education has had on the development of medical
science in America.[25]

Aside from the strategic advantages to be gained from promoting nursing,
there were economic and practical benefits too. Embree calculated that any
programme need not involve large sums of money; a staff of advisors and
assistants in Europe could be maintained for as little as $100,000. At the end of
a five to eight-year period, Embree argued, officers could leave behind them a
legacy of training in bedside and public health nursing in each of the important
countries in Europe.[26] Before any further work was undertaken, however, it was
felt necessary to engage someone with experience in public health nursing to
carry out a more detailed study of conditions in nursing and nurse training in
both hospital and public health work.[27]

After a fruitless search for an appropriate candidate to conduct the nursing
study in Europe, Florence Elisabeth Crowell, an American public health
nurse from the Foundation's Paris Office and Tuberculosis Commission, was
appointed.[28] Although the European programme had closer links with the
Commission for the Prevention of Tuberculosis in France than its American
counterpart, one of Miss Crowell's first assignments was to familiarise herself
with the best American training schools. These were to be used as training
centres for small groups of nurses from Europe for advanced training as a
prelude to assuming leadership positions in their own countries.[29] Toronto and
New Haven were among those North American centres visited in which public
health nursing provided the basis for the university courses for nurses. It is
against the background therefore of the most 'progressive' centres of North
American public health nursing that Miss Crowell's views on public health
nursing in European countries need to be understood. The first stop on Miss
Crowell's itinerary was England.

Colonial consciousness

England was selected as a reference point and natural experiment since it was
believed it represented nursing in its 'most effective state and could . . . serve as
a control and standard for comparison in surveys of less progressive countries'.[30]
Foundation officers believed that countries on the Continent looked towards
Great Britain for their standards and methods.[31] Prominent among Foundation
objectives was to avoid giving the impression that the Foundation was in any
way committed to nurse training in Europe. George Vincent, President of the
Foundation (1917–29) explained his caution to Miss Crowell as 'it is always
better do more than is expected than to disappoint exaggerated hopes'.[32]
Extrapolating reasoning previously applied to medicine, the scope of the

European project was correspondingly designed to concentrate on a small number of strategically located centres capable of exerting influence throughout the Continent. London was perceived by Foundation officers as the gateway to the English-speaking world.[33]

Great Britain was regarded as the exception to other continental countries in terms of its level of development by Foundation officers, since bedside nursing was so well established. But England appealed to Foundation officers for economic, political and cultural reasons: English-speaking fellows could be trained less expensively than in the USA and demonstration projects could potentially be used to set the standards for the British Empire.[34]

Innovation and inertia

The first contribution the Foundation made to nursing in England was the provision of fellowships and travel programmes for three London hospital matrons: Ruth Darbyshire of University College Hospital, Beatrice Monk of the London Hospital and Alicia Lloyd-Still, Matron of St Thomas's and later President of the International Council of Nurses (ICN) in 1925.[35] But Miss Crowell's comments on British, by which was meant English, nursing were far from complimentary. Chief among her criticisms was the Byzantine complexity of the organisation of sick nursing, within which she also included district nursing and health visiting. Many of the difficulties she encountered were attributed to the stagnating effect of tradition and the growth of services by accretion. She argued: 'the halo that surrounds nursing traditions in England has blinded them somewhat to the absence of co-ordination, the lack of logical organisation of various phases of nursing and health visiting work'.[36] She was appalled at the multiple routes into qualifying as a health visitor, which she considered promoted waste and inefficiency. Difficulties in obtaining a clear idea of the content and distribution of health visiting work were compounded by the fact that: 'every county is a law unto itself, every borough, every district. Just as there are health visitors with a jumble of qualifications, so there are counties and boroughs and districts with a jumble of workers and agencies.'[37] Overall, it seemed, training facilities for public health nursing in London and elsewhere were quite inferior to those in the USA, Canada or even France.[38]

A major question in Miss Crowell's mind was just how suitable Britain was as a focus for Fellowship support? The educational and preventive sides appeared inefficiently developed and the social side divorced from the public health work. Unfortunately, training appeared to have been grafted onto old institutions with the result that there were a great many different functionaries performing fragmentary services and no generalised public health nursing in the American sense.[39] While it was all very well for English students to 'muddle through' it was unfair to train students from overseas in such a way and then send them back to work in 'unplowed fields' in their own countries.[40] In concluding her report Miss Crowell returned the pessimistic verdict that 'the incrustation of tradition, of prejudices is thicker and harder than in America, and it takes longer to break through'.[41]

Lighthouses of leadership

Service organisation was a particular source of concern on account of the challenges it presented for developing demonstration sites and practical placements for international students. Embree believed the Foundation should confine its assistance to a few 'lighthouses' and the occasional school that might make a 'real contribution by its influence and training of leaders'.[42] This was consistent with Rockefeller policy more generally, which was less concerned with quantitative production of the rank and file than training of elites. Fruitful learning environments were essential to public health nursing, as Embree argued: 'All of us believe . . . that the work of public health as in the army is done in the field, not in swivel chairs.'[43] Pivotal to the practical experience was the academic standing and status of public health nursing.

University College Hospital (UCH) Medical School and London School of Hygiene and Tropical Medicine (LSHTM) were both institutions in which the Foundation had already invested and were considered by officers as potential foci for educational experimentation in nursing. Under the leadership of the new principal Miss Darbyshire, whom the Foundation considered one of the most progressive leaders in British nurse education, it was hoped that UCH could be used as a centre for reorganising nurse training through affiliation with the University of London. This it was hoped and in keeping with Rockefeller expansiveness, would exercise a revitalising effect upon nurse training, not only in London, and Great Britain as a whole, but on the Continent too.[44] But Miss Darbyshire was sceptical of any possibility of radical reform so long as the General Nursing Council (GNC) was dominated by what she referred to as 'the old ladies of 70 and upwards [who] continue to lead the band and effectively throttle anything that looks like progress'.[45]

An approach to establish public health nursing within LSHTM was also made by Sir Perry Cooper, Dean of Guy's Hospital Medical School, and Miss Rundle, Secretary of the College of Nursing in 1925.[46] The RF had already pledged over £2 million to LSHTM for the development of an institute through the International Health Board (IHN). Dr Andrew Balfour, Director of the LSHTM, confirmed that its resources could be made available for public health nurses but, for reasons that are not disclosed, he added he was not in a position to accept responsibility for their training.[47] Sir George Newman, on the other hand, was opposed to what were referred to as 'nursing complications' with the School of Hygiene.[48] Such 'complications' were evidently based on snobbery. Sir

George reasoned that since the Sanitary Institute was the examining body for public health nursing/health visiting and had no university standing, it was decidedly *infra dig.* for the School of Hygiene to train students who would later be examined by a supposedly inferior body.[49] So although the proposal for a course at the London School of Hygiene flickered with possibilities throughout the interwar period, it ultimately failed to ignite.

But even if organisational problems of placements could be overcome, or affiliation with an institute of hygiene and demonstration districts developed, there was the additional problem of negative social attitudes, even xenophobia on the part of patients against international students. As Miss Crowell noted in her diary 'the great difficulty lies in people's objection to being visited by a foreigner'.[50] But university-based courses in public health nursing were already provided for international students during the interwar period, by the LRCS in London and the RF was far from being first in the field.

Co-operation and competition

Although Foundations and international organisations publicly subscribed to a policy of 'co-operation', the reality was one of rivalry in the field. Miss Crowell, for example, did not mince her words in condemning the Red Cross agencies in Europe as 'slowly dying of dry rot'.[51] Mme Ybrani, Directress of Nursing in Hungary, was no less frank in her denunciation of the Hungarian Red Cross. She fulminated against its conservatism and the 'smug self-satisfaction of its directors'. In her view it was an organisation 'eaten up with vanity and ruined everything it touched'.[52] Within Hungary at least the Red Cross had declared itself the primary provider of nurse training and ordained that any new school should be started under its auspices alone.[53] This made it difficult for the RF to intervene in any context where the Red Cross was already involved.

The low esteem in which particular national Red Cross societies were held may also have provided ammunition for those backers of the LRCS keen to rebuild the organisation after the First World War. Yet the whole ethos of philanthropy ran counter to collaboration, since the reward system was geared towards recognising individual achievement. Sharing rewards detracted from what might be called the 'charismatic credit' or social 'capital' upon which the Foundations relied for legitimisation of their positions as the purveyors of privilege and prestige.

Reluctance to collaborate with potential rivals in the field could be justified by the RF on the basis of confining co-operation to governments and local educational authorities rather than with private agencies.[54] As became apparent at an informal conference between Miss Olmsted, Chief of the Division of Public Health Nursing at the LRCS, Dr René Sand, Secretary-General of the LRCS, Miss Crowell and Mr Embree, the LRCS had very clear ideas about what it wanted: not only to maintain, but to strengthen its role in providing public health nursing education. It was ambitious to extend its work with individual Red Cross societies and governments in addition to giving aid and lending personnel to direct new enterprises and establish fellowship programmes for study abroad. Indeed Miss Olmsted argued that the dual involvement of the RF and the LRCS could only cause embarrassment and confusion. To avoid any such conflict therefore, she proposed that the RF should not undertake any work in nursing, but should express its interest in that field through subventions to the LRCS.[55] This contradicted the avowed intentions of the LRCS as being neither to 'supplant or compete with state or local departments of health . . . rather to supplement their activities'.[56] Embree refused to be drawn into committing the Foundation to taking up any kind of position on the matter, stressing that the RF had not yet decided upon any policy for Europe.[57]

Territorial disputes

The LRCS was determined to adopt the mantle of public health nursing as its own and set the courses in public health nursing, which it already provided in Red Cross Schools of Nursing, upon a rational footing.[58] But it was frustrated by the limits set upon its expansion by the inability of cognate organisations to raise the necessary funds for development. Its problems were compounded by an antipathy towards public funding, which it perceived was associated with a loss of administrative elasticity and exposure to political interference.[59] Like the RF however, the LRCS and the American Red Cross both espoused the co-operative principle, but extended this beyond governmental bodies to other private organisations. Such pragmatism was not without its problems. The sponsorship of nursing initiatives by different philanthropic agencies working independently of each other had led to overlapping functions and duplication of effort.[60] The LRCS may well have been justifiably irritated at the RF's forays into public health nursing: not only did Red Cross societies have a track record in the field but the LRCS had demonstrated its commitment by creating a division of nursing devoted specially to this area.

Universalising education

Initiatives to establish international courses in public health nursing within universities were never the prerogative of the RF. The LRCS had sponsored an international course in public health nursing at Bedford College, London, since 1920. But as the resource base of national Red Cross societies shrank in the late 1920s, course leaders looked towards the Rockefeller Foundation for support.[61] Sixty-seven nurses from thirty-four countries had undertaken the course by 1924 and were allegedly engaged in pioneering work in public health in their own countries.[62] Mrs Cecil Carter, Director of the course, approached Embree for help and advice.[63] But it was unlikely that the RF would become involved with its funding or re-organisation in any way so long as the international course remained at Bedford College under LRCS auspices. Embree had the perfect excuse not to co-operate on account of the Foundation's policy of not supporting 'private' organisations such as the LRCS, but noted privately in his diary that the international course was run by 'unimpressive individuals'.[64] Only when the LRCS had withdrawn from involvement in the international course was the RF likely to step in and provide support.

The LRCS struggled to maintain its support for the course until the mid 1930s when it handed over direction and administration of the international course at Bedford College to the newly formed Florence Nightingale International Foundation (FNIF), in July 1934. The formation of the FNIF had been initially proposed by the redoubtable Mrs Bedford Fenwick, Honorary President of the International Council of Nurses (ICN), at the first Triennial Congress of the ICN at Cologne in 1912.[65] But it did not come to fruition until 1934. Inspired in part by the RF, the FNIF took as its aims educational experimentation, the provision of scholarships to enable nurses from different countries to study in London, the development of facilities for research and the establishment of a chair in nursing at the University of London.

This latter proposal was first raised in a confidential request from Alicia Lloyd-Still to Miss Crowell in 1928. Miss Crowell intimated that it was unlikely that the RF would consider such a request favourably since no suitable candidate seemed to be available and changes within the Foundation made it even more unlikely.[66] It appeared however that Miss Lloyd Still, did have someone in mind: Miss Kathleen Russell, Director of the School of Nursing at the University of Toronto.[67] But there remained the question to how to attract Miss Russell to London.[68] As a first step towards sampling opinion on the need to elaborate educational arrangements within London, the FNIF proposed a study to survey the quality of the Bedford College course and 'post-graduate' education for nurses in London more generally. This might also have the added advantage of creating pressure for the establishment of a chair in nursing. Miss Russell was invited to undertake the study on account of her 'thorough and independent thinking', but was already known to the RF through her work in the Toronto school and had visited England as a Rockefeller fellow in 1925.[69] Miss Russell did not then hold a high opinion of the international course in public health nursing education as it was then practised and was especially critical of what she perceived as its 'amateurish' nature. In her report to the RF she wrote: 'European fellows came from a tradition which favoured theory over practice and would return to assume lady philanthropist roles in their own countries.'[70] It is likely that even if members of the FNIF had been aware of Miss Russell's views, they would still have engaged her on account of a desire either to reform radically or to disband the courses at Bedford College. Her appointment may also have served a further political purpose as a gesture of appeasement to Canada, whose Florence Nightingale Memorial Committee had criticised the scope and content of the courses at Bedford College as ill-equipped to meet the needs of all nurses and poorly designed to translate findings across cultures.[71] In keeping with its social survey tradition, the RF agreed to finance the three-month study.[72]

Miss Russell's report confirmed the need to turn the international courses over to the College of Nursing for administration and teaching and to establish a chair in nursing as the key to setting university standards of nursing education.[73] Such proposals may also have been a practical response to the straitened financial circumstances of the FNIF which had never succeeded in raising the funds it required to endow a chair of nursing or realise even its more modest ambitions.[74] But it was the outbreak of war rather than the report itself which finally provided the excuse to break with tradition and send the international students back to their respective countries. This marked the end of Britain's first flirtation with becoming a 'cosmopolitan' centre for nursing education within a university setting.

Conclusion

By 1938 the general view of nursing in Britain held by RF officers was that nursing had failed to advance as it should have done; that it did not meet the needs of social insurance, preventive medicine or public health.[75] Situating nursing education within higher education was perceived as the only means of raising nursing above the apprenticeship level. Yet no machinery existed with which to co-ordinate the provision of nursing education on an international basis. Some nurse leaders, many of whom had contact with the RF and LRCS, looked towards the ICN to assume a leadership role in regulating the standards of international nursing education. Founded with the intention of establishing regulatory machinery within nursing, the ICN was anxious to harmonise standards of nursing education across member states.

The transcendental nature of the international 'idea' was expressed by Mrs Bedford Fenwick, first Honorary President of the ICN, who asserted that the work of nursing was one of 'humanity all the world over, and it is one, therefore which appeals to women of every land without distinction of class, or degree, or nationality'.[76] Drawing upon the language of the international labour movement, Mrs Fenwick argued that 'if the poet's dream of the brotherhood of man is ever to be fulfilled then surely a sisterhood of nurses is an international idea, and one in which the nurses of the women of all nations, therefore, could be asked and expected to join'.[77] The challenge of universalistic ideals lay in how they could be translated into standardised registration procedures when licensing itself was voluntary and state-specific rather than mandatory.[78]

During the interwar period, the ICN explored the possibilities of establishing common registration qualifications across national boundaries with the International Labour Office (ILO). ICN Secretary Christianne Reimann corresponded with the ILO, requesting a review of the status of international nursing regulation.[79] 'Internationalising' the mobility and migration of nursing labour had been suggested by Miss Maude MacCallum, long-term ally of Mrs Fenwick and representative from Great Britain at the meeting of the ICN's Grand Council in Copenhagen in 1922.[80]

Maude MacCallum, outspoken and founding member of the London-based Professional Union of Trained Nurses in 1920, proposed that each country affiliated to the ICN should collect information on which hospitals in their country would accept foreign probationers for training.[81] The Ministry of Health was also considering the issue in England and Wales. The Aliens Act of 1920 enabled British hospitals to employ foreigners where there was evidence that British applicants could not be obtained and that probationers had no comparable opportunities for training in their own countries, a proviso being made that they would return to their own country after completing training.[82] As a trade-union leader, Miss MacCallum was likely to be sensitive to the wider issues affecting the international labour movement.[83] Although the ICN may have been perceived by some members as a kind of international labour exchange, support for 'internationalising' nursing could also be attractive to professionalisers, keen to use probationer exchange programmes as a lever for establishing national registration machinery.

Yet the subtext of internationalisation could also be read as imperialism. England's inadvertent and passive resistance to Rockefeller blandishments during the interwar period brought with it a dilemma of development. Without external aid, nursing education in Britain stood little chance of 'modernising' from within. Yet acknowledging the need for aid reinforced Britain's declining status as a leading power in international nursing affairs. The politics of patronage however ensured that national interests predominated over inter-nationalist concerns and 'co-operation' remained an aspiration rather than actuality. By the end of the interwar period the RF had ensured it was American standards of public health nursing education which provided a conduit into the university system and eventually in the post-Second World War world, the frame of reference for the international nursing world. This legacy did not die with the interwar period, but has endured into the present. It adds a new and insidious twist to the history of professional imperialism within nursing; one which now comes from within rather than from without.

Acknowledgements

Grateful thanks are extended to the Rockefeller Foundation for awarding me a Grant-in-Aid and Nottingham University Research Committee for making this research possible. Tom Rosenbaum, archivist at the Rockefeller Archive Center, was a treasure trove of information and Charles Webster and Paul Weindling have encouraged me to pursue this research as part of a wider study of the politics of nursing education on both sides of the Atlantic. Thanks are due to the International Council of Nurses Centennial History Project Team. Finally my Head of Department, Jane Robinson, and colleagues at the Department of Nursing and Midwifery Studies, University of Nottingham, have supported me throughout my comings and goings in the Department and I thank them.

Notes

1 RAC RG3/906/2/15, 'Résumé of Rockefeller Foundation Public Health and Nursing Education Activities', p. 9.
2 See R. Kohler, *Partners in Science: Foundations and Natural Scientists, 1900–1945* (Chicago: University of Chicago Press, 1991) for a recent monograph in this area. No comparable volume exists for nursing. Exceptions to this neglect are D. Sheahan, 'The Social Origins of American Nursing and its Movement into the University: A Microscopic Approach' (doctoral dissertation, New York University, 1979); R. Kirkwood, 'The Development of University Nursing Education in Canada, 1920–75' (PhD thesis, University of Toronto, 1988); S. Abrahms, 'Dreams and Awakening: The Rockefeller Foundation and Public Health Nursing Education, 1913–1930' (PhD thesis, University of California, San Francisco, 1992).
3 S. Abrahms, 'Brilliance and Bureaucracy: Nursing and Changes in the Rockefeller Foundation 1915–1930', *Nursing History Review*, 1 (1993), 119–37.
4 D. Fisher, 'The Impact of American Foundations on the Development of British University Education, 1900–39' (PhD thesis, University of California, Berkeley, 1977), p. 152.
5 Sarah Abrahms does mention Rockefeller's European programme in her dissertation but her commentary concentrates on the USA. Paul Weindling makes some reference to the Rockefeller's European nursing programme in his 'Public Health and Political Stabilisation: The Rockefeller Foundation in Central and Eastern Europe between the Two World Wars', *Minerva*, 31 (1993), 253–67.
6 RAC RF 'Annual Report' (1921), p. 208.
7 For an overview of Rockefeller involvement in medical education see E. Fee and R. Acheson (eds.), *A History of Education in Public Health* (Oxford: Oxford University Press, 1992).
8 RAC, RF 'Recommendations of the Conference on Nursing Education, October 1925', RF Docket 24/2/26, Program and Policy, Nursing Education, pp. 1–2.
9 See Fee and Acheson, *Public Health Education*, p. 7.
10 *Ibid.*
11 RAC RF 3/200, 7D/86.53, 'Transcript on Nursing Education'.
12 RAC RF3/906/2/15, 'Résumé of Rockefeller Foundation Public Health and Nursing Education Activities', p. 1.
13 *Ibid.*
14 *Ibid.*

15 RAC RF Source material history, vol. 8, p. 2092. The 36-strong committee had 22 women members, drawn from public health and visiting nurse associations, military nursing agencies and hospital and academic nursing departments. Non-nursing membership included representatives from hospital management, academic departments of education and public health medicine at Johns Hopkins and Yale Universities and government health officials.

16 RAC RF/DR 223, E. R. Embree, Interviews, 1920, Appendix.

17 Little has been written on the history of health visiting in nursing in in England and Wales during the interwar period. For overviews see J. Robinson, *An Evaluation of Health Visiting* (London: Council for the Education and Training of Health Visiting/ English National Board for Nursing, Midwifery and Health Visiting, 1982); R. Dingwall, A. M. Rafferty and C. Webster, *An Introduction to the Social History of Nursing* (London: Routledge, 1988), pp. 173–203; E. Peretz, 'Regional Variation in Maternal and Child Welfare between the Wars: Merthyr Tydfil, Oxford and Tottenham', in P. Swan and D. Foster (eds.), *Essays in Regional and Local History* (Beverley (N. Humberside): Hutton Press, 1992), pp. 133–49.

18 *Nursing and Nursing Education in the United States, Report of the Committee for the Study of Nursing Education and Report of a Survey by Josephine Goldmark* (New York: Macmillan, 1922).

19 RAC RF Minutes, 26/5/20, pp. 20074–6. Edward Embree undertook a study of the European situation in the summer of 1920.

20 RAC RF DR 223, p. 9. E. R. Embree, Interviews, 1920, Appendix.

21 See chapters 2 and 3 in this volume for the tensions between the ICRC and LRCS.

22 RAC RF E. R. Embree Diaries 12.1/1923/13, p. 4.

23 In his diary Embree notes that the ARC Societies and LRCS's were each giving some aid to training of nurses in different parts of Europe but their future was uncertain. The LRCS had indicated that it was keen to expand its activities, even that it should become the administrative agency of all organisations interested in nursing education, but the ARC and chief contributor remained unconvinced of the wisdom of such a proposal; see RAC RF E. R. Embree Diaries 12.1/1923/14, p. 5.

24 RAC RF Source Material History, vol. 9, 11, p. 2203.

25 *Ibid.* p. 2207.

26 *Ibid.* p. 2208. Embree estimated that ten years was the minimum period necessary to realise the impact of the work undertaken by relief agencies. This he argued often faltered on account of sudden and premature withdrawal of support and personnel before ideals could be realised. RAC RF E. R. Embree Diaries 12.1/1923/14, p. 10.

27 RAC RF Minutes, 1/12/20, p. 20152.

28 RAC RF Source Material History, vol. 8, pp. 2056–7.

29 RAC RF Minutes, 6/12/22, p. 22180.

30 RAC RF, 'Memorandum of conversations', 20/12/21-2/122; E. R. Embree, Interviews, 1922, Appendix.

31 RAC RF E. R. Embree diaries, 12/1//14, p. 14.

32 RAC RF Vincent to Crowell, 700C/30/6/22.

33 See D. Fisher, 'The Impact of American Foundations on the Development of British University Education, 1900–1939' (PhD thesis, University of California, Berkeley, 1977), part 2, p. 151.

34 RAC RF Source Material History, vol. 9, 11, p. 2441.

35 RAC RF Minutes, 7/11/24, p. 24266.

36 RAC RF Crowell, 'Memorandum on the Study of Sick Nursing and Health Visiting in England', 1.1/401C/427, p. iv.

37 *Ibid.* p. 77.

38 RAC RF Source Material History, vol. 9, p. 2463.

39 RAC RF Source Material History, vol. 9, p. 2463; G. E. Vincent, Interviews, Paris, 7/7/25, p. 161; semantic as well as substantive differences separated American public health nurses from British health visitors, but nursing is not alone in this matter. Medicine had its own share of semantic struggles, see Fee and Acheson, 'History of Education in Public Health', pp. 8–12.

40 RAC RF Project Report, 401C/26/4/26, Crowell to Mary Beard.

41 RAC RF Crowell, 'Sick Nursing', p. 89.

42 RAC RF Source Material History, vol. 9, p. 2486.

43 RAC RF letter Embree to Crowell, 24/4/23.

44 RAC RF E. R. Embree, Diary series, 12.1.1. 18 Sept. 1923, p. 15.

45 RAC RF 12.1. F. E. Crowell Diaries, 13/2/37, p. 31; for a discussion of the political pressures under which the GNC had to operate see A. M. Rafferty, 'The Politics of Nursing Education, 1860–1948' (DPhil dissertation, University of Oxford, 1992).

46 RAC RF Source Material, vol. 9, p. 2464.

47 *Ibid.* p. 2465.

48 *Ibid.* p. 2466.

49 RAC RF 1.1/700/700C/20/142, letter Crowell to Dr Stroude, 22/8.29.

50 RAC RF F. E. Crowell Diary, 12.1/23/1/29.

51 RAC RF Source Material History, vol. 9, p. 2255.

52 *Ibid.*

53 RAC RF Crowell, 'Report on Hungary', 750C/C10-1.

54 RAC RF E. R. Embree, Diaries, 12.1/1923, Exhibit A. 'Memorandum of Conference between Miss Olmsted and Doctor René Sand of the LRCS and Miss Crowell and Mr Embree held at the Office of the League', 25/7/23.

55 *Ibid.* p. 2.

56 LRCS Archives, Geneva (hereafter LRCSA) 'Nursing', *International Journal of Public Health*, 2 (1921), 640.

57 RAC RF E. R. Embree Diaries, 12.1/1923, Exhibit A. 'Memorandum of Conference between Miss Olmsted and Doctor René Sand of the LRCS and Miss Crowell and Mr Embree held at the Office of the League', 25/7/23, p. 3.

58 LRCSA, K. Olmsted, 'The International Problems of Nursing', *The World's Health*, 4, 3 (1923), 11; G. Kuss, 'The French Red Cross and Public Health', 4, 5 (1923), 20–1; 'Should Red Cross Societies Train Public Health Nurses?', *The World's Health*, 4, 11 (1923), 2–5.

59 LRCSA, 'Nursing', *International Journal of Public Health*, 2 (1921), 639.

60 *Ibid.* p. 643.

61 RAC RF Source Material History, p. 24643.

62 RAC RF1.1/700/700C/20/146, Letter, Director-General to Vincent, 1/7/24, p. 2.

63 *Ibid.*

64 RAC RF E. R. Embree, Diaries, 12.1/1923, Exhibit A. 'Memorandum of Conference between Miss Olmsted and Doctor René Sand of the LRCS and Miss Crowell and

Mr Embree', 25/7/23, p. 1; RAC RF E. R. Embree, Diaries, 12.1/1923/14 'Report of European trip of Edwin R. Embree, Study of Nurse Training – summer, 1923', p. 2.

65 This proposal elaborated upon ideas first suggested by Miss Adelaide Nutting, Principal of Teachers College, New York. See International Council of Nurses Archives (ICNA), Geneva, 'Notes on a possibly International Memorial to Florence Nightingale', Board of Directors, nd.

66 RAC RF Rockefeller Source Material History, vol. 9, p. 2469.

67 *Ibid.*

68 RAC RF 1.1/700/700C/19/139, 'Memorandum of a Conference of G. E. Vincent with Miss E. K. Russell, Director of Public Health Nursing, Toronto Dept of Hygiene and Miss J. I. Gunn, 18/9/25'. Miss Russell had been sponsored by the Rockefeller Foundation in 1925 to undertake a study tour of England.

69 RAC RF 6.1/1.1/22/242; *ibid.* Mary Beard Diary 28/1/36.

70 RAC RF 1.1/700C/19/139 'Travels in Europe, Summer 1925'.

71 A. M. Rafferty, 'The Florence Nightingale International Foundation', Draft Paper, University of Pennsylvania, October 1992, p. 6.

72 RAC RF F. E. Crowell Diary, 9/7/33.

73 RAC RF Source Material History, vol. 9, p. 2470; K. R. Russell, *Report of a Study of the Facilities for Advanced Nursing Education in London, Both Professional and Academic, and of the Future Education Policy of the Florence Nightingale International Foundation* (London: Florence Nightingale International Foundation, 1936); RF 6.1/1.1/22/242 from F. E. Crowell's Diary, 13/2/37.

74 RAC RF F. E. Crowell Diary 12.1.13/2/37, p. 30.

75 RAC RF6/1/1.1/23/262 Letter, George Strode to A. J. Warren, 22/10/38.

76 *Ibid.* M. Breay and B. Fenwick, 'History of the ICN 1899–1909', *International Council of Nurses Annual Reports* (1928–9), pp. 218–19.

77 *Ibid.* pp. 218–19.

78 See Isabel MacDonald's discussion of compulsory state registration of nurses at the 1933 Congress of the ICN at Brussels: ICN Archive (ICNA), I. MacDonald, 'Compulsory State Registration of Nurses', *Congress Reports, International Council of Nurses* (1933), pp. 53–4.

79 I am grateful to Carol Miller for drawing my attention to this correspondence. The interaction between the ICN and other international organisations is currently the subject of further research encompassed within the Centennial History Project of the International Council of Nurses, directed from the University of Pennsylvania and undertaken by a team of historians and consultants from ICN member countries; Joan Lynaugh (Director), Barbara Brush, Geertje Boschma, University of Pennsylvania; Nancy Tomes, University of New York, Stony Brook; Meryn Stuart, University of Ottawa and myself.

80 For further details of the role of the union in radical nursing politics after the First World War, see A. M. Rafferty, 'The Politics of Nurse Education, 1860–1948' (DPhil dissertation, University of Oxford, 1992), pp. 190–1.

81 *Fourth Regular Meeting (Business Meeting) of the International Council of Nurses* (Copenhagen: ICN, 1922), p. 130.

82 PRO London MH55/1447, 'The Employment of Foreign Probationers in British Hospitals'.

83 For a brief discussion of the similarities and differences between the ICN and the International Labour movement see A. M. Rafferty, 'The International Council of Nurses, 1908–22: Professionalising Gender and Engendering Professionalism', Draft chapter presented at ICN Centennial History Project meeting, University of Pennsylvania, 1992, pp. 3–6.

14

Mental hygiene as an international movement

MATHEW THOMSON

Between the two world wars health services in Europe and America began to extend from institutional care of the seriously mentally disordered to cover early treatment of less serious cases, after-care of recovered cases and organised care in the community. Even more ambitiously, there was an expansion of interest in prevention of mental disorder and promotion of environmental conditions to encourage positive mental health among the normal population. A variety of terms were used to describe these new approaches: in Britain a tradition of charitable and local government economic assistance shaped the emergence of 'mental welfare' and 'community care'; in the United States Adolf Meyer adopted the term 'biopsychiatry' to reflect his holistic approach; in France the terms used were 'mental prophylaxis' and 'psychotechnics'; and in the Soviet Union it was 'psychohygiene'. However, the most popular and all-embracing term used to describe these developments was 'mental hygiene'.

The simultaneous adoption of mental hygiene strategies was partially the result of common reactions to social and welfare problems of the interwar period. However, the pace of socio-economic and political modernisation was not even. It is therefore worthwhile considering whether parallel developments were, instead, the result of an international mental hygiene movement. This chapter will consider the extent to which there was an international movement and its interaction with national mental hygiene movements and organisations.

A study of mental hygiene raises some particularly interesting questions about the nature of international health organisations and movements. First, because of the flexible nature of a normatively defined mental health, mental hygiene was very clearly shaped by culture and ideology. Therefore, the influence of international, though, in reality, predominantly American, organisations in spreading mental hygiene can be used to examine the extent to which international health organisations could be a tool of 'cultural imperialism'. Secondly, mental hygiene had a unique relation to international relations. The First World War was seen by many to have stemmed from a European mental malaise, antagonised by the anxieties of prewar national animosity. Therefore, in the post-war years, mental hygienists saw international co-operation – through movements such as mental hygiene – as a prerequisite for mental health. More directly, cultivation of mental health was seen as vital in keeping at bay the aggressive drive for war.[1] However, exacerbating such internationalist hopes, one of the keys to mental hygiene was prevention of mental disorder by restrictive strategies, such as immigration control, which were fundamentally nationalistic and potentially damaging to international relations. Moreover, during periods of political, cultural and economic turmoil, as experienced in the 1930s, there was a danger that mental hygiene movements would turn inwards, manipulating the normative basis of mental health as a tool of nationalism. Finally, international mental hygiene raises important questions about professionalisation, for caught up in the struggle between national and international mental hygiene was an increasingly professional and scientific group of mental health workers who were both part of an international psychiatric community yet dependent on national patronage for their personal success.

The chapter will be divided into three sections, considering in turn the attempts of international organisations to spread propagandist mental hygiene, to attack mental hygiene problems through an international psychiatric research and educational strategy, and to prevent mental disorder through a range of restrictionist mental hygiene strategies. Analysis of the propagandist strategy will focus on the American National Committee on Mental Hygiene and its attempt to develop an international movement. Analysis of the research and educational strategy will consider the international mental hygiene initiatives of the Rockefeller Foundation (RF) and Commonwealth Fund (both American philanthropic organisations). The restrictionist strategy cannot be so easily represented by a single organisation and will be used to show the limitations of international co-operation. The division between these groups and strategies was not absolute but is useful for analytical purposes. Tensions did exist between them yet so did common aims and personnel. The balance between division and unity will determine the extent to which it is justifiable to claim the existence of an international mental hygiene movement.

The propagandist strategy

The US mental hygiene movement centres on Clifford Beers and the National Committee for Mental Hygiene (NCMH), founded in 1908 after the publication of Beers' best selling exposé of asylum abuse *A Mind that Found Itself*.[2] Propaganda was the main strategy of the NCMH: firstly, to fuel the institutional growth of the movement, secondly to change public attitudes towards the insane, and ultimately to educate the public in leading mentally healthy lives.

To a certain extent the shift towards international campaigning in the 1920s was a reflection of American idealistic internationalism in the years immediately following the First World War; a continuation of Wilsonianism in the philanthropic and scientific spheres which should be borne in mind when evaluating the extent of US isolationism. On the other hand, the shift to an international movement should also be interpreted in terms of Beers' personal ambitions.[3] It provided an outlet for his lay propagandist enthusiasm as increasingly he met professional caution in the domestic campaign.

Beers' own accounts, with their dedication to self-publicity, placed him and the NCMH at the centre of the international movement.[4] He had first proposed the formation of an international committee at a 1919 meeting of leading Canadian and US mental hygienists.[5] According to Beers, it was he who actively stimulated the formation of a series of national organisations in Belgium, Britain, France and Australia. He visited Europe in 1923. As an outsider to internal European animosities, Beers could pose as a bridge builder and a charismatic unifying figure in a still politically divided Europe. More materialistically, the US movement promised resources for a major conference. However, because of organisational and financial difficulties this conference was continually delayed. In the meantime European conferences did take place without significant American participation.

Eventually in 1930 the international congress was held in Washington. This Congress was the apogee of the US-centred international movement. The organisation and programme committee behind the Congress were all, apart from the Canadian Clarence Hincks, US mental hygienists. The resources of the NCMH, covering the total cost of $132,721, enabled extensive preparation. A 34-page preliminary announcement was published in four languages: 24,000 copies were distributed in English, 3,000 in French, 3,000 in German and 1,000 in Spanish. With financial aid from US benefactors and foundations, including $10,000 from the Commonwealth Foundation, $10,000 from the Julius Rosenwald Fund and $5,000 from the Milbank Memorial Fund, the NCMH was able to assist the travel of representatives from forty-one countries.[6] Delegates from twenty-two countries with their own national committees attended.[7] In all there was a total of 3,042 official participants. The majority of countries represented were West and East European, but participants also arrived from countries as far flung as the Soviet Union, India, Japan, Siam, Venezuela and the Union of South Africa.[8]

The Congress lasted five days, and the published report made up two volumes and about 1,500 pages. The Congress included the reports on eight special international committees which had been set up to produce comparative studies of mental hygiene provision. These included committees on collection of statistics, standards of institutional care, legal measures and laws, use of psychiatry in prisons and for delinquents, the relation between mental hygiene and welfare, and training in psychiatric social work. Each committee made some tentative recommendations regarding standards and future aims (though these carried no authority) and produced some useful comparative material which indicated the wide range in standards yet the parallel trends between countries.[9] The main part of the Congress was discussion of pre-circulated papers organised in thematic sessions and followed by discussion. In summary, the Congress was a major event in the mental hygiene movement, and this was made possible through the energy and resources of Clifford Beers and the American NCMH.

Despite the apparent success of the 1930 Congress, the next international meeting had to wait seven years. Beers' plan to set up a permanent inter-national institute of mental hygiene at Yale floundered as the Depression hit the NCMH's finances. The 1937 Paris International Congress on Mental Hygiene attracted under 300 participants, the majority of whom were professionals and few of whom were from across the Atlantic. The contrast between 1930 and 1937 can partly be explained by the worsened economic environment which made funding a major conference and travelling long distances more difficult. The political divisions on the European continent exacerbated the situation further. The 1937 conference had been placed in jeopardy by the Spanish Civil War, and the presence of German representatives at the conference exposed the lack of unity in the movement.[10] More fundamentally, the contrast can be explained by the shortcomings which already underlay the congress of 1930. An alternative reading of the international movement raises questions over Beers' story of emerging international unity and US domination. Beers exaggerated the influence of the US movement on the establishment of other national committees. With a donation from the Milbank Fund, the NCMH could provide limited start-up assistance for national movements.[11] Speaker after speaker at the 1930 congress flattered their hosts by acknowledging the influence of Beers' movement. But in reality national movements used the enthusiasm, success and support of the US movement to gain favour and backing from their own governments, professional organisations and general publics in order to bolster indigenous traditions of mental hygiene.

In contrast to the important lay element of the NCMH and its propagandist orientation, European movements tended to be dominated by professionals and to be clinic-orientated. In England, indicating a more professional elitist style, the title of 'National *Council* for Mental Hygiene' was adopted in 1922. England already had a number of well-established groups with significant lay representation, the most important of these being the Central Association for Mental Welfare. The National Council had to avoid infringing on the territory of the established groups and concentrated on providing expert advice rather than serving as leader of the British mental hygiene movement.[12] The leaders of the French League for Mental Hygiene, Edouard Toulouse and Genil-Perrin, were again psychiatrists rather than laymen. In contrast to the US propagandist-centred movement, French energies were directed at the promotion of clinic-based psychiatry in which scientific research was to play a major role.[13]

Somewhat pointedly, Dr G. Heuyer, Director of the Neuropsychiatric Clinic of Paris, presented the virtues of the French model of mental hygiene:

> The Annex Neuropsychiatric Children's Clinic compares favorably with centers of the same kind in foreign countries, and it has already served as a model to various foreign doctors who have preferred the French method, with its strictly medical and psychiatric approach, and who have established centers of neuropsychiatric consultations for children similar to our clinic.[14]

German delegates also tended to be professionals who emphasised research and were ambivalent about lay participation.[15]

The mental hygiene model espoused in the international movement was unrealistic for countries less privileged in financial and educational resources than the United States and some of her Western European partners. For instance, representatives from the Philippines and from Siam admitted that they attended for inquisitive rather than practical reasons, feeling that mental hygiene was not such a serious problem in societies which were at an earlier stage of development.[16] Dr B. Rodriguez Arias, Secretary-General of the Spanish Association of Neuropsychiatry, pointed out:

> Unfortunately, many countries cannot imitate the example – almost always an ideal one – of the United States, for numerous reasons, among others, the generally antiquated organisation of the state, the strong popular prejudices, and limited economic means. Apart from their evident complexity, many of these conditions are so rooted in the mass of the people that a community solution of the problems we have been discussing would call for interminable struggles and years of persevering effort.[17]

Despite this, a Spanish mental hygiene group was set up, adopting the American title as an emblem of their progressive aspirations rather than realistic plans.[18] For countries struggling to assert their national identity, such as Estonia, to claim an interest in mental hygiene was intended to promote their recognition as 'civilised' members of the international community.[19] Backward psychiatric provision could be a stimulus to certain mental hygiene policies. For instance, in a number of Eastern European and South American countries the main focus of mental hygiene was to attack alcoholism and syphilis as a way to offset the potential cost of providing psychiatric services.[20] In Hungary economic hardship encouraged the adoption of mental hygiene and family care of the insane in order to cut the cost of institutional care.[21] The most notable examples of 'family care' were in fact pre-modern – the colony at Gheel in Belgium, in existence since the Middle Ages, and 'boarding out' in rural areas of Scotland.[22]

National mental hygiene movements were also shaped by political environment. In the Soviet Union there was an attempt to establish a mental health movement in the 1920s. Psychiatrists such as A. B. Zalkind looked to German and American models of dispensary care to relieve the strain on overworked party members. But, the political authorities wanted work to be seen as invigorating rather than tiring, the state lacked the resources to establish care for mild mental problems, and party members objected to being seen as neurotic themselves.[23] Therefore in the early 1930s a 'revolution from above' shifted 'psycho-hygiene' away from individual treatment of neurosis towards a broader conception of addressing mental hygiene via social welfare. As a Soviet delegate at the 1930 international congress explained: 'The mental-hygiene movement in Russia goes beyond the limits of psychiatric aid to those who need it and takes part in the organization of the social structure of the commonwealth. Mental hygiene penetrates the whole social fabric of the USSR and takes part in all the progressive steps of social organizations'.[24] At the other end of the political spectrum, in Italy, G. C. Ferrari of the Italian League for Mental Hygiene described Mussolini's regime in terms of its effect on mental hygiene, and saw the regime's encouragement of militaristic 'scoutism' as being of great mental hygienic value.[25] Of course, internal divisions could exist within national political environments. As work on communist mental hygiene in the United States indicates, such political divisions could shape oppositional styles of mental hygiene.[26]

Not only were there indigenous mental hygiene traditions, but there were also non-US channels of international influence. The most important of these was that centring on France. Edouard Toulouse had been advocating his vision of psychiatric reform and open psychiatric hospitals since the 1890s. As early as 1899 he began to campaign at international conferences. Although the formation of the Ligue D'Hygiène Mentale in 1920 was inspired by the example of Beers, it was the continuation of an indigenous French movement of 'psychotechnique' and 'prophylaxie mentale'.[27] In the 1920s the French influence was exported via the Paris international mental hygiene congresses of 1922 and 1927. Rudolf Fabinyi of Hungary saw France rather than the US as the crucial influence.[28] Gustava Riedel, President of the Brazilian League of Mental Hygiene, again stressed the importance of Toulouse in making the Dispensary the centre of mental hygiene organisation.[29] The French dispensary influence was strong in the international organising umbrellas of the League of Nations and the International Committee of the Red Cross which provided further alternative channels of influence to the US-centred movement. In contrast to the NCMH, the Red Cross did provide some material assistance by housing mental clinics in Red Cross centres in Belgium, Japan and Luxembourg.[30] However, mental hygiene was not considered a priority by these other international organisations, thus enabling Beers' international movement to play the leading role.

A third sphere of influence centred on Germany. It has been argued that the German Society for Mental Hygiene, founded in 1928, was an attempt to extend racial hygiene into psychiatry.[31] At the 1930 International Congress, Ernst Rüdin, psychiatric specialist in studies of the genetics of mental disease, and

Wilhelm Weygandt, President of the German National Committee for Mental Hygiene, took the lead in advocating a eugenic approach to mental hygiene and the use of sterilisation for the mentally disordered.[32] Rüdin also spread this message at international eugenics congresses. When the British eugenics movement were lobbying to introduce sterilisation in the early 1930s they turned to Rüdin for scientific backing – sterilisation was already widespread in the United States, but was seen as being less scientifically based.[33] However, also evident at the 1930 International Mental Hygiene Congress are other strands of the German mental hygiene tradition. In the 1920s, Germany saw notable developments in the application of psychology to problems of and assessment of character.[34] The influence of Hermann Simon's physiotherapeutic approach and use of occupational therapy spread to the Netherlands.[35] In 1927 the city authorities in Amsterdam commissioned a survey of mental health care schemes in Denmark and Germany to find a cheaper form of care. As a result, the system of preventive care, 'Fürsorgestelle', in Frankfurt was adopted as a model for the mental hygiene work of F. S. Meijers and A. Querido in Amsterdam.[36] Finally, the development of colonies in Germany influenced a move away from closed institutional care.[37]

The congress of 1930, though impressive in terms of number of countries represented, was less so in the proportion of non-US participants. The best-represented visitor was Canada with 44 delegates. After this Britain and Germany both had 18 and France had 11. No other country had as many as 10 delegates. In total there were 210 foreign delegates, or just 160 if Canada and the US territories of Hawaii, Philippines and Puerto Rico are excluded.[38] Foreign delegates, though under-represented in total, were given a prominent platform. Political divisions were dampened by optimistic internationalism. The two Soviet delegates, despite great problems overcoming political barriers to reach the conference, were greeted with great enthusiasm and curiosity. So much interest was expressed that A. B. Zalkind and Rubinow were given a special session to describe Soviet mental hygiene policy.[39] Despite the interest shown in foreign delegates, many sessions of the Congress were dominated by internal debates between American delegates, or between factions of the psychoanalytic movement. More importantly still, the Congress did not take the opportunity to create permanent organisational structures, set standards in care, regulate qualifications or formulate a unified classification. Perhaps if such concrete steps had been taken the aura of international harmony would have been shattered by exposure of political divisions, national animosities and inequalities of development.

In summary, although the NCMH was the leading actor in the propagandist international mental hygiene movement, it did not simply impose an American vision on the rest of the world. It came up against and interacted with pre-existing mental hygiene traditions. In material terms, the NCMH was able to pay for foreign delegates to attend the 1930 Congress, and provide some fraternal support, but it could do little concretely to shape an international movement.

The research and educational strategy

The RF's interest in mental hygiene began with the funding of the NCMH. In 1909 the NCMH applied unsuccessfully for a million-dollar endowment from John Rockefeller Senior. Shortly afterwards the RF was chartered. A further grant request from the NCMH was turned down. Instead the RF agreed to pay the salary of Thomas Salmon as medical adviser on mental hygiene and loan him to the NCMH as Medical Director. At this time the RF was still seriously considering setting up its own Division of Mental Hygiene. This plan was soon dropped. The Foundation continued to support the NCMH through paying the salary of Salmon and then a series of new Directors after 1919. Support for general expenditure was withdrawn in 1929. However, because of the depressed financial situation of the NCMH, funding was continued reluctantly in other forms throughout the interwar period. In total, the RF contributed $906,100 to the NCMH between 1915 and 1939.[40] Foundation officers were critical of the NCMH's lack of financial independence, but as a result of the dependency relationship gained influence to steer the mental hygiene movement towards research. The Foundation sponsored surveys of the mentally ill and defective, studies in the psychopathology of crime, the development of uniform statistics and classification, and an NCMH survey of mental health services among the European combatants.

After the war, the interest in mental testing and in the international sphere persisted via funding an ambitious project undertaken by the Committee on the Scientific Problems of Human Migration. Though stimulated by fears of immigration of eugenically and mentally unfit Europeans, the range of psychological work undertaken or proposed was vast and went beyond intelligence testing and racial concerns to investigate issues such as character development and emotions.[41] Support for the project petered out in the mid-1920s on the grounds that it lacked focus. However, the breadth of interest was continued in the Rockefeller funding of the Yale Institute of Human Relations. The Foundation made a major investment of $5 million in funding the construction of this institute which was envisaged as a centre for interdisciplinary exchange between law, medicine, psychology and the human sciences.By the mid-1930s similar criticisms of lack of focus and co-ordination had emerged.[42] The failure to make progress in mental hygiene through the human sciences encouraged the Foundation to concentrate on a more scientific approach. Indicative of this shift, the Foundation refused to fund the 1930 international congress, and instead organised a closed meeting of professionals to discuss the state of the discipline.[43]

In 1920 the Foundation had considered the value of directing resources towards psychiatric research. However, under the influence of Simon Flexner it was decided to continue to concentrate on those areas of medicine where knowledge was better developed.[44] The first major step in the emergence of an international programme in psychiatry was to assist the funding of Emil Kraepelin's German Institute for Psychiatric Research in Munich. The inflationary situation in Germany in the early 1920s made it difficult to establish the Institute through German money alone. Aid came from the American expatriate James Loeb of the Kuhn–Loeb banking family who mobilised American-Jewish money. In 1925 Kraepelin and his colleague Plaut came to America in search of further funding. The idea of a research institute outside of a university was not consistent with the Rockefeller policy of encouraging a close alliance between research and medical education. However, the fear that Kraepelin's work would collapse and the belief that the work was of great importance convinced the Foundation to provide financial backing.[45]

The request for funding led the RF to support an international survey of psychiatric research undertaken by Clarence Hincks, Medical Director of the Canadian NCMH, and in the 1930s of the American NCMH. Hincks visited and reported on England, Scotland, France, Belgium, Switzerland and Germany. The reports criticised the lack of scientific work in Britain, whereas they praised Switzerland and Germany.[46] Hincks was impressed with the way in which Kraepelin had shifted his interest from psychiatric nosology and classification to a broad research programme into the scientific roots of psychological behaviour. Hincks was equally impressed by other German research centres. By comparison, he warned that America lagged far behind in the struggle to diminish world mental disorder.[47]

The German Psychiatric Institute initiative influenced a fundamental general policy reappraisal in the early 1930s. Major re-organisation was necessary to rationalise overlapping funding. The problem of overlap was a general one but was particularly acute in the psychiatric arena. At the same time, a reappraisal of the target of funding was undertaken. As a result, what was termed 'psychobiology' became the centre of all Rockefeller efforts. Psychobiology was to be far wider than psychiatry and can be seen as a marriage of the more propagandist mental hygiene concerns of the 1920s with biological research:

> The ultimate aim and the central problem of the programme are the analysis and rationalization of human behaviour. With a sufficiently broad interpretation, therefore, 'psychobiology' is the single principal topic, all the other subjects being viewed as contributory . . . At no time in the past has the likelihood of progress been so great or the need of psychobiological knowledge more urgent. In research upon the anatomy and physiology of the nervous system lies the promise of understanding not only the control of movement and sensation but also essential factors in the emotions of individuals.[48]

In total the Foundation contributed over $10.5 million to psychobiology between 1931 and 1941.[49] This funding helped to shift the emphasis of international mental hygiene from 'speculative' methods and propaganda to science.[50]

Three major justifications were given for the new focus. Firstly, mental hygiene was seen as one of the major medical and social problems facing industrial societies. The cost of care for the mentally ill exceeded that of all other groups of the sick put together. Of even greater cost and importance was the care and control of the delinquent, criminal and educationally backward. Secondly, the Foundation felt that very little psychiatric research of any quality was currently being undertaken and that by channelling all of their efforts in this direction they could make a major impact. Moreover, as bodily diseases became tamed by medical science, disorders of the mind would become the most important area for medical progress. Thirdly, by increasing understanding of the human mind it was hoped to have an impact, not only on psychiatric care, but on the whole of medicine; an understanding of the patient would greatly improve what was seen as increasingly mechanistic general medicine and break down the false dichotomy set up between mind and body.[51] In summary, underlying the Rockefeller programme was the vision that understanding of the human mind was the key to scientific, medical, social and economic progress.

This mental hygienist vision of the RF was to be achieved through an international research strategy. The approach developed at the German Psychiatric Institute was continued, except that the Foundation, as depression and political instability arrived in the 1930s, was less inclined to fund the building or setting up of schemes which it would not be able to control in the long term.[52] Through Alan Gregg at its Paris Office, the Foundation funded scientifically orientated projects which were often led by natural scientists rather than psychiatrists.[53] The influence of Warren Weaver, a physicist, as head of the Natural Science Division, shifted research towards 'vital processes' of life – an attempt to discover the building blocks and forces of living beings.[54] Just as physics was now grounded in understanding of atomic chemistry, medical science was to be based on biochemistry. For psychiatry this meant an understanding of brain chemistry, the effect of the body's hormones on emotions and the influence of genes on intelligence and behaviour. Such research was at the cutting edge of knowledge and the Foundation would fund it wherever there were scientists with the requisite ability.[55] This meant funding research in Europe. Projects were supported in Austria, Holland, Scandinavia and England, but the focus of such work was Germany.

The Foundation's enthusiasm for German research had led it into making some long-term commitments: substantial contributions had been made to the construction of the German Psychiatric Institute and the Kaiser Wilhelm Institute for Brain Research, and several projects were given five-year grants. As early as 1933 this came to be seen as a problem because of political interference under the Nazis.[56] The Foundation was embarrassed by criticism in the US press that it was funding Nazi racial research under Rüdin at the German Psychiatric Institute.[57] In defence, it was argued that this racial research was not directly funded by a Rockefeller grant.[58] Nevertheless, within the German Psychiatric Institute, Rockefeller funding was being redirected towards the expansion of Rüdin's research. In fact, the genetics of mental disorder was one of the main interests of the psychobiology and vital processes programme. Consequently, racial comparisons were seen as a natural testing ground.[59] Elsewhere in Europe, without controversy, the Foundation actively funded research in the genetics of mental disease and defect.[60] The continuation of funding in Germany until 1939 indicates the Foundation's high estimation of the German research. When researchers lost their jobs, due to their Jewish ancestry, the Foundation provided them with assistance and supported the continuation of their research abroad.[61] Through these emigrés, the German biomedical approach was channelled to other European countries. For instance, Edward Mapother, Medical Director of the Maudsley Hospital in Britain, took a series of emigrés hoping that their influence could be a catalyst to British research.[62] The lesson learnt by the Foundation through the Nazi experience was not that the content of the research programme was ideologically unsound, but that it was necessary to develop a policy to avoid the political interference experienced in Germany.

Through small grants and fellowships, rather than institutional endowments, the Foundation gained greater control over the use of its funding.[63] Between 1931 and 1939 the Foundation funded 274 Fellowships, thereby moulding a generation of psychiatric researchers. In addition, 293 small grants under $7,500 were given, rising sharply in 1934 and totalling $668,867.[64] Through the experience of the Paris Office, resources would be targeted at politically stable countries in future. Britain replaced Germany as the ideal.[65] The Foundation was particularly attracted by the role of the British Medical Research Council (MRC). The MRC was a government but non-party body, was biomedically inclined, and aimed to co-ordinate national research.[66] Serving as an intermediary for Rockefeller funding, the MRC protected the programme from political interference, relieved the Foundation of direct responsibility and potential controversy, and promised a commitment to funding after the Foundation had pulled away. It was hoped that similar bodies would emerge to provide an intermediary role in other countries.[67]

Growing RF interest in Britain from the mid-1930s also arose from a shift in mental hygiene strategy. The Foundation had always been unenthusiastic to fund applied psychiatry outside America. For instance, in Britain the clinical work at the Tavistock Clinic gained minimal funding compared to the more research-orientated Maudsley Hospital.[68] As far as the Foundation was concerned, psychiatric practice was the role of national governments. However, the Foundation became increasingly interested in psychiatric education.[69] A great deal of money was spent on encouraging university-centred education in the United States, but dissatisfaction remained over the lack, both of a professional psychiatric qualification, and of psychiatric training in general medical education. In 1933 Ralph Noble, the Australian leader in the international mental hygiene movement, undertook an international survey of psychiatric education for the Rockefeller Foundation.[70] The existence of a professional psychiatric qualification in Britain attracted the Foundation to funding the Royal Medico-Psychological Association, bolstering British training with refresher courses at the Maudsley Hospital, and encouraging institutional doctors to become involved in research.[71] In a sense, Britain was being used as a laboratory to experiment on the development of the profession.

In summary, the Rockefeller mental hygiene strategy shifted over the interwar years from funding of the NCMH's propaganda, to biomedically orientated psychiatric research and finally to professional education. There has been considerable debate about the motivation lying behind Rockefeller international philanthropy.[72] Fisher has argued that 'Rockefeller Officers and Trustees were "sophisticated conservatives" who through the foundations exercised a form of American cultural and economic imperialism.'[73] He depicts funding as a 'proactive' rather than 'reactive' practice.[74] By contrast, the Bulmers' case study of funding of the London School of Economics suggests that the Foundation played a less proactive role and, driven by a desire to avoid political controversy, acted through intermediary organisations.[75] The Foundation's stated aim was to 'benefit the welfare of all mankind'. In terms of the international breadth of psychiatric research funding this ambition would, at least superficially, seem to have been attempted and to some degree attained. On the other hand, very rarely did the Foundation attempt to aid psychiatric practice abroad materially, except when this was integral to research or development of training. Moreover, often underlying the funding of foreign projects was the hope thereby to remedy an American weakness. At times the Foundation did express a more internationalist vision. It was hoped that through aiding Britain influence would reach the whole British Empire,[76] and that funding of a Polish clinic would stimulate psychiatry throughout Eastern Europe.[77] However, this reflected an imperialist 'spheres of influence' vision and rhetoric as much as a desire to 'benefit the welfare of mankind'. Since these peripheral areas were unlikely to aid the grand scientific project, very little money was actually invested. Critics have argued that the Foundation used international funding to spread capitalist and white-Anglo-Saxon-Protestant values.[78] However, what is notable about the psychiatric programme is the rejection of propagandist mental hygiene which would have been the perfect medium with which to dress up ideology and values as science. The Foundation's ideological influence was less direct. The research strategy shifted attention away from social solutions and indirectly diverted resources away from welfare strategies, seemingly depoliticising the problem of mental hygiene. Scientific solutions were depicted as value free and essential for the future of mankind. Consequently, psychiatric scientists were absolved of social responsibility for their actions, and, focusing on long-term scientific problems, had a tendency to neglect the rights of patients, using them inhumanely as guinea-pigs in experiments. The claim that such science was value free was an illusion: in particular, much of the research was based on eugenic assumptions and ideals.

Although the Foundation often simply 'reacted to' existing trends in research, was always loath to make research dependent on Rockefeller beneficence and began to see the intermediary role of the MRC as an ideal, it must nevertheless be concluded that, as one of the most substantial and directed sources of funding, the Foundation did play a major 'proactive' role in shifting the focus of mental hygiene away from a lay propagandist 'movement' to an international scientific programme in the 1930s. This programme was not a 'movement' in the sense of that used for the propagandist groups, especially since it was shaped by a critique of these groups. But the international funding of the RF did help to establish an international network of researchers, bureaucrats and mental hygienists, and in so doing helped to redefine the international mental hygiene movement.

The second American Foundation to play a major role in shaping the interwar international mental hygiene movement was the Commonwealth Fund, which focused on spreading child guidance and psychiatric social work.[79] As such, its aims were closer to those of the propagandist groups than to the Rockefeller research strategy. On the other hand, it shared some of the Rockefeller misgivings about the lay mental hygiene movement. Like the RF, it saw training of professionals as of central importance.[80] It also shared the view that support should be temporary, aimed at areas of existing excellence, and not directly to fund social welfare. As such, the Commonwealth encouraged the trend towards a professionalisation of mental hygiene.

In international terms the Commonwealth vision was far more limited than that of the RF. The only foreign mental hygiene programme it funded was in Britain. This may have reflected the founder's British roots: the Fund announced their British programme as having the aim of 'strengthening mutual amity and understanding between Great Britain and the United States'.[81] Or the choice of Britain may have been because Anglo-American ties were already strong. In terms of cultural and linguistic understanding it would have been far harder to transplant US mental hygiene to the European continent.

The Fund established a fellowship programme to bring British social workers to the United States – the international leader in psychiatric social work. Between 1931 and 1939, fellowships were given to twenty-three social workers. The Fund also gave Fellowships to twenty-one psychiatrists, and organised visits for civil servants to view mental hygiene work in the United States.[82] The

Fund supported the growth of British child guidance clinics in the 1930s, paid the salaries of the officials of the Child Guidance Council which co-ordinated developments in Britain, and encouraged the development of training programmes for psychiatric social workers at the London School of Economics. Undoubtedly, through this funding a strong American mental hygiene influence was stamped on the developing British services.[83] Yet the US influence should not be exaggerated, for British child guidance and mental welfare work, built on strong indigenous roots, took a particularly British shape, and despite the Commonwealth aid was still largely funded by British sources, both voluntary and local authority.[84] In part this reflects the Fund's policy of adapting its programmes to national conditions.[85] However, in reality there was considerable tension as the Fund's officials struggled to impose American models of development. The conditions of growth for the professionalised model were not as favourable in Britain as they had been, with generous Foundation support, in prosperous areas of the United States.[86] In the struggle which ensued the Fund was only partly successful. British mental welfare was split between a small group of trained psychiatric social workers, who assertively followed the professional US model, and a larger corps of less professionalised, often voluntary, mental welfare workers, who followed the lead of Evelyn Fox and her Central Association for Mental Welfare.[87] In summary, as with the Rockefeller role, the emergence of national mental hygiene programmes cannot be interpreted as simply a response to US initiative. The Commonwealth Fund's most important influence was not the imposition of a normative conception of mental health; it was the legacy of a professionalised, science-based framework with which to institute mental hygiene policy.

The restrictionist strategy

Restrictionist mental hygiene aimed to prevent mental illness, mental defect and mental instability through policies such as segregation, sterilisation, prevention of marriage and immigration control. The aim of restriction was to produce a mentally fit population which would benefit the nation eugenically and economically. It has been argued that an international network of advocates of such policies developed during the interwar period.[88] In fact, the nationalist aims of restrictive mental hygiene were not suited to the development of an international movement: encouraging other nations to become more mentally fit would be of no help to national fitness and could, relatively, threaten it, while immigration restriction was based on assumptions regarding the unfitness of foreigners which shattered international goodwill. A further problem with restrictionist techniques was that they aroused controversy, distancing their advocates from the respectable professional aspirations of the mental hygiene movement in the 1930s.

Stimulated by the debate over extending immigration restriction to the USA after the First World War, the Committee on the Scientific Problems of Human Migration had proposed a number of international research projects on migration and mental testing.[89] A preparatory survey was undertaken by Henry Pratt Fairchild. His plan, which was never acted on, recommended sending twenty-four researchers to Europe for a two-year period to gather statistics.[90] Two further international mental hygiene projects were planned but did not materialise. One of these proposed to extend the American research on inheritance of mental ability to 'the racial nests in Europe'. The proposed 'nests', reflecting American anxieties over immigration, were: Yugoslavia; Macedonia and Bulgaria; Ukraine (with its mix of Slavs, Russians and Jews); Finland, Sweden and Norway; Sicily and Southern Italy; and Northern Italy. Notwithstanding the practical problems of co-ordination, the plan threatened to be too internationally controversial to gain support.[91] Consequently, the Committee's work was directed away from practically addressing the migration issue towards scientific psychological research.[92]

At the 1930 International Mental Hygiene Congress the only country to advocate immigration controls openly was Australia. The 'white Australia' policy was depicted by Dr Ralph Noble as an important experiment in eugenics and mental hygiene. However, the defensive tone with which this policy was described suggests that such views were becoming controversial.[93] Noble could look to the mental hygiene movement in the Union of South Africa as an ally.[94] He also hinted that the 'white Australia' policy had relevance to the United States.[95] However, at the 1930 Congress, openly racist American views seem to have been subordinated. Eugenic societies remained a centre for such ideas, but their attitudes towards race and consequently towards immigration control varied according to national context. As Stepan has shown, Latin American eugenicists turned away from the lead of the United States because of objections to US views on race and immigration policy.[96] Once again, the restrictionist strategy proved internationally divisive.

At the 1930 International Mental Hygiene Congress eugenic opinions were still quite widespread. In the late 1920s and early 1930s international eugenics organisations had attempted to spread interest in a policy of voluntary sterilisation of the mentally disordered and defective.[97] But during the 1930s the negative eugenic strand of mental hygiene became more controversial. There seems to have been a further shift towards environmentalist views among American mental hygienists during the Depression. This stemmed from the profound impact of psycho-dynamic theories, and the New Deal political environment which made social solutions more acceptable and strengthened the position of psychological social workers.[98] In personal contact with their clients, and with an interest in protecting their own roles, these professional mental hygienists were often suspicious about hereditarian views of mental illness and hostile towards sterilisation. As in eugenics there was a shift from negative to positive strategies. Instead of compulsory restriction, segregation or sterilisation there was interest in prevention through understanding the psychology of deviant behaviour.[99] By contrast, German advocacy of negative eugenic solutions (already prominent at the 1930 international congress) increased over the decade for such ideas were looked on favourably by the Nazi regime.[100] In particular, a compulsory sterilisation programme was introduced on a scale and breadth not seen elsewhere.[101] Despite this, the Germans remained part of the international movement, attending the last prewar international mental hygiene congress in Paris in 1937. Nevertheless, division over German sterilisation policy at the 1937 Congress, though perhaps not irreconcilable, was shattering the illusion of international consensus and goodwill.[102] A mark of the growing division between the American and German movements was the non-publication of Beers' *A Mind that Found Itself* in Germany, partly because the translator was Jewish, but also perhaps because of the division between the American individualistic and the German racial and communal visions of mental hygiene.[103] In summary, restrictionist issues, which had originally provided practical targets for political campaigning, were increasingly a weakness and embarrassment for mental hygiene as an international movement. In explaining this transition the trend towards professionalisation of mental hygiene was again of central importance.[104]

Conclusion

This chapter set out to explore the extent to which interwar mental hygiene was an international movement. It has been argued that it would be an exaggeration to speak of an international 'movement' in a singular institutional sense. National mental hygiene movements, though stimulated by foreign models, were emerging independently. Secondly, it is too limited a perspective to define mental hygiene as a propagandist lay 'movement'. This should be seen as one strategy towards the goals of mental hygiene. Other strategies have been termed 'research and educational' and 'restrictionist'. The three strategies sometimes overlapped, and sometimes were in conflict. Both within each strategy, and in terms of overall strategy, there was a trend towards the professional and scientific. International, though usually US-dominated, organisations played an important role in internationalising the strategies and creating a new generation of scientists and mental hygiene professionals. Through this process, the lay mental hygiene movement, which had been orientated towards propagandist and restrictive strategies, was gradually superseded by an international network of professionals and scientists dominated by research and psychiatric strategies. Potentially this promised to depoliticise mental hygiene and consequently make constructive international co-operation more feasible. In reality, as the

Rockefeller programme in Germany showed, this was not to be the case. Ultimately, neither through propaganda nor science was the international mental hygiene movement able to overcome the divisiveness of nationalism and maintain the peace and international co-operation which had been seen as a necessary prerequisite for mental health. Nevertheless, after five years of war, and atrocities which owed more than a little to the one path of mental hygiene,[105] a reconstituted international movement again saw mental hygiene and a normatively defined mental health as essential tools in establishing a new world order.[106]

Notes

1 The relation between ideas on mental health and war is explored in D. Pick, *The War Machine* (London: Yale University Press, 1993).

2 C. Beers, *A Mind that Found Itself: An Autobiography* (New York: William Heinemann, 1908).

3 This interpretation emerges in N. Dain, *Clifford W. Beers: Advocate for the Insane* (Pittsburgh: University of Pittsburgh Press, 1980).

4 The account of the American role in the early years of the international movement is reconstructed from a later edition of Beers' autobiography: C. Beers, *A Mind that Found Itself: An Autobiography* (London: William Heinemann, 1923), pp. 310–34; the NCMH journal *Mental Hygiene*; and Dain, *Advocate for the Insane*, pp. 309–40.

5 On the relationship between the US and Canadian movements: T. Richardson, *The Century of the Child: The Mental Hygiene Movement and Social Policy in the United States and Canada* (Albany: 1989).

6 Argentina, Australia, Austria, Belgium, Bolivia, Brazil, Canada, China, Costa Rica, Cuba, Czechoslovakia, Denmark, Dominican Republic, Ecuador, Estonia, Finland, France, Germany, Great Britain, Guatemala, Hawaii, Honduras, Hungary, Iceland, India, Italy, Japan, Latvia, Lithuania, Mexico, Netherlands, New Zealand, Nicaragua, Norway, Panama, Paraguay, Peru, Philippine Islands, Poland, Puerto Rico, Romania, Salvador, Siam, Spain, Sweden, Switzerland, Turkey, Union of South Africa, USA, USSR, Uruguay, Venezuela, Yugoslavia.

7 Committee on Mental Hygiene of the Austrian Society for Public Health, Belgian League for Mental Hygiene, Brazilian League for Mental Hygiene, British National Council for Mental Hygiene, Canadian National Committee for Mental Hygiene, Cuban League for Mental Hygiene, League for Nervous and Mental Diseases of Czechoslovakia, Dutch League for Mental Hygiene, Society for Psychic Health of Finland, French League for Mental Hygiene, German Association for Mental Hygiene, National Society for Mental Hygiene of Hungary, Indian Association for Mental Hygiene, Italian League for Mental Hygiene, Japanese Mental Hygiene Society, New Zealand National Council for Mental Hygiene, South African National Council for Mental Hygiene, Spanish League for Mental Hygiene, Swiss National Committee for Mental Hygiene, The National Committee for Mental Hygiene of the United States.

8 For details on participants and organisation: *Proceedings of the 1st International Congress on Mental Hygiene* (hereafter *ICMH*), Part 1 (New York, 1930), pp. 4–49.

9 *ICMH*, 1, pp. 51–84.
10 Dain, *Advocate for the Insane*, pp. 277–9.
11 Beers, *A Mind that Found Itself*, pp. 327–8.
12 The best source for an understanding of the Council is the British Journal *Mental Hygiene*. British concerns over the lay enthusiasm of US mental hygiene are evident in the report of the Council's Hon. Sec., the psychiatric superintendent Dr J. R. Lord, 'American Psychiatry', *Journal of Mental Science*, 76 (1930), 456–95.
13 Edouard Toulouse, 'The Organization of the Psychiatric Hospital and its Role in Social Life', *ICMH*, 1, pp. 295–342.
14 *ICMH*, 2, p. 553.
15 Hans Roemer, 'To what extent does public opinion help, and to what extent does it impair the work of mental hygiene?', *ICMH*, 1, pp. 266–80.
16 *ICMH*, 1, pp. 120, 128.
17 *ICMH*, 2, p. 85.
18 *ICMH*, 2, pp. 95–91.
19 Professor Puusepp, *ICMH*, 1, pp. 98–9.
20 *ICMH*, 1, pp. 92, 96, 112.
21 *ICMH*, 1, pp. 396–400.
22 *ICMH*, 1, pp. 379–90; G. Gibson, 'The Boarding Out System in Scotland', *Journal of Mental Science*, 71 (1925), 253–63.
23 D. Joravsky, *Russian Psychology: A Critical History* (Oxford: Blackwell, 1989), pp. 336–42.
24 *ICMH*, 1, p. 126.
25 *ICMH*, 2, pp. 95–106.
26 B. Harris, '"Don't Be Unconscious; Join Our Ranks": Psychology, Politics, and Communist Education', *Rethinking Marxism*, 6 (1993), 44–75.
27 Toulouse, 'The Organization of the Psychiatric Hospital'.
28 *ICMH*, 1, p. 104.
29 *ICMH*, 1, p. 349.
30 René Sand, 'Mental Hygiene and World Health', *ICMH*, 2, pp. 232–47. August Ley, of the Belgium League for Mental Hygiene, noted the importance of Red Cross aid: Beers, *A Mind that Found Itself*, p. 314.
31 P. Weindling, *Health, Race and German Politics between National Unification and Nazism, 1870–1945* (Cambridge: Cambridge University Press, 1989), p. 451.
32 *ICMH*, 1, pp. 460–1, 471–88.
33 P. Mazumdar, *Human Genetics and Human Failings* (London: Routledge, 1992), pp. 205–9.
34 U. Geuter, *The Professionalization of Nazi Psychology* (Cambridge: Cambridge University Press, 1993).
35 *ICMH*, 1, pp. 629–38.
36 J. van Linbeek and V. van Alem (eds.), *Querido's Legacy: Social Psychiatry in Amsterdam from 1932 to 1991* (Amsterdam: Department of Social and Psychiatric Epidemiology, Division of Mental Health, Municipal Health Service, 1991), pp. 9–12.
37 *ICMH*, 1, pp. 387, 396.
38 *ICMH*, 1, p. 23.
39 *ICMH*, 1, pp. 144–59.

40 National Committee for Mental Hygiene – Appraisal, folder 362, box 32, series 200, Record Group (RF) 1.1. Rockefeller Foundation Archives (RFA), Rockefeller Archive Center, North Tarrytown, New York (RAC).

41 Folder 629, box 58, series 3, Laura Spelman Rockefeller Memorial Archives (LSRM), RAC.

42 Folder 804, box 67, series 200, RG 1.1, RFA, RAC; J. Morawski, 'Organizing Knowledge and Behavior at Yale's Institute of Human Relations', *Isis*, 77 (1986), 219–42.

43 Norwich Connecticut Conference, 22–5 October 1931, folders 195–6, box 23, series 100, RG 1, RFA, RAC.

44 Letter E.R.E. to George Vincent, 8 March 1921, folder 117, box 2, series 906, RG 3, RFA, RAC; 'Mental Health – History RF Connection', p. 1, folder 193, box 23, series 100, RG 1, RFA, RAC.

45 History of the Kraepelin Institute (1939), folder 58, box 10, series 717, RG 1.1, RFA, RAC. On history of Rockefeller funding of German psychiatry: P. Weindling, 'The Rockefeller Foundation and the German Biomedical Sciences, 1920–40: From Educational Philanthropy to International Science Policy', in N. Rupke (ed.), *Science, Politics and the Public Good: Essays in Honour of Margaret Gowing* (Basingstoke: Macmillan, 1988), p. 131.

46 Hincks to Prof. E. D. Macphee, 27 March 1926, and Hincks to Dr W. Mitchell, 4 April 1926, folder 2, box 1, series 427, RG 1.1, RFA, RAC.

47 Hincks to Edwin Embree, 9 April 1926, folder 2, box 1, series 427, RG 1.1, RFA, RAC.

48 Excerpt from Interim Report to Trustees' meeting, 13 December 1933, pp. 5–6, folder 19, box 2, series 906, RG 3, RFA, RAC.

49 For an account of psychiatric funding between 1931 and 1941: A Gregg, 'Medical Sciences – Program and Policy– Psychiatry', 3 December 1941, folder 19, box 2, series 906, RG 3, RFA, RAC.

50 An important report endorsing the shift towards a more scientific and less speculative approach was: Dean David L. Edsall, 'Memorandum Regarding Possible Psychiatric Developments', 3 October 1930, folder 19, box 2, series 906, RG 3, RFA, RAC.

51 Excerpt from Agenda for Rockefeller Foundation meeting of 11 April 1933, pp. 70–2, folder 19, box 2, series 906, RG 3, RFA, RAC.

52 Excerpt from 'R. A. Fisher – Galton Laboratory', 27 March 1935, folder 117, box 2, series 906, RG 3, RFA, RAC.

53 On Gregg: T. M. Brown, 'Alan Gregg and the Rockefeller Foundation's Support for Franz Alexander's Psychosomatic Research', *Bulletin of the History of Medicine*, 61 (1988), 155–82; D. Paul, 'The Rockefeller Foundation and the Origins of Behavior Genetics', in K. Benson, J. Maienschein and R. Rainger (eds.), *The Expansion of American Biology* (New Brunswick: Rutgers University Press, 1991), pp. 267–73.

54 Robert E. Kohler, 'The Management of Science: The Experience of Warren Weaver and the Rockefeller Foundation Programme in Molecular Biology', *Minerva*, 14 (1976), 279–306.

55 Excerpt from Agenda for Rockefeller Foundation meeting, 11 April 1933, pp. 78–9, folder 19, box 2, series 906, RG 3, RFA, RAC.

56 Extract from R. A. Lambert's Diary, 6 September 1933, folder 56, box 9, series 717, RG 1.1, RFA, RAC. Weindling, 'The Rockefeller Foundation and German Biomedical Sciences', pp. 130–5.

57 Bruce Biven (of *The New Republic*) to Rockefeller Foundation, 20 December 1933; *The American Hebrew*, 2 February 1934, folder 54, box 9, series 717, RG 1.1, RFA, RAC.

58 G. Strode to T. Appleget, 6 March 1934, folder 54, box 9, series 717, RG 1.1, RFA, RAC.

59 Gregg to Plaut, 27 February 1933, folder 54, box 9, series 717, RG 1.1, RFA, RAC.

60 In Denmark Dr A. Wimmer attracted funding to a project on genetics of mental disorder on the basis that the Danish population was small, sedentary, well documented and therefore ideally suited (Wimmer to O'Brien, folder 15, box 1, series 1.1, RG 6.1, RFA, RAC). In Britain the Foundation supported the research of T. A. Munro into the genetics of mental disorder (folder 11, box 6, series 401, RF 1.1, RFA, RAC).

61 Assistance to displaced scholars totalled $34,173: folder 12, box 1, series 803, RG 1.1, RFA, RAC.

62 Mapother to Gregg, 9 January 1934, folder 249, box 18, series 401, RG 1.1, RFA, RAC; Lambert to O'Brien, 8 January 1935, folder 251, box 18, series 401, RG 1.1, RFA, RAC. Emigrés at some time during the period working in London institutions included: Adolf Beck, Erich Guttman, W. Mayer-Gross, Alfred Meyer, Eric Wittkower and Felix Plaut.

63 Kohler, 'The Management of Science'.

64 A. Gregg, 'Medical Sciences – Program and Policy – Psychiatry', 3 December 1941, folder 19, box 2, series 906, RG 3, RFA, RAC.

65 The political reasons for shifting to Britain were presented to the Foundation after Dr Aubrey Lewis' survey of Europe, as expressed by Maudsley Hospital Director Dr Edward Mapother: 'Government Assistance Towards Research in Psychiatry', July 1938, pp. 1–2, folder 355, box 19, series 401, RG 1.1, RFA, RAC.

66 J. Austoker and L. Bryder (eds.), *Historical Perspectives on the MRC* (Oxford: Oxford University Press, 1989); J. Landsborough Thomson, *Half a Century of Medical Research*, 2 vols. (London, 1973 and 1975).

67 Memo of O'Brien to Gregg, 28 January 1938, folder 2, box 1, series 707A, RG 1.1, RFA, RAC.

68 Folder 336–40, box 26, series 401, RF 1.1, RFA, RAC.

69 'The Emphasis on Psychiatry' (October 1943), p. 13, folder 18, box 2, series 906, RG 3, RFA, RAC.

70 'Draft of recommendations regarding education in psychiatry, and steps that might be taken in the immediate future in this regard', Noble to Gregg, 28 February 1933, folder 200, box 24, series 100, RG 1, RFA, RAC.

71 Folder 316, box 24, series 401, RG 1.1, RFA, RAC; Mapother to Gregg, 2 June 1936, folder 248, box 18, series 401, RG 1.1, RFA, RAC.

72 S. Ahmad, 'American Foundations and the Development of the Social Sciences Between the Wars: Comment on the Debate Between Martin Bulmer and Donald Fisher', *Sociology*, 25 (1991), 511–20.

73 D. Fisher, 'The Impact of American Foundations on the Development of British

University Education, 1900–1939' (PhD thesis, University of California, Berkeley, 1977), p. 766.

74 Fisher, 'Impact of American Foundations', p. 721.

75 M. and J. Bulmer, 'Philanthropy and Social Science in the 1920s: Beardsley Ruml and the Laura Spelman Rockefeller Memorial, 1922–9', *Minerva*, 19 (1981), 347–407.

76 O'Brien to Gregg, 20 January 1938, folder 316, box 24, series 401, RG 1.1, RFA, RAC. See Fisher, 'Impact of American Foundations', pp. 724–5.

77 Folder 7, box 1, series 789, RG 1.1, RFA, RAC.

78 Fisher, 'Impact of American Foundations', pp. 708–68; E. R. Brown, *Rockefeller Medicine Men: Medicine and Capitalism in America* (Berkeley: University of California Press, 1979).

79 A. M. Harvey and S. L. Abrams, *For the Welfare of Mankind: The Commonwealth Fund and American Medicine* (Baltimore: Johns Hopkins University Press, 1986).

80 *The Commonwealth Fund – 8th Annual Report for the Year 1925–6* (New York, 1927), pp. 45–6.

81 *The Commonwealth Fund – 9th Annual Report for the Year 1926–1927* (New York, 1927), p. 50.

82 For a list of Fellowships and future careers: 'List of Fellows in Psychiatry and Psychology', correspondence, folder 35, box 3, sub-series Fellowships in Psychiatry and Psychology, Record Group – Mental Hygiene – England, Commonwealth Fund Archive, RAC.

83 Described as 'the psychiatric deluge' in K. Woodroofe, *From Charity to Social Work* (London: Routledge, 1962), pp. 118–50.

84 For a detailed account of adaptation to a variety of English conditions: D. Thom, 'Wishes, Anxieties, Play, and Gestures: Child Guidance in Inter-War England', in R. Cooter (ed.), *In the Name of the Child* (London: Routledge, 1992), pp. 200–19.

85 *Commonwealth Fund Annual Report for the Year ending September 30, 1928* (New York, 1929), p. 65.

86 The spread of child guidance in America was not without its problems: M. Horn, *Before It's Too Late: The Child Guidance Movement in the United States, 1922–1945* (Philadelphia: Temple University Press, 1989).

87 M. Thomson, 'The Problem of Mental Deficiency in England and Wales, c. 1913–1946' (DPhil dissertation, University of Oxford, 1992), pp. 122–49.

88 B. Schreiber, *The Men Behind Hitler* (privately published, London, c. 1975).

89 On the US immigration debate: J. Higham, *Strangers in the Land: Patterns of American Nativism 1860–1925* (New Brunswick, NJ: Rutgers University Press, 1971), pp. 300–30.

90 H. Fairchild, 'Report on Investigation of European Sources of Information on Human Migration', 21 January 1924, folder 635, box 59, series 3, LSRM, RAC.

91 Folder 635, box 59, series 3, LSRM, RAC; Report of Committee on the Scientific Problems of Human Migration, 18 March 1924, folder 630, box 58, series 3, LSRM, RAC.

92 The Canadian movement was also interested in preventive mental hygiene through immigration controls in the 1920s: *A Mind that Found Itself*, pp. 386–7.

93 *ICMH*, 1, pp. 87–9. M. Roe, '"We Can Die just as Easily Out Here": Australia and British Migration, 1916–1939', in S. Constantine (ed.), *Migrants and Empire:*

British Settlement in the Dominions between the Wars (Manchester: Manchester University Press, 1990), pp. 96–120.

94 *ICMH*, 1, pp. 135–7. E. Bradlow, 'Empire Settlement and South African Immigration Policy, 1910–1948', in Constantine, *Migrants and Empire*, pp. 174–201.

95 *ICMH*, 1, pp. 261–2.

96 N. Stepan, *'The Hour of Eugenics': Race, Gender, and Nation in Latin America* (Ithaca and London: Cornell University Press, 1991).

97 *Report of the Ninth Conference of the International Federation of Eugenic Organisations* (IFEO, 1930), pp. 73–91. The interrelation and continuing dialogue between American and German eugenics in the 1930s is analysed in S. Kühl, *The Nazi Connection: Eugenics, American Racism, and German National Socialism* (New York and Oxford: Oxford University Press, 1994).

98 L. Leighninger, *Social Work: Search for Identity* (New York: Greenwood, 1987).

99 On syphilis: Genil-Perrin, 'Syphilis and Mental Hygiene', *ICMH*, 1, 406–38; on alcoholism (against prohibition and for understanding addiction) Forel, *ICMH*, 1, 402; on the need to focus on positive aspects of mental health: Porter Lee, 'The Family as a Constructive Force in Mental Hygiene', *ICMH*, 1, 627–45.

100 *Report of the International Conference on Social Work* (London, 1938).

101 Psychiatrist E. Rüdin, active in the international eugenics and mental hygiene movements, played a key role in the drafting of the sterilisation law of 1933. P. Weindling, 'Compulsory Sterilization in National Socialist Germany', *German History*, 5 (1987), 10–24. It should be noted that even in Germany the negative eugenic/mental hygiene policy raised political objections when directed against party members: Weindling, *Health, Race and German Politics*, pp. 533–9. Moreover it should not be assumed that Nazi mental hygiene was only a form of race hygiene: psychotherapeutic mental hygiene, used as a form of social engineering to encourage character and will-power development, also gained the support of the Nazi regime: G. Cocks, *Psychotherapy in the Third Reich* (Oxford: Oxford University Press, 1985), pp. 98–9.

102 Dain, *Advocate for the Insane*, pp. 277–8.

103 *Ibid.* p. 278.

104 In Germany, the tension between negative eugenic strategies of mental hygiene and psychotherapeutic approaches was also related to a professional struggle between psychiatrists and psychologists: Cocks, *Psychotherapy in the Third Reich*, p. 107; Weindling, *Health, Race and German Politics*, p. 376.

105 B. Müller-Hill, *Murderous Science: Elimination by Scientific Selection of Jews, Gypsies, and Others, Germany, 1933–1945* (Oxford: Oxford University Press, 1988).

106 *Proceedings of the International Conference on Mental Hygiene*, vol. IV (London: H. K. Lewis & Co., 1948)

15

Mobilising social knowledge for social welfare: intermediary institutions in the political systems of the United States and Great Britain between the First and Second World Wars

MARTIN BULMER

We constantly speak about the State or our Society under terms of social organism; more, we talk of the State as if it were a person. But it is a person with a great number of totally detached centres of consciousness; with very little of anything like what could be called a centre of self-consciousness. The individual when we meet him, if he is troubled with any disease, is often painfully anxious to ascertain what his disease is and the way of curing it. But our society sits like a gigantic fat man troubled with all kinds of maladies and diseases in all the various parts of his enormous person; but the pain which each part of the organism suffers is uninvestigated and unremedied because the central consciousness is so remarkably weak. And what we want today is to strengthen the central consciousness that we may both know what are the diseases under which the various parts of the body are suffering and set ourselves with something more of seriousness to investigate the remedy. (Charles Gore, Bishop of Oxford, 1914)[1]

Introduction

The development of the application and use of scientific research – including natural science, medicine and social science – in relation to government and policy-making is a twentieth-century phenomenon. It has occurred alongside a massive expansion in the scope of governmental activity, a vast increase in the size of public bureaucracies and an extension of the authority and involvement of the state into areas which in the nineteenth century were treated as a matter of individual and private responsibility. Nowhere is this more evident than in the field of social policy, where nation states in the industrial world now assume responsibilities inconceivable a century ago. In the fields of health, housing, income maintenance, the personal social services and education, the activities of governments are extensive, in many cases dominating provision. There are different mixes in the different countries, with varying degrees of dominance, but the general trend is unmistakable. In many areas there is too a marked international dimension, some of whose origins are explored in the essays in this volume on medicine, health and welfare. Since 1945, an entire field of international policy, practice and academic research, that of 'development', has emerged as centrally concerned with the international dimension.

In this field as in national social welfare and health, demands for social scientific input to policy-making are nowadays taken for granted. In the recent past, government-funded social science has played an integral part in, for example, the US War on Poverty and its offshoots in the 1960s and 1970s.[2] The state, indeed, is nowadays one of the principal sources of demand for social knowledge. In North America and Western Europe, this substantial presence dates back no earlier than 1960, with the Nazi period in Germany as an exception. In the period considered in this chapter, between 1914 and 1945, this close and integral relationship between social science research and the state did not exist. One of this chapter's purposes is to trace some of the influences which brought social science research to bear on social welfare policy, including ideas about the appropriate extent of state intervention and the role of private philanthropy. This discussion bears on the activities of international organisations and of philanthropic foundations with international programmes, for in many respects they went further than governments of the time in pursuing interventionist policies, and using the institutions of international government and influence to develop social welfare.

Social welfare in Britain and the United States

The quotation at the head of this chapter comes from remarks by Bishop Charles Gore, an influential Anglican active in the Christian Social Union, introducing a lecture by R. H. Tawney on 'Poverty as an Industrial Problem'. Of the 'maladies and diseases' which Gore had in mind in the year of the outbreak of the First World War, the pre-eminent one was poverty. He rightly identified the state as one possible source of measures to tackle the problem, but observed that no coherent state response was forthcoming. This bears on academic interpretations of the expansion of state activity referred to earlier. One influential sociological approach has been to identify the transformation which took place with the growth of the state as an autonomous influence. Skocpol has focused upon the state as an actor in the political system, pointing to the role of career officials as a stratum relatively insulated from ties to dominant socio-economic interests in launching distinctive new state strategies, particularly in times of crisis.[3]

The aim of this chapter is to identify the role and influence of what are termed 'intermediary institutions' in the mobilisation of social knowledge for social welfare, treating these institutions as actors in the political system. Intermediary institutions operate not only within countries but at an international level, where their influence was considerable, and in the case of the American philanthropic foundations, pursued a much more interventionist and ameliorative programme than the American government of the period was willing to contemplate. For example, the Rockefeller Foundation (RF) supported the League of Nations Health Organisation (LNHO) despite the fact that the United States was not a member of the League of Nations (LN).

This account of developments in the United States and Great Britain in the period between 1914 and 1945 is not an historical one, but rather seeks to identify and delineate some of the main historical actors in the development of welfare policy. It abstracts developments in the two societies from their longer-term development in the national context, which may lead to some distortion. Nor, deliberately, does it seek to deal with the impact of external events such as world wars or the Great Depression. The following discussion thus focuses not upon policies promulgated for the improvement of social welfare at particular points in time but upon the institutional means by which social knowledge was brought into being and mobilised between 1914 and 1945.

'Intermediary institutions'

The term 'intermediary institution' is introduced in an attempt to refine our understanding of state activity in the period covered, recognising that a unitary concept of 'the state' does not capture the most significant features of the interaction between knowledge and policy in relation to poverty at this period. 'Intermediary institutions' are more or less organised collectivities formally independent of the state on the one hand and being more than the vehicle of a particularly influential person on the other, which contribute to the process of policy formulation. There are affinities between this conception and Peter Berger's concept of 'mediating structures', which refers to collectivities which lie between, and mediate between, the 'megastructures' of the state and private industry on the one hand and the private worlds of home and family on the other.[4] Some of the institutions considered in this paper, such as settlement houses, social networks linking academics and politicians, and non-governmental think-tanks, clearly fall within Berger's term, but others, such as philanthropic foundations or university departments, are much more part of the world of 'megastructures', though not part of the state.

In the international field, where one is dealing with activities spanning a number of national societies, the term is also applicable but in a slightly different sense. Where one is dealing with relations between nation states, with their own clear boundaries, various institutions may develop, including institutions of international government such as the LN, which seek to co-ordinate activity and mediate between the different national entities. Some of these are institutions of international government, such as the International Court of Justice, others such as the International Red Cross or the Save the Children

Fund International Union (SCIU) are 'intermediary institutions' seeking to mediate between national states at a level other than that of international government.

The influence of intermediary institutions may be exercised through the creation and dissemination of ideas, practical research activity, institutional support for social inquiry, or involvement as collective actors in politics. An understanding of the part played by such collective actors can illuminate the relationship between social science knowledge and state activity at a time when such activity was limited or non-existent. They bridge the academic and policy worlds. Study of them can reveal 'the full array of interconnections between behavioural and social sciences findings and policy making over considerable periods of time'.[5]

Philanthropic foundations

What marks out this period, in the United States in particular, and has immense international significance, is a different source of support, mediating between the state and the citizens, and largely independent of the state, the philanthropic foundation. American philanthropic foundations have played a particularly important part in the development of health on an international scale.

Writing as a child in his autograph book in 1888, Seebohm Rowntree noted down Oliver Wendell Holmes' maxim: 'Put not your trust in money, but your money in trust.' When setting up the Rowntree Trusts in 1904 his father Joseph observed that 'much current philanthropic effort is directed to remedying the more superficial manifestations of weakness or evil, while little thought or effort is directed to search out the underlying causes'. Private philanthropy was the most important source for 'seed money' for developing the basic social sciences, as well as facilitating empirical research on social conditions.

When Mrs Russell Sage sought advice in 1906 on the disposition of her husband's fortune, her lawyer Robert W. Forest, president of the Charity Organisation Society of New York City since 1888, suggested the establishment of the 'Sage Foundation for Social Betterment', having as its object 'the permanent improvement of social conditions'. Its role would be to investigate the causes of adverse social conditions, to suggest how these conditions might be remedied or ameliorated, and to take action to that end. When the Russell Sage Foundation was incorporated in New York in 1907, one of the first projects it supported was the Pittsburgh Survey, with a grant of $27,000 for 'a careful and fairly comprehensive study of the conditions under which working people live and labour in a great industrial city'.[6]

The Russell Sage Foundation activities were specifically oriented to American social enquiry by means of surveys and social intervention. They did not, at this period, support university social science research. On this broader canvas, the most significant body was the group of philanthropic organisations associated with the Rockefeller family, with very significant international interests from the outset. The twelve years between 1901 and 1913 witnessed its coming into being as a new form of philanthropy. Starting with the Rockefeller Institute of Medical Research in 1901, there followed the General Education Board in 1902, the Rockefeller Sanitary Commission in 1909, and the Rockefeller Foundation in 1913, which brought together the International Health Board, the China Medical Board, the Division of Medical Education and the Division of Studies.[7] It was 'a mosaic consisting of its various organisations in medicine and public health, thrown together without thought of integration and without central control'.[8] In addition, the Rockefeller Institute for Medical Research was a separate institution, the Laura Spelman Rockefeller Memorial was founded in 1918, and the International Education Board was set up in 1923. By the end of the First World War, the International Health Board was the most powerful body, due in no small measure to the distinguished leadership of Wickliffe Rose, and its influence continued through the 1929 re-organisation, though by that date it was not the most innovative part of the RF, if still the best endowed.

John D. Rockefeller Sr and his son, John D. Rockefeller Jr, both relied heavily on advisors for the direction which their philanthropic activity was to take. Frederick Gates, Rockefeller Sr's close adviser, placed enormous faith in public health as a panacea for social ills. By 1920 their influence was on the wane, and more adventurous voices were in the ascendant, several of whom had both international orientations and experience. Abraham Flexner was in the process of reconstructing medical education, and in wartime carried out an investigation of prostitution in Europe for Rockefeller Jr. Raymond B. Fosdick, a New York lawyer much influenced at Princeton by Woodrow Wilson, had studied police systems in America and Europe as Rockefeller Jr's man on the Bureau of Social Hygiene, and had headed the Commission on Training Camp Activities for the War Department which sought to tackle some of the public health and social problems associated with war mobilisation. Fosdick was a staunch supporter of the LN throughout the 1920s. In 1915 he and Flexner envisioned a comprehensive programme for social reform through research in criminology, alcoholism, drug addiction, feeble-mindedness, sexually transmitted disease, family structure, incomes policy and delinquency. During the 1920s he advised Rockefeller Jr, was architect of the 1929 re-organisation which created the modern RF devoted to the advancement of knowledge, and was chair of the Trustees of the Laura Spelman Rockefeller Memorial which under its director Beardsley Ruml poured enormous resources into the support of the nascent social sciences.

Thus the Memorial between 1923 and 1929 underwrote much basic social science work at leading institutions such as the University of Chicago, Harvard

University, Columbia University and the University of Pennsylvania. It was also the main source of external finance for the London School of Economics, and funded the New Survey of London Life and Labour.[10] Private philanthropy also played a role in government-sponsored enquiries. Although appointed by the President, the costs of the work of the President's Committee on Recent Social Trends were met by the RF.

What Fosdick, Ruml and the new generation of foundation officials had faith in was the possibility of harnessing science and social science to tackle the problems facing advanced industrial societies, not only at the national but also at the international level. Just as old-fashioned charity had been superseded by the advent of the philanthropic foundation, so the faith of the old guard in public health and medicine as panaceas for social improvement was replaced in time by a more research oriented and sober view of what the foundation could do to foster social improvement.

The RF was not alone. Trusts such as the Carnegie Corporation in the US and the Pilgrim and Rowntree Trusts in Britain also played a part. The Carnegie Corporation, for example, was an independent source of support in a variety of applied social science fields, and an important indirect influence upon public policy through some of the topics which it supported.[11] One of the most important studies which Carnegie financed in the interwar period was the massive examination of the situation of the American Negro by the Swedish economist Gunnar Myrdal, *An American Dilemma*.[12] Like the Rockefeller bodies, the Carnegie Corporation pursued an active policy of supporting activities in Britain (reflecting its founder's Scottish origins).

The international significance of these activities should be underlined. The International Health Board had divided the world up into sectors and saw London as the capital of the British Empire as the ideal place to create strategically placed centres of medical education, endowing the London School of Hygiene and Tropical Medicine in 1922. Donald Fisher considers it unlikely that this institution would have come into existence without the support of the RF.[13] In the social sciences, developments in Britain were heavily dependent upon American philanthropic support, though whether this influence was for good or ill is strongly contested among those who have studied the subject.[14] What is significant is the wider international perspective which it introduced, which developed particularly strongly in medicine and science.

Apart from the war period, there was little government funding available between the wars earmarked for social science. US foundations played a particularly important role in providing 'core' funding at leading private universities, although from the mid-1930s onwards such support was cut back in favour of programme and project grants for more specific proposals, as the foundations made clear that they could no longer continue to underwrite basic development of the higher education system outside the state universities.

Support in Britain was more modest and mainly devoted to direct welfare intervention.[15]

This feature of the interwar period necessitates some revision of the view taken of state structures and social knowledge production. There is continuing controversy about the significance of the social role played by foundations and their degree of disinterestedness in providing support.[16] Foundations at this period were more and more controlled by their professional staff, rather than trustees, who were inclined to take a more detached and long-term view of the social contribution that philanthropic giving might make. Thus Beardsley Ruml at the Memorial staunchly defended a policy of underwriting social science research at selected centres, leaving disbursement of the grants within the university to social science staff at the institution. Studies of this process need to progress beyond arguments about whether or not foundations were the tools of capitalism to understand to what extent they reflected and to what extend they influenced contemporary developments, and in what ways they shaped the development of the social sciences. In particular, what aspirations did they embody as to the application of social science to social problems, and how far was such an emphasis significant in shaping the form of later developments after the Second World War? Whom did the trustees and staff of philanthropic bodies represent, and what was their relationship to academic experts?

Voluntary action and private initiative institutionalised

A focus upon the interconnections between the state and the social sciences may inadvertently direct attention away from the fact that in the first forty years of the twentieth century various forms of voluntary action and private initiative were highly significant – and in many cases more significant than state action – both in social welfare delivery and in studies of social conditions. This chapter is not primarily concerned with the former, but the point should be registered that voluntary activity remained until the Second World War the prime means of delivering certain services to the poor – in Britain, for example, both housing and health care. Such activities mediated between the state and its citizens, but unlike today the state was little involved in promoting the activities. International voluntary activity was also significant. The various national Red Cross societies assumed a higher profile, and the experience of war work in the First World War encouraged individuals like Rachel Crowdy to play an international role. Similarly, Eglantyne Jebb moved from involvement in the Charity Organisation Society to founding the Save the Children Fund International Union.

In studying social conditions, the role of private individuals was of key importance in both America and Britain prior to the First World War and in Britain at least until the Second World War. There has in Britain been a strain of high-minded, disinterested, social concern among the upper and upper-middle classes which was a powerful source of the impulse to social enquiry. In an earlier age it was represented by Charles Booth and the Webbs. Between the wars its most prominent representatives were William Beveridge and Seebohm Rowntree.[17] Such interest was not necessarily political, still less party political, in orientation. Beveridge went to work at Toynbee Hall in 1903 against the wishes of his family and without strong political interest. It was only after *Poverty* had been completed and published that Rowntree became involved in Liberal Party policy-making. The Webbs themselves in the early 1930s turned in an international direction towards the Soviet Union and came to regard communism as providing a model for social planning and reconstruction.

In Britain, local studies of the effects of the Great Depression, such as the accounts by John Newsom and Thomas Sharp of Durham in the 1930s, arose out of humanitarian concern, along with George Orwell's *Wigan Pier*. For some this concern was tinged with radicalism or socialism – Boyd Orr and Titmuss being good examples[18] – but the political impulse was not the primary one. It was much more the response of thoughtful people from comfortable backgrounds to the social circumstances of the working classes. Although their conclusions often pointed to state welfare interventions, the state played no role in stimulating their interest in these issues. Sometimes this analysis of national social issues pointed in an international direction, for example, Boyd Orr developed ideas about dealing with the international agricultural depression while pursuing the improvement of working-class diet in Britain, and was involved in League of Nations attempts to promulgate a World Food Plan. His interests indeed moved increasingly towards international action, and he became the first Director-General of the United Nations (UN) Food and Agriculture Organisation (FAO) in 1945.[19]

In many ways this was a natural transition for him to make. There was clearly a difference between fields rooted in the natural sciences, such as medicine and nutrition, and the emerging social sciences. The scientific basis for the former was stronger, more universal and lent itself to international transfer. Ideas about social organisation and welfare tended to be more society-specific and less well-grounded in a body of academic knowledge. For the most part social investigation before 1940 lacked a clear framework of thought within which it was conducted. The motivations of many of those involved in it were in a broad sense moral, derived from compassion for their fellow human beings and outrage at oppressive social conditions, coupled with a practical desire to change the situation through state action.[20] Much of the interwar effort was carried out beyond the confines of the state, aiming to influence the course of future state activity.

Individual initiatives were institutionalised earlier in the United States, but not in a way that linked them into the state apparatus. The Settlement House movement became a focus for the energies of socially minded women in particular. The Social Survey Movement had close links with social welfare, particularly through the magazine *Charities and the Commons* (later *The Survey*), which Paul Kellogg edited from 1905 until its demise in 1952.[21] Even individual researchers like W. E. B. Du Bois came from academic backgrounds, and after completing *The Philadelphia Negro* he pursued an academic career within a segregated educational system until 1910.

Networks of social science

Between the influential citizen and the state exist social networks that link together politicians, officials, journalists and social scientists and mediate between the state and its subjects. They are informal, but in the development of social policy particularly important. The role of academic social scientists and the institutionalisation of social research in universities is discussed below, but the American pattern (compared to the British) points to greater pluralism within the American political system, a somewhat more distant relation to politics and the existence from quite an early date of competing centres of intellectual influence on policy, both outside and within the academic world. British social researchers, from an early date, had or sought the ear of policy-makers, and as members of a tightly knit social elite centred upon London, fed by the universities of Oxford and Cambridge and later the LSE, the boundaries between social inquiry and influence upon politicians and officials were far more permeable than in the United States.[22]

The role of Toynbee Hall in nurturing social reformers who became officials, journalists, educators and social investigators has already been mentioned.[23] The boundary with party politics was also much more permeable. Rowntree and Beveridge in the Liberal party, the Webbs and Tawney in the Labour party, exercised a not inconsiderable influence. The Webbs exemplified this influence *par excellence*, pursuing an elitist approach to social questions, maintaining extensive social contacts with politically influential members of London Society, being heavily involved in Fabian and Labour Party circles, and devoting their energies to extensive empirical investigations and historical enquiries. Sidney Webb was deeply involved throughout in the affairs of the London School of Economics.[24] R. H. Tawney was also influential. Labour's educational policy, for example, during the minority governments of 1924 and 1929–31, was largely Tawney's creation.[25] He also encouraged younger social scientists later to play an influential role, such as economists Hugh Gaitskell and Evan Durbin and social policy analyst Richard Titmuss, whom he was instrumental in bringing to the LSE. The most important crucible for forging these political links was of course the Fabian Society, a small elite intellectual group of social democrats set up by the Webbs and George Bernard Shaw in the 1890s. It brought together intellectuals and academics supporting the Labour Party, some officials in a private capacity and active Labour politicians. Keith Banting has traced the role which the Society played during the 1960s in influencing social-policy thinking,[26] but its importance in the earlier period in exploring ideas which were embodied in wartime and post-1945 social legislation warrants further study. Again, influences external to the state, closely identified with leading social investigators, were critical in shaping the form of state activity and intervention.

It is true that leading social scientists began to have some influence upon government through official advisory bodies, where they made their voices heard. Beatrice Webb was a member of the Royal Commission on the Poor Laws of 1909, author of the minority report which is now heralded as farsighted but at the time had little immediate effect. R. H. Tawney was an effective member of the Sankey Commission on the Coal Industry in 1919, although the report's recommendations for coal nationalisation were not acted upon for twenty-five years.

The American commission or committee of inquiry as an instrument of enquiry was, up to the Second World War, more independent of government than its British counterpart. Most notable in the United States was President Hoover's commission on *Recent Social Trends*,[27] whose work was directed by sociologist W. F. Ogburn. An earlier local example was the Chicago Commission on Race Relations whose study *The Negro in Chicago*[28] was largely written by black sociologist Charles S. Johnson. Both studies consisted largely of data and their analysis. Though *Recent Social Trends* was officially sponsored, such enquiries were privately financed and independently staffed.[29] In Britain, the private enquiry also played a part. One such was the Pilgrim Trust study *Men Without Work*, directed by a committee chaired by the Archbishop of York.[30] One of the members of the advisory committee was Thomas Jones, erstwhile academic economist, a lifelong socialist and friend of Tawney, but for much of his career at the centre of British government as Secretary to the Cabinet.

The use of such committees raises significant questions about the role of expertise in government in both societies. Karl and Katz[31] have pointed to the ambivalence of Congress about expertise, and the reluctance, prior to 1945, to countenance financing it, preferring to rely on private foundations to perform this function. Economics was the first social science to be legitimated. It has been argued by Guy Alchon that 'there developed, between 1921 and 1933 a three-legged apparatus resting, in different ways, on philanthropic foundations, the National Bureau for Economic Research and the U.S. Commerce Department'.[32] Its goal was to influence microeconomic decision-makers and stabilise the economy as a whole. It steered a middle way between unbridled individualism and state collectivism. The chief actor was Herbert Hoover, first as Secretary for Commerce and then as President, who had launched his public career through the role that he played in international famine relief during the war, and then in Eastern Europe. He held a strong belief in the value of expert advice and its role in achieving better government. In the short term, Hoover's faith was not notably successful, but it germinated the idea for the future that social scientists had a good deal to offer for the understanding of the conditions in which government operated.

In Britain during the First World War, Beatrice Webb, William Beveridge and Seebohm Rowntree had participated in official deliberations on post-war reconstruction, though this was a rare example of an explicit attempt to think through social policy questions which did not recur until the 1940s. Ministers and their officials were in time much more able to accommodate economists. There was during the 1930s a gradual extension of the economic advice available to central departments, laying the foundation for its expansion and consolidation during the Second World War.[33] This was due to various factors: enthusiasm for 'scientific administration', recognition of the scale of the problems the country faced, the growth of the economics profession and the influence of John Maynard Keynes. In social policy, by contrast, the role played by social investigation, whether officially sponsored or not, was much more piecemeal. It provided information to be used by policy-makers, their advisers and their critics, but it did not do so within an integrated framework. It retained this fragmentary character throughout the interwar period. What was more important were the social networks to which some of the leading figures belonged.

The independent scholar

The independent scholar pursuing social scientific themes was by no means a spent force. In the United States, an early classic of sociological research, Robert and Helen Lynd's *Middletown*,[34] was produced under the auspices of the Institute of Social and Religious Research. On the strength of it, Robert Lynd was appointed to Columbia. In Britain, the standard of sociology was borne for a period by that curious duo in the Sociological Society, Patrick Geddes and Victor Branford, who had only the most tenuous academic links. Another curious flowering in the 1930s was Mass-Observation,[35] which sought to develop social observation by analogy with ornithology. In the later 1930s, the early writing on health and poverty of another independent scholar, Richard Titmuss, then working as an insurance inspector, made some impact.[36] Some opportunities arose, particularly as a result of the Rockefeller Foundation fellowships' programme, for European scholars to spend time in the United States and American scholars time in Europe. In the main, these were taken up by those holding academic positions, so they did not improve the lot of the independent scholar.[37]

A focus upon social enquiry and the state needs to attend to how social investigation became institutionalised in non-academic settings. Within government prior to 1940 in Britain and prior to the New Deal in the United States, extensions of statistical enquiry were generally a by-product of administrative change and proceeded at a snail's pace. The main changes were improvements in economic and labour market data, and these by later standards were modest. Probability sampling was not taken up by governments until during the Second World War.

Research centres outside government

Much more significant was the creation, outside of government, of research centres, partly stimulated by wartime activity and partly independent of it. In the United States the National Bureau of Economic Research and the Brookings Institution, in Britain Political and Economic Planning, were organisations of this type, again of an intermediary type. War has been a powerful stimulus to the extension of state activity in the twentieth century, and on a small canvas to the use of social science in policy-making. During the First World War, economists and psychologists were brought into the American federal government to make important contributions, the former in the War Industries Board and the latter in the Army Department. Though this activity ended abruptly with the cessation of hostilities, it was carried forward in the establishment shortly afterwards of the independent National Bureau of Economic Research (NBER) in New York, under the direction of Wesley Mitchell, and in the further growth of psychological testing and its extensive application in education and industry. Such developments represented the first major applications of social science knowledge by government to policy arenas. The NBER was supported by the Carnegie Corporation and the Rockefeller Foundation. Applied psychological research was fostered through private enterprise, beginning with the Scott Company.[38] The Brookings Institution emerged in 1927 in Washington DC out of a merger between three institutions, the Institute of Economics, the Brookings Graduate School and the Institute of Government Research. The first two were set up at the behest of Robert S. Brookings, a St Louis businessman who in middle age, after an abortive attempt to become a concert violinist, turned to philanthropy and put Washington University upon its feet as a major institution. His membership of the War Industries Board during the First World War had convinced him that economic problems lay at the root of most of the world's difficulties, including those of international relations, and that economic research was an important future guide to policy-makers.

Brookings persuaded Henry Pritchett, just appointed head of the Carnegie Corporation, on the board of which he sat, to provide $200,000 a year for five years to establish the Institute of Economics. As head Harold G. Moulton, a young University of Chicago economist, was appointed with an assurance that the trustees would not interfere in the work of the staff. Moulton proceeded cautiously, using better fact-finding and analysis as a prerequisite for policy-making, and urging caution in the drawing of prescriptions for policy from research. Moulton became head of the Brookings Institution when it was formed in 1927.[39]

Institutions like Brookings in America and Political and Economic Planning in Britain concerned themselves with national issues of social welfare and social conditions, since they lacked any adequate general intellectual framework within which social problems, as distinct from the workings of the economy, could be approached. There were additional factors, such as the isolationism of the United States, but such isolationism did not operate in science or medicine, where there was keen interest in the latest overseas advances. The Settlement House Movement was a borrowing of an institutional idea, the Social Survey was a tool of investigation, specific legislative measures could form a model for another society, but the overall conception of social problems tended to be specific to the society, and strongly conditioned by domestic political circumstances.

American studies of poverty, as distinct from studies of housing or health, were few and far between in the United States prior to the New Deal. Studies of the cost of living and the breakdown of expenditure were more common, but with little attention to poverty. A major Brookings study, published in 1934, *America's Capacity to Consume*,[40] was one of the few attempts to look at its incidence and make national estimates. The book was a study of income maldistribution, offering a case for the expansion of purchasing power. Though eschewing the term 'poverty', the study used a family poverty line of $2,000 (an income 'sufficient to supply only basic necessities'). It estimated that 16 million families, about 60 per cent of the total, involving at least 70 million people, received less than that. Rural poverty was clearly identified. The average income of the 5.8 million farm families was only $1,240, and 54 per cent of farm families, containing 17 million people, earned less than $1,000 per year. 'These were the poorest of America's poor. Within fifteen years these people, many of them black, began a mass immigration to cities that dramatically urbanised poverty and provoked anguished talk of a "welfare crisis" in the United States.'[41]

The Brookings Institution was a centre for economic research. Early involvement of political scientists in applied research was less in direct contributions to policy than in studies of the reform of government. Though Charles Merriam was unsuccessful in the 1920s in establishing an Institute of Government Research, because of foundation doubts about the sensitive character of its subject matter, in the early 1930s he and Beardsley Ruml did succeed in establishing the Public Administration Clearing House on the campus of the University of Chicago.[42] In Britain, more characteristic was the establishment in the 1930s of Political and Economic Planning (hereafter PEP), as a non-partisan institute to analyse Britain's social and economic problems.[43] Though bearing some vague cousinly resemblance to Brookings, it lacked initially any systematic social science input, reflecting a British belief that lay members of the elite in influential positions could be their own social scientists. 'Social science', however, is a portmanteau word, which outside universities embraces an applied orientation based in a social science discipline, an interest in empirical social enquiry and performance of the role of policy advisor and consultant. PEP was firmly committed to the last of these three, and in the post-Second World War period developed the second significantly.

The Settlement House movement

The Settlement House movement was important in the development of social welfare. The original settlement, Toynbee Hall in the East End of London, was set up in 1884 by Canon Samuel Barnett, and rapidly acquired both British and American imitators, the most famous of the latter being Hull-House in Chicago. By 1911, forty-six such settlements had been founded in Britain. In the United States growth was even faster, as young Americans like Jane Addams visited Toynbee Hall and returned to found settlements like Hull-House in Chicago, the University Settlement and Henry Street in New York. By 1910 there were more than 400 American settlements.

It is easy in retrospect to poke fun at settlements, for their high-flown aspirations juxtaposed to the reality of 'slumming', for the social distance between their residents and their working-class neighbours and for their relative ineffectiveness in making an impact upon social conditions in the locality. Toynbee Hall, indeed, was built as a 'manorial residence', in nineteenth-century Elizabethan style more characteristic of Oxford than the East End. Yet this urban echo of collegiate life – and its later British and American followers – helped to form the world views of a number of influential figures in public life. Canon Barnett's protégé's included Alfred Milner, Robert Morant, Arthur Salter and William Beveridge, Beveridge indeed being brought in as Sub-Warden in 1903 specifically to sharpen Toynbee Hall's attack on social problems.[44] R. H. Tawney, challenged by the Master of Balliol, Edward Caird, to go and find out why England had poverty alongside riches and do something about it, lived there for over four years beginning in 1903, at the same time as Beveridge.[45] Among Hull-House's leading residents in addition to Jane Addams were Julia Lathrop, later first head of the US Children's Bureau; Florence Kelley, pioneer social investigator and later head of the National Consumers' League; and Edith Abbott, pioneer in social service education. Such settlements were 'ad hoc graduate schools', and it is indeed realistic to see Hull-House (and Toynbee Hall for some of its residents) as a kind of graduate school in social policy before such opportunities existed in universities.

The Social Survey Movement

The scientific social survey as a source of social awareness of welfare issues and their ramifications hardly needs much emphasis, but its intellectual importance as a movement of thought does. Indeed, in the United States it took the form of a Movement, underpinned by support from the Russell Sage Foundation. In 1912 the Foundation had established its own Department of Surveys and Exhibits, headed by Shelby M. Harrison, who had worked on the Pittsburgh Survey, as a clearing house for advice and field assistance in the conduct of surveys and organisation of local exhibits. The peak of activity of the department was reached by 1920: the most significant study undertaken was the Springfield Survey. The Social Survey Movement was sustained by the support of the Foundation, losing its impetus in the 1920s and having virtually disappeared by the mid-1930s.

Some recent studies have emphasised the role of data produced by the state in monitoring changing social conditions.[46] To be sure the census and vital registration were important sources, and some series derived from administrative practice provided indications of underlying social problems, particularly in the labour field.

This is apparent if one turns to developments in Britain after Rowntree. Here the contribution of statistician A. L. Bowley stands out. His five-town survey of poverty (Reading, Warrington, Northampton, Bolton and Stanley) carried out in 1912, used probability sampling and marked a further methodological advance.[47] Like Booth and Rowntree, Bowley's work fed into discussions of state intervention for the amelioration of poverty, but were not reflected in improvements in state data gathering. Indeed, his innovations in probability sampling were first taken up by public opinion pollsters and market researchers in the United States in the 1930s, by American social scientists shortly thereafter, and were only applied in Britain to any extent after the Second World War.

In Britain during the interwar period, there was continuity with the prewar period in the roles played by private investigators and academics in social investigation. To be sure, the role of officials was not negligible, particularly of people like Sir Hubert Llewellyn-Smith, Permanent Secretary of the Board of Trade until 1919, Chief Economic Adviser to the government from 1919 to 1927, and Director of the *New Survey of London Life and Labour*, 1928–35, who earlier had been an assistant to Booth. But the survey movement was sustained by private individuals. Seebohm Rowntree and A. L. Bowley remained leading figures in the study of poverty, E. W. Bakke, Henry Mess and Caradog Jones were important among other practitioners of the local social survey, and Boyd Orr and Titmuss keen students of the social implications of nutrition and ill-health.[48] Academic researchers were more prominent than before 1914, but as before the majority of this work was done outside the aegis of government.[49] The regular updatings of Rowntree's subsistence poverty standard, for instance, which were used by Beveridge in his Report and which became the basis of the post-Second World War National Assistance Board (public assistance) benefit rates, were undertaken by the Oxford Institute of Statistics.[50] Official series were often limited in scope.

Large-scale empirical research, such as the Pittsburgh survey or Llewellyn-Smith's poverty survey of London, required considerable resources to carry them out. A particularly notable feature of the interwar period was the extent to which the State did not contribute financially to the growth of social science. The most important American developments take place at private universities which at this period did not derive support from the federal government or the states. In Britain, the LSE obtained modest finance from government sources. Its most significant developments, in building, consolidating the library and facilitating staff research, were made possible by external grants from elsewhere.[51] The low level of support for social science at other British universities was indeed a consequence of their reliance upon government funding and the low priority accorded, within government and within the academic peer group, to social science.

The nature of the state

This chapter, then, has examined several sources of knowledge impinging upon state social welfare policy, in the period before 1940, philanthropic support, intellectual groups with political affiliations, non-academic research centres, the Settlement House movement and the various social surveys. These intermediary institutions mediated the relationship between knowledge and state social welfare and, in the period prior to 1940 although not after it, had greater salience than developments within government bureaucracies. Any model of the relationship between social knowledge and the origins of modern social policies needs to take account of these mediating influences.

The part played by the state in shaping the agendas of these intermediary institutions was not as great at this period as it subsequently became. These patterns of mutual influence require further study, for certainly the interaction, later in the twentieth century as well as earlier, has been in both directions. Just as social science does not feed smoothly into the decision-making process but is one competing input among many, so societal developments impinge unevenly upon the preoccupations of social scientists. More knowledge does not mean better decision-making. This is evident in the ambivalence which government and social science display to one another, summed up in the phrases 'the uneasy relationship' and 'the uncertain connection'.[52] But it is precisely the argument of this chapter that in the earlier period, prior to 1940, in contrast to the later, the direction of influence has flowed predominantly from social investigation carried on outside the state apparatus to the formation of policy.

One may indeed go further and emphasise what Barry Karl has called 'the uneasy state'. There is a particular danger in extrapolating from the British Liberal government of 1906–14 or a few years of the New Deal, in neglecting the fact that the nature of the 'State' and 'government' was rather different at this period. The United States in the interwar period, as well as having a more diversified system of higher education, was also a more localised and region-alised society than it later became.[53] For the majority of the population the main frame of reference was not a national one, the federal government was weak and moves to extend the authority of the centre slow, cautious and contested. The speed with which the wartime apparatus in Washington was dissolved in 1918 was one sign; the arguments over the scope for planning in the New Deal another. Up until at least the middle of the twentieth century, Robert Wiebe has observed, 'the most useful image of [American] government was that of an empty vessel, a container into which power flowed and formed but which provided nothing of its own. Always an exaggeration . . . the image nevertheless expressed an approximate truth of high importance.'[54] Britain possessed a more centralised system of governance, but prevailing conceptions of the proper scope for state activity remained very conservative. Many of the social investigators discussed earlier addressed themselves at least as much to arguments about the need to extend state activity as to the conditions which gave rise to the necessity for that extension. The tendency for the history of British social policy to be writ-ten in Whiggish terms has obscured this resistance to assuming new responsibi-lities. Throughout the 1930s, for example, the attempts by Keynes to influence Treasury management of the economy turned on the appropriateness of various forms of government intervention. State structures thus made use of the knowledge produced by social scientists but did not actively promote its production. Nor did the state, directly or indirectly, provide employment for social scientists at this period. Much more influential as agenda-setters were those working in a variety of intermediary institutions. The significance of these national developments in the United States and Britain for international activity is that they convey a number of the features of the international scene within national developments.

The relevance of this analysis at the national level for international develop-ments is indirect rather than direct, but significant nonetheless. The importance of intermediary institutions is clear, whether voluntary or academic, at the inter-national level, and the role of philanthropic foundations in nurturing them was considerable. The confidence and determination of American foundations in their mission to reshape the world is striking, even though in the course of the period their emphasis shifted from public health toward science and scientific medicine as the solution to the problems facing mankind. The contested role of the philanthropic foundations in undertaking this task is the subject of keen scholarly controversy. Were they agents of intellectual imperialism and scientific hegemony, or were they more neutral in their effects? Many of the tensions between those active in international organisations and their own governments are mirrored in the tensions between advocates of stronger welfare expertise and intervention and the state. There are also parallels in the kinds of networks developed among those active in the intermediary institutions.

Yet there is also a major contrast between social science for social welfare on the one hand and medicine and health on the other. The latter were or claimed to be sciences with universal application. To be sure application varied according to geography, climate and environment, so what was appropriate in the temperate zones did not necessarily provide a model for the tropical colonies, though so great is American geographical variation that there was usually a model to draw on. The intervention rested upon both a common scientific base and confidence that there were universal solutions. In the case of social welfare both these shared assumptions were more in doubt. The common base was one grounded in empirical investigation rather than theoretical understanding and solutions tended to be specific to particular countries, conditioned by the particular histories and political circumstances of welfare systems in those societies. Internationalism was therefore less in evidence, and less in view as a solution to problems, even though in the Anglo-American world regular interchange continued to be a significant influence.

Notes

1 Introduction by Bishop Charles Gore to R. H. Tawney, 'Poverty as an Industrial Problem', inaugural lecture as Director of the Ratan Tata Foundation, University of London (London: London School of Economics for the Ratan Tata Foundation, 1914).

2 Cf. H. Aaron, *Politics and the Professors* (Washington, DC: Brookings Institution, 1978); R. Haveman, *Poverty Policy and Poverty Research: the Great Society and the Social Sciences* (Madison, Wis.: University of Wisconsin Press, 1987); D. P. Moynihan, *Family and Nation* (San Diego, Calif.: Harcourt, Brace, Jovanovich, 1986).

3 T. Skocpol, 'Bringing the State Back In', in P. B. Evans, D. Rueschemeyer and T. Skocpol (eds.), *Bringing the State Back In* (Cambridge: Cambridge University Press, 1985), pp. 9–11.

4 P. Berger, 'In Praise of Particularity: The Concept of Mediating Structures', in P. Berger, *Facing Up to Modernity: Excursions in Society, Politics and Religion* (New York: Basic Books, 1977).

5 D. R. Gerstein, R. D. Luce, N. J. Smelser and S. Sperlich (eds.), *The Behavioral and Social Sciences: Achievement and Opportunities: A Report to the National Research Council* (Washington, DC: National Academy Press, 1988), p. 148.

6 J. M. Glenn, L. Brandt and F. E. Andrews (eds.), *Russell Sage Foundation 1907–1946* (New York: Russell Sage Foundation, 1947), pp. 210–11.

7 Cf. R. B. Fosdick, *The Story of the Rockefeller Foundation* (New York: Harper, 1952).

8 R. E. Kohler, 'A Policy for the Advancement of Science: The Rockefeller Foundation 1924–1929', *Minerva*, 16 (winter 1978), 480–515.

9 Cf. R. E. Kohler, *Partners in Science: Foundations and the Natural Scientists 1900–1945* (Chicago: University of Chicago Press, 1991), pp. 46ff.

10 For a full account see M. and J. Bulmer, 'Philanthropy and Social Science in the 1920s: Beardsley Ruml and the Laura Spelman Rockefeller Memorial 1922–1929', *Minerva*, 19 (autumn 1981), 347–407.

11 Cf. E. C. Lagemann, *The Politics of Knowledge: The Carnegie Corporation, Philanthropy and Public Policy* (Middletown, Conn.: Wesleyan University Press, 1989).

12 W. A. Jackson, *Gunnar Myrdal and America's Conscience: Social Engineering and Racial Liberalism 1938–1987* (Chapel Hill, NC: University of North Carolina Press, 1990); M. Bulmer, 'The Apotheosis of Liberalism? *An American Dilemma* after Fifty Years in the Context of the Lives of Gunnar and Alva Myrdal', *Ethnic and Racial Studies*, 16, 2 (1993), 345–57.

13 Donald Fisher, 'The Rockefeller Foundation and the Development of Scientific Medicine in Great Britain', *Minerva*, 16 (spring 1978), 20–41.

14 Donald Fisher, 'The Impact of American Foundations on the Development of British University Education, 1900–1939' (PhD dissertation, University of California, Berkeley, 1977); Donald Fisher, 'American Philanthropy and the Social Sciences in Britain, 1918–1939: The Reproduction of a Conservative Ideology', *The Sociological Review*, 28 (1980), 297–315.; debate between Martin Bulmer and Donald Fisher over 'Philanthropic Foundations and the Development of the Social Sciences in the early twentieth century', *Sociology*, 18, 4 (November 1984), 572–87.

15 Cf. H. A. Mess and C. Braithwaite, 'The Great Philanthropic Trusts', in H. A. Mess, with C. Braithwaite, V. Creech-Jones, H. Jennings, P. Jephcott, H. King, N. Milnes, T. Morgan, G. Williams and H. E. Williams, *Voluntary Social Services since 1918* (London: Kegan Paul, Trench, Trubner and Co., 1948), pp. 172–87.

16 Contrast R. F. Arnove (ed.), *Philanthropy and Cultural Imperialism* (Bloomington, Ind.: Indiana University Press, 1980) with B. D. Karl and S. N. Katz, 'The American Private Philanthropic Foundation and the Public Sphere, 1890–1930', *Minerva*, 19 (1981), 236–40 and B. D. Karl and S. N. Katz, 'Foundations and Ruling Class Elites', *Daedalus*, 116, Part 1 (1987), 1–40.

17 Cf. J. Harris, *William Beveridge: A Biography* (Oxford: Clarendon Press, 1977) and A. Briggs, *Social Thought and Social Action: a Study of the Work of Seebohm Rowntree 1871–1954* (London: Longmans, 1961).

18 Cf. J. Boyd Orr, *As I Recall* (London: McGibbon and Kee, 1966) and M. Gowing, 'Richard Morris Titmuss', *Proceedings of the British Academy*, 61 (1975), 1–30.

19 Boyd Orr, *As I Recall*, pp. 118–20, 157ff.

20 G. Himmelfarb, *The Idea of Poverty: England in the Early Industrial Age* (New York: Knopf, 1984), pp. 526ff.

21 C. A. Chambers, *Paul U. Kellogg and 'The Survey'* (Minneapolis: University of Minnesota Press, 1971).

22 P. Abrams, *The Origins of British Sociology 1834–1914* (Chicago: University of Chicago Press, 1968).

23 See S. Meacham, *Toynbee Hall and Social Reform 1880–1914: The Search for Community* (New Haven, Conn.: Yale University Press, 1987), p. 45.

24 A testament to his belief in the power of empirical social investigation. Webb hoped that study of the social sciences would 'break up economics', replacing analysis of concepts by collection and analysis of facts. See W. Beveridge, *The London School of Economics and Its Problems 1919–1937* (London: Allen and Unwin, 1960), p. 109.

25 R. Barker, *Education and Politics 1900–1950: A Study of the Labour Party* (Oxford: Clarendon Press, 1972).

26 K. Banting, *Poverty, Politics and Policy* (London: Macmillan, 1979).

27 President's Research Committee on Social Trends, *Recent Social Trends in the United States* (New York: McGraw Hill, 1933).

28 Chicago Commission on Race Relations, *The Negro in Chicago* (Chicago: University of Chicago Press, 1922).

29 On the financing of the commission, see D. Fisher, *Fundamental Development of the Social Sciences: Rockefeller Philanthropy and the United States Social Science Research Council* (Ann Arbor, Mich.: University of Michigan Press, 1993), pp. 96–111.

30 Pilgrim Trust, *Men Without Work* (Cambridge: Cambridge University Press, 1936).

31 Karl and Katz, 'Foundations and Ruling Class Elites'.

32 G. Alchon, *The Invisible Hand of Planning: Capitalism, Social Science and the State* (Princeton, NJ: Princeton University Press, 1985), p. 3.

33 See D. Winch, *Economics and Policy: A Historical Study* (London: Hodder and Stoughton, 1969) and S. Howson and D. Winch, *The Economic Advisory Council 1930–1939: A Study in Economic Advice during Depression and Recovery* (Cambridge: Cambridge University Press, 1977).

34 R. S. and H. Lynd, *Middletown* (New York: Harcourt, Brace and Co., 1929).

35 A. Calder, 'Mass-Observation, 1937–1949', in M. Bulmer (ed.), *Essays on the History of Sociological Research* (Cambridge: Cambridge University Press, 1985), pp. 121–36.

36 R. M. Titmuss, *Poverty and Population* (London: Macmillan, 1938).

37 S. Cohen, 'Foundation Officials and Fellowships: Innovation in the Patronage of Science', *Minerva*, 14, 2 (1976), 225–40; E. Arlene Craven, 'Patronage and the Direction of Research in Economics: The Rockefeller Foundation in Europe, 1924–1938', *Minerva*, 24, 2–3 (summer–autumn 1986), 205–22.

38 Cf. R. T. von Mayrhauser, 'The Manager, the Medic and the Mediator: The Clash of Professional Psychological Styles and the Wartime Origins of Group Mental Testing', in M. M. Sokal (ed.), *Psychological Testing and American Society 1890–1930* (New Brunswick, NJ: Rutgers University Press, 1987), pp. 107–63.

39 D. T. Critchlow, *The Brookings Institution 1916–1952: Expertise and the Public Interest in a Democratic Society* (De Kalb, Ill.: Northern Illinois University Press, 1985).

40 M. Leven, H. G. Moulton and C. Warburton, *America's Capacity to Consume* (Washington, DC: Brookings Institution, 1934).

41 J. T. Patterson, *America's Struggle Against Poverty 1900–1980* (Cambridge, Mass.: Harvard University Press, 1981), p. 16.
42 Cf. B. D. Karl, *Charles E. Merriam and the Study of Politics* (Chicago: University of Chicago Press, 1974).
43 Cf. J. Pinder (ed.), *Fifty Years of Political and Economic Planning: Looking Forward 1931–1981* (London: Heinemann Educational, 1981).
44 Harris, *William Beveridge*, pp. 48–9.
45 R. Terrill, *R. H. Tawney and his Times: Socialism as Fellowship* (London: Andre Deutsch, 1974), pp. 31–5.
46 Roger Davidson, *Whitehall and the Labour Problem in Late-Victorian and Edwardian Britain: A Study in Official Statistics and Social Control* (London: Croom Helm, 1988); M. Lacey and M. Furner (eds.), *The State and Social Investigation* (Cambridge: Cambridge University Press, 1993).
47 A. L. Bowley and A. R. Burnett-Hurst, *Livelihood and Poverty* (London: Bell, 1915).
48 E. W. Blake, *The Unemployed Man* (1932); H. A. Mess, *Industrial Tyneside: A Social Survey* (London: Benn, 1927); D. Caradog Jones (ed.), *The Social Survey of Merseyside* (London: Hodder and Stoughton for the University of Liverpool, 1934, 3 vols.); J. Boyd Orr, *Food, Health and Income* (London: Macmillan, 1937); Titmuss, *Poverty and Population*.
49 Cf. J. Stevenson (ed.), *Social Conditions in Britain between the Wars* (Harmondsworth: Penguin, 1977).
50 P. Townsend, 'Measuring Poverty', *British Journal of Sociology*, 5 (1954), 130–7.
51 See Bulmer and Bulmer, 'Philanthropy and Social Science in the 1920s' and the forthcoming centennial history of the London School of Economics and Political Science by Lord Dahrendorf, to be published by Oxford University Press, which discusses the significance of this funding and its interpretation.
52 Cf. G. M. Lyons, *The Uneasy Partnership: Social Science and the Federal Government in the Twentieth Century* (New York: Russell Sage Foundation, 1969); L. E. Lynn, Jr (ed.), *Knowledge and Policy: The Uncertain Connection* (Washington, DC: National Academy of Sciences, 1978); see also M. Bulmer (ed.), *Social Science Research and Government: Comparative Essays on Britain and the United States* (Cambridge: Cambridge University Press, 1987).
53 B. D. Karl, *The Uneasy State: The United States from 1914 to 1945* (Chicago: University of Chicago Press, 1983).
54 R. H. Weibe, *The Segmented Society: An Introduction to the Meaning of America* (New York: Oxford University Press, 1975), p. 132.

Index

Cambridge History of Medicine

Health, medicine and morality in the sixteenth century *edited by* CHARLES WEBSTER

The Renaissance notion of woman: A study in the fortunes of scholasticism and medical science in European intellectual life IAN MACLEAN

Mystical Bedlam: madness, anxiety and healing in sixteenth century England
MICHAEL MACDONALD

From medical chemistry to biochemistry: The making of a biomedical discipline
ROBERT E. KOHLER

Joan Baptista Van Helmont: Reformer of science and medicine WALTER PAGEL

A generous confidence: Thomas Story Kirkbride and the art of asylum keeping, 1840–1883
NANCY TOMES

The cultural meaning of popular science: Phrenology and the organization of consent in nineteenth-century Britain ROGER COOTER

Madness, morality and medicine: A study of the York Retreat, 1796–1914 ANNE DIGBY

Patients and practitioners: Lay perceptions of medicine in pre-industrial society *edited by*
ROY PORTER

Hospital life in enlightenment Scotland: Care and teaching at the Royal Infirmary of Edinburgh
GUENTER B. RISSE

Plague and the poor in Renaissance Florence ANNE G. CARMICHAEL

Victorian lunacy: Richard M. Bucke and the practice of late-nineteenth-century psychiatry
S. E. D. SHORTT

Medicine and society in Wakefield and Huddersfield 1780–1870 HILARY MARLAND

Ordered to care: The dilemma of American nursing, 1850–1945 SUSAN M. REVERBY

Morbid appearances: The anatomy of pathology in the early nineteenth century
RUSSELL C. MAULITZ

Professional and popular medicine in France, 1770–1830: The social world of medical practice
MATTHEW RAMSEY

Abortion, doctors and the law: Some aspects of the legal regulation of abortion in England
1803–1982 JOHN KEOWN

Public health in Papua New Guinea: Medical possibility and social constraints, 1884–1984
DONALD DENOON

Health, race and German politics between national unification and Nazism, 1870–1945
PAUL WEINDLING

The physician-legislators of France: Medicine and politics in the early Third Republic, 1870–1914
JACK D. ELLIS

The science of woman: Gynaecology and gender in England, 1800–1929 ORNELLA MOSCUCCI

Science and empire: East Coast fever in Rhodesia and the Transvaal PAUL F. CRANEFIELD

The colonial disease: A social history of sleeping sickness in northern Zaire, 1900–1940
MARYiNEZ LYONS